Jill Liddington is co-author of *One Hand Tied Behind Us*, which quickly became a suffrage classic and author of *The Long Road to Greenham*, which won the Fawcett   k Prize in 1990. She is a Fellow of the Royal Historical Society and an H   ry Research Fellow- at the University of Leeds. She lives in Mytho   yd, West Yorkshire.

REBEL GIRLS
Their fight for the vote

JILL LIDDINGTON

virago

VIRAGO

First published in Great Britain in 2006 by Virago Press

7 9 10 8

A CIP catalogue record for this book
is available from the British Library.

ISBN 978-1-84408-168-4

Typeset in Spectrum by M Rules
Printed and bound in Great Britain by
Clays Ltd, St Ives plc

Papers used by Virago are from well-managed forests
and other responsible sources.

MIX
Paper from
responsible sources
FSC® C104740

Virago Press
An imprint of
Little, Brown Book Group
Carmelite House
50 Victoria Embankment
London EC4Y 0DZ

An Hachette UK Company
www.hachette.co.uk

www.virago.co.uk

CONTENTS

Chronology and Organisations   vii
Preface   xi
Introduction: Edwardian ancestors   1

Part One: Dawn 1903–1906

1 Daughter: Adela Pankhurst   17
2 New woman: Mary Gawthorpe   32
3 Suffragettes released: Adela and Mary   53

Part Two: Landscapes and Communities 1906–1907

4 Tailoress and writer: Lavena Saltonstall   81
5 'Baby suffragette': Dora Thewlis   107
6 Painting the valley: Florence Lockwood   135

Part Three: Hearts and Minds 1907–1911

7 Votes for Women everywhere: Mary Murdoch and
the Coates clan   163
8 'Womanly endurance': Edith Key and Lavena Saltonstall   179
9 Banners and vanners: Isabella Ford and her sisters   193
10 'A genius for revolt': Adela and Mary again   215

Part Four: Mavericks and Democrats 1911–1914

11 Such smashing girls: Leonora Cohen   231
12 Pillar-boxes and beefeaters: Molly Morris and Leonora   246
13 Pilgrims and fugitives: Florence Lockwood and
Lilian Lenton   261
14 Unsafe City: Leonora, Lilian and Florence again   286

Part Five: Afterwards 1914–2005

15 Living with the memory   299
16 Rebel Girls: writing narrative history   313

Appendices

1 Suffrage detective: tracking the evidence   325
2 Rebel girls: biographies   337
3 Bibliography and sources   351
4 List of illustrations   357
5 Acknowledgements   360
6 Abbreviations and Notes   362

Index   394

CHRONOLOGY AND ORGANISATIONS

CHRONOLOGY

1902 Deputation of Yorkshire textile workers with suffrage petition to Westminster.

1903 Oct: Women's Social and Political Union (WSPU) formed by Emmeline Pankhurst.
Oct: Leeds Arts Club formed by Alfred Orage; Isabella Ford and Mary Gawthorpe join.

1905 Oct: Christabel Pankhurst and Annie Kenney at Free Trade Hall, Manchester.

1906 Jan: General Election: Liberal landslide; Campbell-Bannerman Prime Minister. WSPU moves down to London.
May: Deputation to Campbell-Bannerman.
June–Jul: Adela Pankhurst at Belle Vue and Boggart Hole Clough, Manchester.
Oct: Emmeline Pankhurst leads demonstration at opening of Parliament: arrests include Adela Pankhurst and Mary Gawthorpe.
Nov: Suffragette prisoners released and travel to Huddersfield by-election.
Hebden Bridge (fustian weavers) and Halifax (tram workers) strikes start.

1907 Jan: Suffragettes arrive in Hebden Bridge.
Feb: NUWSS 'Mud March', London.
     Women's Parliament demonstration: arrests.
Mar: Lavena Saltonstall and Dora Thewlis arrested, Westminster.
June: Colne Valley by-election with Victor Grayson; Florence Lockwood a witness.
Autumn: Women's Freedom League formed.
Nov: Hull West by-election, Mary Murdoch carries the NUWSS colours.

1908   Feb: Women's Parliament: arrests include Lavena Saltonstall.
Apr: Asquith becomes Prime Minister
June: NUWSS procession with embroidered banners, and WSPU rally.
   NUWSS caravan tour of Yorkshire dales.
Oct: Leeds: Prime Minister Asquith heckled.
   Sheffield: Adela (WSPU Yorkshire organiser) disguised as kitchen-maid.

1909   Spring: Lloyd George's 'People's Budget' rejected: political crisis.
Summer: NUWSS caravan tour of Yorkshire dales, with Isabella Ford.
Jul: Imprisoned suffragettes begin hunger striking.
Autumn: Government introduces forcible feeding of hunger-strikers in prison.

1910   Jan and Dec: General Elections: Asquith's Liberal government confirmed in power.
Adela Pankhurst campaigns in Scarborough and the Dales.

1911   Summer: Conciliation Bill; Women's Coronation procession.
Nov: Asquith announces manhood suffrage bill.
   Window-smashing raids, Leonora Cohen imprisoned in Holloway.
   By end 1911 both Adela Pankhurst and Mary Gawthorpe leave WSPU.

1912   Jan: Labour Party votes to support women's suffrage: labour–suffrage pact.
Mar: WSPU window-smashing raids, Lilian Lenton takes part.
May–June: NUWSS's Election Fighting Fund to support Labour candidates.
Autumn: Pethick-Lawrences expelled from WSPU.
Oct: Christabel Pankhurst, from exile in Paris, edits the *Suffragette*.

1913   Jan: Speaker of House of Commons announces no suffrage amendment to reform bill.
Feb: Leonora Cohen smashing attack at the Tower of London.
   WSPU arson attacks, including Kew Gardens, Lilian Lenton accused.
Apr: 'Cat and Mouse' Act: suffragette 'mice' released from jail on licence.
June: Death of Emily Wilding Davison; Doncaster trial; Lilian Lenton escapes.
June–Jul: Florence Lockwood in Budapest; NUWSS suffrage pilgrimage.
Nov: Asquith visits Leeds; Leonora Cohen to Armley gaol.

1914   Adela Pankhurst 'banished' to Australia. Outbreak of war.

1916   Mary Gawthorpe and mother emigrate to United States.

1918   End of the war. Women over thirty win the vote.

1928   Women over twenty-one win the vote. Death of Emmeline Pankhurst.

1931   Sylvia Pankhurst's *The Suffragette Movement* published.

ORGANISATIONS

ILP   Independent Labour Party.
            Formed 1893; led by Keir Hardie MP.
            In 1900 ILP joined with trades unions to form the Labour
            Representation Committee (which later became the Labour Party).

NUWSS   National Union of Women's Suffrage Societies.
            Formed 1897; led by Mrs Fawcett.

WSPU   Women's Social and Political Union.
            Formed 1903; led by Emmeline and Christabel Pankhurst.

WFL   Women's Freedom League
            Formed 1907; Teresa Billington-Greig and others broke away from
            WSPU.

EFF   Election Fighting Fund
            Set up by NUWSS 1913 to support Labour candidates at by-elections.

DEFINITIONS

Suffragists   Campaigned for votes for women constitutionally i.e. within the
                   law.
Suffragettes   Campaigned for votes for women, adopting militant tactics i.e.
                   involving breaking the law.
Adult suffragists Wanted votes for *all* adult men and women (by abolishing the
                   property qualification).

MAPS

Map I: Yorkshire and the Pennines   6
Map II: Textile communities of the West Riding   82
Map III: Mapping the Huddersfield and Colne Valley Suffragettes   108
Map IV: North and East Ridings: North York Moors and Yorkshire Wolds   206

Writing this Preface coincided with my standing for the first time ever as a candidate in my local community – largely to stop more BNP councillors being elected. I was out campaigning. Feedback on the doorstep is always sobering, especially when voters say 'I'm not going to vote: they're all the same'. Friends claim that when I meet women intending not to take part in elections, I respond: 'but suffragettes *died* so that you could have the vote'. I do not. Partly because, as a suffrage historian, I know that the campaign for the vote was much wider than Emily Wilding Davison's martyr's death at the Derby race-course; and so much broader than the leadership of Emmeline Pankhurst which inspired such suffragette daring and bravery.

The Edwardian Votes for Women campaign was everywhere. It spread out into every town; it walked down every street; it entered every home; it was discussed – and argued over – across kitchen and dining-room tables up and down the land. It encompassed the courageous suffra*gettes*, whose militant actions often landed them in prison to endure hunger strikes and even forcible feeding. And it embraced those self-effacing suffra*gists* who so dreaded public speaking; their constitutional campaign had them mounting soap-boxes in market squares and even taking their suffrage caravan out to the remotest dale, the most sea-swept fishing harbour. It included those whose own brave rebellions went quietly unrecorded: arguments with fathers, whose political loyalties or patriarchal certainties blinded them to their daughters' undemocratic lack of the vote. This book is written to honour all those Edwardian campaigners whose small acts of enormous courage so often went uncelebrated.

One Hand Tied Behind Us: the rise of the women's suffrage movement (1978) which I wrote with Jill Norris told the tale behind the Pankhurst headlines, the story of the radical suffragists of Lancashire, women weavers and winders who took their campaign out to factory gate and cottage door. They were women whose confidence to demand the vote for themselves sprang from their jobs in the great cotton mills and from their political experience in the new labour movement. They championed radical ideas but, increasingly critical of Emmeline and Christabel Pankhurst's tactics as militancy escalated, they remained suffragists. Rather than the suffragettes' Women's Social and Political Union (WSPU) they preferred the constitutional tactics of Mrs Fawcett's great National Union of Women's Suffrage Societies (NUWSS).

Since the 1970s, new perspectives have enriched and widened our understanding of women's history and gender history. Alongside, a recent slew of Pankhurst biographies has kept suffragette history to the forefront. So as well as 'celebrity suffrage', we now know more about the lives of ordinary women campaigners, of how their private experiences shaped their public actions.[1] We also know about local and regional suffrage histories beyond just Lancashire; these challenge or even overturn the conventional London-centred narratives, notably Sylvia Pankhurst's 1931 *The Suffragette Movement*: well-known national figures retire to the shadowy wings or disappear, to be replaced centre-stage by fresh new actors.

However, in the years since *One Hand*, the suffrage history of the vast Yorkshire region – with its west, north and east ridings making it by far the largest of the English counties – remained unrecorded and unwritten. In *Rebel Girls*, my research across this region has thrown up completely new figures. They are decidedly not the politically-experienced radical suffragists of Lancashire's cotton towns, but daring 'rebel-girl' suffragettes – usually aged between sixteen and twenty-five – who time and time again hurled themselves against the intransigent Liberal government.

They rejected the deadening expectations and conventions of their Victorian elders. They demanded new rights and new freedoms. They wanted the educational opportunities enjoyed by some of their brothers and comfortably-off sisters; they wanted freedom to work and the right to a living wage; they wanted freedom to love, the right to challenge double standards of sexual morality, and the freedom to turn their backs on 'marriage as a trade'. They saw it as a battle of youth and energy, spirit and beauty, against the confining compromises of their parents. As they put all this into campaigning practice, their Edwardian lives were transformed for ever by the personal politics of their volatile Votes for Women experience.

This is at last the piece of the suffrage jigsaw that has been missing for so long. Campaigners had apparently disappeared without trace, their children and even grandchildren now passed out of sight. Then, recently,

exciting new electronic research techniques and original discoveries of neglected manuscript collections, both in the UK and the United States and
Australia, has meant that these remote Edwardian ancestors could at last
be rediscovered. For most of the rebel girls, never heard of before, their
freshly unearthed stories had been completely forgotten.

Two examples. The cover picture depicting the arrest of 'Baby
Suffragette' was catapulted onto the popular newspaper front-pages in
spring 1907. This striking photograph had been reprinted in one or two
popular suffrage histories.[2] Now we can give this anonymous suffragette a
name: Dora Thewlis. And we can reconstruct her life. She was a sixteen-
year-old weaver from Huddersfield, and her imprisonment and her
treatment by the 'paparazzi' of the day changed her life for ever. Second,
dancer Lilian Lenton waited till her twenty-first birthday – then determined to burn two buildings a week until the Liberal government granted
women the vote. One of these empty buildings was in Doncaster and, by
tracking Lilian's story through 1913 newspaper reports, her dramatic court
appearance, and her even more melodramatic escapes from houses in
Leeds and Scarborough, a fresh story for these frenzied years can at last be
pieced together.

All this detective sleuthing began to add up to an excitingly new and
dramatic panorama of the Edwardian suffrage experience. Disparate shapes
when assembled together shifted into recognisable patterns and into an
untold suffrage history. Shimmering into view was a newly designed set, a
fresh script and a fresh cast of actors: rebel girls.

The stories told here focus largely on eight rebel girls all born between 1881
and 1891: the forgotten Pankhurst sister Adela, and Mary Gawthorpe from
Leeds; tailoress Lavena Saltonstall from Hebden Bridge and Dora Thewlis;
Molly Morris in Sheffield and Lilian Lenton; Alice Schofield from
Middlesbrough and Violet Key-Jones from York. They all entered the
Edwardian century as shadowy figures: shy, awkward, unconfident girls
frustrated by their confined horizons. They were young, idealistic and
impatient, often vulnerable and sometimes confused, yet determined and
extraordinarily courageous. Then, as their own words and their photographs show, they were transformed rapidly – sometimes almost
overnight – into daring, fearless combatants taking on the Liberal government. The rebel girls invented the rules as they went along and sometimes
their impetuous plans went awry. The political context they found themselves in was highly volatile, with the authorities attempting to contain

them. As the battle with the state intensified, they inevitably ended up in extremely perilous situations – in court, forcibly fed in prison, and eventually even as fugitives on the run.

Alongside the rebel girls campaigned more experienced women, recently married and bringing up young children – such as Leonora Cohen from Leeds. And the picture is completed by accomplished suffragists such as painter Florence Lockwood in the Colne Valley and doctor Mary Murdoch of Hull. We follow them out to the Yorkshire dales and isolated harbour-sides, in caravans and on pilgrimages, as they campaign to win hearts-and-minds.

So the aim of *Rebel Girls* is to tell two stories. The first recounts how the lives of these Edwardian girls were transformed by their passionate Votes for Women commitment. The second story takes regional form. It returns the rebel girls to their own communities, for they inhabited a Yorkshire landscape, they had local roots. I have selected Yorkshire partly because that is where I live; partly because it makes the strongest contrast with its better-known neighbour Lancashire; and partly because this vast region has so far eluded suffrage historians. Yet Yorkshire, especially its industrial West Riding, remains as crucial for suffrage historians as Lancashire; and I return to this comparative theme in the final chapter.

If *One Hand* – tracking the suffrage movement from its mid-Victorian beginnings in Manchester through to 1906–7 – represented Part I, *Rebel Girls*, opening around 1905–6, just as imprisonment of Yorkshire suffragettes began to grab the newspaper headlines, is the long-awaited Part II.

The story starts in the textile towns of the West Riding: Dora Thewlis, Lavena Saltonstall and others sprang from their industrial communities around 1906–7, and are evoked by the phrase 'community suffragettes'. The narrative then moves to cities like Leeds and Sheffield, with individual militant mavericks such as Lilian Lenton and Molly Morris repeatedly taunting and evading the Liberal government.

The tale of this dazzling generation of campaigners is possible to tell only a full century later. *Rebel Girls*, based upon innovative research techniques and newly discovered evidence, shifts little-known actors from the shadowy wings to well-lit centre-stage; a new drama and chronology emerge, offering a fresh narrative history of women's suffrage.

Edwardian Ancestors

Queen Victoria died in January 1901. Her raffish son Albert Edward, so long waiting in the wings, succeeded her. The coronation of Edward VII in autumn 1902 was a resplendently imperial ceremony. Edward Elgar was invited to compose a *Coronation Ode*, and for its finale he used the powerfully percussive rhythmic beat of his first *Pomp and Circumstance* march. The king apparently suggested Elgar's stirring melody be provided with appropriate words. The finale of the *Coronation Ode* lyrics – 'Land of Hope and Glory/Mother of the free./How may we extol thee, who are born of thee?' – so resonated with the Edwardian patriotic *zeitgeist* that it was even sold as a separate song-sheet. It rapidly became a second national anthem, both words and music instantly recognisable a full century later.[1]

The coronation's glorious music fits with our inherited image of Edwardian England. Vita Sackville-West's novel *The Edwardians* (1930) celebrated the *jeunesse dorée* enjoying the lavish country-house life of her childhood at Knole, a sprawling Tudor palace set in a spacious park. More recent popular histories similarly conjure an Edwardian world of willowy duchesses and sleekly plump politicians.[2] Certainly, the power that the great land-owning aristocracy wielded still remained vast. At the turn of the century the Prime Minister, Lord Salisbury, leader of the Conservatives, sat in the hereditary House of Lords, rather than in the elective House of Commons (though he was the last prime minister to do so). Britain remained governed by an almost cosy two-party system, closely ingratiated into court circles. Pleasure-seeking Edward VII relished fashionable European watering-places – such as Marienbad, where he struck up a strategic friendship with Sir Henry Campbell-Bannerman, leader of the Liberals.

However, beneath the vivid 'land of hope and glory' beat, a rather different imperial theme was unfolding. From autumn 1899 in South Africa, Britain had been fighting white Boer settlers in a protracted war. When the besieged frontier town of Mafeking was relieved, it prompted hysterically jingoistic celebrations back home. At the 1900 'Khaki' General Election, the 'mafficking' craze kept Salisbury and the Conservatives in power. However, when Boer farmsteads were burned and Boer refugee women and children were herded into makeshift concentration camps, those Britons already anxious about going to war became outraged by this brutality. Liberals were divided: imperialists like Herbert Henry Asquith (soon to become Prime Minister) supported the war, while rising Welsh orator David Lloyd George opposed – as did, from the sidelines, the small new socialist Independent Labour Party (ILP). Among suffragists, patriotic Mrs Fawcett, leader of the National Union of Women's Suffrage Societies (NUWSS) supported; Quaker and ILP member Isabella Ford of Leeds opposed.[3] Until peace arrived in May 1902, opinion was so bitterly polarised that it affected even children at school. In Manchester, leading ILP member Emmeline Pankhurst opposed: amid rampant patriotism, her youngest daughter Adela had a book thrown in her face in the classroom. At ILP meetings in Huddersfield, Edith Key's husband, standing on a horse-drawn lorry stationed in the town square, spoke against the war: so unpopular was this that their two sons had to be withdrawn from school.[4] These bitter divisions would echo down the years.

The Boer War highlighted other fissures cutting across Edwardian England. It revealed the appalling levels of poor health among young men volunteering for military service in South Africa: up to one in three was rejected as too small or too slight, prone to rheumatism, or suffering weak lungs, heart trouble or bad teeth.[5] How could the empire, 'mother of the free', be defended against its enemies by recruits unable to fight effectively? They might be 'born of thee', but this scare about the health of the British race shone an alarming spotlight on working-class motherhood.

These turn-of-the-century currents added up contradictorily: resplendently imperial, yet wracked with poor health; complacently united against the foe, yet bitterly divided.

Certain Edwardians left a prolific record of their lives. Arthur Benson, who wrote the words 'Land of Hope and Glory' for Elgar's music, kept a four-million-word diary running to 180 volumes. Less prolific, Florence Lockwood in Colne Valley kept a diary upon which she drew in writing her autobiography. Autobiographies are certainly invaluable: Mary Gawthorpe's *Up Hill to Holloway* also lets us into the very intimate heart of her Leeds upbringing.

There are of course yawning gaps in the written record, with little surviving evidence of how the majority of Edwardians lived. Up to the 1970s, just a generation ago, it was still possible to talk to elderly Edwardian men and women, and to ask them about their lives before the First World War. Paul Thompson's *The Edwardians* (1975) offers an oral history based upon some five hundred recorded interviews with survivors of this generation.[6] But now, into the twenty-first century, taping direct suffrage testimony of Edwardians is no longer possible. Mary Gawthorpe for instance died in 1973; also from Leeds, Leonora Cohen, often dubbed 'Britain's oldest surviving suffragette', reached an extraordinary 105 years old, dying in 1978. So when a younger suffragette, Victoria Liddiard, a veteran of a 1912 window-smashing raid, finally died aged 102 in 1992, we could be fairly certain no one else survived her.[7]

However, an additional extraordinarily powerful tool for historians is now available: the 1901 hand-written household census, recording individual personal data. This is publicly released 101 years later, so the census recorded shortly after Queen Victoria's death was duly made available in January 2002. The 1901 information also all suddenly became accessible through new electronic internet search; this was complemented by electronic searches for birth, marriage and death certificates, plus the digitalisation of late-Victorian censuses. *The Lost World of Mitchell and Kenyon*, archive film revealing the forgotten vibrancy of Edwardian street life, with young workers all grinning happily at the camera as they pour in their thousands out of northern mills, rounded off these new people's history sources.[8]

For suffrage historians, the empowering advantage of being able to access electronic data on-line is that it readily makes available the personal details for *every* household and *every* person, however 'ordinary' and however frequently they moved. Unlike written evidence, an Edwardian need not have been a literate diarist or memoirist to be recorded; nor, in contrast to oral testimony, do they need to be a survivor – much beyond 31 March 1901.

Web-site searches immediately reveal, with striking poignancy for the 'rebel girls' and their families, the harshness of the enormous chasms of inequality spanning late-Victorian and Edwardian England. This is brought home starkly by the pattern of female domestic servants; high infant mortality rates; a family's fragile dependence upon its male breadwinner; and regional inequalities, notably between north and south.

The employment of female domestic servants in a Victorian household could make the difference between a comfortable home life and a less com-

fortable one. In one elegant north Leeds suburb, Isabella Ford's family of
well-to-do lawyers, with its six daughters and two sons, employed a gov-
erness plus five living-in servants. Then when Isabella was ten, the family
moved still further out of the city, to spacious Adel Grange, one of
Yorkshire's 'brass castles'; here the Fords employed a cook, a lady's maid,
two housemaids and a kitchen maid, two gardeners and a coachman.
Similarly, radical barrister Richard Pankhurst, his wife Emmeline and their
family, living at 8 Russell Square in London when Adela was a young child,
employed three living-in servants: a nurse, a cook and a housemaid.[9] The
household census also makes clear, of course, that most households did
not 'have' servants to make their lives more comfortable, and that the daily
lives of those responsible for housework remained hard, demanding and
repetitive.

A search through successive household censuses can also reveal alarming gaps. A child's name recorded on the 1891 census can have disappeared
by 1901. The frequency of infant and child deaths parallels the Boer War
health alarms; these small-scale family tragedies often stemmed from pre-
ventable health causes – poverty, poor diet and inadequate public health
provision. Memories of child coffins pepper the early chapters in this book:
few families escaped. Indeed early deaths affected upper-middle-class families too: Isabella Ford had two sisters who died young, and the Pankhursts'
elder son died aged four.

With no welfare state (beyond a harsh Poor Law system with its dreaded
workhouse) and little to rely on in hard times to keep them from starving,
most late-Victorian families relied heavily upon the wage of their male
breadwinner. If he died, his wife and children were left to fend as best they
could. Even Emmeline Pankhurst when widowed in 1898 discovered this
the harsh way. Richard, so ready to lend his radical-barrister skills to every
needful socialist cause, had failed to make a will and Emmeline was suddenly left with little – except debts. She faced a brutally abrupt awakening.
The family – Emmeline, Christabel, Sylvia, Adela and Harry – had to move
to a smaller home in Manchester and, within weeks, Emmeline had
resigned her unpaid role as a Poor Law Guardian and taken a salaried post
as Registrar of Births and Deaths.

For many families, financial anxieties grew in the face of multiple
problems. Doctors' bills had to be paid: debts easily mounted in working-class families. The stories presented here are threaded with
hopelessly idealistic fathers, or feckless fathers who drank into the
meagre housekeeping money; of mothers, prematurely aged, who had

to bring up the children on the earnings from their needle. Children witnessed all this in the home, and such harsh childhood experiences certainly had profound effects on Mary Gawthorpe and Leonora Cohen in Leeds. It meant that as the new century dawned they were determined it should promise better; and, as the Conservative government's energy dribbled away, that a new Edwardian government must bring in a real welfare reform agenda to tackle the worst of family insecurity and poor child health.

These deep fissures running through late-Victorian and Edwardian England – domestic service, child health, family insecurities – also had a strong regional dimension, distinguishing the north of England from the south. A regional profile of female servants makes this clear. Within the industrial West Riding of Yorkshire, only eight per cent of households in the 'worstedopolis' city of Bradford employed one or more female servants, and the figure for Huddersfield was just ten per cent. However, across most of London's residential West End, the figure rose well above twenty-five per cent.[10]

The great northern urban belt running from the North Sea in the east across to the Irish Sea in the west included some of England's biggest cities. Of the dozen major towns outside London, most lay along this stretch: Hull and Sheffield, Leeds and Bradford, Manchester, Salford and Liverpool. Within the West Riding, Leeds and Sheffield had been granted city status in 1893 and Bradford and Hull followed in 1897. The population of Yorkshire, with its three ridings, spread over a vast 3.9 million acres, was still growing: it rose by eleven per cent between 1891 and 1901, from 3,600,000 to nearly four million. And that of the heavily industrialised and congested West Riding (itself alone 1.7 million acres) increased by thirteen per cent between 1891 and 1901, from 2,760,000 to just over three million.[11]

Yet the sprawling Yorkshire region also contained dramatic contrasts: the West Riding, for all its industrialisation, still included isolated hill towns in a landscape little changed since the Brontës lived there. The great North and East Ridings remained largely rural; here rural wolds and sleepy dales' villages fed into Edwardian visions of an older pastoral England. *The Secret Garden* (1911) opens poignantly with the lonely orphan-heroine travelling to her new Yorkshire home in the middle of nowhere across Missel Moor, and being told 'It isn't fields nor mountains, it's just miles and miles and miles of wild land that nothing grows on but heather and gorse and broom'.[12]

*

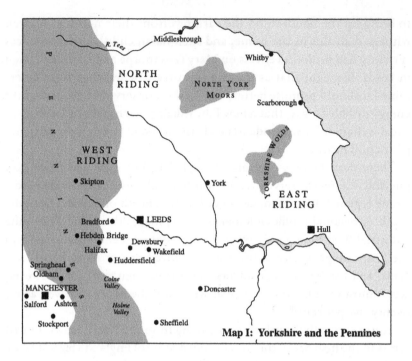

Map I: Yorkshire and the Pennines

For individual families, vivid personal meanings lay behind such abstract population distribution statistics. There were dramatic migrations of people not only from rural south to industrial north, but also countless smaller journeys criss-crossing the region, families constantly packing up to move from country to town. Particularly in the Pennine West Riding, the central industrial landscape of this story, plentiful textile jobs persuaded families to uproot from the land and to move into towns. This pattern of frequent, undramatic economic migrations – for a better job, for a bigger rented house – was typical of working-class families such as that of Dora Thewlis and her suffragette mother, Eliza.

The majority of those rebel girls who became community suffragettes either worked in a textile mill or in linked manufacturing jobs: Dora Thewlis was a weaver in Huddersfield, Lavena Saltonstall a fustian clothing machinist in Hebden Bridge. Otherwise they worked in occupations such as shop assistants, which indirectly depended upon the factory population. Of those later maverick militants, Leonora Cohen initially helped her mother, a skilled needlewoman, with garment-finishing at home in Leeds; she later became a skilled milliner, making wire hat-shapes and intricate hand-tucking for the luxury hat trade.

Within the three Yorkshire ridings, of the 1,166,000 men and 446,000 women recorded, as occupied, no fewer than 126,000 men and 149,000 women worked in textiles, with a further 41,000 men and 68,000 women in clothing, tailoring and millinery. In other words, fourteen per cent of working men and an extraordinary forty-nine per cent of working women had jobs in either the textile or associated clothing industries.[13]

It was the landscape of this textiles territory which shapes the early part of this suffrage story. Across a landscape of dark millstone grit flowed the great rivers, into which tumbled smaller streams, cutting deep valleys in the Pennine hillsides. Alongside the major rivers ran the man-made canals, and on the banks of both rivers and canals stood the great stone-built textile mills and factories.

This industrial north was *the* cradle of the suffrage movement. And while the suffrage history trigger-spring lay with Manchester, capital city west of the Pennines, the textile communities of Pennine West Riding, notably the Huddersfield and Halifax areas, provided the crucible where were forged the early community suffragette campaigns.

Edwardian girls like Mary Gawthorpe and Lavena Saltonstall observed the harsh and confined lives of their late-Victorian mothers – and wondered. Their mothers' educational opportunities had been so limited, illiteracy almost commonplace: the mothers who signed their daughters' birth certificates with just a cross included those of Dora Thewlis's mother Eliza (1860) and Annie Kenney (1879). Alongside, a double moral standard concerning sexual behaviour still prevailed; at least one suffragette's mother had to employ a lawyer to pin down the slithering father of her illegitimate baby and to persuade him to sign an 'Agreement as to Child' to pay maintenance if he wished his paternity to remain discreetly hidden.

Late-Victorian legislation began to usher in reforms. The great 1870 Education Act, by introducing free compulsory elementary education, had triggered the building of big new schools by local School Boards. The education offered might often have been over-crowded, noisy and repetitive. Yet, as *The Intellectual Life of the British Working Classes* (2001) argues, it opened up to the coming generation of late-Victorian Board School children the opportunity to enjoy learning about other worlds, of reading as a pleasure, of writing as a power.[14]

Women have always written, and now opportunities to be published were widening. Modest Isabella Ford was among those who tried her hand at fiction. Published in 1890, her first novel was, Walt Whitman was informed, 'quite a success'; but reviewers dubbed it over-detailed. The second, exploring young women in bohemian London (her sister Emily had been an art student at the Slade) had a mixed reception. Of her third novel, *The Times* crushingly dismissed her talent as 'needs developing'.[15] In the new century, Isabella became yet more self-effacing in her forties, turning from novel-writing to labour politics and women's suffrage.

However, with more freelance outlets opening, Edwardian women grew able to put their own writing on a more professional basis. Born in 1892, Anglo-Irish Rebecca West was among the most witty and successful. She had her first piece of journalism – a letter to *The Scotsman* on 'Women's Electoral Claims' – published when she was still at school; and from 1911 when she was nineteen, her pieces appeared regularly in the adventurous *Freewoman*, plus the socialist *Clarion* papers; and she began writing her second novel, *Adela*.[16]

But for most women emerging from the Board Schools, it remained difficult to write your way out of the mill or clothing workshop; whatever their ambitions, they had no option but to keep their dreams as dreams and to stay with the 'day job'. So it was the Edwardian suffrage campaign that now gave the greatest fillip to women's writing. Here was their cause, here was their subject, here was the opportunity to dip their feminist pens in vitriol and take on all critics. Lavena Saltonstall had her fair share of the suffragettes' devastating wit, writing in the evenings after finishing at her clothing machinist job. One anti-suffragette, styling himself 'Pankson Baines', took her on in the newspapers, and must have been relieved when imprisonment forced Lavena to curtail the escalating correspondence.

Opportunities were also opening up for women artists. The landscapes painted by Florence Lockwood, who too had earlier been a student at the Slade, captured the rich landscape grandeur of her rural-industrial Colne Valley. Florence also went on to design Huddersfield's beautiful suffrage banner for public display. Indeed, the Votes for Women campaign prompted Edwardian designers, artists and embroiderers to rise to the needs of the processional hour. It promoted their work to a new public.

Successive reform acts – 1832, 1867, 1884 – had given additional men the parliamentary franchise. By the turn of the century, most adult men could vote at parliamentary elections: probably about sixty to seventy per cent of them satisfied the electoral requirements of owning or renting property.[17] This brought skilled working-class men into the constitutional fold. Mary Gawthorpe's father, a leather worker in Leeds, not only had the vote but was taken on by his employer, a prominent local Conservative MP, as an

1. The Colne Valley, Slaithwaite, 1922, painted by Florence Lockwood of Linthwaite, watercolour.

efficient Party organiser who could drum up the working-class vote at elections. As a child Mary remembered house-to-house canvassing and substantial election teas; but her mother was less sanguine about 'the politicals' – especially when her husband 'sat long hours with political cronies in this or that public house'.

Growing numbers of women could vote, and even stand for election – but only for local government. With an increasingly wider local government franchise, even married women could count. Emmeline Pankhurst was elected to both her local Board of Guardians and later to the Manchester School Board. It was deemed perfectly seemly for Edwardian women to concern themselves with local philanthropic affairs – a natural extension of their traditional charitable sphere, whether single, married or widowed. Yet women should *not* concern themselves with state governance including, as it did, defence of the 'wider still and wider' empire and declaration of war; after all, women did not even fight. Their exclusion from full citizenship continued decade after decade.

It was not for want of asking. As early as 1832, an independent Yorkshire woman, Mary Smith, who satisfied the then demanding property qualifications, had even dared petition Parliament – through Henry Hunt MP, veteran democrat champion of the 1819 Peterloo Massacre. Since then, a women's suffrage movement, born in the 1860s, had – thanks to some far-sighted women supported by John Stuart Mill MP – taken every opportunity to put its requests for enfranchisement to Parliament.

The natural home of the new women's suffrage movement lay in pro-gressive Liberalism such as Mill's, and its natural home was Manchester. Here it was led by pioneer suffragist Lydia Becker, with the support of rising radical barrister and active Liberal, Richard Pankhurst, champion of every progressive cause. And in the 1890s Richard and Emmeline became actively involved in a new Women's Franchise League, which campaigned that the demand for the vote should include married women, not just single women and widows.

Leeds was rather overshadowed by energetic Manchester. Nevertheless, the roots of the Leeds Women's Suffrage Society, formed in 1890, also lay in progressive Liberalism. Its support largely came from the city's professional elite – who had now moved up out of the congested city centre to quiet elegant suburban streets like Springfield Mount, home to merchants and 'share-brokers'; or migrated further north to Headingley or even out to Adel. No family epitomised this progressive suffrage elite better than Isabella Ford's, now living out in the country at spacious Adel Grange. Like that other lawyer's family, the Pankhursts, the Fords supported every late-Victorian reforming cause: anti-slavery, Josephine Butler's 'contagious diseases' campaign, women's education – and, of course, suffrage. Along with her sister Bessie and their sister-in-law, Isabella helped form the Leeds Women's Suffrage Society.[18] Yet this Suffrage Society was more than just a Ford family club. Its president lived at the top of Springfield Mount, and here hosted some of its afternoon drawing-room meetings; among the Society's earliest members was Agnes Sunley, wife of a poorly paid factory packer, who had earlier been employed as a suffrage petition worker, collecting signatures round working-class districts of Yorkshire.[19]

From the early pioneer days of Lydia Becker and the Women's Franchise League, the suffrage movement had met continued frustrations: private members' bills in the House of Commons repeatedly failed for lack of government support. In 1893 however, friends of suffrage like Isabella Ford and Mrs Fawcett, widow of a leading Liberal politician, determined to win wider public support. They organised a Special Appeal to be signed by women only, 'of all Parties and all Classes', including industrial women workers, and they set about collecting signatures. In Manchester, this new wave of suffrage energy attracted a recent graduate, Esther Roper, who took on the daunting secretaryship of the important Manchester Society. Her father had left school at eleven for factory work and then been taken up by the Church Missionary Society; after he died, CMS supported Esther at Owens College, and she graduated in 1891. This unorthodox background gave Esther a refreshingly new perspective on suffrage: she took the Special Appeal to the factory gates and into working women's homes. Though self-effacing, she even organised a demonstration of over five thousand people in Manchester's Free Trade Hall, with Richard Pankhurst and national leader Mrs Fawcett on the platform. Then, from 1897, Esther was joined in Manchester by charismatic Irish poet Eva Gore-Booth, and together this impressive pair took suffrage campaigning into the new century.[20]

Yet for *our* story, it is Isabella who now grows in significance. With remarkable courage, she had begun to move away from her family's Liberalism, and had even joined the socialists in Leeds. Isabella and her sister Bessie, disillusioned with Liberal employers' hypocrisy after the defeat of the great Manningham mill workers' strike in nearby Bradford, had joined the ILP at the very first opportunity.[21] The ILP supported trade union campaigns, and Isabella championed the tiny struggling Leeds tailoresses' society, plus women textile workers in Yorkshire, so poorly organised compared to Lancashire, supporting local women's strike actions. As an experienced traveller who 'had' languages, Isabella even began to represent trade unionists at international gatherings, though she found public speaking nerve-racking. In acknowledgement of her selfless labour campaigns, her modest portrait even appeared in the *Yorkshire Factory Times*.

2. *Isabella Ford,* Yorkshire Factory Times *supplement, 1 November 1889.*

Isabella experienced real difficulty in helping working women make economic gains when they still completely lacked a constitutional voice. She increasingly turned to *political* solutions, and in 1897 helped set up the National Union of Women's Suffrage Societies (NUWSS) led by her friend, dignified Mrs Fawcett.

For the first time women's suffrage had an effective countrywide organisation, particularly strong in the Manchester area. Here, the northern suffrage revival encouraged Esther Roper and Eva Gore-Booth to join with local women trade unionists and to take their radical tactics one step further. They would launch a suffrage petition to be signed only by women working in Lancashire's great cotton mills. All such women contributed to the country's wealth, were subject to its industrial legislation, yet none of them could vote for the MPs who made those laws. At a national level, the name of the newly formed Labour Representation Committee highlighted this political anomaly: working men demanded to be represented in Parliament.

Esther and Eva launched their suffrage petition in May 1900 in Blackburn, where no fewer than 16,000 women worked in the weaving mills. Petition workers, like experienced mill worker Selina Cooper, were recruited; they trudged down cobbled back streets to collect names from women just home from a day's work, and stood patiently in mill yards with their sheets ready for signature. This painstaking work paid dividends: by spring 1901, these radical suffragists had persuaded no fewer than 29,359 Lancashire women cotton workers to sign; and in March the giant petition was taken down to Westminster — where it was presented to sympathetic MPs, with speeches from cotton trade unionists.[22]

Unlike Esther Roper in Manchester however, Isabella's Leeds campaign was disadvantaged. She was joined by no Eva Gore-Booth; she lacked Esther's strategic links to the city's university and she lacked the hinterland of well-organised, politically experienced women textile trade unionists across Lancashire that Esther could call upon. Nevertheless, fired by the success of the Lancashire women cotton workers' petition, Isabella's attention now turned to Yorkshire. Here suffragists aimed to collect signatures from the less well-paid, poorly organised women textile workers the other side of the Pennines. The arguments for citizenship were growing ever stronger with the increased economic presence of working women. There was international pressure now, as suffragists in northern Europe noticed that women were already able to vote in certain Australian and American states. And so, as the new century dawned, the hopes of the women's suffrage movement were rising – even across Yorkshire.

As Elgar's stirring music and Benson's imperial words echoed around England, many of the rebel girls growing up in the 1890s and yearning for wider possibilities began to encounter a new spirit that would transform their lives. Often it was a charismatic Votes for Women speaker: Adela Pankhurst listening to her own mother, Mary Gawthorpe hearing Christabel Pankhurst at the Labour Church in Leeds, Lavena Saltonstall coming across women orators in Halifax. New possibilities, only wishfully dreamed of earlier, began to open.

Edwardian writers were entranced by the possibilities heralded by such a 'Piper at the Gates of Dawn' vision.[23] Few captured better than Rebecca West this enticing promise of new life and new freedoms. In her novel, significantly entitled *Adela*, West's heroine, whose wealthy uncle refuses to pay for her university education, is confined to a humdrum typing job in an ugly city. 'Adela' then travels by train across England's countryside, and she:

Felt a pleasure in the mere fact of existence quite new to her . . .

As she looked wildly over the fields, she saw that a road crossed the plains to the little town . . . Somehow this road fascinated her. It seemed the most desirable thing in the world to walk along by the bent alders in the lively winds: to become for a time a part of the joyful traffic of the plains . . . And in the morning to go forth again to somewhere lovelier and more distant to find pleasanter and kindlier people.

For the first time in her life she felt fully the desire for the open road . . . Her cheeks flamed. Overcome by a passion quite as sharp and fiery as any lust, she turned swiftly to make her way out of the station on to that road.[24]

Elgar's melody had captured the new Edwardian *zeitgeist*. At the new century's dawn, the rebel girls welcomed the open road.

PART ONE

Dawn

1903–1906

CHAPTER 1

Daughter: Adela Pankhurst

1903–1906

A blue plaque by the front door of 62 Nelson Street, Manchester reads: 'Emmeline Pankhurst (1858–1928) and her daughters Christabel and Sylvia, founders of the suffragette movement, lived here 1897–1907'. Emmeline Pankhurst, iconic founder of the suffragette movement, is a household name. And everyone has heard of her eldest daughter Christabel, brilliant tactician, and Sylvia, talented artist and the movement's historian. Yet there was also a third daughter, Adela, largely erased from suffrage histories and so forgotten.

The youngest of the three Pankhurst sisters, Adela was just eighteen years old when the Women's Social and Political Union (WSPU) was founded at her family home on Saturday 10 October 1903. Adela boasted neither her mother's poignantly elegant charisma, nor Christabel's incisive lawyer's mind, nor yet Sylvia's powerful political writing skills. But, the first teenage suffragette, she was recognised by Edwardian contemporaries as the most original and 'most intelligent of that family'.[1]

At an impressively young age, Adela became a powerful open-air orator who could hold and win the rowdy Edwardian crowd. Scarcely out of school, she took off across Lancashire and Yorkshire, sent by her mother to convert the north to votes for women. And she continued to play a key role in the suffrage campaign for the next eight years.

Adela was born on 19 June 1885 in Manchester, third daughter of Emmeline and Richard Pankhurst. When Adela was a baby, the family moved down to London, where their Russell Square home became a mecca for every advanced political thinker: socialists, freethinkers, Italian anarchists.[2] A son, Harry, was born in 1889, but seems to have been too young to accompany his three sisters for the holiday to Clacton on the Essex coast – and to the photographer's studio by the pier.[3] This well-known photograph taken about 1890 records a solemn Adela about the time of her fifth birthday, staring out at the camera.[4]

3. Centre: *Adela Pankhurst, about her fifth birthday, Clacton-on Sea, c.1890.*
Left: *Christabel.* Right: *Sylvia.*

In Russell Square, Adela spent much time downstairs with the three servants, sitting on a high steel fender in front of the fire, enjoying 'the company of the "proletarians" in the kitchen'. Older, cleverer Christabel and Sylvia 'moved in the firmament above me, as two remote but brilliant stars. They could do everything that was worth doing . . . go out with father and mother; even to meetings, which I imagined were delectable' – for her mother was busy in the drawing-room upstairs with meetings of the new Women's Franchise League.[5]

Then in 1893, the Pankhurst family moved back north and the three sisters were sent to the fee-paying Manchester Girls' High School. Adela, just eight years old, felt lost at this large elite school and hated it.

This was also the moment when her parents abandoned their progressive Liberalism for Keir Hardie's newly formed visionary Independent

Labour Party (ILP). Socialism rather than women's suffrage now became the Pankhursts' creed. Throwing herself into this new cause, Emmeline was elected on an ILP ticket to the local Board of Guardians, responsible for administering the Poor Law; she attended weekly meetings to oversee the workhouse and provision of outdoor relief. Richard, who despite poor health did not stint himself either, also stood as an ILP candidate at the General Election, though unsuccessfully.

Adela's parents were passionately involved in socialist 'free speech' campaigns in Manchester. 'Most of my early recollections are political', she wrote later:

> Our home now became the centre of active political life, local comrades came to arrange political events and speakers visiting the city were entertained by us . . . One small girl, who sat quieter than the quietest mouse, lest she should be observed and banished . . .
>
> My parents mixed freely in all these activities and this was almost the only social life we knew.[6]

Christabel and Sylvia could enjoy the rage for bicycling, popularised by the socialist Clarion Cycling Clubs. The two younger children felt excluded from these activities:

> I grew more and more oppressed and listless day by day. Harry, too, was pale and delicate, repressed and miserable. He got his share of teasing but less than mine and with less animosity. My sisters took little notice of him. He was small and unimportant and they, with their cycling and socialist interests, by this time nearly grown up.
>
> Father and mother must have been worried over Harry . . . but they did not think of the one thing needful; that my mother should give up her public work and devote herself to her only son. It would have been treason to the Cause . . . One excitement followed another in public life. Strikes, elections, free speech demonstrations, public bodies – but we two younger children drooped, more and more.[7]

Certainly, around the time of her eleventh birthday in June 1896, Adela felt so badly neglected she even ran away from school. She was discovered and brought back; but, possibly suffering some kind of a nervous breakdown, she refused to speak. To deal with this silent rebellion, her parents took Adela away from the High School and sent her to stay with an aunt in Aberdeen. Afterwards, some of the teasing at home seemed to cease, and she began to enjoy school rather more. But, Adela reflected later, 'Experiments are very dangerous things and this one of my parents in raising their children on the "class struggle"', left its mark.[8]

Adela's sense of forlornness deepened. By summer 1898, her father's health had deteriorated, and Emmeline had taken seventeen-year-old Christabel to Geneva to stay with an old family friend. While they were abroad, Richard suddenly grew desperately ill. Sylvia was left to cope with the crisis and summoned doctors. Harry and Adela – who had only just had her thirteenth birthday – watched at the bedside of their dying father, until Sylvia sent them off to school. On 5 July 1898, his wife not yet arrived back, Richard Pankhurst died. The effect of such a sudden bereavement on Adela was profound. She reminisced much later that her father died when she was 'about nine'; the bereavement must indeed have made her feel like a far younger child.

The household plunged into deep mourning. In their distress, Emmeline and Sylvia clung to each other. At the funeral, Richard's coffin was accompanied by thousands on foot plus the Clarion Club on bicycles. Emmeline had chosen for his headstone Walt Whitman's words: 'Faithful and true and my loving comrade!' The legacy of Richard's political idealism was magnetic: 'The loss of our father had the effect of intensifying in all of us the desire to carry out, through our lives, the object of his [beliefs,] and our mother was most anxious to keep his ideals always before us'.[9] It was a great deal for Adela to live up to.

In fact, Emmeline – widowed young, losing the lodestar of her life – now found her late husband's unworldly idealism tempered by far more immediate practical considerations. Richard had failed to leave a will. Debts mounted. Emmeline took on a salaried Registrar's post. And the family moved to a smaller house – from the leafy Manchester suburbs to 62 Nelson Street, elegant but in the built-up Oxford Road area near the city centre. She also had to look hard at the cost of her children's education. Christabel, taking part-time courses at Owens College (later Manchester University), reluctantly helped her mother in the 'art' shop Emmeline had opened. And, luckily, Sylvia won a free studentship to Manchester's School of Art.

Emmeline could no longer afford the High School fees for thirteen-year-old Adela, who was sent to a nearby Board School, Ducie, massive, gaunt, in red-brick.[10] For the daughter of a barrister, however radical, the education here was a very abrupt contrast to all Adela had been familiar with. She was cut off from her friends; her scalp became infected with lice. On advice from her sister, Emmeline removed Adela – who returned to the High School. Here, a new headmistress supported Adela's interest in history, and even encouraged her to work towards an Oxford scholarship. However, Emmeline (hotly supported by Sylvia) opposed this on the grounds, they claimed, that Richard would have seen a women-only college at Oxford as a betrayal of his lofty ideals.

Amid the grieving household's gloom, Emmeline was again elected for the ILP, this time to the Manchester School Board – ironically, to help oversee local schools just like Ducie. With their mother politically engaged again, the three younger children spent endless evenings on their own at Nelson Street, missing not just one parent's loving attention but now both.

The household census offers a snapshot of life inside semi-detached 62 Nelson Street in March 1901. Recorded as head of the household was of course forty-two-year-old widow Emmeline Pankhurst, Registrar of Births and Deaths. Twenty-year-old Christabel was listed as working as 'manageress for art [shop]', and eighteen-year-old Sylvia as an art student. Then there is fifteen-year-old Adela and eleven-year-old Harry, both still at school. Ellen Coyle, twenty-five, cook, was assisted by housemaid Mary Leaver, twenty-eight. Additionally there were Emmeline's two brothers: Walter, an accountant, helped his sister keep the art shop books, while Herbert (who helped lighten the family gloom) was a book-binder manager; and there was a second Herbert, a fourteen-year-old nephew. The two uncles seemed to help along the genteelly impoverished Pankhurst household, though adding to its congestion.

Correspondence between an anxious Emmeline and the administrator of the fund established after Richard's death to provide for the children's education and maintenance reveals the effect of her financial worries on Adela. From late 1902 these payments, Emmeline learnt, were to be reduced. Furious, she complained that not only was she sending money each month to Sylvia (now studying art in Venice), but she also needed the full payments to enable Adela to 'continue at the High School preparatory to going to the [Owens] College', for her daughter had a 'distinct literary gift'. Then at the end of 1902, the dismal wrangle still unsettled, Emmeline's nightmares grew:

My youngest daughter has fallen ill with diphtheria & scarlet fever. I have been compelled to isolate her by sending the other members of the family away and as I cannot nurse her myself because of my official work as Registrar I have had to engage a trained nurse.

This is of course a great trial and anxiety to me and also a source of great expense.[11]

Adela was sent away to convalesce while the house was disinfected. In January 1903, the payments at last restored to the old level, Emmeline added in her letter, 'You will I am sure be pleased to know that my girl is nearly well again. She goes to her grandmother on the Isle of Man next week'.

On Adela's return, Emmeline – paying rent for rooms elsewhere and uncles Herbert and Walter no longer living in Nelson Street – found school fees undoubtedly a hurdle again. Financial stringency was required. That spring it was decided that seventeen-year-old Adela could no longer remain at the High School. She must leave. At Easter, she accompanied her mother to Paris to bring a reluctant Sylvia back to Manchester, partly to help in the shop; meanwhile Christabel was being coached for matriculation to Owens College. Years later Adela wrote to an old suffrage friend that she stayed at school 'until I was nearly 16 [17] & only left to let Christabel go to the university & Sylvia to stay abroad after her travelling scholarship was exhausted', her own education sacrificed for theirs.[12]

Respectable jobs were distinctly limited for impoverished Edwardian girls: office work, shop work, possibly teaching. Adela may have had the door slammed shut on her formal education, but she remained as feisty and resourceful as any of the Pankhursts, and had listened to Emmeline's School Board stories. She made enquiries and, for a barrister's daughter, made an odd choice – to become a lowly pupil teacher. This system provided an ill-paid apprenticeship consisting of rather haphazard training while helping teach younger Board School pupils. Adela found that by passing a preliminary examination, she could become an 'Article 50' teacher in an elementary school – and so serve 'the people'.

While nourishing a private desire to write fiction, I set my mind on becoming a teacher, in order to gain an entrance to the people's schools, where I thought I could find a sphere of usefulness. I thought that, presently, I could write a novel based upon my experiences, which would shake the capitalist system to its foundations . . .

In 1903, I left school to enable my sister Christabel to take her law course at the university, and took her place [in the shop?] in assisting my mother, spending about two years at home, reading, writing and thinking a great deal . . .

I read everything I could lay my hands on concerning the social evil, and a desire to begin my career as a crusader for social righteousness was stirring in me. I began to urge my plan of entering the Education Department upon my mother who, not having descerned [sic] my real intentions, did not think it a good opening. My mind was so set upon it that I won her reluctant consent to interview Mr Wyatt, the Director of Education myself, to whom I put my case, literally trembling with eagerness.

In due course I was appointed to a school as a supplementary teacher at £30 a year and I felt I had taken the first step along the road I had so long wished to travel. I was, at last, one of the working masses who were to redeem mankind.[13]

Adela added: 'Poor mother was very much grieved. She had an artist and a lawyer among her children and considered an elementary school teacher rather a come-down'. Emmeline now knew from experience about Board School teacher drudgery. And for Adela, it was too difficult to swallow all her disappointment about her lack of real training. (Years later, one of her old suffrage friends wrote: 'Adela was just a pupil teacher and she told me [she] never had a chance to go in for teaching in the proper way, which I gathered she would have liked to do'.)[14]

Her school was in Urmston, a working-class suburb beyond Salford (and so not part of her mother's jurisdiction). This Board School was much smaller than fearsome Ducie, the classes less noisy; eighteen-year-old Adela would catch the 7 a.m. train for long demanding hours in the classroom, returning home to study so that she could pass 'the necessary examinations – which I very easily did, once I had an insentive [sic] to exert myself. The work I put in was tremendous, teaching all day, studying all night and speaking at weekends. Strangely enough my delicacy seemed to disappear – my cough vanished, the stoop in my shoulders straightened up'.[15]

Indeed, from this point on, Adela seemed to really enjoy her new sense of fulfilment and independence. She later summarised her life: 'the pay was poor; the hours long, but I was happy'. And by then Adela certainly was 'speaking at weekends'. For not only the socialist ILP but also the women's suffrage movement both nationally and in

Manchester, had found new political energy and new sources of popular support.

Esther Roper, now joined by Eva Gore-Booth and experienced mill workers like Selina Cooper, had launched the Lancashire women textile
workers' petition in 1900, and in spring 1901 they took it down to
Westminster. It was just at this point that Christabel Pankhurst, bored
with helping out in her mother's shop and rather at a loose end, began to
attend courses part-time at Owens College. At a poetry lecture she met
Eva and Esther, and was soon captivated by Eva's infectious charm.
Christabel became a frequent visitor in their household. Esther, aware of
her own hard-won university education and impressed by Christabel's
quick brain, suggested to Emmeline that her eldest daughter train as a
lawyer. Christabel now began to read law at Manchester University,
thanks to Esther. Indeed, the three women went on holiday together to
Venice in 1902. This relationship filled a real vacuum in Christabel's life,
her imagination fired by what she recognised as their 'women's suffrage
revival'. In 1901 she joined the North of England Society for Women's
Suffrage (as the Manchester organisation was now called), becoming one
of its regular speakers at ILP meetings. In summer 1903 she watched as
Esther, Eva, Selina Cooper and other working women formed a new
group: the Lancashire Women Textile Workers' Representation
Committee. Its title echoed the newly organised labour movement's logic
and tactics.[16]

By early 1903, Christabel, brought up in a household infused with ILP
idealism, was growing impatient with the slow progress on suffrage and
with the labour movement's lacklustre support. ILP visitors to the
Pankhursts became subjected to 'a weary ordeal of chatter about women's
suffrage', and Christabel even went public in Keir Hardie's *Labour Leader* with
her criticisms of ILP timidity.

Meanwhile, Emmeline had proposed a suffrage resolution at the 1902 ILP
conference. She was herself also now working closely with Eva Gore-Booth
on local schools issues, and would have heard of their new suffrage committee. Emmeline, more than Esther and Eva whose focus lay with women
trade unionists, saw the ILP as *the* way to win Labour support, and decided to
set up her own separate Women's Labour Representation Committee.
However, once Christabel told her mother it sounded too like the
Lancashire Women Textile Workers' Representation Committee, Emmeline
changed its name to the Women's Social and Political Union – WSPU. She

invited a number of local ILP women to 62 Nelson Street on Saturday 10 October 1903.[17]

It was an historic occasion. Later Pankhurst histories have talked up the WSPU's independence of all political parties, its newness and being women-only. This certainly makes for a stirring story, but is not necessarily very good history.[18] The earliest accounts record the WSPU as not only distinctly low-key, but also as essentially a small pressure group within the ILP. Which is what it then was.

Adela's Australian biographer, Verna Coleman, suggests that, at eighteen years old, Adela 'could claim to be the youngest member of the original group that gathered for the first meeting of the new society'. Other writers are more cautious. However, as this meeting was held in her own home and Saturday was not, after all, a school day, it is highly likely Adela was present. The meeting was in Emmeline's small but elegant parlour overlooking a small side garden. As the youngest there, Adela probably played a junior or background role, perhaps helping Mary Leaver to bring in chairs and open the front door, or assisting Ellen Coyle with carrying pots of tea. We shall never know: no WSPU records were kept then. Fragmentary evidence has however survived from much later in Adela's life, when she reminisced to an old suffrage friend, 'I only got myself into the Suffragette movement to get my mother and Christabel out of a hole. I didn't mean to take up politics as a career . . . I was very young and inexperienced'.[19] Suggesting chairs and teapots.

Most importantly, 10 October 1903 was as significant a turning point in Adela's life as had been her father's death and the abandonment of her scholarship hopes – and infinitely more positive. Yet exactly what she did in the early WSPU remains hazy. This is partly because initially the WSPU, just one small local suffrage group among many, remained almost indistinguishable from the ILP, being virtually a socialist ginger group for suffrage.[20] And partly because biographers, keen to suggest Adela was soon out addressing suffrage meetings, overlook the fifteen hours' toil in a pupil teacher's day; in fact, she was working hard memorising her notes to gain needed qualifications: 'I passed my exam in a few months. My mother was happy about it . . . I think she was fond and proud of me in those happy days . . . [But] to my mother, I am sure my teaching was not a career, but a way by which money could be earned for the great work of agitation'.[21]

Teresa Billington, also a pupil teacher, was one of the WSPU's earliest recruits. Visiting Nelson Street, she found the family 'missionaries in unity in a home in which the mission came first and everything else existed on a lower level'. At WSPU meetings, 'Mrs Pankhurst or Adela would arrive with three or four favourable replies . . . and the speakers would be allotted', often to sympathetic ILP branches.[22] Adela was probably able to squeeze in ILP meetings near home, especially at Tib Street in Manchester city centre, a favourite socialist open-air stump. This was a good time for her, working well with her mother while Christabel studied for her law exams.

Then in February 1904 Christabel had managed to get a platform seat at a Liberal meeting in the Free Trade Hall: she interrupted rising politician Winston Churchill to move a women's suffrage amendment. Though she had to sit down, Christabel could see the effect it had on the leading Liberals – a well-chosen target, since they were likely to form the next government.

In the autumn Sylvia left Manchester for London and the Royal College of Art. However, in spring 1905, just when Adela might reasonably think her home was less crowded, another new suffrage recruit arrived. Mill worker Annie Kenney from Springhead near Oldham had been drawn into the WSPU by Christabel. Childlike Annie had just lost her mother and, utterly bereft, was welcomed at Nelson Street by the Pankhursts, whom she adopted as her substitute family, inspired by Emmeline and falling under Christabel's sway. They asked Annie to stand for a local textile trade union position, which had not entered her mind before, and she was elected to the committee.[23] For the WSPU, this was immensely useful, as Esther Roper and Eva Gore-Booth had already shown. A woman trade unionist, claiming to speak for tens of thousands of voteless mill workers, carried far greater political clout than, say, a humble pupil teacher.

Adela and Annie initially worked well together. Yet for Adela, still catching the early morning train out to Urmston and struggling with teaching plus studying, this had the makings of a difficult situation. One older sister had gone, but within months another rival for her mother's attentions had arrived. Also, independent-minded Teresa Billington now gave up teaching: Emmeline had arranged for her to work as the ILP's first woman organiser – possibly a rather tantalising prospect for Adela too. It was about this time that she fell ill again, this time with pleurisy.[24]

Meanwhile, Emmeline's frustration mounted at the lack of suffrage progress. In May 1905, a private member's bill was presented in Parliament, but once again it was talked out, despite lobbying by Emmeline and other suffragists.

Then in June, not long after Adela's twentieth birthday, school broke up. The holidays at last gave her *time* – a luxury in such short supply for the past two years. And with the summer weather, the small WSPU branched out more widely, though still very dependent on ILP branches' support and Hardie's *Labour Leader* publicity. Emmeline spoke locally on women's enfranchisement, as did Sylvia (back home for holidays) and Harry. Beyond Manchester, Annie Kenney spoke near Oldham, while Christabel even ventured out to Grimsby and Middlesbrough, selling Hardie's 'Plea for Women's Suffrage'. Adela's favourite stump remained Tib Street, yet by the end of the summer she had also gone with Sylvia and Annie out to fairgrounds in Ashton and in Oldham. She might be the youngest and still haunted by personal insecurities, but Adela certainly could hold her own as a stump orator. Later, she rather sweepingly conjured up these times:

> From a shy, somewhat melancholy girl I became, before I was nineteen, a self-confident woman who could hold crowds of thousands . . . All I wanted was a piece of chalk and a 'lorry' [low, flat wagon] because I was too small to speak off a soap box and all by myself I could rouse any district.[25]

Then, once the autumn term started again, all this went quiet – for a short while.

A general election was expected, with a new Liberal government predicted. And on Friday 13 October, 1905, again at the Free Trade Hall, leading Liberal politicians Winston Churchill and Sir Edward Grey were billed to speak. Christabel Pankhurst and Annie Kenney obtained two tickets. It turned out to be a legendary occasion. At question time Annie Kenney jumped up from her seat to interrupt this packed meeting of the Liberal party which, after all, boasted that it was the party of democratic reform. She shouted, 'Will the Liberal government give women the vote?' When she was ignored, Christabel and she unfurled their 'Votes for Women' banner, whereupon both women were hustled out. Christabel, with her legal training, knew she had to do more. She apparently spat at one of the policemen. This worked. The women were arrested and had to appear in court.

Adela undoubtedly knew of this daring plan beforehand and, although not in the hall, certainly remembered being caught up in the ensuing blaze of publicity: 'Next morning, every newspaper in the United Kingdom published accounts of the incident under staring headlines . . . But the evening

papers had the biggest thrill, for the elderly magistrate, with a lack of fore-
sight common to his species, delivered the law and the Liberals into the
hands of these two young girls by sending them to prison.'[26]

Christabel was sentenced to seven days and Annie to three in
Manchester's Strangeways prison. 'The excitement which prevailed was
intense', Adela added. Then, to welcome them both back from gaol, the
ILP organised a protest meeting in the Free Trade Hall; it was advertised by
the *Labour Leader*, with not only the two ex-prisoners speaking but also
Emmeline, Esther Roper, Eva Gore-Booth and Teresa Billington. As Adela
recalled, 'The very fact that the largest hall in one of the greatest cities of
the Empire was filled to overflowing to consider the question of votes for
women was a triumph . . . A roar of applause burst forth and, as my sister
and her companion stood facing the great audience, they were cheered and
cheered again.'[27]

Hannah Mitchell, another new WSPU recruit, added: 'The North was
roused, and neither Sir Edward Grey nor his Party were ever able to damp
down the fire they lit on that October evening in 1905'.[28] The suffrage campaign had overnight sped into a new gear.

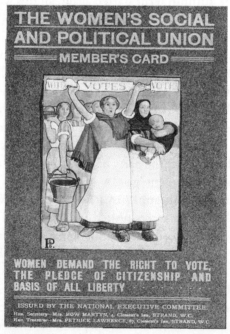

4. *WSPU Membership Card designed by Sylvia Pankhurst c.1906.*

However Adela, busy teaching, still struggled to squeeze politics into any free time. Poignantly, even on New Year's Eve 1905, she was among the 'small band of faithful' braving the cold weather to speak at Tib Street.

By now the WSPU had dispatched Annie Kenney down to London, better to attack Liberal politicians in the run-up to the General Election. Then, in January 1906 the WSPU moved its headquarters from Manchester to London. This shift of WSPU focus seemed to free up Adela to flex her own suffrage muscles and to respond to the greater demands on her:

It fell to my lot to become more and more active in the movement since Annie went to London and my sister [Christabel] was nearing her final examinations. I had often to take my mother's place when she found the demands [on] her were beyond her time and strength.

When I think how young I was and how inexperienced in life, I marvel at her faith in my good sense and capacity, when she sent me travelling long distances from home to address meetings, not only in halls, but out of doors, without the least doubt that I could acquit myself well in any circumstances which arose. At that time, I saw nothing strange about a small, round faced girl of less than twenty years of age, standing before great crowds, to address them on the great questions of the day. As a matter of fact, I forgot all about myself, and thinking only of the movement, I generally found the hour or more for which I had been speaking had slipped away and neither I nor the audience were aware of it.[29]

We do get a strong sense that from this point, spring 1906, Adela came into her own, her apprenticeship years at last over. She even wrote a poignant short story for *Labour Leader*: its heroine, Geraldine Horsely, was all that had been denied Adela by family circumstances. Geraldine had just come 'down from Oxford' and she aimed to set up an experimental school – helped by her father, a 'progressive' Liberal mill-owner. In their luxurious home, Geraldine 'sat with her parents over the fragrant log fire' outlining her plans. But her father refuses his permission. Geraldine ought to have other priorities now, he tells her firmly:

'To succeed politically, I have to entertain many distinguished men here in my house. Your duty lies there. You are young and pretty, well educated and talented in a womanly way, and what you have to do, Geraldine, is to please – I repeat it, to please'.[30]

Open warfare rumbles between father and daughter. Geraldine is tempted by noble self-sacrifice. Then one night her mother enters her bedroom. By the flickering fire she 'knelt beside her chair, and laid her head on her daughter's knees' – warning Geraldine against marrying a man with whom she has nothing in common. Her mother confesses her own marriage had been a compromise: her impoverished parents had urged her to assure herself 'of a home and a protector'. So, mother now warns daughter, 'live your own life, be responsible for your own actions, right or wrong'. Emboldened, Geraldine replies:

> 'Dear mother . . . I am strong enough now. I will be free, and if I must give
> up my school, I can do good work teaching in another . . . I will let in the
> light, the light of a new day, mother, for you and for me' . . . The mother
> and daughter watched the wild March dawn brighten over the hills.

Adela had frequently yearned for the intimate confidences Geraldine enjoyed with her mother. But there the parallel ends. For Adela's parents' marriage had scarcely been a soulless compromise; nor would they have pushed their daughters into expedient marriages. But though Adela's parable might lack narrative subtlety, and her own family experience be unconventional, yet it sheds a shaft of light on her dreams of freedom and loving relationships, and a new future for women glimpsed in 'the wild March dawn'.

As well as this writing, Adela also deputised for her mother at speaking engagements: at a Yorkshire ILP branch, making 'a fair substitute' for Emmeline to a good audience; and she spoke on women and socialism in both Salford and the Peak District.[31] For Adela, as with the early WSPU hopes, socialism and suffrage remained intimately entwined. She was now part of the team and was able to deal imaginatively with heckling crowds:

> Sometimes, my meetings began in a very rowdy fashion; mobs of boys and
> men would gather round the box or chair on which I was mounted and pelt
> me well with eggs and tomatoes or over-ripe oranges, but I generally met
> them with good enough humo[u]r to win their silence and I would end up
> by having an enthusiastic hearing. I am and always was incapable of think-
> ing out a joke beforehand, but sometimes I saw quite spontaneously, the
> humorous side of things, which was very helpful with an obstreperous
> crowd. Once, I remember in Bradford, I had a particularly tiresome and

narkish interjector, who eyed me sourly, from under a lamp post, and kept up a running fire of disparaging interjections; at last he said: 'If you were my wife I'd give you a dose of poison'. 'No need of that, my friend' I replied cheerfully, 'If I were your wife I'd take it'. The audience yelled with delight and my tormentor left the meeting early.[32]

CHAPTER 2

New woman: Mary Gawthorpe
1904–1906

Coincidentally, over the other side of the Pennines also on Saturday 10 October, 1903 – the day Emmeline Pankhurst formed the WSPU – Leeds Arts Club opened *its* doors to newest thinking of a different sort. Inspired by charismatic intellectual Alfred Orage, the Club introduced Yorkshire's greatest city to *avant garde* modernist culture, including European writers such as Henrik Ibsen and provocative new thinkers, notably Friedrich Nietzsche. The Arts Club recruited among the 'professional proletariat': elementary school teachers like Orage, craftsmen such as printers and compositors.[1] And among those magnetised by the Arts Club magic was Mary Gawthorpe, just four years older than Adela Pankhurst, who had also left school to become a humble pupil teacher. It was Orage's new world of Nietzschean philosophy that inspired Mary to burst free of her restrictive Victorian upbringing and, even more decisively than Adela, to reinvent herself as an Edwardian 'new woman'.

Nellie Gawthorpe, as she was then called, was born on 12 January 1881 at 5 Melville Street in Woodhouse, north Leeds, and grew up in red-brick-terraced working-class respectability. Mary always remembered every detail of that first family house. Downstairs, in front of the fireplace stood the heavy wooden tub (later replaced by a larger zinc bath), in continuous use on Saturday evenings. The floor was covered with coconut matting and a home-made rug; her mother's invaluable sewing machine, also always in use, stood to the left of the fire to catch the best light. Upstairs were two bedrooms. Four daughters and a son were all born in the big bed; they appeared at regular intervals over a dozen years, 'controlled entirely by Nature's rhythm'. Lacking indoor toilets, the bedrooms contained 'the sanitary indispensables for night use' – the alternative being a dark walk up Melville Street to fearsome communal outdoor closets. The Gawthorpe house was safe, domestic, familiar. '"Home is where Mother is" was supremely true in our home, where Mother was rarely absent'.[2]

Nellie's mother, Annie, had worked in a mill from the age of ten, until she could be taken out to help her sister, a dressmaker. Nellie's father had hoped to become a teacher but had had to follow his father into a leather works. John Gawthorpe now worked as a currier at one of the tanneries in smoky Buslingthorpe, just below Melville Street and alongside Meanwood Beck, which flowed down into the River Aire in the city centre. This north Leeds neighbourhood contained no fewer than a dozen leather works and textile mills.[3] As a young child Nellie, close to her father, would go on errands to his work. She negotiated the narrow paths between pits full of soaking skins, passed where the skins were tanned; she skirted the 'fleshing shed' and the great furnaces, and climbed up into the building where she watched her father, wearing a giant buffer on his right arm, draw the tanned pieces across to ensure the leather's suppleness before they were transformed into boots and shoes.[4]

An energetic Anglican, John Gawthorpe was also choir leader and Sunday school superintendent at nearby St Michael's Church in Buslingthorpe. His employer, W. L. Jackson, was an eminent Leeds Conservative MP. When most men had the right to vote, an efficient working-class Conservative organiser who could drum up the votes was highly prized; so, at election time, Nellie's enterprising father 'did not curry leather, he electioneered', being employed as one of Jackson's ward agents. 'But part-time leather worker and part-time political worker was a demoralising combination, particularly as Mother only half tolerated the politicals' – especially when it began to affect the household budget and the orderliness of Annie's respectable temperance home. Her husband 'sat long hours with political cronies in this or that public house . . . coming home later and later'.[5]

Nellie's warm childhood years were short-lived. Her father committed a 'glaring indiscretion', possibly fuelled by political alcohol. A 'black cloud' descended on the family 'and Dadda was It'. Nellie's mother could not forgive 'what Father had done to her home'. His church involvement began to fade. Problems mounted. When Nellie was seven, two of her sisters died (first baby Alice, then ten-year-old Lucy). Other serious family illnesses followed: scarlet fever, pneumonia, typhoid fever. Doctors were forever in and out of the Gawthorpe house and their fees had to be paid. Debts mounted – as did tensions between her parents, and ten-year-old Nellie became abruptly aware of what was unspoken; she recalled one night:

> I am standing by the fire. Mother is also standing there. Father has just come in – he is late for tea, the evening meal. He is explaining himself and Mother says, 'Stop maudlin!' . . . Mother looks at me. Something that can be felt drops into me and I know that Father, whose teetotalism I have strenuously maintained in the school yard, for no beer is drunk in our home, is not teetotal, as indeed someone has said.
>
> Looking backwards I see that as the moment of transformation when I was first led to take, silently, Mother's side . . .
>
> Mother did look [at me], and though I did not know all that the look might have said . . . a half-conscious resolve had formed. My soul affirms and remembers the very words: 'When I am twenty-one', it called itself.[6]

'Twenty-one' spelt independence. But for the moment Nellie attended St Michael's church school (rather than a newer Board School) down in industrial Buslingthorpe. She fondly remembered singing and scripture, sewing calico and knitting cuffs. She progressed to a top class, reached only by those not forced to leave and become half-timers: half day in the mill, half at school. By the age of thirteen, most Leeds girls left school to become domestic servants or tailoresses; a lucky handful might even become clerks or teachers. In 1894 Nellie, an able pupil, sat for a scholarship to the Higher Grade (i.e. secondary) School, and was awarded a two-year free scholarship – but without maintenance costs:

> This was entirely unsatisfactory to Father. The scholarship was not accepted on these terms. Though I had given plenty of signs that I was by way of being a teacher, I had never consciously claimed my calling. Father it was who decided the issue and solved the problem of [my] getting more education and more money. I was to be a pupil-teacher then, at his own St Michael's. Father presented the proposal, and without any hitch it was accepted . . .
>
> With Father and Mr Brown [head teacher], I signed the articles of my four years' apprenticeship . . . I was thirteen years and some months and I was to begin teaching at once. One day I was a pupil. Next day I was a pupil teacher.[7]

Probably helped by Nellie's extra wage, however modest, the Gawthorpe family – parents, Nellie, her brother Jim and older sister – then moved to a slightly larger house nearby, 30 Jubilee Street. As a pupil teacher, Nellie had to work hard. She was assigned to a class in the Infants' school (where she was disconcerted by one teacher's sly innuendos about 'Father'). 'Those were', she recalled, 'rather forlorn days'. Every morning, after an evening's studying, Nellie rushed her breakfast and raced to school: she and the two other pupil-teacher girls had a lesson from 8 to 9 a.m. with a college-trained teacher. Afterwards, Nellie taught her pupils everything, from scripture to sewing, history to recitation. Though much of it was 'drudgery and grudgery', she also taught herself to play the school's old-fashioned harmonium; she made friends with other pupil teachers, and she won an education prize – the first of many.[8]

Then, halfway through this apprenticeship, Nellie, along with the only other pupil teacher to survive the regime, began half-time attendance at the Pupil-Teachers' Centre opposite Leeds' imposing town hall. Her small childhood world suddenly expanded. The Centre was in the impressive stone-carved offices of Leeds School Board, built as a monument to municipal pride. 'What a revolution as well as a revelation', she remembered, 'there was no hardship in this'. Nellie shared classes with older Board School teachers, and here encountered grammar, algebra and formidable mental arithmetic. Saturday mornings at the Central Higher Grade School on Woodhouse Lane included science, French and solid geometry. 'Always, in halls of memory, I sit at these Saturday classes in half-galleried, sunlit rooms . . . decidedly hollow inside but even more hungry for all the instruction I could hold'. Inspired, Nellie excelled, winning more prizes.[9]

Among the pupil teachers Nellie met there was Ethel Annakin from Harrogate, daughter of a well-to-do builder. Ethel went on to teacher training college in Liverpool, something Nellie longed to do 'above all things in the world'. In 1899 she passed the Queen's Scholarship with distinctions. Though both the Centre principal and her aunt offered to pay her college expenses, it meant two years without a salary. The alternative, working towards the Government Certificate for non-college-trained teachers, entailed continuing as before: teaching by day and studying by night. Nellie felt agonisingly torn. Annie Gawthorpe, old beyond her years like so many hard-worked Victorian mothers, experienced a difficult menopause, losing all her teeth by the age of forty-five. In the end Nellie felt 'it was my duty to stand by my Mother, whose health was frailer and frailer with each passing brush with the reality which was Father'.[10] Tensions between her parents had certainly grown even sharper: Nellie could see these problems increasingly troubling her hard-pressed mother.[11]

5. *Nellie Gawthorpe, aged 18, 1899, wearing a 'mother-made blouse'.*

So Nellie stayed at St Michael's, where she had been – child and pupil teacher – for fourteen years. But her apprenticeship was ended. Aged nineteen, her annual salary was raised to £45. She soon found another job, teaching at a boys' school in Beeston, south Leeds, and earning £50 as an assistant mistress, again in a church school. 'It was my first major, independent act', and 'did not please Father when he heard of it.'[12] Every day Nellie got up early, to take two trams – down into the city centre, across the River Aire and out to Beeston. She taught the older boys: only a few years separated them from their teacher, and some even towered over her for she remained small. Nellie summed it up: 'I loved teaching, loved the little lads, raced from one end of the city to the other, then down to the certificate classes . . . back home once more, reading, coming and going and going and coming, one blessed thing after another'.[13]

Nellie's family was also changing. Their father was drinking more despite spasmodic efforts to stop, even signing the temperance pledge of the moderate drinker. But his trouble was deep-seated and John Gawthorpe could not afford to drink at all. Whatever was left from his wages (sometimes little indeed after a drinking spell), there were at least the two daughters' small earnings for their mother to fall back on. Then Nellie's elder sister married in autumn 1900.[14] 'Father's increased fellowship with the politicals' meant Nellie often took the place in the household he had earlier occupied. In the evening, she would study at the kitchen table at 30 Jubilee Street, her books spread out, with her mother seated opposite.

At about ten o'clock, Annie would shoo her daughter upstairs; then Nellie heard:

> Heavy creaks travelling up the stairs. Father!
>
> Home at last! There is some recrimination not always audible as to words, but distinctly hearable, coming from the parental room across the landing . . .
>
> When a particularly distressing passage at arms seemed in progress one night, it occurred to me with the force of revelation that I ought to invite Mother to my bed . . . Mother was of my way of thinking and there we were. We all went to sleep. This happened two or three times . . .
>
> One night the pattern was rudely broken. We had not settled down when Father entered the room, my room, without knocking, an unspeakable outrage, I informed him. Father demanded Mother's presence in their room . . . Crossing his legs in what seemed to me an ungodly pose, reminding me more of a satyr than my Father, in spite of the largeness of the shirt he was wearing . . . Mother . . . suddenly left my bed, followed by Father . . .
>
> [My] naïvety was genuine. Nineteen at the time . . . I had no conscious knowledge of the drama in which I seemed to take part . . . Had I known by direct communication, I should most likely have . . . put up a stiffer fight on Mother's behalf, which, re-informed by the hidden objective 'when I am twenty-one', might have won the battle of the beds on that puzzling night's first round.[15]

Nellie celebrated her longed-for twenty-first birthday in January 1902. And in the summer she passed the final examination.[16] This, rather than the birthday itself, was the milestone to celebrate. She at last could liberate herself from her father's hold. She took singing lessons. She began to have fun, joining a popular church-based pierrots group, dressing up in white costumes, black pom-poms and face patches.[17] She grew increasingly confident and attractive and acquired two boyfriends.

However, her father's unreliability worsened during 1902. In a North Leeds by-election, his employer, Conservative MP Jackson, was defeated by the Liberal, manufacturer Rowland Barran. Given a political payments-by-results system, this was disastrous for the Gawthorpes' family budget. Payments had to be kept up on the family piano; Jim had to leave school and get a white-collar job.

By summer 1902, it became clear that Jim and Nellie alone were contributing to the home, not their father. Annie, now aged fifty, grew weaker. Divorce, or even legal separation, was scarcely available to work-ing-class families. Respectable wives of men who drank their wages had few options. Nellie surveyed this hopeless domestic scene and took the initia-tive:

> I decided to move to Beeston Hill, to live as well as teach there. I carried the major part of the family with me, sweeping Father along with the rising tide . . .
>
>   'When I am twenty-one' is maturing now faster than can be thought. How could the Father like this transplantation? It was now his turn to take the long journey. He was fifty-two and had lived in Woodhouse all his life. He was markedly sober just now, receiving my two boy friends with thoughtful gravity . . .
>
>   Father announced one day that as for him, he was going back to Woodhouse. What could this mean but that here was it, the unknown but wished-for crisis . . . of 'when I am twenty-one'. With unbelievable speed the rest of Father's family acted. He had no sooner declared himself than the three of us – Mother, brother and I – were united. And we were united against him, Father. I went to the Vicar; and now I told him what I could not tell him before . . . We would leave Father to his own devices, no less . . . [The Vicar] was helpful and not critical. He advanced my salary a few days.[18]

They found a smaller house nearby, loaded up onto a one-horse cart all their modest possessions – clothes, Annie's faithful sewing machine, the precious family piano, Nellie's notebooks – and moved. After twenty-seven years of marriage, Annie just left a private note for her husband by the clock on the mantelpiece. Nellie recalled, 'We left him . . . The work was done. We had left Father.' The next day a policeman visited the house; terrified, Annie peered at him through the letterbox; he eventually departed. Nellie had run away from home: she would meet her father only once again.

At Beeston, there was much paper-hanging and whitewashing. Annie looked years younger. Nellie felt exhilarated by her new freedom and the political independence that went with it: 'I was the householder, the rent payer, thus qualified for the municipal vote'. After all the long appren-ticeship years, up she bubbled.[19]

The effect was like a cork fizzing out of a bottle. Of the two boyfriends, Nellie chose the reticent one 'whose friendly eyes I liked better'. Thomas Birtwhistle Garrs lived nearby and was a compositor on the *Yorkshire Post*,

6. Thomas Birtwhistle Garrs.

a skilled printing job. With a father not unlike Nellie's, he already had his share of breadwinning. While she had been absorbed with Annie's problems, Nellie had asked Thomas Garrs to stay away. He was, one mother reported to the other, miserable, and Nellie now turned to Garrs again. Annie was close friends with him from the start. From a very musical family, he was a fine baritone, while Nellie herself had developed into a mezzo-soprano and began to take singing lessons at Leeds College of Music. Together they would play baritone classics, and then Garrs would have to hurry away to the *Yorkshire Post* night shift to operate his linotype machine (which speeded up the laborious type-setting process). An engagement was announced and Nellie even sent off to London for furniture catalogues, imagining the rooms they would live in after marriage. She always referred to him as 'F.L.' – First Love. It was all part of 'living in that brave, mad, beautiful year [1902] when I was twenty-one'.[20]

It was to be a *very* long engagement. In February 1904, Nellie's teaching probation was at last over: she received the coveted Government 'parchment' and proudly became a fully Certificated Assistant Mistress, paid £60. It had taken her ten hard years. Perhaps not unsurprisingly, she fell ill, afterwards recuperating first at the seaside and then in the Yorkshire country, where she and Garrs developed a taste for walking. Continuing to study, Nellie began attending Leeds University's newly founded extension lectures and became labour delegate to its committee.[21]

Garrs, a thoughtful craftsman, opened up a new world of ideas for Nellie. The Anglican church school system (and with it the Conservative Party) had provided her childhood with its ideological framework. With this went patriotic support for the Boer War. But Garrs had other notions. Stimulated by his persistent questions, Nellie:

> began a determined self-analysis, examining to the best of my ability the basic influences of my life. Instead of being the conservative I had imagined myself, I discovered I was not basically conservative but leaned to labour. More than leaned . . . The discovery was pure velvet, not a hardship. I seemed to be all set that way. The Labour Movement, it now seemed to me, was in aim and method all I had hitherto known as practical Christianity. I took to the new ethics like a duck to water . . . If this was initiation into the requirements of a new age, then First Love was unquestionably my first teacher and initiator.[22]

For Nellie Gawthorpe and Thomas Garrs the labour movement initially meant not the Pankhursts' ILP, but the Labour Church. Founded in 1891, it offered all the comradely fellowship of a chapel but without any other-world theology. Few inspired this idealistic socialism more vividly than Whitmanite writer Edward Carpenter, living near Sheffield – and his hymn, 'England Arise':

> *England Arise, the long, long night is over,*
> *Faint in the east behold the dawn appear;*
> *Out of your evil dream of toil and sorrow*
> *Arise, O England, for the day is here.*

On Sunday mornings Nellie and Garrs attended the Leeds Labour Church, conveniently situated nearby on Dewsbury Road; around this, Nellie recalled, 'trails of Edward Carpenterian glory were still shedding lustre of first origins'. On Sunday evenings, after Garrs had left for his night shift, she attended alone. 'But I was not lonely. How could I be lonely among the comrades who accepted me as warmly and fully as I accepted them?' With them she sang:

> *The people, Lord, the people!*
> *Not thrones and crowns, but men!*[23]

This was a time of tremendous growth within the labour movement. The couple soon joined the local ILP. Although formed in nearby Bradford, the ILP was weak in Leeds. This was partly due to the industrial diversity of the city, with fractured trade unions; hence the strength of local Liberalism – which at the 1900 'Khaki' General Election had won East Leeds from the Conservatives, then gone on to sweep up at the North Leeds 1902 by-election. Herbert Gladstone, son of the great Liberal prime minister and MP for West Leeds, was the rising star.

Nellie rose fast within the small local ILP, buoyed by her abilities and political energy; she became vice-president and responsible for a woman's page in *Labour News*, 'our local baby weekly'.[24]

It was also about this time that Nellie, after some to-ing and fro-ing, began to alter her name to the more sophisticated 'Mary' Gawthorpe. And before long, under her new name, she found herself agreeing to give two Sunday speeches; she went to enormous lengths to prepare her talk on 'The Child under Socialism'. She also encountered Ethel Annakin again, now a college-trained teacher and moving in ILP circles. Then, in 1904, Mary went to hear cool twenty-four-year-old law student Christabel Pankhurst talk at the Labour Church on how 'political enfranchisement must precede social regeneration'. Mary spoke a few words to her afterwards; but the first labour issue of the day then was unemployment and by October 1904 Mary had been drawn into public meetings on the feeding of needy children.[25]

With school every day and more examinations, by mid-1905 Mary was again exhausted, and asked for a transfer out of the smoky city. So, during the summer holidays the regular Gawthorpe trio – Mary, Jim and Annie – made the trek westwards out to the countrified edge of Leeds – and Mary's new Board School, Hough Lane in Bramley. Here, from their new house at Warrell's Mount, the kitchen looked out over open fields. This move was another turning point for Mary. She joined the local rambling club, with its winter *conversaziones* and limelight lectures. She spoke from the regular labour stump – bravely, given that most of her pupils came from Liberal families; and she got on to the National Union of Teachers' committee. Her transformation to Mary Gawthorpe, Edwardian new woman, was well on the way when Thomas Garrs introduced her to the Leeds Arts Club and so Alfred Orage.[26]

Leeds was by far the most cosmopolitan city in Yorkshire. Its diverse economy supported a rich mix of occupations: textile mills, for sure, but also the large tailoring and clothing industries, and the commercial firms with their clerks; there were also government officials, lawyers and doctors, artists and musicians, printers and even writers. And it was a city that had accommodated waves of immigrants – first from Ireland, settling in the congested courts and tenements down by the polluted River Aire; they were later joined by Jewish refugees fleeing anti-Semitism in Russia and eastern Europe.

Less dramatic migrations came from rural England. Among them was Alfred Orage. His family was impoverished (yet another drinking father), his mother widowed. Orage was rescued from a *Jude the Obscure* destiny by a well-placed local patron who had spotted his talents, given him the run of his well-stocked library and sent him to teacher training college. In 1893, aged twenty, Orage had arrived in Leeds to work as a certificated assistant in a school in the Irish community. Shocked by the slums, he wrote an imaginative essay on Leeds and the view looking down to the river from its northern slopes:

> Yonder, down there, the infernal pot is boiling, and the steam hangs like a nightmare over the city . . . The Aire is simply a huge sewer: it has the filth of Leeds in suspension . . . It has been transformed into the oily-flowing mud stream, into whose waters no fish may dare venture, on whose banks no leaves can breathe, no trees may grow.[27]

Orage, also an admirer of Edward Carpenter, joined the ILP, giving lectures to local branches on Shelley's poetry and writing book reviews for *Labour Leader*. But quixotic Orage had scant patience for either ILP collectivism or the drill-like School Board curriculum. Married to an art student, he read voraciously and became attracted to theosophy, yet still felt intellectually isolated. Then, fortuitously, in 1900 in a second-hand bookshop, Orage bumped into Fabian lace merchant-cum-freelance journalist Holbrook Jackson. Jackson was impressed by the powerfully charismatic presence of Orage, then given to wearing hand-woven flame-coloured silk ties. His 'life was a process of getting tired of persons, ideas and movements', for Orage 'was always <u>neo</u>'. This was a meeting of like minds. They shared a fascination for George Bernard Shaw, and Jackson introduced Orage to the German philosopher Friedrich Nietzsche, then little-known in Britain; he lent Orage his copy of Nietzsche's aphoristic *Thus Spake Zarathustra*; with its subversively brilliant declaration that 'God is dead! . . . I teach you the Superman', it came to

Orage as a stunning revelation.[28] Nietzsche, Orage held, 'did for moral-ity what Copernicus did for astronomy': he created a new movement in Europe. God was replaced by superman, beyond ordinary mortals, whose will was no longer constrained by slave morality or mass collectivism. Nietzsche wrote equally provocatively about relationships between men and women:

> Everything about woman has one solution: it is called pregnancy . . .
>
> Man should be trained for war and woman for the recreation of the warrior . . .
>
> Let woman be a plaything . . . Let your hope be 'May I bear the Superman!' . . .
>
> The man's happiness is: I will. The woman's happiness is: He will.[29]

While Orage did not embrace the full 'superman' extremes, he certainly helped popularise Nietzsche's philosophy in England. Orage wrote:

> As the . . . advanceguard of the world-will, he certainly looked upon man as pre-eminently the warrior and . . . the will to power. Correspondingly, woman was the principle of conservation and the will to live. Yet . . . the will to live is no more than the ground and condition of the will to power; and as representing these, woman is the ground and condition of man . . . While man is a means to the world-will's purpose, woman is a means to man.[30]

Orage and Jackson, from shared discussions and pilgrimages to Edward Carpenter, discovered there were others hidden away across Leeds, 'dream-ing similar dreams to ours'. From these intellectually adventurous beginnings sprang the Leeds Arts Club, inaugurated on Saturday 10 October, 1903. It was based very centrally next to the town hall, its prem-ises shared with an engraver and an artist, a printer called Marx and a surveyor called Ovid Umpleby. What could be better? The first of the Club's Saturday afternoon discussion meetings was a talk given by Orage on Nietzsche. Apparently, 'the local bourgeoisie were flabbergasted when the shocking views of such as Nietzsche, Ibsen and Shaw were acclaimed in their midst'.[31]

Thomas Garrs had the highest praise for the Club's cultural possibilities. The subscription was however 10/6d [52p] and membership was by election.

Despite these hurdles, Garrs and Mary joined the following year, one of Garrs' sub-editors at work acting as their sponsor. Mary found one of the greatest of the Club's attractions was its book collection, available to any member wishing a quiet browse. Yet her education, so laboriously acquired, had scarcely prepared her for this heady draught of cutting-edge European culture. She found the Club:

> Was as unique, as distinguished a group then . . . as I have met anywhere since . . . It was stimulating, refreshing and nourishing to be a member . . . It often seemed that in its own sphere the Leeds Arts Club could not have been bettered . . . The Club . . . had the germ of a new future, not necessarily to be matured in London, but . . . a community right on the spot.[32]

Among Mary's treasured possessions was a Leeds Arts Club syllabus: it opens with Orage on 'The Mystical Doctrine of Democracy' one Saturday afternoon, followed by an evening *Conversazione* – plus summer excursions, a literary and a musical group. And then there was also Orage's own spell-binding magnetism. On one occasion, Mary recalled:

> At last I screwed up courage one Saturday afternoon and spoke a few words. When the gathering broke up for scattered conversation, Orage came to me with a word of thanks . . . Orage the catalyst would always endeavour to stimulate or provoke discussion . . . The fishing was always delicately done and you could not please Orage better than by taking hold.[33]

Orage could shock. One day Mary, taking him a message, was shown upstairs by his sister to his book-lined study:

> Before I knew it, he had pulled me to him and had said 'Kiss me' . . . I was led . . . to do exactly what Orage asked, or commanded, that is, I kissed him . . .
>
> Swift as lightning, the taker of the kiss gave a little laugh, an elated tri-umphant laugh . . .
>
> At the first moment I told F.L. what had happened, not knowing what to make of it . . . He listened in silence, and in silence the incident passed.

Later, Mary, on a similar errand, refused to go upstairs, despite the mocking laughter, but subsequently:

It did seem that Orage was going out of his way to pull me up at this point and that. 'But I am not afraid,' I answered to some straight question or other. 'You will be,' said he . . . I countered with, 'But I am free, I feel free'.[34]

In Mary, determined not to let her new opportunities go to waste, Orage had met his match. By winter 1905–6 she was buffeted on a wider scale by 'two regular winds . . . No doubt about the strength with which they blew, those Labour and Women's Suffrage winds'.[35] Along with all her other commitments, Mary raced from meeting to meeting that winter; but it soon became clear that it was not the labour movement but women's suffrage that would change her life dramatically. Given the strength of both winds, it was natural that Mary Gawthorpe would encounter Isabella Ford.

Isabella, Bessie and Emily Ford had all joined the Leeds Arts Club. As a writer, Isabella, particularly interested in drama and in Ibsen, joined its management committee. If Orage, with his Nietzschean mysticism, represented one strand of the Club's thinking, then politically experienced Isabella Ford represented another: committed to trade unionism, political inclusion and widening citizenship. Mary Gawthorpe had already been sent a copy of Isabella's 'industrial women' pamphlet, and although she does not say so, it is highly likely these two active ILP women now met each other at the Leeds Arts Club.

The turn-of-the-century suffrage movement in Leeds largely remained rooted in the progressive Liberalism of elite professional families like the Fords. Isabella now occupied a unique position in Leeds politics. Friendly with Edward Carpenter, she had left her family's Liberalism and joined the ILP. Isabella championed women trade union members in West Yorkshire and, as a founding member of the Leeds Women's Suffrage Society and a friend of Mrs Fawcett, had helped set up the National Union of Women's Suffrage Societies (NUWSS) in 1897. Yet the slog for Leeds' struggling trade union women was often unrewarding; Isabella's fiction writing had scarcely been successful; and possibly comparing herself with her painter sister Emily, now exhibiting successfully, Isabella in her forties wrote no more novels. The scrapbook she kept ended abruptly about 1901–2: the rest of the pages remain tragically and tellingly blank.[36] She grew more personally reticent, too, yet at her most effective, Isabella remained an *éminence grise* of the Edwardian labour and suffrage movements: always quietly supportive and enabling.

Fired by the success of the Lancashire women textile workers' suffrage petition of March 1901, Isabella turned her attention to Yorkshire and the collecting of signatures from the poorly paid women textile workers her side of the Pennines. She encouraged others to step forward. In Leeds, Agnes Close, secretary of the tiny Tailoresses' Union, stood on an orange box in the market and, she said, persuaded 2,800 of the city's 3,000 women textile workers to sign.[37] The campaign began in June 1901. Meetings were held in Colne Valley's tiny hillside villages just above Huddersfield; petition workers made their way to every small cluster of mills. This petition campaign was extraordinarily successful: no fewer than 33,184 Yorkshire women textile workers signed. By February 1902, one suffragist was writing proudly to another, 'Isabella Ford told me they were getting on splendidly with the Yorkshire working women eager to sign. So the Yorkshire and Cheshire sig[nature]s exceed those sent up from Lancashire last year'.[38]

On Tuesday 18 February, Isabella accompanied the deputation of working women with their great petition down to Westminster. It was carried triumphantly into the House of Commons, where they were greeted by ten MPs; eight women made short speeches; Isabella – nobody's fool when it came to the soft-soaping of 'sympathetic' Liberal politicians – recorded how they:

> were answered politely, and even cordially, by some of the MP's present, but the usual vagueness of expression employed on such occasions rather opened the women's eyes . . . Their backs began to stiffen a little.
>
> It is only in the House that a proper idea of the attitude of the nation's representatives about women can be found, for there disguise seems unnecessary. We all felt it as we hurried along the passages to Committee Room No 13. It was written on the faces of the members we met.[39]

The petition presented, Keir Hardie, always a strong champion of women's suffrage, took the women on tour of the House. Afterwards, they drove to Chelsea Town Hall for a public meeting, presided over by one of Hardie's fellow Labour Representation Committee MPs: in a powerful speech, Hardie asserted the importance of suffrage to working-class women.

Meanwhile, the October 1903 *zeitgeist* of the WSPU and Arts Club also caught up the NUWSS. It organised a national convention to ensure women's suffrage was raised at the next general election; within a year it had set up scores of new local suffrage committees and established an impressive election fund of £2,500. This was at last the beginning of a *national* suffrage organisation with real teeth: it had funds of its own and more control over local societies. However, the NUWSS's achilles' heel was that it remained, as even its own historian recognised, 'irrationally optimistic about the Liberal Party'. As the prospect of a general election and a new Liberal government drew nearer, this would pose an increasing challenge for the NUWSS, especially in a strongly Liberal city like Leeds.[40] It made it much more difficult to build upon the success of the 1902 Yorkshire suffrage petition.

Isabella was rising nationally within the ILP, and this brought her into closer contact with the Pankhursts. She supported both organisations, speaking in Sheffield in November 1903 for the NUWSS, along with Christabel Pankhurst for the new WSPU. She also took part in a London debate in 1904 organised by Sylvia, with Margaret Bondfield, labour organiser and adult suffragist (who argued that women's suffrage would only benefit privileged women). And Isabella wrote a strong letter with Emmeline Pankhurst in *Labour Leader* on women's suffrage. Certainly, from here on, Isabella prioritised women's suffrage over the labour movement.[41]

In January 1905 Isabella gave a talk at the Leeds Arts Club on 'Woman and the State', chaired by Alfred Orage. Well versed in suffrage heritage, Isabella explained how in Celtic tribes women had held the franchise, and their right to hold public office decayed only from the eighteenth century; however, now the tide was turning and women were reasserting their public rights.[42] Mary Gawthorpe, just twenty-four, must have attended, but what she thought of Isabella is unknown. For sure, Adel Grange was far, far removed from her Bramley elementary school classroom, and Isabella's independent income from Mary's wage. Such class differences had proved an unbridgeable gulf in the past. But now, successive governments' denial of the vote to every Edwardian woman – however well travelled with however many languages – became an increasing bond for mid-life Quakers and busy, impatient rebel girls alike. There was powerful solidarity in shared political exclusion.

This came dramatically to a head in Manchester's Free Trade Hall on Friday 13 October, 1905. The news sped over the Pennines that Christabel Pankhurst and Annie Kenney had been imprisoned for demanding votes for women at the Liberals' rally. 'An Uproarious Meeting', ran the *Yorkshire Evening Post* headline the next day and, later, 'Miss Pankhurst released from gaol'.[43] Both Isabella, and Mary (up with the news, being engaged to a newspaper worker) were elated. Isabella, in Hull for a NUWSS conference, jumped on a train to Manchester specially for the fiery ILP protest meeting. There, she told the audience enthusiastically that 'the newer and more revolutionary ideas and methods are gradually supplanting the older and more subservient ones, for women are beginning to realise what freedom really means'.[44]

Mary herself could not attend, but she was profoundly impressed by Christabel's daring action:

> The clarion note translating this need into the practical politics of the oncoming General Election was sounded when Christabel Pankhurst and Annie Kenney were first arrested . . .
>
> I heard and answered that call instantly, as soon as the news that the two women submitted to imprisonment rather than pay a fine was reported in the press, next day. According to my opportunities, I said, writing to Miss Pankhurst in Strangeways Prison, if it was necessary to go to prison in order to win the vote, I was ready. That declaration brought me into direct, immediate contact with Christabel . . . She now followed me up with a barrage of press cuttings.[45]

The WSPU had up till then been almost exclusively Manchester-based, with only a few excursions beyond. For Mary, on the other hand, 'I was rather solidly Leeds and Yorkshire'. She watched the advertisements for local Liberal parliamentary candidates, began writing letters to the press and was even 'prepared to act on my own'. Mary did not have to wait long for an opportunity. On 6 November, Herbert Gladstone MP, destined for high government office, spoke in his constituency. Mary went along, probably accompanied by Thomas Garrs for protection, and by Agnes Sunley who lived locally. Mary reported her Gladstone encounter in *Labour Leader*, adopting the impishly ironic tone increasingly characteristic of the WSPU:

> Mr Herbert was very humorous over the question of women's suffrage, sending his Liberal supporters into fits of laughter at the mere suggestion of the question. Successive questions on our part only resulted in extracting from the West Leeds member that he 'would not pledge' himself, though 'he saw no reason why women should not vote'.

Immediately, Mary began to be noticed. Agnes Sunley sent her a postcard:

Many thanks for your action at [the] meeting & subsequent letters. W[omen's] S[uffrage] seems to have entered a new phase now as women go to prison for it. Let us hope that the Manchester incident is the beginning of the end.[46]

According to another Arts Club member, vivacious Mary was certainly 'endowed with a power of repartee and wit which was unequalled even by Christabel Pankhurst'. Her years of drudgery had not blunted her natural vivacity, and she had doubtless learnt from Arts Club stylists like Orage. Mary's letters to the press in the run-up to the January 1906 General Election pointed out pithily that the main political parties were calling upon voteless women members yet again to get the vote in. Mary wrote in *Labour Leader* about this bitter irony:

Through the whole length and breadth of the country, the help of women is being sought by each and every party . . . Are they welcomed as comrades and co-workers, respected as future voters, or are their services merely valuable on the score of that odious factor (still rampant where gilded irresponsibility does not want liberty) – 'influence'? . . .

When Mr Herbert Gladstone was asked his opinion on November 6th last, in Leeds, he said that the Parliamentary machinery (six million votes) was 'already' large and cumbersome, and that if women were enfranchised, they would be 'eligible for all offices' etc, just as men were. Why not? . . . Why should not . . . Miss I O Ford, Mrs Pankhurst, and others we could mention, be considered in the light of [as] possible Parliamentary candidates?

Mary then added, with Nietzschean fervour:

Those who are really in earnest must be willing to be anything or nothing in the world's estimation, and publicly and privately, in season and out, avow their sympathy with despised and persecuted ideas, and their advocates, and bear the consequences.[47]

In Manchester at the same time, Adela and Sylvia Pankhurst, Annie Kenney and Hannah Mitchell were turning up regularly to heckle local Liberal candidate Winston Churchill, leading to nightly pandemonium. The WSPU had shifted suffrage rhetoric from traditional reasoned requests to persistent and urgent demands. Even historians critical of the Pankhursts acknowledge the significance of this: 'Emmeline and Christabel grasped instinctively the necessity to escape the "realism" that inhibited action by lifting their sights and creating a sense of *inevitability* about their ultimate success. Herein lay their genius as leaders'.[48] In Leeds Mary managed to challenge every election candidate with questions on Votes for Women, admitting later that, 'If not asking strictly according to Manchester [model] where the reported lively suffrage doings were mostly confined, still the asking [the question] caused a mild sensation in the home environment'. The level of 'sensation' depended on whether the constituency was being defended by a Liberal MP (as four out of five in Leeds were, including North Leeds where her luckless Father would have been battling against Rowland Barran MP).

Mary kept up her barrage of letters to Leeds newspapers into New Year 1906. In the face of criticism about WSPU tactics, she mildly reasoned that, as 'an unenfranchised British subject',

> . . . whatever women may do at public meetings in their zeal for a right cause does not affect the issue [of justice].
>
> I do not advocate the 'smashing' of meetings, nor do I defend unfair interruptions, yet it must be remembered that women have a real grievance, and the man disturber has at least – his vote.[49]

Even Mrs Fawcett was now alerted to Mary's daring propaganda: Isabella Ford, as organising secretary of Leeds Women's Suffrage Society, wrote enthusiastically to her that:

> A little teacher in Leeds tells she has been to all the candidates' meetings. Her 'young man' went too to protect her – and she gained the sympathy of the meeting in each case, in spite of 'chuck her out' cries being raised. She has extracted a ?written promise from H. Gladstone finally to vote for our Bill.[50]

Isabella was less patronising than she sounded, as Mary remained diminutive, while the reference to Gladstone typified Quakerly optimism. These two Leeds women were now – at last – in regular contact, with Isabella writing Mary a postcard, urging: 'Do fix something for Miss Rowlette [NUWSS speaker in Yorkshire]. She is so good on w[omen's] suff[rage]: and you can have her for no charge. A cottage meeting is better than nothing. How about teachers?'[51]

*

General Election polling took place on 15 January 1906 in Leeds. The out-come was four Liberal MPs and, for the first time, a Labour MP, James O'Grady, in the strongly Irish East Leeds constituency. By the end of January, the sheer enormity of the Liberal landslide became clear. With this new Liberal government, it is in hindsight apparent that Christabel Pankhurst's tactics – aiming for the heart of power, the Liberal leadership – made better sense than simply relying on cottage or teachers' meetings. However, in the post-election euphoria, Mary Gawthorpe, heroine of the hour, now received so many ILP speaking invitations that she was, she said, 'able to satisfy Miss Ford, including teachers in Miss Rowlette's itinerary'; and during spring 1906, Isabella and Mary addressed a number of local meetings together. Nominated by its organising secretary, quiet but effec-tive Isabella, Mary joined the committee of the Leeds Women's Suffrage Society, part of Fawcett's larger NUWSS.[52]

In February, Christabel Pankhurst came to Leeds and spoke on suffrage, warning that nationally the Liberals were still exploiting their women elec-tion workers. Isabella offered her hospitality at Adel Grange. After she returned home, Christabel sent Mary a note asking her to write to key Labour politicians – O'Grady MP, ILP orator Philip Snowden, now MP for Blackburn and married to Ethel Annakin – asking: 'what the Labour mem-bers have done and are going to do this session for women's franchise. From what I have heard it is quite necessary to keep an eye on them . . . J K H[ardie] is the [only] one who really wants to help'.[53]

Mary remained whirled up in a mass of meetings – everything from ILP to University Extension Committee, trade union to suffrage – mainly in the Leeds area; but she was already becoming well-known across the West Riding, travelling out to Keighley, Wakefield and beyond. And she was also still writing to the newspapers. She responded to a *Yorkshire Weekly Post* arti-cle, 'Where a Woman Fails', which had pontificated that a woman's main loyalty is to people she loves, not to principles: they may be loveable angels but women are less just, trustworthy and honest than men. Mary's hack-les rose, and she retaliated head-on with 'How Women Will Succeed'. Here, conscious of the contrast between her mother's confined life and her own freedoms and more equal relationship with Garrs, she offered her personal social and economic analysis:

The average woman's life is still hedged in by artificial conditions, and her natural aspirations are still bound down by artificial and arbitrary laws and customs . . .

Women, as a sex, are still . . . and are everywhere taught that the broader race-life, or welfare of future generations, does not concern them; that a strict confinement to home life or self-preservation should be their only goal . . .

Small wonder is it then that, living a life of such utter dependence, she fails to acquire that 'perfect sense of justice' which we are to believe all men possess; that having her duties narrowed down to the four walls of her home, she cannot keep a secret – for secrets do not bother the woman who is allowed a refreshing and illuminating glimpse into the outside world . . . You cannot expect a sense of honour (implying thorough self-respect) from a person who, though deemed an angel, is not fit to be trusted . . . who is not credited with sufficient intellect to mark a voting paper correctly, or sufficient justice to weigh rival claims . . .

Not in the differentiation of the sexes does the future weal [welfare] of races lie, but in co-education and co-operation throughout life . . .

Woman as a law-abiding subject must be made a self-respecting citizen, with a direct voice in the affairs of the world . . . As potential citizens with a raised status in life, they will not practise the vices of the slave – dissimu-lation, petty tyranny, 'influencing' and the like – but as free and responsible women will develop just in proportion as more justice and more freedom are meted out to them.[54]

CHAPTER 3

Suffragettes released: Adela and Mary

1906

From January 1906 through to the outbreak of war in August 1914, suffrage campaigners had to aim their fire at a Liberal government. The General Election and its landslide victory returned a triumphant 401 Liberal MPs to the House of Commons: ever afterwards, Liberal spirits would be buoyed up by the rallying call 'Remember 1906!'

The new government was elected on a wave of reforming promises: to tackle those Victorian scourges of respectable family life – childhood ill-ness, unemployment, poverty. Both Mary Gawthorpe and Adela Pankhurst had first-hand experience not only of child deaths but also of a male breadwinner's fecklessness or reckless idealism. And both women had seen in their Board School classrooms the effects of poor diet and insecu-rity on their pupils. The social reforms introduced from 1906 onwards included therefore both the feeding of school children and medical inspec-tion in schools. In the longer term, Lloyd George as Chancellor of the Exchequer aimed for more radical reforming measures, including old age pensions and a National Insurance scheme to help workers (though not their families) during illness and unemployment.

The new Liberal government – dependent upon the votes of working men and upon some powerful trade unions like the miners – also brought in reform of laws that had previously crippled union activity. There were now in the Commons no fewer than twenty-nine Labour MPs (including of course Keir Hardie, Philip Snowden, James O'Grady, and leading figure Ramsay MacDonald). But despite their presence and energetic ILP cam-paigning, there were distinct limits to the government's reforming zeal. The Liberal party remained dependent on the financial backing of its wealthy elite members who provided the bulk of its leadership. Prime

Minister Henry Campbell-Bannerman, son of a Glasgow businessman, not only wintered at Marienbad but also spent his summers in a Scottish castle, like other upper-class land-owning Edwardian gentlemen.[1] With business interests heavily represented in the Commons, there was still no government-backed momentum to abolish the half-time system of child labour. In the industrial north, such a measure would have been unpopular with both employers and working-class families so reliant upon children's weekly shillings. In addition, the Liberal and Labour election victories depended upon a secret electoral pact between Herbert Gladstone for the Liberals and Ramsay MacDonald for Labour. While the pact was unknown to ILP members, its existence helps explain Labour MPs' support for such an extremely moderate Liberal reform programme to tackle underlying inequalities.

Suffragists and suffragettes alike also found that the dramatic change of government brought only limited hope. Their 'friends' in the Commons – Keir Hardie plus some sympathetic Liberals – still seemed largely confined to backbenchers, who wielded only meagre influence. Suffrage campaigners' arguments were often met by forceful stone-walling from adult suffragists who claimed they wanted votes for all men and women (as some genuinely did) and anything 'less' would merely further privilege well-to-do women.[2] And suffrage was scarcely high on the government's legislative agenda: in the crowded parliamentary timetable, ameliorative social and economic reform took priority over women's citizenship demands. In the high expectancy of spring 1906 the politically wise learnt not to hold their breath on suffrage.

Among the suffragist campaigners, Liberal women found themselves in the trickiest of dilemmas, wanting Campbell-Bannerman's government to legislate, yet embarrassed by the WSPU's militancy and heckling. So when women's suffrage was not included in the King's Speech in February setting out the government's programme, loyal members of the Women's Liberal Associations were exhorted to be patient and to recognise that other reforms were more urgent.[3] Mrs Fawcett's NUWSS renewed its optimistic faith, sustained by high hopes of Campbell-Bannerman. Leeds Women's Suffrage Society, cleaving to its traditional Liberal roots, produced a leaflet giving 'Eight Reasons Why Women Want the Vote'; its first argument was, 'Because it is the foundation of all political *liberty* that those who obey the Law' should 'have a voice in choosing those who make the Law'.[4] Such Liberal suffragists believed that closeness to the new government gave them at least a foot in the Downing Street door.

Meanwhile, the WSPU, less prepared to be well-behaved and patient, moved its headquarters from Manchester down to London to be better placed for barracking the government. This attracted further publicity: in January the *Daily Mail* dubbed them 'suffragettes'; and the *Daily Mirror*, launched shortly after the WSPU formation, found these suffragettes provided their cameramen with interesting news photographs. In April the WSPU's new militant tactics included noisy interruptions from the Ladies' Gallery in the Commons when Keir Hardie presented a women's suffrage resolution; this angered even Hardie.[5]

Despite these differences of suffrage strategy, planning went ahead for a joint deputation to Campbell-Bannerman on 19 May. Impressive plans were drawn up between the NUWSS, WSPU and women's Liberal and temperance organisations, plus Lancashire radical suffragists and the Women's Co-operative Guild representing working-class married women. Altogether 400 women were present, representing over a quarter of a million. Eight women spoke at the deputation, including the Guild president and Emmeline Pankhurst for the WSPU. Campbell-Bannerman expressed sympathy but was mindful of Conservative electoral gains if just the few women satisfying the property qualifications were enfranchised; hinting at Cabinet opposition, he claimed he could make no pledges and indeed could only 'preach the virtue of patience'.

Extremely disappointed, women marched to Trafalgar Square for a rally before returning home.[6] The WSPU, feeling thwarted, vowed to escalate the heckling of ministers. Suffragette militancy would soon sweep up both Mary Gawthorpe and Adela Pankhurst. For both of them, 1906 was a year of tumultuous non-stop campaigning. In other respects, this affected them differently. The WSPU had sprung dramatically into life at Adela's home when she was just eighteen, her education cut off *before* she had been able to enjoy a training like her elder sisters. On the other hand Mary, now aged twenty-five, had gained her teaching qualifications before Christabel's imprisonment inspired her to action. With a gap in age of four-and-a-half years, Mary was buoyed by an infectious self-confidence compared to the more fragile identity of Adela, not yet twenty-one. At the same time, Mary was acutely conscious of the differences in background between the Pankhurst and Gawthorpe homes, the one a 'splendid family with all that achievement, education, learning', while suffragettes like herself came 'very, very much from the ranks, [with] strain, struggle, economic pressure, incessant sickness in the home'.[7] Together, however, they embarked on a totally new and exciting existence, working as peripatetic WSPU organisers, despatched across the county to stir up the demand for Votes for Women.

Nominated by persuasive Isabella Ford, Mary remained a committee member of the Leeds Women's Suffrage Society (i.e. NUWSS); indeed Mary and Isabella, with their overlapping Leeds activities – Arts Club, ILP, suffrage – were now in close contact. Shortly after the Campbell-Bannerman deputation, Mary was invited by Isabella to tea at Adel Grange. It turned out to be less of a relaxing social occasion, more of a tricky political meeting. Also present was Isabella's ILP friend (and Mary's one-time fellow student) Ethel Annakin, now Ethel Snowden; as the wife of an MP, Ethel was far more aware of Westminster political currents than Mary, unfamiliar with London.

We have only Mary's reminiscence of this uncomfortable encounter of Leeds suffragists. Isabella was the questioner, Mary recorded: 'At that otherwise innocent tea I was put through my paces in a way to which I had no clue . . . I was virgin soil in the weighty matters of cliques and struggles for leadership.' Mary's autobiography disingenuously claims this tea-time was a strangely 'unexpected attack', ostensibly because she had not asked permission for her *Yorkshire Weekly Post* article.[8] This is unlikely. More probably Isabella and Ethel felt disappointed and betrayed by recent suffragette interruptions in the Commons when Hardie had presented his suffrage resolution; they wondered how women were to win the vote with such counter-productive tactics, and perhaps hoped Mary might influence Christabel and Emmeline.

All of them remained in the ILP, but Isabella felt torn between her older suffrage friends like Ethel Snowden, and those like Mary who supported the newer militancy. But despite these tensions over the Adel teapots, the immediate outcome was cooperation over suffrage tactics. Mary agreed to help organise Leeds Women's Suffrage Society's open-air 'Camp Stool' meetings, at which seats were sold or hired for a penny [0.5p]; she even drew in her mother. So, one summer week her diary noted three 'C.S.' meetings in Leeds, a Teresa Billington meeting in Town Hall Square, another English-Yiddish one for Jewish workers and a Tailoresses' meeting, plus another – doubtless negotiated by Garrs – of Leeds print workers (the last two with Isabella as well as Mary speaking).[9]

But for Mary the most significant of these summer Leeds meetings were those addressed by well-connected and wealthy philanthropists, the Pethick-Lawrences. Frederick Pethick-Lawrence, a socialist barrister friend of Hardie's, published his own *Labour Record* which reported the suffragette campaign extremely sympathetically. These socialists were very recent and passionate converts to suffrage, with Emmeline Pethick-Lawrence becoming the WSPU's efficient and invaluable treasurer.

Mary not only organised the Pethick-Lawrences' meetings, as the *Labour Record* noted, but also 'enlivened them with her ready wit and effective repartee'. She was, Frederick wrote later, 'a roguish little maid who could flatten out an interrupter at one of her meetings, and yet leave him amused though perplexed'. After one meeting in Bramley, Mary and her mother invited the Pethick-Lawrences home. Before they left the Pethick-Lawrences glimpsed, propped up on the Gawthorpes' piano, Cecil Sharp folk songs. There was immediate shared enthusiasm. Mary began to sing. 'These are the ties that bind', she wrote later; both Mary and her mother 'knew we had met real friends'. Mary came to a decision:

> So swelling the surge, so swift the movement, so imperative the demand, so peremptory the challenges, the tide swept one along . . .
>
> It may be objected: what about school? Believe it or not . . . I had resigned from the Bramley Council School. With no prospects whatever I had resigned, a child of this awakening storm which was piling wave upon wave, carrying a school of human corks of whom I was one, into some unknown harbour.[10]

Garrs probably felt doubtful about such a reckless move as resigning. However, Mary did not throw herself into the WSPU immediately. Rather, she joined Mrs Ramsay MacDonald and the Women's Labour League; the labour movement rather than suffrage offered her national campaigning opportunities, and through the League Mary took part in a deputation to the Minister on the feeding of school children.[11]

Meanwhile, Adela remained up north: 'My heart was with my own people in Lancashire and Yorkshire, with the poor and downtrodden, the fallen women and the neglected children.' Yet it was an odd time for her: 'Some dear friends I made but saw little of them. Annie Kenney was the first and closest of these. Annie, in those days, largely shared my views and enthusiasms, but she was a greater favourite than I was at [WSPU] Head Quarters . . . and . . . was greatly beloved by Mr and Mrs Petheck [*sic*] Lawrence . . . and . . . practically their adopted daughter.'[12] Adela once again was made to feel she did not quite match up, while the Pethick-Lawrences petted Annie Kenney, who so neatly fitted the WSPU political bill, Adela recalled.

For Adela the contrast between her everyday school-teaching drudgery and the new suffragette life with its promise of freedom was growing stark. With the WSPU campaign of challenging Liberal cabinet ministers continuing, this tension soon came to a head. On Saturday 24 June, just days after Adela's twenty-first birthday, Winston Churchill and Lloyd George planned a great public rally in Manchester, less than a mile from Nelson Street. Belle Vue was the pleasure park where as a child Adela had often gone to see the monkeys and watch the fireworks. She now bravely returned, less pleasure than political purpose on her mind:

> Seven of us were told [to go] off to interrupt [sic] this meeting with our persistant [sic] question: 'When will the Liberal Government give votes to women?' It was arranged that we should take up our seats, singly, throughout the hall and stand up, one by one at intervals. I had the post of danger, in a front seat, and was to take the last turn. Since the first meeting in the Free Trade Hall, the women had interrupted several meetings at which Cabinet Ministers were present, and the Liberal stewards had gained an unenviable reputation for their rough handling of the suffragists.[13]

For Belle Vue, Adela had borrowed her mother's best hat and silk coat. The hat was trimmed with roses and had a wide brim which hid her face, and the high collar of her coat helped the disguise. She was accompanied by a tall, scholarly-looking man, probably a local socialist, there to lend solidarity. Also attending for the WSPU were a Mrs Morrissey from Liverpool, and Hannah Mitchell – who had also borrowed a smart suit and stylish hat from a friend to go unrecognised by the Manchester Liberals. Hannah later wrote:

> Elaborate precautions were taken to keep out the militants, most of whom were well known by then . . . I was shown to my 5 shilling seat by an obsequious steward, and soon recognised in the 10 shilling seats Adela Pankhurst . . .
>
> We had a definite plan . . . We rose, one at a time, as our appointed man [Liberal speaker] was getting well under way with his speech, displayed our banners and called out the question:
>
> 'Will the Liberal Government give the vote to women?' holding up the meeting until we were put out, more or less violently. Then, when all had

settled down again, and the next speaker was well away, another woman
rose and repeated the procedure, and in turn was bundled out . . .

I was thankful to be second out. Adela was the first to be ejected . . . and
I followed Adela [outside] who was in the grip of a big burly officer, who
kept telling her she ought to be smacked and set to work at the wash tubs.
She grew so angry that she slapped his hand, which was as big as a ham. For
this she was charged with assaulting the police, as well as obstruction . . .

At the police station . . . they questioned us, and wrote descriptions,
which we tried to foil by covering our faces, or looking steadily at the
floor.[14]

So Adela Pankhurst was among the first suffragettes to be arrested after
Christabel and Annie Kenney at the Free Trade Hall, and was certainly the
youngest.[15] The ILP in Manchester organised a defence fund and arranged
for a solicitor. Eleven days later, on Wednesday 4 July, the women appeared
in Manchester's city-centre Minshull Street Police Court. For Adela
Pankhurst, as for Hannah Mitchell, it was a first court appearance. Both
women felt defiant. Their case was heard by a stipendiary (i.e. professional)
magistrate who, Hannah Mitchell felt, was not unsympathetic:

He listened gravely to the recital of our misdeeds, and . . . imposed on each
a nominal fine: mine was half-a-crown [12.5p]. Adela, who was supposed to
have assaulted her giant captor, was fined ten shillings [50p], but the magistrate's quizzical glance from the slight, girlish figure to the burly constable,
seemed to me to speak volumes . . . We all refused to pay the fine . . . [and]
were brought back into court, and given three days, that is Mrs Morrissey
and myself. Adela was awarded seven days' imprisonment, she having
assaulted the 'law'.

We were then taken below to await the arrival of the prison van.
Someone brought us a jug of tea, and told us that six women had been sent
to prison that day in London for ringing the Prime Minister's door bell, and
refusing to leave Downing Street.[16]

All Adela's preceding experience over three years of WSPU campaigning
had been preparation for this dramatic and testing moment. Strangeways
was the same prison regime her elder sister had endured just nine months
earlier: an ugly prison dress, oversized heavy shoes, hairpins taken away, a
prison cap, a badge with the number of the cell, a straw mattress, empty-
ing slops, tin mugs, regimented exercise. To Hannah Mitchell's annoyance,

her husband paid her fine: 'Most of us who were married found that "Votes for Women" were of less interest to our husbands than their own dinners', she wrote later. Adela served her sentence, remaining in prison a further four days all on her own after Mrs Morrissey was released. Alone, Adela was appalled by the plight of the other women prisoners, many of them prostitutes, but nevertheless concluded that imprisonment was bearable if you had a degree of outside support percolating inside the walls: 'I was released on Monday morning and I was glad enough to go home to a good breakfast. My mother had come [up] from London to meet me and in the evening a great meeting of welcome was held in St Stephen's Square'.[17] For once in her life Adela could feel her mother was truly proud of what she had achieved.

A meeting was arranged for the following Sunday, 15 July, at Boggart Hole Clough, the Manchester park which had made news with a 'free speech' arrest of Emmeline Pankhurst a decade earlier. Adela, Hannah Mitchell and the Morrisseys were billed to speak as released suffragette prisoners. Keir Hardie and Mrs Pethick-Lawrence came up from London. Adela recalled dramatically how they set off:

> On a beautiful Sunday afternoon we arrived to find the ground densely packed with people. The meeting place is like a great cup – the Boggart's Hole – and the speakers stand at the bottom and talk upwards to the audience.

Mrs Pankhurst opened the meeting by asking the crowd to join in singing 'England, arise, the long, long night is over'. Hannah, who was to speak from one of the platforms, recalled signs of hostility from the start. After Hannah and Adela outlined the attitude of both main political parties to women's suffrage claims, the chair, a local ILP orator, challenged the restive crowd:

> 'Now then, you Tory troglodytes and medieval Liberals, what are you going to do about it?' We soon knew what the mob was going to do: there was a concerted rush and the group round the Chairman was separated. We were on sloping ground, and in danger of being pushed downhill by our assailants, most of them young men who were behind us.[18]

Hardie, the chair, and other ILP men tried to protect them. Frederick Pethick-Lawrence reminisced, 'the rowdies – who seem to have been the

football members of some local Radical [i.e. Liberal working men's] clubs –
proceeded to deliberately set upon the women. Several of them, including
my wife, were very seriously hustled, and Miss Adela Pankhurst was very
nearly trampled under foot' – intentionally. Adela vividly recorded what
happened next:

> Suddenly several gangs of young men, with straw hats and sticks appeared
> at the top of the steep banks, densely packed with the people. Heedless of
> consequences, these gangs rushed down upon us sending the crowds pell-
> mell upon us; they then linked hands and surrounded us and dragged each
> of us separately to the top of the steep bank and began to drag us about the
> park. The two men had me, one by each arm, and a gang of youths pressed
> on us from all sides. They tore off my hat and ripped my clothes half off my
> back and struck at my head and face. I had a cut over my eye caused by a
> stone, flung by a cowardly ruffian and both of my cheeks were bleeding
> from being constantly bumped against my captors' shoulders.[19]

Their opponents had decided those women, Hannah and Adela, who
had interrupted the Belle Vue meeting were now fair game. Flower beds,
grass and even trees were trampled down as Adela and the others were
swept along, 'rushing hither and thither amid the dense crowds'. Several
times women tried to rescue her but without success. Hannah, who
caught glimpses of Adela across the crowd, had a similar experience. A
woman reporter came to help:

> Together we tried to reach Adela who was surround by a crowd of roughs,
> while an older man on the fringe of the gang was shouting indecent sug-
> gestions . . . At last a group of men fought their way to me and Adela,
> having to beat off our assailants with their bare fists in order to get us out of
> the Clough. The crowd followed yelling like savages. Someone opened the
> door of their house and drew us inside. We were glad to take shelter.[20]

Adela was eventually rescued by the police and later 'was taken to a
small house in a street which ran beside the Park, where I found my
mother and Mrs Pethick-Lawrence, with their supporters, all unhurt, but
surrounded by excited Press reporters, who had begun to realise the dramatic possibilities of the movement'.[21] To her increasing frustration, Adela
still had to return to work the next day:[22]

It may seem very odd to my readers that, after this exciting episode, I turned up at school on Monday morning and taught all day, without thinking very much of anything but my scholars and my work . . .

Within a few weeks of making my protest . . . I gave a model lesson to the Inspector and sat my first teachers' examination . . . I felt the hono[u]r of the militant women was at stake and . . . I was gratified, a few weeks later to receive a Government notification that I had passed in all subjects. This ensured my position as a fully fledged 'Article 50' teacher in charge of a class and I was appointed to a city school in a working class suburb of Manchester . . . Three or even four different classes were taught in a central classroom, which created a terrible hubbub and confusion very trying to the nerves . . .

Now, while I passed my time in the fusty school room with my grimy pupils, surrounded by a labyrinth of dreary slums, the process of . . . stuffing these very unclean heads . . . seemed very slow, compared with the policy of the enfranchisement of women, which was promised to do so much for us.

For the moment, Adela spent her 1906 summer holidays organising in the north.[23]

During that summer the WSPU's future direction was becoming clearer. In London, Australian suffragette Dora Montefiore, a home-owner, who had been on the Campbell-Bannerman deputation, refused to pay her taxes and barricaded herself into her house: the 'Siege of Fort Montefiore' gained considerable press coverage.

At the end of June Christabel Pankhurst gained her law degree and set off for London to take charge of the campaign and develop its political strategy. She then went up to Cockermouth near the Lake District, where a by-election had been called for August. Meanwhile, after her Leeds 'Camp Stool' meetings, Mary Gawthorpe also rushed north, in response to a 'hurry call' from Ramsay MacDonald's wife. So Mary arrived at Cockermouth on behalf of the Women's Labour League, to speak in support of the Labour candidate, a miners' leader. Christabel's eyes were, however, set on future strategy not on past allies. At Cockermouth, almost overnight the WSPU's political line lurched – from being a small suffrage group intimately aligned to (and receiving considerable support from) the ILP and labour movement, to becoming a politically independent group, refusing to support not only the Liberal candidate, but also now the Labour candidate. So was it still possible to speak on both labour and suffrage? Mary ruefully admitted later, 'now what I ran into [was] not so much a snag as a seething cauldron . . . The Cockermouth Election was a hot spot for me'.[24]

The two organisations that Mary thought she could work for – the WSPU and the Women's Labour League – were moving apart. When the WSPU headquarters heard that she was in Cockermouth representing the League, 'an emissary was sent up to ask me to join them'. However, Mary recalled, 'I could not see my way to join the WSPU' – for she liked both Keir Hardie and Cockermouth's Labour candidate: she still wanted both Votes for Women *and* a labour victory. Why not? After all, it was what she had now been working towards for almost a year. However, this divergence of old allies had far wider repercussions than just Mary's personal dilemma. There was furious correspondence in the *Labour Leader*: Mary wrote that *she* supported the Labour candidate (believing 'there is no salvation for women but in Socialism') while at the same time supporting Christabel and the WSPU. She resisted being forced to choose between her two political objectives.[25]

In the event, the Conservatives won the by-election; and tense relationships between WSPU and ILP were patched up – for the moment.[26] Mary returned from Cockermouth to 'streams of labour meetings' across the industrial West Riding. Her Sundays were dictated by railway timetables, with 'strange intervals, long waits, sometimes a stay overnight'. Meanwhile, down in London Isabella Ford kept Mary informed on the slow progress of women's suffrage. However, Mary had seen clearly at Cockermouth 'the difference in status between men with votes and women without', that little could be achieved without full citizenship; and she was beginning to grow impatient with the NUWSS's diplomatic suffragist tactics.

In mid-August she was invited to London by Emmeline Pethick-Lawrence. On Mary's arrival at their barrister's flat, Emmeline was sitting at her desk. She 'lifted her head and looked at me . . . It was a full moment. Nothing was said but I knew I was nearing a great decision. I knew what the answer would be. I had written to Christabel less than nine months ago that I was ready to go to prison if that was necessary in order to win the vote. Now the tide of ineluctable choice had caught up with me and there could be no retreat.'[27]

Mary was poised to switch her personal loyalties from Labour to the WSPU. Her political transformation was due partly to Emmeline Pethick-Lawrence's 'look'; and Mary also came into close contact with inspiring

Emmeline Pankhurst who also had a profound effect on her. Mrs Pankhurst told Mary that, if she lived over again, with her five children coming in quick succession, she would not change one iota. Mary did not forget that, comparing this with her own mother's more difficult and tragic married life. There was a great deal for Mary to think about: 'My own engagement [to Garrs] had not matured to the point of marriage and now it was having to take care of itself.' Her days of 'First Love' and the Leeds ILP were drawing to a close. 'The actual proposition was made, and I returned to Bramley as an organiser of the Women's Social and Political Union.'

It was a major change. Mary's mother, who had helped with the 'Camp Stool' meetings, was silently apprehensive that the Gawthorpes' recently acquired relative security was being threatened yet again by unpredictable forces. When she left Bramley, Mary promised to send her mother half her weekly wage. Garrs did not say much either: 'He was uneasy and approving, all at the same time'. Elsewhere in Leeds, Orage – when he learnt the news – while politically supportive in the abstract, was probably at the more personal level just bemused.[28]

The WSPU had more work than it could handle. Like other campaigning organisations, including the NUWSS, it recruited and employed about six organisers; so Mary now joined Christabel, Teresa Billington and Annie Kenney.[29] The WSPU planned meetings for Mary in Manchester; here she visited the Pankhursts' Nelson Street home, probably meeting Adela for the first time, and noticed how 'an almost silent absorption invested each remaining occupant, for the family was already scattered abroad'. In August, Mary spoke at an open-air meeting to welcome Annie Kenney back from Holloway, and to deal with Manchester's hecklers she turned on the men and said: 'My dear friends, you have got votes. I am fighting for mine; give me a chance. I come from Yorkshire, and I want to go back with a good impression of Manchester people'.[30]

Mary was soon off to Liverpool, then back to Leeds in preparation for an Emmeline Pankhurst visit, 'for now the time had come to line up my native city in the new order' – Votes for Women. Here, she may have had help not only from her mother but also from her elder sister and small nephew, happy 'when helping Auntie's Suffragette work'.[31] She was then sent down to rouse Sheffield, visiting Edward Carpenter's home. Though the poet was out Mary met his disciples, and bought her first pair of sandals; however, when the attentions of an elderly fruitarian simple-life disciple persisted, Mary signalled '"Help, help"' to Leeds, 'and F. L. came on the run. [When] the fiancé was introduced, his kindly presence cleared the atmosphere without the need of stronger measures'. From Sheffield, Mary moved to Huddersfield and on to south Wales (picking up speaking tips from the more practised Teresa Billington) then was ordered to London for the opening of Parliament in October.[32]

7. *Mary Gawthorpe, Leeds, February 1908.*[33]

Annie Kenney relished being despatched here and there by the WSPU leadership. She later wrote, 'No one will ever surpass Christabel for tactics . . . We were all placed as though she was playing a serious game of political chess, her opponent being Parliament. I never had the least objection to being moved about on the political chess-board, and even if I, as a pawn, was captured, I knew she would soon recover lost ground'.[34]

In the summer holidays, Annie had been sent to Scotland. Adela joined her, returning to her school classroom in the autumn. Yet, increasingly, WSPU campaigning absorbed her time and energies: she recalled later how she 'worked my way through England, a lonely girl but happy in my way'.[35] Then in September Adela was in Bolton near Manchester, where women weavers were on strike in protest against new working conditions. From here, she wrote her first report for *Labour Record*, recounting how the weavers had been out for eight months, with 'blacklegs' (strike breakers) imported from elsewhere, with no knowledge of weaving. Adela's report was knowledgeable, if a little homilistic, about the unemployed and low-waged sweated workers 'the noise of whose drunken revelry filled the once respectable streets'. Significantly, though, even with Christabel now in charge of post-Cockermouth WSPU policy, it was only in the final paragraph that Adela turned to suffrage:

> One lesson all the women have learned during their adversity [is] that the law-making for themselves, their husbands and children, cannot be safely entrusted to the capitalists and employers. They are demanding the Parliamentary vote in order to secure direct representation of their labour in Parliament, and to build up a State where the interests of the whole community are cared for, and so to put an end to the possibility of strikes for ever.[36]

Adela gave out a slightly different message from that of Mary Gawthorpe, and most certainly from Christabel, who now disentangled the WSPU from its labour origins and prioritised suffrage above all.[37] Yet within a few weeks both Adela and Mary met again at the historic opening of Parliament on Tuesday 23 October.

8. Adela Pankhurst, 1908

The WSPU organisers – Annie Kenney, Teresa Billington and Mary Gawthorpe – were all young Lancashire or Yorkshire women who had left home and the north to work for the WSPU; they wanted first to take London by storm and then, hopefully, win over the Liberal government. Often they were inspired by politically experienced women: Annie Kenney by Emmeline Pankhurst (and of course Christabel); Mary by Emmeline

Pethick-Lawrence and by Emmeline Pankhurst's unforgettable presence. For Adela, still tied to her Board School, her relationship with her mother had always been painfully complex, but she was undoubtedly inspired by her example (as well as by her father) and was moved that her mother had travelled up to greet *her* on her release from Strangeways.

These narratives of admiration, conversion and transformation of rebel girls were central to the unfolding dramatic WSPU story (and in direct contrast to Isabella Ford's quiet behind-the-scenes persuasion within the Leeds Suffrage Society).[38] Teresa Billington, herself probably the most independently-minded of the WSPU organisers and most certainly an Edwardian 'new woman', captured the almost semi-religious worship of such young suffragettes. Her wickedly vivid portrait depicts one of their innumerable north-south train journeys; the conversation on board had been prompted by Charlotte Despard, another experienced philanthropic ILP member in London who had just joined the WSPU leadership:

'Do you suppose' asked one girl when the train was halfway up England, 'that Mrs Despard has ever committed a sin?'

There was an angry protest from one end of the carriage and then a shout of laughter.

'You are a very dear infant,' said I . . .

What followed now was an earnest discussion of the amazing goodness of this newly-met associate of ours . . . stumbling words of admiration . . .

'She was born saintly,' declared Annie Kenney.

'Then,' suggested Adela, 'she would never be tempted to do anything evil' . . .

'How dull,' said I . . .

Mary Gawthorpe struck for harmony. 'Did you ever ask yourself,' she said, 'whether it was better to be born good or to struggle into goodness?' . . .

'This calls for philosophy, Mary's favourite concern. Go to it!' I said. They did . . .

'What you are considering is whether Mrs Despard or Christabel is the greater saint' [said an Irish voice] . . .

I suggested . . . 'Both fighters, brave, daring – which is a special kind of bravery – both committed to service, both gallant'.[39]

This conversation, Teresa Billington says, took place in October 1906 – perhaps on the journey to plan the daring protest at the opening of Parliament on Tuesday 23rd. In London, Mary was staying in the

Pethick-Lawrences' flat in Clement's Inn. Adela increasingly chafed at her classroom commitments, so routine compared to the excitement of Votes for Women. It seems that this historic protest at Parliament was *the* turning point at which she decided to commit herself once and for all to the suffragette campaign, and to give up her teaching job, as had Mary Gawthorpe and Teresa Billington before her:

> I found myself increasingly eager to get into the fight, and when I read of the great strides the movement was making in London . . . I became more and more consumed with a desire to be present.
>
> Something stronger than myself seemed to drive me along and in a rash moment, I wrote for a day's leave of absence . . .
>
> I wish that I could convey to my readers an impression of that wonderful [rail] journey and my still more wonderful arrival in London in the early dawn of a summer [autumn?] morning. If I had the art of conveying to you what I felt when I waved good-bye to my dear tall brother [Harry] who carried my sea-grass basket to the railway station, somewhere about midnight . . .
>
> I, in a home-made coat and skirt, home-trimmed hat, with a month's salary in my Dorothy bag, had set forth to regenerate mankind . . .
>
> I was rushing into it and the express train, tear along at what speed it would, was too slow for me.[40]

Adela would have arrived just in time for a final planning weekend, on 20–21 October, packed with meetings and speeches. Adela, Mary recalled, 'made a great hit' with a speech about women's role in the evolution of peaceful civilisation, bringing in (perhaps remembering her family's opposition to the Boer War) 'plenty of references to fighting and killing'. Mary too was beginning to be recognised as an accomplished speaker. Her strong voice had already come to the notice of the WSPU leadership – which now picked her out for a particularly demanding role:

> As we left Clement's Inn after lunch, Tuesday, October 23, I had something to think about. I had newly learnt that at the House of Commons I was to begin the protest meeting in the Lobby itself, if the request for Government support was refused. While the greater [WSPU] membership was outside the House of Commons, a pledged delegation was now in the outer lobby awaiting the return of Mrs Pankhurst and Mrs Pethick-Lawrence from the inner lobby where they were interviewing the Liberal Whip.[41]

Along with Adela and Mary was Mrs Cobden-Sanderson, daughter of Richard Cobden, the Victorian champion of free trade and cheap bread. The northern rebel girls were now joined by a few well-connected respectable London ladies. Together they had gained admission by asking to see particular MPs (often Labour members). The central lobby was crowded. Charlotte Despard explained the strategy later that day to the *Daily Mirror*:

> We got in simply to determine whether the Prime Minister will give us a Bill this session. We went as a deputation, and one of our number tried twice to a send a note to the Whip, asking him to get a pronouncement from Sir Henry [Campbell-Bannerman] as to his intentions. After some trouble it was taken in, and the Whip went to the Prime Minister, who said it was absolutely impossible. The Whip came out, and very courteously informed us what the answer was. We asked: 'What about next session?' and he simply shrugged his shoulders, and said: 'Impossible'.
>
> Then someone said the time had come for action.[42]

It was then half-past four. The suffragettes suddenly sprang into action. First Mary jumped up on to one of the velvet settees and began to address the astonished lobby crowd: 'Men who have the vote, and women who want the vote . . .' but she was dragged down before she could get further.[43] Charlotte Despard started a protest about women not having the vote. Chief-Inspector Scantlebury, a giant of a policeman, was momentarily taken aback by this sudden action – but speedily recovered himself. He pushed his way through the jostling crowd to the settee and, the *Daily Mirror* lobby correspondent reported, 'lifting one of the women just as if she was a bundle of clothes, bodily carried her, kicking and screaming, down the steps', and deposited her before returning hot and breathless to the lobby. The *Labour Record* took up the story: 'The women formed up round her, but the police dragged her down. Then Mrs Despard . . . took her turn, then Mrs Cobden-Sanderson, then others. All as they spoke were hustled out with rough hands and bundled into the street. There they started to hold a meeting of protest. And it was there that the arrests took place'.[44]

A deputation of women from the East End produced another scrimmage outside at the Strangers' Gallery. Mary herself wrote:

Getting arrested was not so easy as it sounds. After the struggle in the Lobby, and well do I remember the combined grip of Mrs Pankhurst and Mrs Pethick-Lawrence holding me on to the seat as House of Commons policemen pulled at my person in two directions at once. I was most literally in the hands of the law. Once dislodged, it was nothing at all for a couple of six-footers to convey my one hundred and four pounds [weight] to the Members' entrance where I was thrown out.

There were now two sets of battles, one continuing in the Lobby as Mrs Despard, and Mrs Cobden-Sanderson were succeeded by others, one at a time, who, as they were ejected into the street, began as many speeches of protest, on all fronts, so that outside the House it was pandemonium itself. With every new speech, the gathering crowds would rush in that direction. I was still making speeches, had to make three, climbing to the railings at different points, before I was arrested.[45]

The peaceful opening of Parliament had definitely been disturbed. Next day, the front-page headline of the *Daily Mirror* trumpeted 'Riotous Suffragettes Evicted after an Onslaught on House of Commons'; in its report the paper told how they waved white flags inscribed 'Votes for Women', proclaiming 'Down with the tyrants!'[46] Adela later claimed she was arrested simply for standing in the lobby of the House, saying nothing.

Though Charlotte Despard and Emmeline Pankhurst remained free, ten other women were finally arrested – including Mary Gawthorpe and Adela Pankhurst, Emmeline Pethick-Lawrence and Mrs Cobden-Sanderson, Annie Kenney, Teresa Billington and Dora Montefiore. They were all immediately taken to Cannon Row police station. Dora Montefiore remembered them as excited and dishevelled militants, the younger suffragettes with their hair tumbled down and clothing torn; she tried to tidy them up to make them look more presentable. Charged with using abusive language with intent to cause obstruction, they were identified and 'stared at by special police'. Frederick Pethick-Lawrence agreed to stand bail. Eventually, after agreeing not to return to the House of Commons that night, the women were let go and returned to their London accommodation, where Mary Gawthorpe remembered 'hectic sleeplessness and fatigued awakening'.

Quite early the next day, Wednesday 24 October, they appeared at Westminster Police Court. Messrs Cobden-Sanderson and Pethick-Lawrence (who reported it all in his *Labour Record*) managed eventually to gain admittance to the court after repeated requests. It became clear that the police could produce no evidence of the abusive language charge. Moreover, the voteless women accused refused to recognise the jurisdiction of the court, composed as it was solely of men administering man-made laws. Dora Montefiore even defiantly held up an 'income tax siege' banner. The magistrate, however, bound them over to keep the peace for six months, and they were led down to the cells below, it reputedly taking two constables to move Adela from the dock when they were charged.[47] Mary somehow managed hurriedly to write a picture postcard to her mother who was anxiously waiting news back in Bramley. The postcard (apparently with a portrait of Dora Montefiore and the slogan 'Taxation without Representation is Tyranny') stated, 'This is being written in the Police Court. We are refusing to acknowledge the power of the Court to judge us'.[48]

Meanwhile, Sylvia Pankhurst had entered the court to protest about its non-jurisdiction. She was hastily thrown out, arrested, charged, convicted on the spot, given the option of a fine or prison for a fortnight, and chose prison. Mary added 'all this happening while we were awaiting further developments in the cells below to which we had been sent. Now we were brought in, one by one. We were warned that we must find surety [security] for £10 or to go to prison for <u>two months</u>. Like Sylvia [we] all chose prison'.

After this sentencing, the women were all taken back to the cells, and the full dreariness of prison's official routines began to close in on them; as Mary put it, 'long waits, drab routine, fatigue, endurance, endurance, fatigue'.[49]

The eleven women waited in the Black Maria to be taken away. Frederick Pethick-Lawrence went round to each one asking for a message for the public. Mary remembered, 'I was feeling rather whizzy by then but managed to write, "It is not only the vote we are fighting for, but everything that is involved in the giving of the vote to the women of England"'. Incensed at what had happened, Pethick-Lawrence added, significantly, in his *Labour Record* report that ten out of the eleven women were members of the ILP, who each had 'given all that she had to give for the men, for the women, for the children of her race' – alluding to those elected on to School Boards or as Poor Law Guardians. He added, to shame his male readers, 'The vote is a small thing in itself, but it is the key to the whole world'.[50]

The springless Black Maria rattled them across London to Holloway. It was dark and sombre by the time they arrived. Each had to go through the full routine of being recorded as a new prisoner; undressed, identified (e.g. by eye colour). Diminutive Mary was allocated a prison dress so vast she constantly tripped over in it; with no garters, her stockings were billowing heavy coarse wool, weighing down her feet and ankles. The prisoners' cells consisted of cement floors and wooden plank beds. From a rather limited prison library, Mary selected the fattest volume, which proved to be Thackeray's *The Virginians*. 'This Novel is thus forever associated with that prison cell and the single, caged light before which I sat'.[51]

It was the unprecedentedly harsh length of the prison terms that caught public attention. The following day, papers like the *Daily Mirror* splashed this sensation across its front page: 'Riotous Suffragettes Sentenced to Imprisonment at Westminster Police Court'. The WSPU's number of active sympathisers grew.

Importantly, help came from certain key NUWSS suffragists. Conciliatory Mrs Fawcett was prepared to offer support to the eleven imprisoned women, and for that support to be public. On Thursday 25th, Walter McLaren, a staunchly supportive Liberal MP, wrote to her: 'I feel quite as you do. I think the old Suffrage Societies should support these plucky women, and I will gladly support you in trying to have a Demonstration in their favour'. Mrs Fawcett immediately wrote to *The Times*, saying that the militant women had been insulted and abused, yet 'they have done more during the last 12 months to bring it [suffrage] within the realm of practical politics than we have been able to accomplish in the same number of years'.[52] Fawcett's generous support carried considerable weight.

Nor did the husbands and families of the imprisoned women have any intention of letting their sense of outrage go without vigorous public protest. T. J. Cobden-Sanderson immediately wrote an impassioned open letter about the imprisonment of his wife, the daughter of Richard Cobden, 'the man who gave you the cheap loaf'. Equally passionate, Florence Fenwick-Miller, who had been on the School Board in London, immediately wrote to *The Times* on behalf of her imprisoned daughter, Irene:

> I appeal to the men of England, Ireland and Scotland! . . . I appeal to the men who were only a week or two ago signing a document intended to shame the Tsar of Russia for governing his people without representative parliamentary institutions.
> Was this, all of it, sheer hypocrisy? . . . Surely amongst you there are

enough right-thinking and feeling [men] to effectually tell your so-called Liberal Ministry that its women political prisoners, if not released, shall, at any rate, not be treated as common felons? . . . Surely there must be thousands of men who will be ashamed to nestle into their comfortable beds to-night, after their good evening meal, knowing that for this cause eleven noble women are sleeping on straw in solitary dark cells, fed on the harsh food that you offer men of the criminal classes as a deterrent from further crimes . . .

Who are these women? . . . You have got in prison two of the daughters of the late Dr Pankhurst, a gold medallist of his University . . . Then you have got my girl, Irene.[53]

Though the prisoners themselves at the time were not aware of it, such letters caused a great sensation. And thanks to the unceasing efforts of Pethick-Lawrence, Cobden-Sanderson and Keir Hardie, the eleven women were eventually designated as political prisoners (i.e. treated not as second division convicted prisoners but as first division prisoners) – a recognition imprisoned rebel Irishmen had fought for earlier. Although they still had to wear prison clothes, this change of status meant the women could enjoy wider letter-writing, reading and visiting privileges. Mary was able to read Mary Wollstonecraft's *Rights of Women*; Thomas Garrs and Annie Gawthorpe could now visit her:

> F. L. now accompanied Mother to London on the strange errand of visiting daughter and sweetheart in prison. The sparkling ring which I had been wearing was in temporary custody of the authorities. Bereft of all that signified 'daughter', I faced my astonished parent in an outlandish get-up, miles too big for me, the veriest figure of fun. Mother's dismay would have been comic had she not been crying at the same time. 'But' I rallied her, 'this is not a Parisian dressing establishment.' At which she smiled through her tears.[54]

That night, while Garrs returned to the *Yorkshire Post*, Annie Gawthorpe, undoubtedly on her first trip to London, stayed as guest of Charlotte Despard.

It is less clear what visitors Adela Pankhurst received, and whether Emmeline, Christabel, or perhaps Harry, visited the two younger sisters in prison. As Adela began to endure her two months incarceration, she sent an undaunted message to the outside: 'Fight till We Win'. She even wrote a reflective essay, 'Thoughts in Prison', for the *Labour Record* about having given up her teaching job after years in the classroom to campaign for as abstract a political principle as the franchise:

> What becomes of the little girls in the dreary elementary schools, where the State sends millions of diverse young creatures . . . ?
>
> I had asked this question of myself before; as a school teacher I had been trying for years . . . to stave off the inevitable answer in their individual lives. I had felt the hopeless futility of my work. Now, in prison, as the question came to me again during the long hours when I was left alone, it seemed to me that for the first time in my life I was <u>doing</u> something which would help.[55]

For Adela, those winter weeks in Holloway – like her first imprisonment that summer – were a sacrifice that helped make sense of so many of her earlier struggles, both personal and political. For all the women prisoners, the first, second, third, fourth week of incarceration dragged on – to mid-November. The prison door had clanged shut, and remained shut. But in the world outside Holloway, there was a different story.

Locked up in gaol were not just northern rebel girls like Annie Kenney and Adela Pankhurst. No. The prisoners now included highly respected well-established middle-class women, some with useful connections – as the newspaper-reading public and even the Liberal government soon found out.

Of the letters posted to Mrs Fawcett over the next few weeks from NUWSS suffragists, most – but not all – supported the militants' action. Already the WSPU had turned some sympathisers into critics: Esther Roper and Eva Gore-Booth did not disguise their alienation at seeing brawling at Westminster; and Dora Montefiore was also disillusioned with the dishevelled suffragettes and now broke with the WSPU.[56] Mrs Fawcett nevertheless planned a banquet to honour the suffragettes' release. More broadly, England was shocked by the imprisonments – not only by who had been incarcerated, but also the cruel length of time: two months. Shockwaves reverberated the length and breadth of the country. Newspaper readers began to hear of the WSPU, and to listen to the reasoned arguments of the suffragists.

Then the Liberal government found itself confronted by an exceedingly unwelcome challenge. A by-election was called in November in Huddersfield when the MP, a Liberal, resigned. The government certainly wanted to retain the seat, but there would be a three-way contest, with Conservative and Labour candidates challenging the Liberal. For the WSPU, this by-election offered the perfect opportunity for publicity and propaganda about the government's hypocrisy and brutality. For the Huddersfield NUWSS branch, generally Liberal sympathisers, it was a chance to raise the claims of women's suffrage.

Huddersfield was well served with a magnificent railway station and good rail links to London and Manchester. Emmeline Pankhurst and Hannah Mitchell, who arrived on Tuesday 20 November, were among the first to descend on the town; Emmeline spoke that night at the market cross on the WSPU's determination to oppose every Liberal candidate. She angrily told the crowd how the suffragettes had been treated in the Commons' lobby, adding how utterly inconsistent it was that Mrs Cobden-Sanderson, daughter of the Free Trade hero, should be sent to prison for merely asserting women's claims to suffrage. Hannah Mitchell recalled that the two of them 'roused so much interest that at the close we had enough volunteers to bill [post] the town the next day . . . The Huddersfield campaign was a wonderful experience, like putting a match to a ready-built fire. The Yorkshire women rose to the call and followed us in hundreds'.

Meanwhile, the NUWSS branch held a meeting on Thursday morning: it announced that, as all three candidates supported suffrage, it would take no part in the by-election, and that it did not endorse the suffragettes' action. Esther Roper and Eva Gore-Booth for the Lancashire Women Textile Workers' Representation Committee, supporting the Labour candidate, also arrived and organised open-air meetings.[57] It was the full suffrage cast.

It was a tricky time for Campbell-Bannerman's government, lest the voters of Huddersfield actually began to take notice of Mrs Pankhurst's attacks and the Liberals lost their seat. Saturday's *Daily Mirror* ran with 'Suffragettes: Baby-Kissing Tour to defeat Huddersfield Liberal candidate'. The WSPU placed an advertisement in the *Huddersfield Examiner*: 'Working Men of Huddersfield, will you allow the Liberal Government to treat the women of this country so unjustly?' The government panicked – and on Saturday evening sprang the early release of the suffragette prisoners. The women were having supper in their cells when the surprise order suddenly arrived and, as they had served only half their sentence, they were dazed and excited. They were released from Holloway. If the government had made a bad mistake, it was a propaganda gift for the WSPU. Asked about the government's reasoning, Annie Kenney replied, 'We have our own opinion about the Huddersfield election. Some of us are going there tomorrow – a detachment of the gentlest among us'.[58] After a jubilant welcome meeting at Caxton Hall, they jumped on a train north.

In Huddersfield on Monday, suffragettes had chalked on the pavements: 'Votes for Women. Prisoners arrive at 3 p.m. today'. Hannah Mitchell had booked all available halls, which were packed even before the train was due. A great crowd gathered around the station for the arrival of the released suffragettes. Eventually, after a missed train connection, Mary and Annie appeared. The *Daily Mirror* reported, 'No women in history have ever had a wilder and more enthusiastic reception than did Miss M. E. Gawthorpe and Miss Annie Kenney'. The square outside the station was crowded with 4,000 people; women waved handkerchiefs from windows, people yelled and clapped as Annie and Mary mounted the lorry serving as a platform. Christabel Pankhurst 'humorously suggested that the Liberal Government had something to do with the travelling arrangements that had delayed the expected ladies'. Afterwards, Christabel, Annie and Mary proceeded arm-in-arm up the main street, followed by cheering crowds; tramcars had to halt until the procession passed. Hannah Mitchell recorded, 'Huddersfield honoured itself that day by the welcome it gave those women'.[59]

There were only a couple of days to go before polling. On the eve of election day, the Lancashire Women Textile Workers' Representation Committee paraded through the town centres with placards appealing to electors to vote for the Labour candidate. The suffragettes drove round the constituency in a horse-drawn wagonette, distributing leaflets as they went, with their placard urging electors to 'Oppose the Government that imprisons women, and vote against the Liberal candidate,' and stopping regularly to make short speeches.

Mary Gawthorpe found the sudden transition from prison to platform took its toll: she suffered a severe nose-bleed and almost lost her voice. However, on one occasion, while busily engaged, she became aware of someone bowing formally to her. 'I looked carefully and met the eyes of my Father, eyes gleaming a trifle sardonically . . . All this in a flash. I ignored him completely. But I knew he was proud of his belligerent offspring.' Mary never knew whether John Gawthorpe was in Huddersfield anyway for the Conservatives, or had gone knowing his daughter would be there.

For election day, Wednesday 28th, the WSPU positioned themselves at the polling station and outside the Liberal candidate's committee rooms, urging electors to vote for anyone but him. Under a banner headline,

'Today's Election At Huddersfield – Suffragettes Hard At Work', the *Daily Mirror* front page carried a large photograph of amused mill workers reading the suffragette slogans chalked on the pavements.[60]

The Liberal machine in Huddersfield in fact remained hardly dented. When the Liberals claimed their electoral victory, the suffragettes were very disappointed, though they tried to sound upbeat, claiming, 'We have given the Government such a fighting as they have never had before. We have frightened them into letting our sisters out of prison'.[61] But the result represented a relief to the fence-sitting local NUWSS suffragists, alienated by self-publicising ex-prisoners and hopeful about their newly elected Liberal MP.

9. Mary Gawthorpe cheered by a huge crowd of boys and girls, Huddersfield by-election. *'Yorkshire ought to be jolly well ashamed of itself', she said.* Daily Mirror, *30 November 1906.*

1906 had been an unforgettable year for both Adela Pankhurst and Mary Gawthorpe: they had travelled on new journeys that neither could have predicted. The Liberals might have held Huddersfield, but the by-election campaign – hard on the heels of public protest against harsh gaol sentences – had far-reaching effects. One immediate repercussion was in Huddersfield itself, where passionate suffragette enthusiasm welled up overnight. And more broadly across the West Riding, women began to sit up and take notice of Votes for Women. The suffrage movement had so far been limited mainly to cities and major towns; the WSPU scarcely operated outside Manchester and London. Now the campaign spread wide and spread fast – most especially out to the small Pennine textile communities nearby – like Hebden Bridge and Halifax.

PART TWO

Landscapes and Communities
1906–1907

CHAPTER 4

Tailoress and writer: Lavena Saltonstall
1906–1907

Our story now plunges into the closely-knit local communities at the industrial heartland of Yorkshire's West Riding. Unlike more cosmopolitan Leeds, these small towns and villages lying at the Pennine foothills had grown prosperous on textile manufacturing and closely linked occupations: clothing and engineering. In 1906–7, from the small isolated town of Hebden Bridge and nearby Halifax, sprang a cadre of rebel girls who worked in the local clothing factories or worsted mills. But unlike those imprisoned after the Commons' lobby protest who so often went on to write their memoirs, these community suffragettes had, until recently, disappeared without trace. They flashed meteor-like across the Edwardian sky, leaving only a trail of glowing stars. Tantalisingly elusive, Lavena Saltonstall, unsung suffragette heroine of Hebden Bridge, wrote no autobiography and left no personal papers or photograph (though, thankfully, her letters to the press have survived). She slipped through the commemorative suffragette net and passed away without her descendants' celebration of their remarkable suffragette ancestor. A story untold – till now.

Historians need to piece together these biographies: the rebel girls were not limited to better-known suffragettes like Mary Gawthorpe. For a regional study of the Votes for Women campaign, Lavena and her friends are central. Luckily, the suffrage detective can now reconstruct their stories from a rich mix of sources, illuminating even 'Lavena the Obscure'. And importantly, Lavena – like Rebecca West – could wield a wicked pen. She found the most effective way to make her point against die-hard opponents was wittily, stroppily and in print. In her powerful writings, only recently unearthed, we can now hear her distinctive voice, still as clear as a bell a century later.[1] So Lavena's story springs from this new and original research, previously difficult to access and thus utterly neglected.

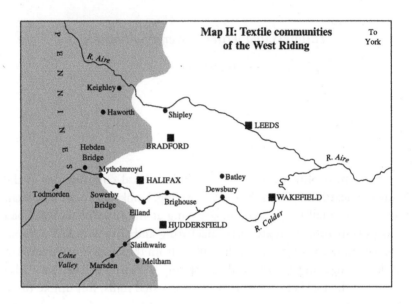

Map II: Textile communities of the West Riding

Lavena Saltonstall was born in September 1881 at Rawholme, just outside Hebden Bridge, in a short row of small stone cottages with a cobbled communal courtyard behind. Her birthplace looks down a steep grassy slope to Hebden Water, rushing down to swell the River Calder. Flanked by wooded hillsides towering above, it offered an idyllically beautiful landscape for childhood.[2]

Lavena was the second daughter of Mary and John Saltonstall, who worked as a fustian dyer in the local textile trade. (Fustian, made from cotton, had more threads per inch, making it an extremely hard-wearing cloth suitable for corduroy or moleskin work trousers.) Hebden Bridge specialised in fustian dyeing and sewing, mainly in small-scale firms. Of local men and boys, nearly half worked in fustian manufacture and the clothing trade.[3] Despite its rural setting, Rawholme was just a few minutes' walk upstream to a dyeing and finishing firm, where John Saltonstall undoubtedly worked. Like so many other local people, he grew up in one of the old hilltop hand-loom weaving and farming hamlets that peered down on the town, moving downhill to the valley-floor steam-powered mills and fustian clothing factories that were turning Hebden Bridge into a small late-Victorian boom town.[4] More unusually, a desperate Mary had fled south from Scotland with an illegitimate child: her daughter Emily was five years old when she and John married.[5]

Rawholme grew congested for the growing family; and by the time Lavena was four, they had moved again. Like so many other working-class families, the Saltonstalls were small-scale economic migrants, flitting repeatedly between rented accommodation, hearing of a better job, or needing more room when a baby arrived. Lavena's story of successive flittings can stand for thousands of others.[6] For each removal they probably loaded their modest possessions — a few clothes, perhaps a table and a couple of chairs, a bed — onto a one-horse cart, trudging uphill and down in its wake. Or they may have borrowed one of the many barrows used for wheeling fustian 'pieces' round the town, from manufacturer to cutter, from dye-works to warehouse.

First, the Saltonstalls moved into a neat, prosperous town-centre street. Here, possibly in attic lodgings, Lavena's brother William was born. Soon, however, an industrial building boom, prompted by direct rail links to Leeds and Manchester, engulfed the street's residential respectability: large fustian clothing factories appeared, plus a cotton mill, dye works and iron works. Perhaps because it was becoming an unhealthy environment for a baby, the family moved up-hill towards the ancient handloom settlement, Heptonstall. Here brother Richard was born. Shortly they moved again — this time up on the opposite hillside to Wood Top, a rural-industrial hamlet with a dye works and mill pond for the steam engine; here John Saltonstall would have found a better dyeing job and here Lavena's sister Amelia was born. Half-sister Emily was now out working as a 'fustian tailoress machinist'.[7] The views along the River Calder were stunning, but isolated Wood Top was very bleak in winter and, before Lavena was thirteen, the Saltonstalls had moved yet again — this time to an old stone terrace down by the River Calder. Their low-lying house must have been damp: here five-year-old Amelia caught a tubercular disease and, despite being taken to hospital by their mother, died of convulsions. John Saltonstall, now promoted to foreman fustian dyer, earned a better wage, and the family moved higher above the river to a solid two-up-two-down house. But here in 1896 nine-year-old Richard fell ill with intestinal consumption and died at home. Lavena was fourteen.[8]

In this Pennine community, household sanitation remained primitive and indoor toilets rare; clean water was at a premium and sewage disposal rudimentary. Farmers still manured fields draining down the hillsides to the town below, polluting drinking water drawn from street pumps. Local officials regularly sent samples for analysis, but the results, despite references to 'excrementitious matter', and 'urinous water', were not sufficiently lethal for the magistrates to condemn the water. Typhoid fever regularly broke out. Such epidemics affected children particularly, sometimes fatally. Local schools closed for weeks on end in the winter due to scarlet fever.[9]

It is unclear which school Lavena attended. What is more certain is that she had to leave at the earliest opportunity. She would undoubtedly have liked to stay on at school, to become, say, a pupil teacher, for we know from her later writings how keen was her hunger for learning. However, Lavena's tenth birthday fell in September 1891, and it is likely she began as a half-timer shortly after. (The act raising the age to eleven was not passed until 1893, and to twelve in 1899.) There were hundreds of half-timers attending local schools.[10]

Lavena's meagre wages would have helped fund the family's last few moves to better housing. She now followed Emily into the fustian clothing trade; indeed, she had little option, for there were precious few local alternatives to a job in tailoring. In Hebden Bridge at the turn of the century, of the 1,670 women and girls recorded as occupied, seventy per cent worked as tailoresses. There were over two dozen local factories operating as clothing manufacturers and wholesalers, many of them small workshops or family factories, mass-producing hard-wearing corduroy, whipcord or needlecord trousers.[11]

On leaving school, a half-timer like Lavena would sit next to a more experienced woman, learning without pay for a few weeks, then graduating to half-pay; eventually she went 'on for herself', sewing less complicated garments at piece rates (i.e. payment by a 'piece'). The process was simple: woven lengths of cloth were cut in bulk to a pattern, and the cloth and lining for each garment was passed to a machinist who completed all processes (i.e. the garments were 'made through'). Girls such as Lavena sat either side of narrow tables down long alleys, sewing – mainly trousers in standard sizes. Each girl worked her own sewing machine, probably still powered by a foot treadle. A male tackler would supervise, and the women entertained themselves with hymn-singing. Hours were usually 6 a.m. to 6 p.m., with meal breaks, plus Saturday morning, making fifty-six hours per week, with few holidays. Average weekly wages for

10. *Women sewing in machine room, Hebden Bridge; note scissors hanging from their belts.*

women on piece-work went up to fifteen shillings [75p], compared to hourly-paid men earning twenty-five shillings [£1.25]. In other words, tailors earned nearly double the women. Certainly, compared to the twenty-one-shilling wage of a Lancashire woman weaver, trade union organisation remained very patchy and pay was low. Clothing was notoriously a sweated industry, and its piece work relentless. Local parents might determine that their daughters should not enter the clothing factories, but there was little choice but to do so.[12]

When Lavena Saltonstall was growing up in Hebden Bridge at the turn of the century, 'fustianopolis' was a compact out-of-the-way town with its own local accent; it was proud of its distinctiveness from other communities along the Calder valley: Mytholmroyd or Todmorden. With powerful traditions of self-help and voluntary organisation, the right brass band could be mustered for every occasion; a church or chapel stood on many street corners, as did half-a-dozen neighbourhood co-operative stores. With its clock-tower and specialist departments (grocers, drapers), the handsome new Co-operative Hall stood tall in the town centre. The co-operative movement flourished locally, providing profit-sharing shopping and its own Co-op Society Reading Room.[13] There was even a large and successful manufacturing co-op, Nutclough Mill. These two buildings gave Hebden Bridge its distinctive skyline.

11. Hebden Bridge: showing Unity Street (sloping top right) with the Saltonstalls' end-terrace house and, just visible, the 'tin tab' roof. Below are weaving sheds and mill chimney; the Woodend landscape had little changed since Lavena lived there.

Lavena's nineteenth birthday fell in September 1900: she had probably been at work about eight years. By then the Saltonstalls had flit once again – to a larger three-storey end-terrace house in an industrial suburb, Woodend, above Nutclough Mill. Here, stacked up the hillside were terraced rows inhabited by cotton weavers and fustian clothing machinists, tailors and boot-makers, with even the errand boy a 'fustian errand boy'. There was a co-op store at one end of Unity Street, facing Woodend Wesleyan Mission hall, a corrugated-iron tabernacle, or 'tin

tab'.[14] Here lived nineteen-year-old Lavena, 'Machinist (Fustian clothing) tailor'; her forty-five-year-old father John, 'Foreman Dyer
(Fustian)'; forty-five-year-old mother Mary; and her brother William,
now aged fifteen, who had been able to stay on at school as a pupil
teacher (perhaps because he was four years younger than Lavena, or
because it was easier for a family to 'afford' for a boy to stay on at school).
Twenty-five-year-old Emily, still a fustian tailoress, had left the family
home and now boarded nearby.[15]

Lavena seems to have felt keenly the town's extreme isolation: even the
seven-mile journey to Halifax would have been a rarity, for she was twenty
before the new-fangled electric trams from Halifax managed to reach as far
out as Hebden Bridge. Such a tightly-knit community combined the
advantages of rootedness with the disadvantage of stifling expectations. For
girls these were firmly fixed: destiny decreed working in the fustian clothing factory followed by marriage. Certainly, Lavena's own hard-working
mother had devoted her married life to maintaining working-class domestic respectability at home. The Saltonstall family was apparently very
conventional, probably Church of England, and in all likelihood supporting the Conservative Party; and Lavena became drawn desultorily into the
Conservatives' 'Primrose Dame' tea-parties, perhaps as much for social as
political reasons.[16]

Educational opportunities for working-class girls were limited: male
cutters attended evening classes in 'Cloth Dissection' or 'Tailors' Cutting',
but the curriculum was distinctly segregated, with women teachers offering 'Starching and Ironing', needlework and cookery both 'Household' and
'Middle Class'.[17] These years of confined horizons, long hours and harsh
conditions were already beginning to chafe. Later, Lavena reflected back on
this time and wrote lambasting this frustrating lack of options, wit over-
coming bitterness but not suffocating anger:

As I am a tailoress many people think it is my bounden duty to make
trousers and vests, and knit and crochet and sew, and thank God for my station in life.

I am supposed to make myself generally <u>useless</u> by ignoring things that
matter – literature, music, art, history, economics, the lives of the people
round me and the evils of my day. They think I ought to concern myself
over clean doorsteps and side-board covers – things that don't matter so
much . . .

In my native place the women, as a general rule, wash every Monday, iron on Tuesdays, court on Wednesdays, bake on Thursdays, clean on Fridays, go to market or go courting again on Saturdays, and to church on Sundays. There are exceptions, of course, hundreds of exceptions, but the exceptions are considered unwomanly and eccentric people.[18]

Sadly, we do not know whether Lavena did 'go courting' then (though if she did, unlike Mary Gawthorpe, she obviously did not encounter an 'F.L.'). Nor do we know exactly the shape her life was taking between 1901 and 1905–6 when she was around twenty-three or four years old: these are five missing years.[19] We do, however, get a sense that a great deal had happened since 1901 when she was living with her family in Unity Street: the arrival of the electric trams to Hebden Bridge heralded an opening up to new ideas for its fustian tailoresses – as the story of Lavena's friend and neighbour Lilian Cobbe makes clear.

Like Lavena, Lilian Cobbe, daughter of a maltster and corn miller who had come north from Suffolk, became a half-timer; and also like her, Lilian and her younger sister Louie worked as tailoresses in one of the local fustian clothing factories. Such women workers remained poorly organised up to the turn of the century but, at New Year 1900, twenty-nine-year-old 'fustian clothing finisher' Lilian Cobbe bravely joined the Amalgamated Union of Clothiers Operatives (AUCO) branch, recently formed in Hebden Bridge. Eight other women and girls joined with her, each paying three-pence a week in dues, half the rate of men.

The branch, however, remained precarious: Lilian and the others let their membership lapse. But after the General Election in January 1906, the mood of reform, with a Sweated Industries Exhibition held in London in May, touched even Hebden Bridge, with women speakers visiting there. Also in May, a charismatic trade union organiser arrived: she persuaded a dozen women to pay their 3½d each and –join the AUCO branch. Among them was Lilian Cobbe, who became the tailoresses' unofficial leader, determined that they should be sweated and voiceless no longer.[20]

Christabel Pankhurst was another speaker who arrived to stir things up: in March, Christabel spoke to the ILP annual meeting of the Sowerby division, Lavena and Lilian's own constituency. The *Hebden Bridge Times* reported Christabel's speech: 'So long as women have not votes, they are not free, and they are socially and industrially in subjection', and she accused the Liberal government of forsaking its pledges to women.[21]

This rising mood of confidence and assertiveness rubbed off on to Lavena. Increasingly, she refused to accept her mother's confining domestic expectations:

> The majority of girls are brought up by well-wishing parents to earn their living, to become thoroughly domesticated, to behave respectably, go to Sunday school and read religious books, all with a view to one day getting married. The 'getting married idea' is the most important one in most girls' lives. No account is taken of the fact that just as faces are different, so are temperaments.[22]

She determined to resist her family's conservative politics and, even if it meant getting into trouble at work for being too outspoken, she decided to *do* something – herself, *now*:

> Being a tailoress, and living in an age when poverty, vice and disease are stalking through the land and attacking particularly the people of my class, I have decided to abandon the so-called womanly accomplishments and have something to say about these evils.[23]

Lavena now took a more radical step than either Lilian Cobbe or her own half-sister Emily. In a dramatically defiant gesture of independence, when she was about twenty-three, Lavena gave up her machinist job and left damply claustrophobic Hebden Bridge. She moved seven miles along the valley to larger Halifax, where she became a weaver, which, while noisier than the clothing factory, paid better wages. And she became a boarder in a suburban street along with other cotton mill workers.

In Halifax, Lavena encountered a new and wider world. She made friends with a group of confident women there who indeed did 'show a tendency to politics, or to ideas of her own' without the slightest misgivings. Lavena, grown dissatisfied with 'Primrose Dame' teas, was moving fast towards the labour movement and suffrage campaigns.

Laura Wilson, fearless and feisty, became Lavena's closest friend. Their backgrounds were not dissimilar: Laura's father was a dyer's labourer and her mother had put only a mark (rather than a signature) on her daughter's birth certificate. Laura herself, a worsted coating weaver, had married George Wilson, a machine tool maker, in 1899. Now aged twenty-seven, she lived with George and their young son in a terraced house. Given the

Saltonstalls' constant traipsing and flitting, Lavena looked upon the Wilsons as skilled craft workers, prudently stable.

Around the corner lived Mary Taylor, wife of a metal worker, with a grown daughter. Mary's husband Arthur had lost his job ten years earlier due to victimisation of labour supporters. Like James Parker (now a Halifax MP), Arthur had been an ILP 'rising star'; secretary of the engineers' union and active in Labour Church, he was a Labour councillor; and Mary, now aged forty, was elected a Poor Law Guardian – so both were senior figures in the vibrant local labour movement.[24] Both Wilsons and Taylors were active in Halifax's strong ILP branch, and it was into their neighbourhood that Lavena escaped from Hebden Bridge and now found herself lodgings.

A clear picture of the radical world of Edwardian working women in the Halifax ILP begins to emerge. In autumn 1905, just before suffragette militancy erupted, Christabel Pankhurst came across to speak at the ILP branch, Laura Wilson chairing the meeting. By March 1906 when Christabel, now better known, returned, this time for the ILP nearby, the socialist-suffragette excitement in the air was clear. Mary Taylor was soon demanding Votes for Women at the ILP national conference, and when a Women's Labour League branch was formed in Halifax, Laura, Mary and Lavena all naturally became key members.[25]

Meanwhile Lavena kept in touch with friends in Hebden Bridge, moving easily between the two communities. This meant she was well positioned for the events which now exploded; these were to be the making of the local suffragette movement, transforming Lavena Saltonstall's life.

In Halifax at midsummer 1906, a tramway accident killed an 'Irish harvest man'. The tram driver Chadwick was dismissed by his employers, Halifax town council. His unfair dismissal looked like victimisation. The issue festered, and was reported at length in the local press as a matter of direct public interest – along with low wage and safety issues – for everyone now used electric trams, the gondolas of the people. This community dispute was obviously discussed by Laura Wilson, Mary Taylor and Lavena Saltonstall, and Lavena was emboldened to write to the papers. This was the first of her many public letters. She turned her pen scathingly against 'the brilliant idea which brought one-man [tram]cars into hilly Halifax', an 'example of someone's laudable attempt at municipal economy in reducing the number of tramway-men'.[26]

Aghast that an elected council proved such an unfair employer, the

Halifax tram workers came out on strike. The dispute brought into public notice the close-knit Women's Labour League network of Laura Wilson, Mary Taylor, Lavena Saltonstall. They organised two meetings for Annie Kenney, now famed as 'one of Mr Asquith's prisoners'. The WSPU, with its strategy of spotting a local industrial dispute, seized the opportunity. One Saturday afternoon, Annie arrived – and mounted a furniture-moving dray before a 200-strong audience. Lavena must have been in the audience, listening intently. Annie's speech glided guilelessly from the tram dispute to the demand for the vote: 'As a factory girl, as one who has helped build up trade unionism, if I know how to fight for a living wage, I can help fight for women's political freedom'. That evening at an ILP meeting, Laura Wilson proposed the resolution – 'Like Miss Kenney, I have lived the life of an ordinary working girl' – followed by Annie, who mocked Herbert Asquith for his having to scurry away from suffragettes.[27]

Certainly, when Annie came to write her memoirs, it was industrial communities like Halifax that remained most vivid in her romantic imagination:

> The wildest parts of the Yorkshire and Lancashire moorlands were the parts from which we received most recruits. This was owing to the women being versed in Labour politics. Many, many are the happy evenings I have spent in some lonely cottage on the edge of the moors, not many miles from the famous 'Wuthering Heights'. The wife would have returned from her mill-work, having tramped miles during the day, the husband would also be at home. Tea would be served, hot muffins, tea-cake, sometimes cold ham, and a real good pot of tea. The fire would have been lit by a good-hearted neighbour, and the hearth cleaned. The lamp would be burning, and we would talk about politics, Labour questions, Emerson, Ruskin, Edward Carpenter, right into the night . . . The sense of companionship that creeps around one, sitting in front of a rosy fire with kind people, is beautiful. When I retired I would listen to the wind whistling and howling over the moorland, and live all over again that world-read romance 'Wuthering Heights'.[28]

The strike quickly intensified, triggering open-air meetings around the town. Lavena herself was now billed as a speaker, but, knowing she was a better writer than speaker, she sent a self-mocking letter, which was read out instead: 'I cannot tackle an audience of above two, including myself . . . I have no wish to become acquainted with the old apple and other ancient missiles which would be my lot if I consented'.[29] The crowd was less reticent. A tram-men's brass band led a procession from Halifax towards Hebden Bridge; and, with the council digging its heels in, a systematic community trams boycott was organised, adopting the slogan 'Walk and win'. Mary Taylor walked or even cycled to her Guardian meetings.

All this somehow did persuade Lavena to speak. On Monday 17 September, the Women's Labour League arranged a meeting, with the three friends taking the platform before a large crowd 'seething with excitement'. Mary promised belligerently that women 'can settle both the Town Council and the Tramways Committee'. Lavena herself was now 'greeted with acclamation' being 'known to the audience through her letters to the Press'. She rose to propose the resolution supporting the strike, provocatively urging the restraining of any 'blacklegs' (strike-breakers) 'in all ways open to us'. But Lavena remained a nervous speaker: she 'could only say one or two words and apologise for her inability to make a public address', and, although 'the women were in ardent sympathy with her', she had to sit down. Laura and Mary, more experienced, proposed to widen the trams boycott to shop-keepers and this met with loud applause. Mary added, 'We shall walk barefoot if there are no stockings to be bought except from [anti-strike shops]'. The resolution was carried unanimously, with all women standing – a moving sign of community solidarity.

Two days later, they held a meeting near Lavena's boarding house; Laura proclaimed that now 'only middle-class' people were riding on trams. With their banner, 'Women support your husbands for a living wage', the meeting even attracted six detectives. Slogans were daubed on the door of the wife of a tram-strike 'blackleg'. Another Women's Labour League open-air demonstration drew a crowd of 800, gas lamps casting eerie shadows through the darkness. Mary urged, 'Let us boycott these blacklegs', and the crowd walked in procession to the Trades Club. Next day, 500 people gathered: this time, Mary 'walk and win' Taylor, who had been teased about cycling to her Guardian meetings at the Workhouse, rang a small hand-bell. Laura, who said she had tramped so much her feet were blistered, 'hoped working men would walk until they were bow-legged rather than submit'.[30]

All this took place against a summer and early autumn of suffragette militancy. The arrests of Adela Pankhurst and others at the Liberals' meeting in Manchester and the crowd violence at Boggart Hole Clough had all been reported in the papers like *Labour Leader*. At the same time, the Halifax women were accused of encouraging people to smash windows. So, with the suffragettes in mind, Poor Law Guardian Mary now publicly retorted:

I've been told a score of times that I ought to be locked up. I am not going to be . . . It's been said if they get me under lock and key the strike would be settled. If they lock me up, there are 600 or 700 women left, and the magistrates will have to deal with them. But I am not going. Prison life is not good enough for me.[31]

Laura was equally unyielding: 'If Mrs Taylor and I are responsible for the bother, why did they [police] not take us? I am not anxious to go to prison, but if I can do any good by going to prison I am willing to go'. And Lavena accused the Christian ministers, who had gone to tram workers' homes to persuade them back to work, of themselves being agitators – as were the magistrates. 'I have been fighting for justice. I wish you had in Halifax a few [radical] parsons such as there are in Hebden Bridge', she said.[32]

In October, with the strike still unsettled, Annie Kenney returned to Halifax. She would have reported her earlier meeting back to WSPU headquarters, and been encouraged to nourish such fertile ground. Certainly, this time, addressing the crowded Women's Labour League meeting, her speech was more strategic, her political rhetoric melding the strike issue to women's demand for the vote. She sympathised with the men out on strike: 4½d an hour was absurd as a living wage and Annie went on:

If I lived in Halifax I would refuse to pay a penny toward the trams. (Applause) If the men of Halifax will band themselves together, they will set Halifax on fire with enthusiasm and will be bound to win in the end. It is always the same, both with men and women – those who are building up the wealth of the community have to suffer unless they take a determined stand. Women must get their political freedom, so that at the next election they will be able to express their opinions through the vote, and send men to the House of Commons to make better laws than we have today. Women realise there is one law for the rich and another for the poor. Women have thought too much of men and too little of themselves. Remember Mr Asquith would not receive a deputation from women, and he sent three [of us] to prison . . . We [suffragettes] could make him afraid . . . If [we] ran a candidate for East Fife [his constituency], Mr Asquith would be turned out.[33]

The women's suffrage resolution, proposed by Laura, was agreed and Annie Kenney hurried back to London. Then, within days, startling news from Westminster arrived: newspapers headlined 'Irrepressible Women.

Ten Suffragettes Go to Prison' – including, of course, Annie, Adela Pankhurst and Mary Gawthorpe.

Coincidentally, alongside the tram strike, in Hebden Bridge a dispute of fustian weavers also loomed. The issue was low wages: local weavers argued that they received ten per cent less than those in Lancashire. Weavers in Ashworth's mill struck. Non-union weavers accepted the employers' offer of two and a half per cent; however, defiant union members met in the Co-operative Hall, appointed a strike committee and, supported by Todmorden and District Weavers' Association, started mill collections. Soon, over 200 weavers came out, and the Association rented the late-Victorian 'tin tab' Woodend mission room near Lavena's old home, meeting there daily to organise the strike.[34]

A weavers' strike touches a community less directly than a tram dispute. The strike nevertheless escalated into a community conflict like the Halifax battle. The Hebden Bridge weavers were pitted against local employers, usually living nearby – and against the 'knobsticks' they hired to run the looms and so break the strike. During November, 'knobsticks' leaving work were hooted at and their doors pelted with mud. Stones were thrown at Ashworth's house, breaking some windows and just missing his wife. The police presence was strengthened with both plain-clothes and mounted men. 'The masters' (employers) sued for breach of contract over forty fustian weavers at Ashworth's Mill; supported by the Weavers' Association lawyer, they slugged it out in court.[35] Battle was joined in rural Hebden Bridge – where traditional grievances tapped into rawer emotions and near-violence bubbled near the surface.

In November 1906, the nearby Huddersfield by-election was made the more dramatic with the imprisonment of the suffragettes. Laura Wilson went across, 'to support the political party for whom I have worked for fourteen or fifteen years; but hearing the women speak in Huddersfield, I became converted on the question of votes for women . . . I recognised at that election that we must either march with our regiment or remain behind, and I am determined to march with my regiment'.[36]

By then the WSPU, helped by the publicity generated by the Westminster arrests and harsh sentences, was trying to develop into a national organisation based on local branches. The precedent here was democratically-run organisations like the NUWSS and ILP; and indeed many of the WSPU branches remained intimately rooted in ILP culture based in ILP strongholds like Halifax.

Nothing more vividly conjures up the inspiring moment of this late-1906 groundswell of support for the WSPU than the ILP *Manifesto* rushed out for the imprisoned suffragettes. From Leeds, Ethel Annakin Snowden invited women ILP members to sign the manifesto, hastily circulated to branches, and to send her a postcard.[37] (Though given the WSPU lurch away in the Cockermouth by-election, there was consternation in ILP circles: was this invitation, issued by the wife of a leading MP, official ILP policy? There must have been brisk discussion in the Snowden household. The *Labour Leader* editor, no longer so sympathetic to the WSPU, reassured readers the invitation was 'purely personal' and not official.)[38]

MANIFESTO
To the Women's Social and Political Union.

WE, THE UNDERSIGNED WOMEN OF THE INDEPENDENT LABOUR PARTY, DESIRE TO PLACE ON RECORD OUR WARM APPRECIATION AND HIGH ADMIRATION OF THE WORK DONE FOR WOMAN SUFFRAGE BY THE WOMEN OF THE SOCIAL AND POLITICAL UNION. IN PARTICULAR DO WE ADMIRE AND CONGRATULATE THE BRAVE WOMEN WHO HAVE HAD THE COURAGE TO SUFFER IN PRISON FOR THEIR CONVICTIONS, AND WE ASSERT, WITH THEM, OUR PROFOUND BELIEF THAT NO REAL AND LASTING PROGRESS WILL EVER BE MADE APART FROM THE COMPLETE ENFRANCHISEMENT OF WOMEN.

12. Manifesto to the Women's Social and Political Union, *ILP, New Year 1907.*

In local ILP branches like Halifax, however, members' response to the *Manifesto* invitation was extremely enthusiastic. Twenty-two women signed, headed, naturally, by Mary Taylor and Laura Wilson.[39] Among the other signatories was twenty-seven-year-old Dinah Connelly, a woollen weaver, married to Charles Connelly, a skilled stonemason. Like Laura Wilson,

Dinah was now bringing up young children, and the Connellys lived not far from where Lavena boarded.

With the ILP *Manifesto* support came a phenomenal growth of WSPU branches in late 1906, from a handful to four dozen. Halifax became a key branch. Mary Gawthorpe, as an organiser constantly criss-crossing the country, was despatched to Halifax, for the WSPU was casting round for promising bases in the northern industrial heartland. Annie Kenney had already reported back on her encouraging reception; the tram dispute provided a golden opportunity; and the lively Women's Labour League with its fearless women speakers seemed keen to link the local volatile conflict to women's demand for the vote. As the local paper put it, 'Women's suffrage is in the air, and Halifax is being infected with the germ'.

So at New Year 1907 Mary Gawthorpe arrived at Halifax station, met by Laura Wilson who offered her hospitality. She was hurried up to the Wilsons' house. Mary's first WSPU meeting, on Thursday 3 January, was a day-time 'cottage meeting' in the Wilsons' own home. No records survive, but Mary Taylor and Dinah Connelly would have been present, listening as Mary Gawthorpe outlined WSPU aims and methods, including militancy and 'opposition to whatever government is in power, until such time as the franchise is granted'. A second, more formal, evening meeting was held in Halifax Socialist Club for women like Lavena who worked during the day. Here, at this momentous occasion, the Halifax WSPU branch was formed. No fewer than seventeen women enrolled, with Laura elected secretary.

Suffragettes were news. Next morning, the local press reporter visited the Wilsons; he found Mary Gawthorpe, still at breakfast, bubbly with optimism. She was four feet, ten and three-quarter inches tall, weighed only just over six stone, and had hazel eyes and, ever the WSPU organiser, was 'plainly attired, with fountain pen fastened to a leather case to her dress'. Asked about prison, debonair Mary, 'with a merry twinkle in her eye', was characteristically voluble:

> Oh, yes, and it was fine. There is nothing I enjoy better after scrubbing out the cells etc than the tea which was provided. But just imagine, I earned 10s 5d [52p] by knitting socks . . . We [WSPU] are making converts hourly . . . Even when . . . we are compelled to yield to the strong force [police], we have one weapon left with which to fight and we use that freely. That is our tongue.[40]

The Halifax WSPU branch looked out local opportunities for suffrage propaganda – and seized them. It did not have to search far. Hebden Bridge and its six-months-old fustian weavers' strike provided an important local example of the grassroots growth of the early WSPU.

In the face of intense community pressures the strike remained firm, the masters now 'importing' knobstick weavers from further away to keep their looms running. At 5.30 p.m. knobsticks leaving Salem Mill accompanied by police were jeered by hostile crowds. Amid threats, a scuffle broke out. A big crowd groaned as the knobsticks appoached. Six summonses were issued.

Lavena, moving to and fro between Hebden Bridge and Halifax, was well placed to monitor all this conflict – and to act. Perhaps through Mary Gawthorpe, she contacted the WSPU and arranged for a visiting suffragette speaker to link the weavers' conflict to votes for women. The speaker despatched was Emmeline Pankhurst herself. (Emmeline's own account made the visit sound spontaneous: she says she first heard of the strike when passing through Hebden Bridge by train, and had made some enquiries: 'When I heard that this struggle had gone on six weary months I felt there was some work for us to do'. In that urgent moment, perhaps both explanations, Lavena's planning and Emmeline's coincidence, were true.)[41]

A meeting on labour representation for women was arranged by Hebden Bridge Trades Council; this quickly became caught up in the strike. Emmeline arrived – accompanied by Jennie Baines, a suffragette from Stockport (who had recently been arrested outside the Commons and sentenced to fourteen days in Holloway), plus of course Mary Taylor and Laura Wilson, known locally through the Halifax tram strike.

To the striking fustian weavers the name 'Emmeline Pankhurst' would have evoked both a pioneer labour champion and founder of the suffragettes, an elegant widow whose family had braved even prison for their political beliefs. The exact balance – socialism and suffrage – might have been perceived rather fuzzily; but in the volatile political tension of the moment, that seemed not to matter. Emmeline promised inspiration, hope and national recognition for the weavers' claim to a living wage.

Early evening on Monday 28 January, 1907, a procession of 400 weavers – headed by a brass band composed just of those members of the Hebden Bridge and Heptonstall bands who were themselves out on strike – wound its way ceremoniously from the Weavers' Institute at Woodend and down into the town. Here, the swelling crowd packed into the hall overflowed into meetings outside. The band played the hymn 'Beautiful Zion', with the peaceful audience (among which a dozen police helmets were visible) singing. 'The scene was unparalleled in the history of Hebden Bridge', the local paper summed up epically.

Emmeline Pankhurst had to perch on a wooden staircase running up outside the town-centre Bridge Mill. Lilian Cobbe, as a leading clothing trade unionist, took the chair. Mary Taylor tried to keep the impatient crowd entertained, for Emmeline had to speak at no fewer than three overflow meetings. But it was worth waiting for: Emmeline brought not only her polished oratory but also a wider international perspective to her expectant listeners:

> It is evident that the quiet persuasive methods . . . do not always succeed, and the time comes when these methods need something more to back them up. I realise that here in Hebden Bridge the time has arrived when you want something of an aggressive kind if you are to bring the weary struggle to an end. My experience at Bolton [weavers' strike] and elsewhere has taught me . . . that if you make your injustice known, public indignation will be aroused, and you will win.
>
> In Australia they have legally-constituted boards of arbitration to settle such matters . . . This all came about through women's suffrage; when women get the vote they send a different type of men to Parliament, with the result that trades disputes are settled by arbitration, and strikes and lockouts are unknown . . . From information gleaned I am convinced the weavers of Hebden Bridge have a strong case . . .
>
> If Labour representation in Parliament is necessary for men it is still more necessary for women, who are ground down and are the bottom dog always. This is why we agitate so much and make so much noise. We demand the right of women to choose our representatives in Parliament . . .
>
> Do you think you can get a legal minimum wage out of members of Parliament who are masters themselves, or connected with firms of employers? You in Hebden Bridge have sent a Liberal to Parliament and a Liberal says he is in favour of freedom and all that kind of thing. Yes, he is – for men, but not for women . . . Women are at present quite intelligent enough to pay their taxes, but they are not considered intelligent enough to put a cross on a voting paper and place it in the ballot box . . .
>
> My advice to the women of Hebden Bridge is to fight loyally in the strike and set to work to get the power that the men have got, and do away with strikes and lockouts.[42]

Emmeline sat down to cheers. Her rousing speech, suggesting the vote would end such industrial conflicts, had brilliantly elided the local industrial dispute and women's political demands. Mary Taylor added that, from her experience of the Halifax tram boycott, 'You are sure to win if you will stand shoulder to shoulder . . . We want all you women to come out and show the masters that you are not going to have it.' Jennie Baines reminded the audience of her fourteen days in Holloway, and said she would stay for a while in Hebden Bridge to help: 'If the women will rally around me, I will explain to them our methods of fighting for women's franchise, and the way to end the strike'. And Laura Wilson concluded, proposing a resolution following Emmeline's pleas for conciliation boards as in Australia, and this was carried unanimously. The meeting broke up, with knots of people standing about afterwards peaceably discussing the strike and the memorable evening.

Meanwhile, however, weavers leaving the mill of another local employer, Roger Shackleton, were still being mobbed by strikers. A few even clambered up to Shackleton's home near Heptonstall, where 'assailants' showered down large stones, breaking three windows and an easy chair inside. Afterwards, 'marauders' ran down the steep fields towards Hebden Bridge.

Emmeline left town: but her meeting seems to have stirred violence. On Tuesday 29th, a crowd pursued weavers leaving Salem Mill; the police lining the route suddenly wheeled around to form a cordon across the road and the crowd had to retreat. Another large crowd led by suffragettes set upon the weavers employed by a William Thomas and mauled them. Weavers were escorted home by an angry throng singing 'Count your Blessings', accompanied by loud groaning; the crowd then climbed up to Shackleton's house with more hooting, returning to a town-centre meeting addressed by Jennie Baines. Afterwards, they called out 'To William Thomas's'. Singing 'Beautiful Zion', they marched up the steep winding road to Thomas's house, where hymns and songs were interspersed with scary groaning and hooting. (Thomas said later that at ten p.m. he went out in his slippers to his front garden, where the crowd shouted at him and a snowball was thrown.) All this despite heavy snow and a keen biting wind.

On Wednesday night the town was even more crowded as the knobstick weavers left work, and strike supporters were again driven back by a strong police cordon.[43] Jennie Baines received a court summons for 'watching and besetting' (intimidation) at the homes of both Shackleton and Thomas.

Feeling isolated and needing reinforcements, she contacted the WSPU. Adela Pankhurst and Mary Gawthorpe were dispatched.

On Thursday, Laura Wilson returned to Hebden Bridge to speak at an open-air meeting and distribute handbills; she too was summonsed for 'unlawful assembly'.

Adela Pankhurst arrived, along with Mary Gawthorpe. Mary was met at Hebden Bridge station by a posse of forty policemen. She asked a constable if anything exciting was going on, but 'he only looked at me mysteriously'.

Then on Friday 1 February, the strikers again met at the Weavers' Institute and, headed by a band, walked in procession, looping down through the town to the large Co-operative Hall, gathering crowds as they went. Every seat was taken by 7 p.m. Bandsmen played 'Lead kindly light' and the audience sang enthusiastically. Pinned up on the platform, much to the audience's amusement, were the summonses for Jennie Baines and Laura Wilson. Lilian Cobbe presided and Adela moved the resolution condemning the employers – Shackleton, Thomas and Ashworth – and calling upon Parliament to introduce a legal minimum wage to make such strikes unnecessary. Like her mother four days earlier, Adela chided the weavers for electing a Liberal at the last election. And she went further, exhorting her audience with belligerent socialist rhetoric:

> You can run the mills without masters, but the masters can't run mills without workers. I ask you to see [visit] the employer himself. I propose that you go with me at the close of this meeting, accompanied by the band, to see Mr Thomas. (Laughter, cheers.) We will tell him what the men and women of Hebden Bridge think of it, and will tell him in no quiet way either. He will very soon want to stop the strike if we go often enough . . .
>
> Picketing – trying to persuade the knobsticks to come out – is supposed to be lawful, but when you go before a bench of magistrates composed of employers, it does not matter what the law is; they change it and make it what they like. You should have thought about that when the election was on. It is too late now. The women have to come in again and remedy your mistakes . . . I advise you to go on persuading the knobsticks to come out . . .
>
> When I was summonsed I did not pay my fine. No, I went to prison! You will never win a strike by paying fines . . . Go to prison, and every paper in the country will know about it, and back you up. I believe you have got to look to the women to lead you.

Laura Wilson likewise said she would 'show the men of Hebden Bridge how to go to prison . . . Going to prison was not such a horrible thing, after all. There was a going to prison that was glorious, and this will be an instance'. And musical Mary Gawthorpe, who conducted the band during the collection, added that it was the masters who were the real culprits, and she predicted that Hebden Bridge would soon become famous. Like Adela, she had been to prison and also exhorted them: 'Have the courage of your convictions, and, if necessary, go to prison. Prison is not bad, after all; it is very nice! And I don't mind going again! It is different altogether, going for a principle'; and, to applause, Mary moved the resolution, demanding the Liberal government enfranchise women in the coming session of Parliament. At the end, as the audience rose, Adela sprang to the front of the platform. To cheers she incited them: 'Now my turn's come. If you will come with me, we will take the band and see Mr Thomas'.[44]

This was incendiary fill-the-gaols oratory, either naïvely optimistic or disingenuously calculating in inciting the weavers to brave imprisonment. In Edwardian Britain, it was one thing for a Cobden-Sanderson or a Pankhurst to be sentenced to Holloway and to trigger correspondence in *The Times*; it was quite another for a low-paid Yorkshire weaver to refuse to pay his fine and be sent to Armley gaol. He might merit a paragraph in the local paper if he was lucky.[45]

However, at about 9.30 p.m. the laughing crowd poured down the stairs, with Mary and Adela arm-in-arm at the front. They all filed outside.[46] The streets were crowded and in darkness; Adela addressed an overflow meeting from the Co-op stores' doorway. A procession headed by suffragettes climbed up the winding icy road. At William Thomas's house, they found constables guarding the door, with police lined across the road. The band played 'Beautiful Zion' once again; Adela addressed the huge crowd, encouraging them to 'hoot Mr Thomas' and this was echoed by Mary Gawthorpe. Jennie Baines announced to cheering that she was ready to go to prison. The crowd moved further up hill to the home of a second employer, where there was more hooting. Then they slithered down the hill to the town again, and up the Heptonstall side to Shackleton's house, 'swelling their numbers and bringing people to their doors to look curiously upon the unusual scene'. Police were again in position. The crowd sang with gusto; suffragettes appealed for hooting. 'It was a memorable night, and will not be forgotten for a long time to come', concluded the local press. Adela, writing a report for Pethick-Lawrence's *Labour Record*, offered a more euphorically upbeat account:

It was there, on the great snowy hills, under the deep star-lit sky, that the working men and women vowed that the old order of things should end and the new begin; that the day when the few should live upon the labour of the many had drawn to a close; and that the day of true liberty for men and women was dawning.[47]

However, the dawning was scarcely painless. On Monday 4 February, two of the striking weavers appeared in the magistrates' court, accused of unlawful violence. The weighty Lancashire textiles trades unionist, David Shackleton MP, alarmed at suffragette incitement of his members, arrived in Hebden Bridge and condemned the violence. Letters critical of the suffragettes began to appear in the local press. Nonetheless, even on the eve of their trial, Adela Pankhurst and Jennie Baines continued to address open-air meetings.

On Thursday 7 February, Jennie Baines and Laura Wilson appeared before Todmorden magistrates. In the crowded court sat sympathisers, including Adela Pankhurst (though probably not Lavena who would have lost a day's pay). Jennie, accused of 'watching and besetting' at the homes of both Thomas and Shackleton, defended herself. She claimed the windows were broken the night before she arrived, and her only aim was women's suffrage. The magistrates unhesitatingly returned a guilty verdict, sentencing her with a forty-shilling fine or fourteen days. Jennie retorted, 'I refuse to pay on principle, because I do not acknowledge the justice of laws administered by men until women get the vote'.

Laura Wilson, accused of 'violent and inflammatory' speech (unlawful assembly) was equally defiant. 'I object to the constitution of the Court because it is constituted of men only. I demand to be tried by my peers', and to know why there were still no women lawyers. A police sergeant, reading out her words from his notebook, alleged that she said, 'If you cannot get justice by fair means get it by foul', and that the handbills she distributed were seditious. Laura admitted the meeting had been 'a little bit lively', that she had distributed handbills, and that, as it was held open-air, she had spoken in a loud voice. But, she alleged, the police had been anxious to make an arrest – unfairly, as 'I have the cause at heart that I am fighting for'. Sounding absolutely fearless, Laura tried to summon Adela as a witness, but the clerk ruled against this. Laura too was found guilty and bound to keep the peace for six months, on sureties of ten pounds or imprisonment for fourteen days. She retaliated: 'I shall not find sureties to keep the peace . . . I shall not pay any fines or costs imposed on me by men who do not allow me to have a woman in Court to plead with me. I refuse to be bound over'.[48]

That afternoon both women were taken by train to Leeds' forbidding Armley gaol, the first suffragettes to be incarcerated in a Yorkshire prison. They were seen off at the station by a handful of sympathisers. That night in Hebden Bridge, Adela plus Laura's husband George Wilson justified what had occurred: the only way to settle strikes was by labour representation in Parliament. (However, while still defiant, there was no longer the fill-the-gaols incitement: two imprisonments were sobering enough.) Even though their son was only five years old, George's loyalty to Laura during her imprisonment contrasts with Hannah Mitchell's experience: 'Most of us who were married found that "Votes for Women" were of less interest to our husbands than their own dinners'.[49] George Wilson's commitment vividly illustrates how suffragette militancy within local West Riding communities sprang from labour movement solidarities which the WSPU could conveniently tap into.

Nationally, early 1907 was a time of tremendous WSPU optimism and growth. The leadership exhorted sympathisers that, 'The help of every woman in the country is needed now if the fetters are to be struck off that keep women a subject race.'[50] It was indeed about this time that a Hebden Bridge WSPU branch was formed. On the night of Saturday 9 February, just two days after Jennie Baines and Laura Wilson were carted off to Armley, a local mass indignation meeting was held.[51] The joint Hebden Bridge branch secretaries were Edith Berkley, another experienced fustian clothing machinist, and Louie Cobbe, Lilian's younger sister.[52] Within a few weeks, WSPU branches sprang up like mushrooms along the Calder Valley: not only in Hebden Bridge and Halifax, but in smaller communities like Elland too.

Also during this exciting weekend, there were hurried secret discussions about a 'Women's Parliament' demonstration in London planned by the WSPU for Wednesday 13 February. Mary Taylor would go. Lavena Saltonstall was prevented by her job from joining in and would have regretted this, for she was now a totally committed suffragette. Lavena even found herself at the sharp end of the local anti-suffragette backlash. She was certainly keenly aware of how a single woman, out earning her living independently of her family and speaking her own mind, was viewed by the local community. Later she recalled with vehement passion:

Should any girl show a tendency to politics, or to ideas of her own, she is looked upon by the majority of women as a person who neglects doorsteps and home matters, and is therefore not fit to associate with their respectable daughters and sisters. If girls develop any craving for a different life or wider ideas, their mothers fear that they are going to become Socialists or Suffragettes – a Socialist being a person with lax views about other people's watches and purses, and other people's husbands or wives, and a Suffragette a person whose house is always untidy. If their daughter show any signs of a craving for higher things than cleaning brass fenders or bath taps, they put a stop to what they call 'high notions'.

Who is going to tell these mothers that daughters were not given to them merely to dress and domesticate? Who is going to tell them that they have a higher duty to perform to them than merely teaching them house-work? – Who is going to tell them that it is as cruel to discourage a child from making use of its own talent or individuality as it would be to dis-courage a child from using its limbs?[53]

In fact, the local backlash against socialists and suffragettes grew unpleas-antly personal. Women who would not compromise paid the price. Lavena's friend Laura Wilson was released from Armley, welcomed by, among others, Dinah Connelly.[54] On Friday 22 February there was a packed meet-ing organised by Hebden Bridge Trades Council in her honour. Lavena Saltonstall was there of course, along with Jennie Baines and Hannah Mitchell, plus Louie Cobbe and Edith Berkley, as joint WSPU branch secre-taries. To loud applause, 'heroine of the evening' Laura repeated how she objected to 'the trade union of lawyers' sending her to prison. She pro-claimed, 'If they could sentence me for thinking, I would have to be sentenced for life', and told the local reporter, 'I went to gaol a rebel, but I have come out a regular terror', believing that, as 'the first suffragette to be placed in a Yorkshire gaol', she had done a great deal 'to rouse the North of England'.[55]

Lavena herself meanwhile launched into bitter correspondence in the *Hebden Bridge Times*. With her witty, punchy writing style, she angrily gave as good as she got in exposing male political hypocrisy. She wrote from her Halifax lodgings:

Sirs – Some of the male members of the community of Hebden Bridge seem to be unduly alarming themselves because a handful of suffragettes came down to condole with the weavers for being on strike. Surely, if women are not intelligent enough to vote, they cannot be expected to show much tact during their sojourn among the strikers . . .

Poor men! If they are so susceptible to the wiles of woman, they cannot, any more than women, be capable of having a vote. One of our 'Votes for women' champions [Laura Wilson] has been entertained just lately in one of His Majesty's institutions for distributing 'seditious literature'. Foolish person! Had she forgotten that men are safeguarded on every part by Church and State, while women are left out? There is nothing for them to do except obey laws over which they have no hand in the making . . .

Go into the Houses of Parliament you men (women are not admitted now). How many bills are passed for the benefit of anyone excepting the aristocratic Lord so-and-so or the self-made millionaire and landowner? . . . If we could see the domestic lives of some of these critics who are adverse to women having votes, no doubt we should see more than ever the desirability of women having votes . . .

So now, ye critics, be not alarmed – all will work out in favour of the Suffragettes.

Yours sincerely,

L SALTONSTALL[56]

Meanwhile, a man called Pankson Baines (presumably an anagram, perhaps a lawyer, possibly both) lampooned Lavena in the next issue of the *Hebden Bridge Times*. In Halifax, he said sardonically, Lavena had been 'launched from obscurity into dazzling fame' by championing the tramway men, and now she 'comes forward to champion her friends the suffragettes'. He adroitly posed three pointed questions. Did the suffragettes come to Hebden Bridge uninvited, and what good did they do the weavers? Do suffragettes have domestic lives at all? And did Lavena really believe the best way to enfranchise women was to besiege Parliament violently?

Lavena immediately responded. It was a dual purpose campaign, by arrangement, she said, and did no harm to the weavers. She went on, 'All my friends (the suffragists) lead domestic lives which may be held up as "models" of cleanliness'. And she objected to his accusations of violence: the suffragettes went in orderly procession, while men behave far worse at elections. Giving women the vote would rid England of the 'sweating system' and child labour; 'Oh! Yes! Pankson Baines, we will vote'.[57] In Edwardian England the issue of female domesticity, and by implication, whether an independent suffragette was marriageable, drove to the core of the argument about womanliness.

Pankson Baines retaliated sarcastically: either the suffragettes were uninvited, or came by arrangement. And were they not just using the weavers' strike to their own advantage? Lavena again hit back, suspecting Pankson Baines had something of the legal about him. She explained, 'I made the arrangements partly [for suffragettes to come] ... It was an understood thing'; and their main motive was purely women's suffrage. She added that when men agitated for the vote they had burned down buildings. Pankson Baines then lunged back at the 'curious genus known as the suffragette family'. He still maintained there was a contradiction about exactly why they came: Mrs Pankhurst said it was chance and that they were not invited, while Lavena ('her devoted recruit') says they *were*; they could not both be right, and the suffragettes merely exploited the strike for their own ends.

Pankson Baines might have won the battle but Lavena Saltonstall was still fighting a wider war – for the main issue remained: how precisely to win Votes for Women. Within a matter of months, Lavena's life had been transformed. Hers was one of the small acts of enormous courage: speaking in public, inviting Emmeline Pankhurst, taking on Pankson Baines, later going to London, suffering imprisonment. By March 1907, Lavena, rebellious tailoress-turned-weaver-cum-writer, had been swept up into the thick of national events. She had travelled down to Westminster and taken part in the suffragette action there. As the next chapter recounts, she was among those arrested, her prison number D2, 18. In Holloway, Lavena apparently did not let her writing skills lie: she reportedly kept a journal during her time in prison which, alas, has disappeared.[58] However, Pankson Baines' final riposte has not: their vitriolic correspondence ended with Pankson Baines sarcastically thanking Lavena for her advice, his gratitude 'only increased by the fact that Lavena and two of her Hebden Bridge comrades are ... languishing in prison ... I bid farewell to Lavena, the Modern Martyr'.[59]

For the suffragettes hurrying over the Pennines from Manchester, the West Riding textile communities provided their nearest urban communities. WSPU uprisings were not limited just to Halifax and Hebden Bridge, with their local industrial disputes, but were echoed across a wider community – notably in Huddersfield and the Colne Valley. And of these, the case of 'baby suffragette' Dora Thewlis proved particularly controversial.

CHAPTER 5

'Baby suffragette': Dora Thewlis
1907

Over 500 ILP women signed the *Manifesto to the Women's Social and Political Union* published at New Year 1907. Of these, 136 came from the West Riding of Yorkshire and a further 146 from Lancashire: together they added up to well over half of all signatories. And of the fifty-eight WSPU branches now sprung up across the country, almost a quarter lay in Yorkshire – mainly within the West Riding textile towns.[1] For such Pennine textile communities in northern England were *the* heartland of early WSPU support. Their very names – Halifax and Hebden Bridge, Bradford and Keighley, Leeds and Dewsbury – conjured up countless bales of wool, the racket of looms, the whirr of sewing machines.

Few of these early WSPU branches showed more fervent Votes for Women enthusiasm than Huddersfield. After its November 1906 by-election, accompanied by the melodramatic release of suffragettes from Holloway, no fewer than forty-eight local ILP women signed the *Manifesto*. And when the Huddersfield WSPU branch was formed in December, about fifty women immediately gave their names. They then remained constantly in the eye of the political storm because in July 1907 another by-election, this time in nearby Colne Valley, thrust the busy Huddersfield suffragettes into the national limelight once again. In contrast to the unreported heroism of Halifax and Hebden Bridge, Huddersfield suffragettes operated in the full glare of the national press. News reporters and photographers tracked their every move, reflecting suffragette derring-do back next day to an eager tabloid-reading public.

By surprise good fortune, a rare hand-written branch minutes book has recently been discovered; we now know more about the Huddersfield members than about those of any other WSPU branch outside London.[2] This archival survival allows us a unique opportunity to identify precisely the Yorkshire women who became suffragettes, to learn what they thought and the shape of their intimate friendship networks. We can pace their neighbourhoods up their terraced streets, following the vivid trail of Huddersfield's nest of suffragettes. We can eavesdrop on their lives as they were suddenly swept up in the dramatic events of the suffragette spring of 1907, and thrust into heroic prominence for just a few dramatic months. For they were no 'caste apart'; they were distinctly 'ordinary' women living in unremarkable hard-working wool mill communities.[3]

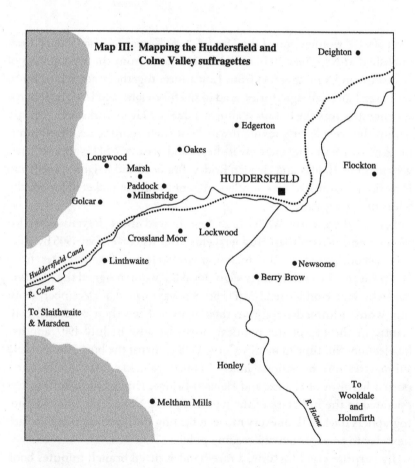

Map III: Mapping the Huddersfield and Colne Valley suffragettes

Huddersfield took the palm as a West Riding textile centre. Bradford was dubbed 'worstedopolis', Hebden Bridge led in fustian; but Huddersfield on the River Colne was the only major West Riding textile manufacturing town with a canal skirting close around it. This waterway linked it directly to Wakefield and the Humber estuary in the east; and, as the canal climbed up the Colne Valley into the Pennines, to Lancashire in the west. Later, the railway line between Leeds and Manchester followed the canal along the Colne, crossing its tributary valleys on a series of dramatic viaducts. These direct communication links positioned Huddersfield very favourably compared to Halifax, or even Bradford, and stimulated intense mill-building.

The majesty of these stone-built mills along canal and river bank captured the imagination of painters, photographers and architectural historians ever since. Strung along a waterfront of under four miles stood over six dozen textile mills, one every hundred metres; and large industrial buildings were even more densely packed around the town itself. These mills spun long wool fibres and then wove the spun yarn into wool and worsted cloth – especially popular tweeds, to be sewn into ready-made suits and coats in Leeds.[4]

It was these towering mills clustered by the canal wharves that pulled hard-working families into late-Victorian Huddersfield to look for work and a living wage. They came mainly from the surrounding rural areas, travelling under ten miles, though a few made more dramatic migrations. Within these families, it was the women – wool weavers themselves or married to a mill worker – who now so exuberantly demanded the vote. Risking arrest and even imprisonment, their lives were suddenly transformed by suffrage. Initially, however, their experience was shaped by the world of mill work and by the socialist politics that sprang from this industrial experience. Two key families – the Keys and the Thewlises – illustrate this story.

Edith Key was born in January 1872 in Eccleshill near Bradford. Her mother, Grace Proctor, probably a local mill worker, registered the baby's birth. However, Edith's birth certificate left the name and occupation of the father blank. Edith's 'putative' (reputed) father was Joseph Fawcett, a well-to-do mill owner who, it seems, had seduced eighteen-year-old Grace. When baby Edith was just ten weeks old, both parents signed a formal lawyer's 'Agreement as to Child', whereby Joseph agreed to pay Grace two pounds for the expenses incurred at the birth, plus a weekly allowance of two shillings for Edith's maintenance until she reached thirteen years old, or died. For her part, Grace swore that she would not, 'so long as the said payments of Two shillings every week shall be punctually made as aforesaid take any proceedings to affiliate the said Child or otherwise molest sue or disturb the said Joseph Fawcett' about baby Edith. And to this legal undertaking was added, as an afterthought, a careful codicil that, if Joseph defaulted on these weekly payments, Grace could, after four weeks, apply to the magistrates 'for an Order of Affiliation upon the said Joseph Fawcett as if this Agreement had not been entered into'. Grace signed the document with a faltering signature and Joseph with his more confident pen, Grace adding a second wobbly signature for receipt of her two pounds.[5] Thus Joseph reluctantly acknowledged his paternity, knowing he had hanging over him the fear of devastating scandal if he reneged on his weekly payments. For her part, Grace knew that so long as the payments appeared each week, she must never contact the father of her baby.

Then when Edith was five, Grace gave birth to another baby, Ethel – also with no visible father. Fortunately, however, Grace had three sisters nearby. The eldest, Hannah Proctor, kept house, while the two younger, Martha and Emily, worked as worsted weavers. The three aunts took nieces Edith and Ethel – but not sister Grace – into their all-female extended family. Instead, Grace, now in her mid-twenties, lived in the Britannia Inn in the centre of Bradford with the widowed pub landlord and his children. Here she worked as a general domestic servant – a skivvy – pulling pints, washing glasses, scrubbing floors, perhaps pondering her misfortune and the hypocrisy of 'gentlemen'; probably visiting her growing daughters on her day off.

It is easy to lose sight of Edith as she grew up, shunned by her father, separated from her mother, brought up by her aunts. All we know of her late-Victorian childhood is that by about the age of ten, probably with her aunt Martha, she had moved to Huddersfield; here, apparently, Edith worked as a child half-timer. In 1885 when she reached her thirteenth birthday, the Clerk of the Huddersfield School Board formally requested from Bradford a copy of Edith's birth certificate, allowing her to leave school and work full time. By the time she was nineteen, Edith, living on the outskirts of Huddersfield, worked as a knotter, probably preparing the wool warp threads ready for the weavers' looms.

Along the way someone had spotted Edith's musical talent and encouraged her to develop it. Rather like Mary Gawthorpe with the Leeds Arts Club, Edith joined the Huddersfield Choral Society, a hub for provincial cultural life where she met a particularly talented musician.

Frederick Key, son of a Lincolnshire farmer, was a very unusual man. At the age of six, he had been blinded by an arrow while playing 'Robin Hood'.

Blindness was treated unsympathetically by the Victorians but Frederick was rescued from this bleak existence when he was sent to a Midlands institute for the blind, where he learnt newly introduced braille. Aged ten, Frederick then went to a more advanced school for the blind in London, and here developed his considerable musical abilities, qualifying as an organist and piano tuner. Afterwards, he apparently toured England and Europe as a concert artist and singer, appearing as guest soloist with the Huddersfield Choral Society – where he met Edith. Her life was to be happily transformed – by a man whose creative talents outweighed his loss of sight.[6]

Nineteen-year-old Edith and twenty-eight-year-old Frederick, 'pianoforte tuner', were married in March 1891 in an Independent Chapel in Huddersfield, with Aunt Martha acting as a witness. Initially, they settled down by the River Colne at Paddock where their elder son Lancelot was born, and later moved to West Parade near the town centre.[7] It was always going to be an unconventional household, but the recollections of Lancelot and his younger brother Archie suggest it was certainly a happy home. Lancelot remembered that, around 1898, aged about six, he:

> . . . went on tramp with my blind Father throughout . . . Lincolnshire . . . and a part of Yorkshire selling sheet music. I remember the homecoming because my Mother had a feast of fried bread for us to eat. It tasted fine after our long tramp. Afterwards my Father set up in piano dealing at No 43 West Parade . . . [and] managed to struggle on.

Enterprisingly, Frederick had opened a music shop, repairing and tuning pianos, while trying to compose music and even run a small music academy: 'Dad's creative talents literally poured from him', Archie recalled. As the business prospered, Frederick grew more interested in socialist politics, becoming friendly with ILP orators like Philip Snowden. On Sundays, the sons recalled, 'father would preside at open-air meetings in Huddersfield, speaking from a horse-drawn lorry' stationed in the town square.[8] Indeed, the first issue of *The Worker* featured Frederick not only giving a talk on socialism but also advertising his pianos with the inspiringly secular motto 'Harmony in the home is more to the live man's taste than the prospective songs of angels'.[9] For behind (and above) the shop lived the Keys. Edith, along with bringing up their two sons, ran the financial side and kept the accounts. From here, it was a short step to her joining the WSPU, becoming secretary and efficiently taking the branch minutes.

*

The Thewlis family story has a less troubled beginning. Eliza, born in 1860 in rural Suffolk, was among those late Victorians whose family migrated north in search of a better life – in the textile factories of Meltham Mills, a hill village perched near Huddersfield, where Eliza found work as a 'mill-hand'. She met James Thewlis, a wool weaver from nearby Cartworth, a rural textile village further up the Holme Valley. In February 1880, in a Wesleyan Chapel in Huddersfield, nineteen-year-old Eliza, heavily pregnant, married twenty-year-old James.

Their daughter Mary was born in May, followed by at least three other daughters and a son. Like the Saltonstall family, the ever-growing Thewlises moved house regularly around the area. When Dora was born in May 1890 they were living in Honley, a small industry-in-the-country town where James worked as a woollen weaver. The Thewlises felt increasingly hard-pressed. Eliza, now thirty, returned to the mill; both she and her ten-year-old eldest daughter, Mary, worked as thread doffers. And baby Dora seems to have been boarded out with relatives or friends while her mother was working.

The family's many moves included Slaithwaite up the Colne Valley; and later across the Pennines as economic migrants heading for higher wages. Here in Lancashire they found cotton mill jobs – James as a weaver, twenty-year-old Mary as a rover, and the three younger daughters as assisting adult weavers. Ten-year-old Dora was still at school; little Mabel and toddler Minnie were at home. Women cotton weavers earned about one-third higher wages than West Riding women wool weavers, enabling Eliza to keep out of the mill.[10] But the Thewlises did not settle and within a few years had migrated back to the West Riding. Finally, the itinerant family moved to a neat stone mid-terrace house on the outskirts of Huddersfield. The Hawthorne Terrace neighbourhood, overshadowed by the inevitable railway viaduct, was of course dotted with woollen mills. Here, along with other family members, Dora, too, got a job as a weaver. And the family, all low-waged industrial workers, also became drawn into the local labour movement.

When we meet her in 1907, Dora is sixteen, earning almost a pound a week, and a child of labour sympathisers only too happy to speak their minds. 'We have brought her up in Socialistic and progressive beliefs', Eliza proclaimed proudly. 'Ever since she was seven, she has been a diligent reader of the newspapers, and can hold her own in debate on politics'.[11] And from their Hawthorne Terrace home, mother and daughter, Eliza and Dora, were well-poised to throw themselves into suffragette action.

Two final suffragette family stories may be told more briefly. Elizabeth Pinnance, born in Paddock about 1879, left school at ten to work as a half-time rug weaver. In 1899 she married Bob Pinnance, a cloth-presser; with their three children, the Pinnances moved around the lower Colne Valley near Milnsbridge, then a small but bustling community. It had not only a Liberal Club but also its own Socialist Club: here ILP members Bob and Elizabeth sent their children to its Socialist Sunday School. Bob, a trades union organiser, was blacklisted by local mills and had to find work in Lancashire where trade unionism was stronger. Their grandchildren remember Elizabeth, a smart well-presented woman, having a little 'house' business after her husband's victimisation, selling lemonade from home and developing her business skills.[12] By the time the WSPU branch began, the Pinnances were living near Paddock and this is the address that appears in Edith Key's list of branch members.

Annie Sykes, probably born in Lockwood in 1880, was the daughter of a sizer and beamer, and by 1907 was working as a housekeeper.[13] She is one of the Huddersfield suffragettes whose story remains unrecorded.

It was Edwardian families like those of Dora Thewlis, Edith Key, Elizabeth Pinnance and Annie Sykes, clustered around the mills of Huddersfield and the Colne Valley, which people this suffrage story. Certain themes emerge strongly from such family histories. Households depended heavily upon textile manufacture, notably wool weaving: even Frederick Key's music business relied upon pianos paid for directly or indirectly from wool wages. Wool manufacturing processes bred every kind of craft specialism: mills were bedevilled by custom-and-practice hierarchies dividing men's work and wages from women's. There was continuing hostility to working women; the Yorkshire Warp Twisters even fought two successful strikes to prevent women entering their craft. The antipathy was strongest against married women (though those like Eliza Thewlis had little option but to work).[14]

This made union organising extraordinarily unrewarding – as Bob Pinnance had found. And no one knew these difficulties more keenly than Ben Turner, ex-half-timer from the Holme Valley; with his friend Allen Gee, he helped build the General Union of Textile Workers. A hardworking union official, he wrote:

I persuaded our union to widen out its ranks and take in as members all grades of textile workers . . . It took a bit of doing, for there was and is yet some snobbishness in working-class ranks. The weaver was looked down upon by the overlooker . . . A woollen spinner and a woolsorter despised the company of men in ordinary grades of labour . . . The woolsorter had his special chair in his snug at his customary public house and a wool-comber or a labouring factory worker had to be above the ordinary if he was allowed in that place . . .

When I tried and got our union to agree to take the guinea [£1.05] a week man and the 12s [60p] a week woman as well as the £2 a week man and the 25s [£1.25] a week mender, it wasn't all easy, for the spinner felt himself a different class from the piecener [young assistant], a cog above the weaver, and a long way over the willeyer and fettler who did the hard preparatory work in the mill.[15]

Such minutely-observed job sectionalism might now seem comical, but was only too real for lowly weavers like Dora Thewlis. Alongside these craft gradations, trade unions were also hampered by the large number of small firms, often rural and isolated, where employers exerted paternalistic sway over their workers, blacklisting trouble-makers. Individual mills paid their own wage rates, making comparisons difficult; and great power within the mills lay with overlookers (managers), a bulwark against trade unionism. In such a low-wage economy, union members could only afford a low contribution, so the union's income was little more than a few pounds a year. As Ben Turner expressed it, 'We were all poor folks, with poor incomes and poor trade, and hadn't the vision we ought to have had'.[16] As late as 1910, there were only 4,500 members, very few of them women. For every one woman member in a wool trade union, there were in contrast twenty-seven members of the well-organised women cotton unions.

All this had major political repercussions. The growth of the Labour Party, bringing together trades unions and smaller socialist groups like the idealistic ILP, was slow in the Huddersfield area. However, the ILP made up for this, supporting a vibrant ethical brand of socialism and local socialist clubs. It was this inspirational 'religion of socialism' belief that the world could be a better place for all, that attracted Frederick and Edith Key, Dora and Eliza Thewlis, Bob and Elizabeth Pinnance and Annie Sykes. So, to counteract the Liberal daily *Huddersfield Examiner*, the rival *Worker* was funded by the local ILP.[17] It reported on the Socialist Sunday Schools, the brass bands and processions. And it publicised meetings – such as that of Mrs Pankhurst at Milnsbridge Socialist Club in January 1906.

At the 1906 General Election, Huddersfield and its neighbouring constituencies remained a sea of Liberalism. There was no divvying up of seats by the secret electoral pact as there was in two-member Halifax or multi-member Leeds. Rather, Liberal values permeated all. On Huddersfield Borough Council, Liberals could easily outvote Conservative and Labour councillors.[18] In Milnsbridge one Liberal family, the Crowthers, active Congregationalists, owned half the mills, as well as having a hand in running local banking, the chamber of commerce, the wool manufacturers' association, freemasons' lodge and the Colne Valley Liberal association – giving the community the nickname 'Crowther Village'. Elsewhere, local Liberals effortlessly intermarried into non-conformist families (often Congregationalist), with their temperance, self-help and thrift, and, of more earthly use, control of the influential *Examiner*.[19]

The local Women's Liberal Association was growing into one of the largest in Britain. And the Huddersfield NUWSS branch was, unsurprisingly, run by Liberal sympathisers: its inaugural meeting was held in the Temperance Hall, and the Huddersfield Liberal Women's Association secretary, Helen Studdard, was elected a key committee member. Although both Allen Gee and Ben Turner were active supporters, the suffragist emphasis locally was on dignified reform rather than flamboyant action.[20]

At the Huddersfield by-election in November 1906, the Liberals predictably again held the seat – with the Labour candidate, fighting on the ethical-socialist slogan 'all things socially needful should be socially owned', merely pushing the Conservative into third place. It was into this political context that the suffragettes, suddenly released from Holloway, exploded. Naturally, the by-election also drew in sympathetic local ILP women – including Eliza and Dora Thewlis. Eliza, never hesitant to blow her own trumpet, was soon claiming, '[Dora] and I were the first Huddersfield people to assist Mrs Pankhurst in the recent by-election'.[21]

It was from this rich if volatile political mix that the following month Ethel Annakin Snowden's invitation to sign the ILP *Testimonial* appeared in the *Labour Leader* (see illustration 12, page 95). Huddersfield was apparently one of the places where this caused tensions in the ILP branch: was it an official initiative or just a personal one? Certainly, it is easy to imagine discussion in the Key household: Edith keen to sign, and Frederick, an adult suffragist, arguing against. In the event, Edith did sign (though only one other Huddersfield woman joined her) while the Thewlis mother-and-daughter team did not. However, two miles away, the small Milnsbridge Socialist club was more welcoming, with over two dozen women signing. With even smaller Flockton, three miles away, producing a further nineteen signatories, suggesting that in their haste women just signed where they could, this gave a total of forty-eight locally.

While the signatures were being collated, there were further suffragette arrests at the House of Commons. Just after these imprisonments the Huddersfield WSPU branch sprang into life. Emmeline Pankhurst returned to the town, accompanied by the full WSPU panoply: Annie Kenney and Adela, Hannah Mitchell and Anne Cobden-Sanderson – for such communities were crucial to the WSPU's current propaganda strategy. The meeting, held in Huddersfield's imposing town hall on 18 December, was opened by Emmeline. Consummate politician that she was, she stated that, despite the by-election controversy, the WSPU had aroused real interest in the enfranchisement of women locally, and the main reason for her returning now was:

> To reap the fruits of the work at the by-election. We hope to form a branch of the WSPU . . . Think of the women in Holloway gaol tonight . . . [and] at Christmastide . . . Women went to prison last Thursday, and again on Monday night, and will continue to go to prison until the Liberal party is compelled to carry the principle it professes, and to enfranchise women of this country.

Adela proposed the women's citizenship resolution, seconded with jocular irony by Hannah Mitchell: prison would soon be so full of women that there would be no room for the ordinary drunk and disorderly man. Anne Cobden-Sanderson thanked Huddersfield that she was not still imprisoned, having been released for the by-election. As daughter of the 'cheap bread' radical feted by Liberal leaders (including Campbell-Bannerman and Winston Churchill), she had been well positioned in prison to ponder the hypocrisies of a Liberal government which 'had lost touch with the common people, finding itself more comfortable and more at ease in the drawing rooms of the rich'. Annie Kenney urged 'young women of the town to come out and join the movement, so that your mothers' lives can be easier and happier'. The speeches were greeted with applause, and at the end of the meeting, when the Huddersfield branch was formed, about fifty women put their names forward.[22]

Luckily, because efficient Edith Key kept the membership list at the back of her minutes book, we know a lot about these founder-members. At the head is Edith's name and address as branch secretary. The committee included Eliza Thewlis, living nearby at Hawthorne Terrace. (Eliza later declared she was elected founding president, but this claim did not make its way into the branch records.)[23] Over the page is the name 'Miss Dora Thewlis' among the long lists of members. Other committee members were clustered along a one-mile stretch of Colne Valley between Crossland Moor and Paddock. In just a few streets in Lockwood there was a veritable nest of suffragettes, with Mrs Annie Sykes and her aunt Miss Ellen Beever just ten minutes' walk apart. The WSPU branch sprang from the tight-knit wool-mill communities skirting Huddersfield.[24]

To start the branch off, in January 1907 Adela Pankhurst came and spoke at Marsden Mechanics' Hall. At Berry Brow Labour Club, Mary Gawthorpe tackled the tricky question of 'Adult Suffrage or Women's Suffrage?', adroitly arguing for recognition of the equality of the sexes as the first step, and later spoke on 'Lessons from the Raids and from Prison Life', urging those sympathetic to the movement to become members of the local branch.[25]

Nationally, the WSPU planned a march from Caxton Hall to Parliament for Wednesday 13 February, the day after the King's Speech at the opening of Parliament. Branches were invited to select 'delegates'. WSPU organisers in the north – Adela Pankhurst and Mary Gawthorpe – sought out women willing to risk arrest and so endure prison sentence. Who from fledgling Huddersfield was brave enough to go as branch 'delegate'? We can imagine suffragettes hastening from house to house for hurried conversations – encouraging, cajoling, agreeing, planning. In the end, four women agreed to put themselves forward, including Annie Sykes and her aunt Ellen Beever.[26] Mary Taylor from Halifax also volunteered. How much was really explained to the 'delegates' remained hazy: later Ellen Beever said that 'the majority were unaware of what they would be called upon to do', but went prepared to obey the instructions of the WSPU leaders.[27]

Hasty arrangements were made to subscribe 'towards the housing of provincial women' so that they could be offered overnight hospitality in London. Then on Monday 11 February, the WSPU held secret meetings at which 200 'delegates' were divided into fourteen groups, each with a leader.[28]

At 3 p.m. on Wednesday 13 February the 'Women's Parliament' duly met in Caxton Hall; it was crowded to overflowing. The resolution condemning the omission of women's suffrage from the King's Speech would be taken direct to the key offender – the Prime Minister himself. Emmeline Pankhurst's cry of 'Rise up, women!' was met with shouts of 'Now!' And a 'deputation' of 400 women formed itself into a four-deep procession, led by Charlotte Despard and accompanied by police. They marched into the spring sunshine, singing:

Rise up, women! for the fight is hard and long;
Rise in thousands, singing loud a battle song.
Right is might, and in its strength we shall be strong,
And the cause goes marching on.
Chorus: Glory, glory, Hallelujah.

At 4.30 p.m., as the procession approached Westminster Abbey, police attempted to break it up into small groups. The marchers refused. As they continued to push forward, constables on foot began seizing women and shoving them down side streets and alleys. Mounted police started riding through the ranks of women to disperse them. Rain fell and women put their umbrellas to vigorous use. Just outside the House of Commons, suffragettes again and again charged the massive door. Police horses backed into the swaying, heaving crowd. Women were scattered and re-formed. The struggle lasted several hours. Increasingly bedraggled women hurled themselves repeatedly against police lines. 'Women began to fight like tigers', commented one reporter. In the pandemonium helmets were knocked off. By 7.30 p.m. no fewer than thirty-four women had been arrested.[29]

Earlier, Ellen Beever and Annie Sykes found themselves in a second group. Ordered to be ready for action by 5.45 p.m., they made their way to the Commons' entrance. This aunt-and-niece team, looking out for each other in the mêlée, managed to keep together most of the time but were occasionally divided by the crush. Separated from Annie Sykes and on her own now, Ellen Beever asked to see the Huddersfield MP, but was intercepted by an official and refused admission. With suffragette wit, she later defiantly told a local reporter:

I tried again and again to secure an entrance, only to be repulsed every time . . . As the officer turned round, smiling, I tried to slip into the House, but they were too sharp for me. Having lost sight of my niece, I went in search of her, and found her a little further on the street, being protected by a police inspector, because of the crowd and crush. The police officers were of a very good-humoured sort, and appeared to be enjoying themselves. I slipped my arm into that of my niece to support her. This kind, guarding officer was joined by another, a rather big fellow, and together they escorted us along the streets in a kindly, protecting way. They did not tell us where we were going, nor that we were their prisoners. In fact, we never suspected we were under arrest until they took us into the police office, and there informed us . . . that we should be charged with obstructing the footpath and the police in the execution of their duty . . . [But] it was the crowds, and also the police, who were obstructing the footpath, and not the suffragists.[30]

A second batch of twenty-three women (including Ellen Beever and Annie Sykes, and later Christabel Pankhurst and Mary Gawthorpe) had been arrested. Frederick Pethick-Lawrence arranged bail. By ten o'clock, the scrimmage was over. Altogether fifty-six women had been taken; this time it was no longer limited to WSPU leaders or just a handful of women. Indeed, what is remarkable is they were mainly young women in their twenties or thirties, often from the north. 'Most of the prisoners were working-class women from Lancashire, Glasgow, and Yorkshire', reported the *Daily Mirror*, 'and the mingling of dialects made a strange element in the hubbub'.[31]

From now on, women were to be barred from St Stephen's Hall, unless accompanied by an MP. The next day, there were front-page photographs in tabloids, headlined 'Police Brutality to Women. Unnecessary Violence Used in arresting Suffragettes. Women Kicked'. There were reports of women who clung to the railings being forced away and so receiving bruising; of 'merciless' mounted police who enjoyed riding women down. WSPU headquarters responded with cosmopolitan braggadocio: 'We are going to get a lot of big, strong mill-girls up from the North as soon as possible, and then these policemen – the brutes – will find they have different people to handle'. Among those who wrote to complain was Ben Turner, protesting that:

> Mounted police rode down women on the footpaths and drove them from the street islands[?] under the heads of the omnibus and carriage horses . . . The abusive language of some of the police was most scandalous . . . Against these proceedings, last night in Westminster, I emphatically protest.[32]

And the next morning, Thursday 14, after a two-hour sitting at the crowded Westminster police court, no fewer than fifty-three women were sent to prison, bringing the total number of suffragette martyrs to ninety-five (more than doubling the number imprisoned in 1906). Among them were Ellen Beever and Annie Sykes, who both received the lightest sentence of 7/- [35p] fine or seven days. They chose prison. Afterward Ellen reported laconically:

> It was a very quiet affair as far as my niece and myself were concerned. We were each fined 7s . . . We went to Holloway prison in the 'Black Maria',

singing 'Glory, glory, hallelujah/And the cause goes marching on.' . . .

We were second class prisoners, with separate cells . . . I was put to making hardened sheets . . . Dry brown bread [to eat] – no knife to cut it – and tea, which was more like tin than tea. Horrid stuff! . . . [But] I am not sorry I have been a prisoner for the good and noble cause. Indeed, I am glad to have suffered in its interests.[33]

A full quarter of the suffragettes arrested came from the West Riding: Huddersfield and Halifax, plus Bradford, Leeds and Sheffield. Even the *Huddersfield Examiner*, which had so far held aloof, could no longer sustain its news blackout now that local suffragettes had hit the national front pages. A reporter visited Ellen Beever and Annie Sykes at home after their release; but he was, we sense, instructed to keep his tone jocular. After all, it was a *Liberal* government that these uppity women had challenged. So he set forth 'not without trepidation' and tracked down Ellen, who vividly recounted her experiences. The reporter wrote down her debonair remarks but left, he said, glumly contemplating a future with 'a Parliament and a Cabinet dominated by women, especially by women holding the opinions which this determined suffragette so cheerfully and frankly avowed'.[34] Annie Sykes added she was 'sorry I did not do a bit more and get fourteen days' in prison.

Overnight, even in Huddersfield, newspaper readers discovered suffragettes were not just by-election 'specials' or women based only in London or Manchester. They lived in your community, down your street, they might be on your very doorstep – or even a member of your family. These early Yorkshire suffragettes were 'ordinary woman', certainly 'not a race apart'.[35]

Nationally, the first WSPU *Annual Report*, proclaiming 'The Needs of the Hour', drew upon the empowering language of mid-Victorian liberalism, notably John Stuart Mill's *The Subjection of Women* with its parallels with slavery. It ratcheted up the moment of exhilaration and the glorious cause for which:

The help of every woman in the country is needed now if the fetters are to be struck off that keep women a subject race, and the barriers broken down that bar the way to their development, and arrest the evolution of the race. If women will unite together now, regardless of class distinctions and of all differences of political creed . . . they will win their political right . . . [through] the greatest agitation of modern times, and the most significant.
Edith How Martyn   Emmeline Pethick-Lawrence   Christabel Pankhurst.[36]

Buoyed by such powerful political rhetoric, the WSPU grew success-fully. More branches sprang up across the country, now reaching five dozen. One MP, Dickenson, had his suffrage bill coming up for its second reading. What should the WSPU do if the Dickenson bill was not supported in the Commons by the government? With the February demonstration having gained so much publicity, the suffragette spirit was rising. A second demonstration should be arranged. Annie Kenney's memoir, if somewhat vague and romantic, captured the mood:

> The idea was to get the Lancashire and Yorkshire factory women to come to London in clogs and shawls and march on Parliament . . . Adela and I were sent off as recruiting sergeants, our territory being Lancashire and Yorkshire. We had a wet, wild and stormy campaign. Not only was the weather stormy but the tempers of some of the men whose wives we had coaxed or con-vinced into giving in their names for the deputation were stormy too. We told them it meant arrest . . .
>
> The wildest parts of the Yorkshire and Lancashire moorlands were the parts from which we received most recruits . . .
>
> No deputation that I helped to work up gave me such supreme joy, sat-isfaction and happiness as did the deputation of March 20th, 1907.[37]

These were certainly extremely heady days for Huddersfield WSPU. On 5 March in Huddersfield's Friendly and Trades Club, a confident Eliza Thewlis chaired a meeting with Annie Kenney and Hannah Mitchell. 'The time has come when we ought to arise and assail our opponents' position. Prisoners have been taken from Huddersfield, and there are others ready to go and suffer if a[nother] batch is required', she exhorted her audience. And the meeting, condemning the brutality, urged support for Dickenson's bill that Friday as a government measure. Ellen Beever, just released from prison and equally pugnacious, declared, 'Women can not do better than force our way into the legislature and have a spring-clean of our injustices.' Annie Kenney added that suffragettes:

> are blamed for their [militant] methods, but our mothers and grandmoth-ers have been fighting for 50 years, and we, the grandchildren, must adopt different methods, and until men recognise women as worthy of the vote I will not work for any man at an election . . . I will never be satisfied until I see a thousand Yorkshire and Lancashire women clattering their clogs on the floor of the House of Commons.

In an incendiary speech, Hannah Mitchell also exhorted her audience to rebel against the Liberal government with direct confrontation:

> We are living under male legislation and male administration. The woman [taxpayer] helped pay for the mounted police who were used to trample us down. We might with profit imitate the tactics of the men. We might pull down the railings at Hyde Park, and then go for the Church dignitories . . . The working men will go to sleep until the next general election, but the women will go to London and wake them up.[38]

All this oratory won laughter and applause: dizzying political rhetoric in an excitable suffragette spring. There was wild optimism about imminent victory, or, if the campaign took a little longer, women would fill the gaols. At the end of the meeting, volunteers were requested for 'the next London crusade' in a fortnight's time. Four names were handed in as 'delegates', with one or two others weighing pros and cons.

On 8 March, the Dickenson bill received its second reading in the House of Commons: the Ladies' Gallery was closed as a precaution. The bill was talked out. The WSPU would indeed march again on Parliament. In the event, ten women agreed to go down from Huddersfield to London – they included Dora Thewlis, Elizabeth Pinnance and Ellen Brooke; aged twenty-two and so not much older than Dora, Ellen, daughter of a hardware dealer, came from rural Wooldale.[39] Again, in rapid conversations with friends and neighbours, women weighed the odds, offering the 'delegates' courage.

On Tuesday 19 March the Huddersfield contingent set off. Eliza Thewlis and Edith Key accompanied them on the 9.33 a.m. train as far as Manchester. Here they breakfasted, and were joined by the 100-strong Lancashire 'clog and shawl brigade'. Then mothers said farewell to daughters, aunts wished nieces well. The 'delegates' left on the noon train, from a station packed with supporters, with bouquets 'presented to the women who were journeying to do and dare for the vote'.[40]

On Wednesday 20 March, amid heightened expectancy, there were impassioned speeches and great excitement at Caxton Hall. Viscountess Harberton volunteered to lead several hundred marchers to Parliament. But once again the House of Commons was defended, this time by over 500 constables. Lady Harberton proceeded alone with the petition. Old Palace Yard suddenly bristled with police. From 4 p.m., just as Big Ben struck, battalions of women rushed repeatedly at this architectural symbol of exclusive citizenship – but without success. Constables stood shoulder to shoulder, with an inspector yelling instructions. Police lines held. Caxton Hall became a refuge for exhausted women. Ever the lawyer, Christabel Pankhurst urged them to 'get inside the Lobby, inside the House itself, sit down next to Sir Henry Campbell-Bannerman; if you can, seize the mace', symbolic of parliamentary authority and elective democracy.[41] 'Many delegates were present from the North of England', reported the *Daily Mirror*, 'and from the stronghold a constant stream of reserves were hurried up to take the place of those dispersed and arrested'.[42] The determination to reap greater success than in February was palpable.

The second fight begun at 5.30 p.m. After each arrest, crowds rushed in the wake of the cabs speeding off to Cannon Row police station. Back up in Huddersfield, Edith Key monitored the arrests like an army general; she received 'two wires from the front'. The first said 'Beginning fighting today, all well so far', and in the evening, 'We have done well. Huddersfield branch four in already'.[43]

Indeed, by 10 p.m., seventy-five women had been arrested. They included three from Halifax – Lavena Saltonstall, Laura Wilson and Dinah Connelly; two from Hebden Bridge – Lizzie Berkley and Lilian Cobbe; and no fewer than seven from Huddersfield – including Dora Thewlis, Elizabeth Pinnance and Ellen Brooke. Altogether seventeen women from the West Riding were arrested, with two from Bradford and two from Sheffield; plus one man – none other than Alfred Orage, now living in London.[44] What was striking was how young the suffragettes were: the average age was twenty-seven. The typical occupation given was weaver, plus tailoress.

Pethick-Lawrence was again busy at Cannon Row police station, bailing out suffragettes at two pounds a head. The protest had been extremely successful in capturing press interest. The following day, Thursday 21 March, Britain woke up to front-page headlines blaring: 'Suffragettes Storm the House – Desperate Encounter with the Police – Wholesale Arrests', accompanied by a page of photographs. One depicted Lady Harberton's lone figure entering the House to see the Prime Minister, and three showed individual suffragettes caught as they were being arrested.

The main picture blazoned across the tabloid front page captured a rather dishevelled wild-looking girl, her dark hair flying, shawl swirling from her shoulders, skirt placket undone in the scrimmage. Both her arms were outstretched as helmeted police, unfazed by the hubbub, escorted her away. She scarcely reached their shoulders. The caption below noted the photograph 'shows one of the attacking party struggling in the grasp of two burly constables'.[45] This rebel girl was unnamed, and people wondered who she was.

On Thursday, the seventy-five arrested suffragettes appeared in Westminster Police Court before a slightly tetchy magistrate, Horace Smith. He told one woman to stop 'jabbering'. Ellen Brooke from Wooldale challenged him, asking 'if walking quietly was disorderly conduct?' A girl who tried to show her Votes for Women flag received a sharper sentence. For the first time, some of the suffragettes were defended by a barrister, who pleaded that women had every right to go into the Commons to see an MP on legitimate business. Cross-examining a constable, the barrister elicited the admission that an order had been given to stop every woman from entering at Palace Yard: only men were allowed through. When they heard this, 'there was a chorus of indignant "Oh! Oh!s" from the back of the court', instantly suppressed, rising from sympathisers shocked at bare-faced government hypocrisy.

The police prosecuting lawyer, an imperious Mr Muskett, asked whether 'these misguided women', trying 'to change the Constitution by unconstitutional means, should [not] be more severely dealt with'. In fact, the sentences meted out were – monotonously – twenty shillings [£1] or fourteen days: for Dinah Connelly and Lavena Saltonstall, Laura Wilson, Lizzie Berkley and Lilian Cobbe, and other Huddersfield suffragettes like Elizabeth Pinnance.[46]

Ellen Brooke and Dora Thewlis were remanded. It was the latter, by far the youngest girl arrested, who had now hit the headlines. Dora 'the little mill-hand' had reached her sixteenth birthday the previous May. In court 'in her mill dress', she 'looked a pathetic figure', her face only partially visible, her 'bright, laughing eyes looking out at the magistrate'. Papers reported with some delight for their avid readers the dialogue between Dora, indignant Horace Smith and pompous Muskett:

'Dear, dear me!' said Mr Smith with surprise, when he heard the evidence. 'I see you are only seventeen'. Afterwards he found that she was a year younger.

'You are only a child. You don't know what you're doing'. The lassie laughed quietly.

'It's a great pity you should have been brought up here [into court]. Where do you come from?'

'Huddersfield' was the meek reply.

'Who let you escape from Huddersfield?'

The Daily Mirror

THE MORNING JOURNAL WITH THE SECOND LARGEST NET SALE.

| No. 1,057. | Registered at the G.P.O. as a Newspaper. | THURSDAY, MARCH 21, 1907. | One Halfpenny. |

SUFFRAGETTES STORM THE HOUSE—DESPERATE ENCOUNTER WITH THE POLICE—WHOLESALE ARRESTS.

The suffragettes made a most determined onslaught on the House of Commons yesterday afternoon, and many arrests were made, as all efforts to persuade the demonstrators to go away quietly failed. (1) Shows one of the attacking party struggling in the grasp of two burly constables. (2) Lady Harberton (a prominent suffragette) entering the House to see the Prime Minister. (3) and (4) Two more demonstrators being quietly but firmly led away by the "men in blue."—(Daily Mirror and Half-Tones.)

13. Daily Mirror, *21 March 1907*. Top left caption: *'One of the attacking party struggling in the grasp of two burly constables'*. Bottom left: *Lady Harberton entering the House to see the Prime Minister.*

'A lot did'. And the eyes danced merrier than ever as she turned to her friends at the back [of the court].

Muskett: 'I don't know who pays the expenses of all these poor women and girls'.

Horace Smith: 'The child cannot be a delegate or anything else. She doesn't know what she is doing. You ought to be at school. It is really a shocking thing that you should be brought up to London to be turned loose on the London streets to come into collision with the police. It is disgraceful. Where is your mother?'

'But I come for [represent] my mother and sister, not for myself'.

Smith: 'But you ought to have come with your mother. It is shocking.'

Muskett: 'Will this poor child promise to go back, though I don't think it is any good trying to help or reason with this class of woman. It is absolutely futile'.

Smith: 'Will you go home, my girl?'

Dora: 'I don't wish to go back, sir'.

Smith: 'But you can't stay in London all your life.'

Dora: 'I shall remain here as long as they [WSPU] want me'.

Smith; 'I repeat it is disgraceful, and the matter ought to be taken notice of. Here is a young girl of 17 [16] enticed from her home in Yorkshire and let loose in the streets of London to come into collision with the police. It is disgraceful for everybody concerned. The child shall be remanded [in custody] till Wednesday [six days], and I shall communicate with her parents'.[47]

This court dialogue when shorn of its comic-opera touches reveals two truths about Edwardian England. First, men like Horace Smith had not the remotest understanding of child labour, let alone the half-time system so widespread in the north. His pontification is tragically revealing about the dimensions of inequality. Second, Smith saw 'young girls' and 'London streets' as having only one possible reading: moral looseness and semi-prostitution. The word 'entice' says it all: Dora had been 'enticed' down onto the London streets, in her turn to 'entice' innocent young men. As 'Pankson Baines' had once goaded Lavena Saltonstall on suffragettes' dubious domesticity, so it remained unthinkable for *respectable* women to demand citizenship by taking to the streets.[48]

Horace Smith did indeed write to Eliza and James Thewlis: his letter reached Hawthorne Terrace on Saturday morning. It 'spoke of the great risks the girl ran in coming up to London under such circumstances and unaccompanied by her parents'. He apparently added that next Wednesday, when she would be returned home, 'her fare would be paid out of the poor-box'. Eliza and James were incandescent with indignation at being so patronised. 'She is not penniless, as she has money of her own which she has saved out of her earnings of £1 a week', they told the *Huddersfield Express* reporter, and Dora was quite capable of taking care of herself. Eliza vigorously explained her daughter's progressive upbringing: as a regular newspaper-reader, she could 'hold her own in a debate on politics' and thoroughly understood the women's citizenship cause:

> She and I were the first Huddersfield people to assist Mrs Pankhurst in the recent by-election, and it was mainly through our efforts that the Huddersfield branch of the WSPU was formed. I have the honour to be the president of the branch, and intended going to London, but circumstances prevented me. Dora at once said, 'Let me go, mother. I am quite capable. I understand what I am fighting for, and am prepared to go to prison for the cause. I feel that women ought to have their rights, and it will be an honour to go to prison'.
>
> Naturally I hesitated owing to her age, but I knew she would be surrounded by friends, and I consented, and the union [WSPU] accepted her as a delegate. I travelled to Manchester with her, and placed her in the care of the officials . . . The magistrate had no cause for saying that she was turned adrift on the streets.[49]

Eliza also wrote a revealing letter to Dora in prison:

> Dear Child
> I am very proud of the way you have acted, so keep your spirits up and be cheerful. You ought to have told the magistrate, when he said you were too young and ought to have been at school, 'What about working at Huddersfield [on] a loom for 10 hours at a stretch?' You know what you went to London for, and what you are doing. You are a member of the Women's Social and Political Union, who are looking after you, so do your duty by the WSPU.

Together, James and Eliza not only wrote to the WSPU headquarters confirming that they upheld their daughter's conduct, they also replied in no uncertain terms to Horace Smith's homily. They were keenly aware of economic arguments for the vote:

> We find ourselves in agreement with his Honour when he says that girls of seventeen [sixteen] ought to be at school. But we respectfully remind his Honour that girls of Dora's age in her station of life are in this part of

Christian England compelled [in their] thousands to spend ten hours per day in health-destroying factories, and the conditions and regulations under which they toil for others' gain are sanctioned by law, in the making of which women have no voice.

What wonder is it if Dora should have turned a rebel and joined hands with the dauntless women who risk life and liberty in the hope that thereby justice may the sooner be conceded to their sex . . .

Dora journeyed to London with our consent and approval, her mother accompanied her as far as Manchester, leaving her there in the hands of friends in whom she had every confidence. In these circumstances it is not our intention to bring discredit on our daughter's action by accepting the advice tendered in your communication . . .

Yours faithfully,
James L Thewlis, father
Eliza Thewlis, mother.[50]

However, in Holloway, Dora as the youngest was separated from the others, apparently even from Ellen Brooke; she was given a bath and a prison number, put in prison clothes, and taunted. Dora began to grow pallid. A local reporter interviewing her in prison certainly gave the impression of how pathetically grateful she was for a visit:

'Oh, I'm so glad to see you', she cried. 'I feel so lonely here. I want to go back home. I have had enough of prison . . . Since I have been here [five days] nobody has been to see me or write to me. Everybody has forgotten me. It is too bad. My only comfort has been derived from a couple of letters which I have received from home . . . [including one which said] 'We all keep on saying, "I wish Dora were here". George Taylor (my sister's young man, Dora explained) does not like the idea of your going to prison. He says you see no danger in anything. Cheer up.' . . .

'Since I was thirteen years old, I have been one of the main workers at our Huddersfield [WSPU] branch, and shall continue to fight at home, but in a quiet and ladylike manner. But never again to London, unless they let us enter the House of Commons like ladies, with the policemen bowing down to us.'[51]

However much embellished by the reporter's journalistic flourishes, Dora Thewlis embodied both pugnacity and pathos. Thursday's *Daily Mirror* front page again published her arrest photograph; and inside,

another Dora portrait, neatly hatted and scarfed, 'taken a short time previous to her arrest', perhaps by WSPU headquarters. And it was this
media limelight that gives us a posed studio photograph of Dora, looking rather startled; like the earliest photograph of Mary Gawthorpe, it
suggests how unusual it was still for girls like Dora to have their portrait
taken.

14. Dora Thewlis, DailyMirror, 28 March 1907.

Appearing in court again on Wednesday 27th, Dora was sent home by
Horace Smith, who appointed an elderly wardress to accompany her.
Further inside Thursday's *Daily Mirror* ran the headline 'Baby Suffragette
Goes Home': a news reporter had tried to track Dora's every step north-
wards. This Sherlock Holmes pursuit was swathed in the prison's 'utmost
secrecy'. Dora was smuggled out of the courthouse by the back way in a
four-wheeler, and driven to King's Cross station to catch the two o'clock
train north. The forbidding wardress deterred anyone from talking to
Dora, and shook her fist at the photographers who followed them,
allegedly calling them cads. Edith How-Martyn and Charlotte Despard,
who had both anxiously sat in court, suspected Dora would go by an earlier train. They guessed correctly and turned up on the platform. While the
wardress bought the tickets, Edith How-Martyn snatched a few
encouraging words with Dora. Then 'baby suffragette' was whisked into a
third-class carriage. The whistle blew and the train got up steam. 'It was too
much for the girl. Pushing her wardress on one side and getting to the

window she snatched one kiss from Mrs Martyn and waved her hand'.[52]

When she arrived back at Huddersfield station, Dora sprang out of the carriage and was handed over to her mother by the wardress. Her three sisters (despite one of their 'young man's' reservations) greeted her warmly but, ominously, no other local suffragettes had come to the station to greet her. Branch members seem to have felt alienated that Dora's childish escapade had turned their citizenship campaign into an irresponsible dispute about 'enticement' and sexual disrepute. Indeed, as the Thewlis family left the station, there was winking from railway porters, while some hobbledehoys shouted vulgar remarks.[53]

A local suffragette released from Holloway prison was, however, still a sufficient novelty for reporters to be despatched to Hawthorne Terrace and 'the simple surroundings of the suffragette's home'. Eliza defiantly told them, 'Of course she is a baby compared with the others . . . When she is eighteen my daughter will again go to London to assist in the raids on the House of Commons, and so will I. If necessary she will go to prison'. And Dora, quickly regaining her buoyancy, told the *Daily Mirror* journalist that 'she had not carried her fight far enough, and was ready to go back to London' – at which point her father quietened her. Thursday's headline ran, 'Young Huddersfield Suffragette Tells of Her "Torture" in Prison', and the journalist hyped up her tragic Holloway saga. 'Now lying unwell at her home', Dora said prison had caused her health to break down: the doctor had been called. Indignant, Eliza and James planned to bring the matter 'before the notice of the Home Secretary':

> 'They tortured me. I can see it all now', said Dora brokenly, in an interview yesterday. 'They tried to break my spirit, and they succeeded. They held me up to ridicule as a "baby" and a "child", and treated me like a criminal rather than a girl under remand . . .'
>
> Dora has one request to make to the world in general: 'Don't call me the "Baby Suffragette",' she said. 'I am not a baby really. In May next year I shall be eighteen years of age. Surely for a girl that is a good age?'

The local paper drew the story to a philosophical close: 'In years to come, when she is a reminiscent old woman, Dora will have a great tale to tell of her experiences at Westminster'.[54] More immediately, sixteen-year-old Dora, thrust suddenly into the public eye by the press, understandably found it too much to bear. Thereafter she went very, very quiet.

*

For those suffragettes with young children, prison brought additional difficulties: Elizabeth Pinnance's husband certainly supported his wife's actions
and looked after the children while she was in Holloway. By early April, the
majority of women sentenced to fourteen days were released and returned
home. Edith Berkley and Lilian Cobbe returned to Hebden Bridge. Lavena
Saltonstall, Laura Wilson and Dinah Connelly went back to Halifax to tell of
their ordeal, and celebrate with a reception tea at the Socialist Café.
Returning home, Elizabeth Pinnance remembered that 'it was much worse
when I came back to Huddersfield'; as suffragettes speaking at meetings, 'we
got used to having fish-heads and tomatoes thrown at us'.[55]

This was indeed a time for reassurance and reappraisal. Huddersfield
itself held a WSPU mass meeting with its 'ten martyrs' sitting on the platform – including Elizabeth Pinnance, Ellen Beever, Ellen Brooke, Annie
Sykes, and of course Dora Thewlis. Hannah Mitchell, Annie Kenney and
Nellie Martel all spoke – plus Laura Wilson, who said she had already suffered imprisonment twice that year, first in Armley due to the Hebden
Bridge strike and then in Holloway for demanding the vote; she added how
proud she felt that so many women she met in Holloway came from
Huddersfield.[56]

The WSPU also courageously held an open-air meeting in Marsden
market place up the Colne Valley. A crowd had gathered by the time Eliza
Thewlis, introduced as the mother of Dora, began speaking. Hecklers jos-
tled Ellen Beever, Elizabeth Pinnance and others. The mob then armed
themselves with decayed vegetables from a nearby refuse heap and began
to pelt the suffragettes – who stubbornly continued their meeting for
almost an hour. The mob then ran up a lane, hurling eggs and banana
skins. Fleeing suffragettes ran across a fairground towards the home of
Mary Scawthorne, and once inside barred the door. Rioters threw stones
and even half-bricks, cracking one of the door panels. It began to rain: the
'natural aversion of rioters to water caused them to disperse', noted a
reporter laconically. Mary Scawthorne was indignant that no one curbed
the mob. As the women had passed a political club, heads apparently had
popped out of the windows and the suffragettes were booed; men in the
crowd were heard encouraging boys to drown out the speakers' voices.
Suffragette meetings were certainly growing rowdy. The anti-suffrage
crowd now felt it had a licence to disrupt.

Nationally, the WSPU thrived on the oxygen of publicity. Yet while we
know a good deal about the London-based narrative, local networks have

largely remained clouded in obscurity. But in Huddersfield, for nearly two years from May 1907, the survival of a WSPU minutes book shines an invaluable shaft of light on branch activity. The book opens with a meeting held on Tuesday 14 May, neatly minuted by Edith Key. It records a well-organised, very energetic branch meeting weekly, its procedures formally (indeed almost bureaucratically) ultra-democratic. The branch even rotated the woman presiding at the meetings, each of which was held in a different member's house.[57] After the Westminster frenzy of February and March, the minutes book plunges us right back into the very everyday life of community suffragettes.

The first meeting opened with discussion on affiliation to Huddersfield Friendly and Trades Club; the branch bravely planned an outdoor meeting at the town's Market Cross: Laura Wilson would be invited to speak and failing her, Hannah Mitchell. In the event, Laura Wilson, Eliza Thewlis and Edith Key spoke, and the occasion raised 8s 5d [42p]. At a meeting held at Edith's house behind the family music shop, affiliation to the Friendly and Trades Club was raised again and – obviously a tricky subject – again postponed. Nellie Martel was invited to speak at another open-air meeting in St George's Square in front of Huddersfield's magnificent station, 'and that the Speaker stand on a lurry'. (The branch's most unusual member, Bertha Lowenthal, daughter of a prosperous German-born wool merchant, who lived at the spacious Grange in Huddersfield's residential suburb Edgerton, would 'entertain' Mrs Martel.)

So far, so routine. Then in summer 1907 the Huddersfield area found itself swirled into yet another political storm. A by-election was called for Colne Valley. WSPU members unanimously agreed to postpone all regular branch business until after the contest, and a big meeting with Adela Pankhurst was planned.[58] Huddersfield suffragettes threw themselves with wild enthusiasm into supporting the by-election's dashing independent socialist candidate, Victor Grayson. He attracted not only Emmeline Pankhurst's support but also the attention of national press photographers.

Scarcely had Grayson's election passed (the drama of which is traced in the next chapter) than the minutes book records discordancy within this WSPU branch, tensions which had only been hinted at till then. On 30 July a resolution was passed which Edith Key then duly (and, one suspects, with a certain degree of personal relish) dispatched to Hawthorne Terrace:

August 5 1907

Dear Mrs Thewlis

As secretary of the Huddersfield Branch of the WS&PU it is my unpleasant duty to inform you that the following resolution was unanimously passed at our last Branch meeting. 'This meeting decided that Secretary write to Mrs Thewlis explaining the feeling of the Branch [towards her] and asking her to work agreeably or resign from the Branch'.

I do not find any difficulty in explaining the motives of the members in deciding to pass the above resolution; as although to a woman they recognise your gifts as a speaker and your undou[bted] usefulness as such, they feel that your power to persuade [deleted, 'sway' added] the members to certain actions tends in many cases to over-ride their better judgement. In second place the feeling is that much unpleasant contention results whenever matters arise in which you seem determined that your will shall rule.

And thirdly, the members feel sure that if you could only realise as they do that the membership of the Branch and its influence is being rapidly reduced, mainly on account of the above reasons, you would, as a woman desirous of seeing the Branch flourish and its influence grow, do your utmost to make our business meetings pleasant memories in the bitter struggle for justice for women.

I am

Yours in the cause,

and Edith Key signed her name. Edith had scarcely used diplomacy to spare Eliza's feelings. We can only speculate exactly what Eliza had done. It was probably her overpowering stridency, her insistence to reporters of her key role in the WSPU, and her inflammatory rhetoric of militancy (though other local suffragettes seemed to have echoed this).[59] Her daughter Dora's adolescent mood-swings had perhaps seemed a self-indulgent weapon with which to do battle with the government. Thewlis, mother and daughter, no doubt seemed to other members to be publicity-hungry egoists, forever claiming the branch as their own.

Infant *cause célèbre* Dora had indeed not only hit the tabloid front pages but had even been careless enough to remain there. Her notorious photograph with its dishevelled hair and open placket had been bad enough at the time of the arrests. Now, to rub salt into a wound, celebrity Dora had been turned into a postcard. A commercial firm – Shamrock of Paternoster

Row, London – had spotted a marketing opportunity to exploit the suffragettes' curiosity value. Its merchandising tactics even included burying
Dora's Yorkshireness, making her into something more recognisable for
southern purchasers, a 'Lancashire lass'. So, for those Edwardians who were
now regular senders of picture-postcards, the image of 'baby suffragette'
could now be purchased in shops, slipped into pillar-boxes and posted up
and down the country. All this happened to one rebel girl in high-summer
Huddersfield.

15. 'A Lancashire Lass', Shamrock postcard.

CHAPTER 6

Painting the valley: Florence Lockwood
1907

WSPU tactics had shifted away from local industrial disputes to more direct political targets. Suffragettes continued to heckle ministers brave enough to venture outside Westminster. From Huddersfield, 'anti-government cru-saders' travelled to Leeds and Batley when cabinet ministers were advertised to speak: the minutes book records that they 'gained admission to their meetings, and aided in putting such Ministers to confusion'.[1] By 1907–1908, however, it was increasingly clear that Campbell-Bannerman's Liberal gov-ernment was *not* going to give the required support to push through a bill to enfranchise women. A longer-term strategy needed to be thought out.

It was also becoming obvious that more richly imaginative propaganda was now required to win Votes for Women. To persuade Parliament, suf-fragettes and suffragists alike had to win the argument with the public out across the country. In every city, suburb and isolated village, down every street, across kitchen tables and in drawing rooms throughout the land, they had to *persuade*. They had to capture Edwardian hearts and minds. Women must be persuaded to show – visibly – that, yes, they personally *did* want the vote; and they had to convince Edwardian men – the majority of whom did, after all, already possess that most precious of powers, the par-liamentary vote. Indeed, a few such men – newspaper editors, local town councillors or freemasons, publishers, barristers, local Liberal leaders – held influential positions and must be targeted.

While the WSPU's inspiring suffragette frenzy at Westminster and in communities like Hebden Bridge and Huddersfield continued, so too did a second parallel campaigning strand. The NUWSS, led by quietly concilia-tory Mrs Fawcett, had now survived its first decade. Its attitude to militancy ranged from the supportive (Fawcett had held a banquet at the Savoy for

released suffragettes in December 1906), through the diplomatically tolerant, to the outright alienation of some women's organisations by such
antics. A NUWSS network of branches now flourished; there were thirty-
three local societies, with seven across Yorkshire including Leeds and
Bradford, Huddersfield and Hull, York, Barnsley and Whitby.[2] Through a
new International Woman Suffrage Alliance (IWSA), the NUWSS was
linked to suffragists in the United States, Australia and Europe. And it now
went further to win the propaganda battle.

In January 1907, an Artists' Suffrage League was formed, the first such
society of professional women working in the creative industries. The
League quickly became the art power-house of the suffrage movement: its
key members had graduated from the Slade in London's Bloomsbury, and
included Isabella Ford's sister Emily, who had begun exhibiting and had her
own studio in Chelsea. Crucially, the Artists' Suffrage League helped the
NUWSS stage its first public demonstration – on 9 February, just days
before the WSPU's Women's Parliament demonstration. This procession
through London initiated what historian of suffrage pageantry Lisa Tickner
rightly named 'an impressive and unprecedented sequence of public
demonstrations', whereby 'suffragists developed a new kind of political
spectacle'. Scheduled for the opening of Parliament, the 'Mud March' (as
it became known, for obvious reasons) was indeed a highly innovative
women's procession. (However, in order to ensure the inclusion of the
British Women's Temperance Association and of the Women's Liberal
Federation, so well positioned to exert leverage on the government, the
invitation had not been extended to the WSPU.)[3]

It was the very first time that such respectable Edwardian women had
taken to the streets. Yet remarkably, 3,000 women took part. The procession was headed by Mrs Fawcett and Lady Frances Balfour, Lady Jane
Strachey (president of the Women's Local Government Society) – and Dr
Edith Pechey-Phipson, the medical pioneer. As early as 1869 at the age of
twenty-four, Edith had become one of the first half-dozen women to win
the right to study medicine at Edinburgh University, in the face of sexual
harassment and hostility, including a 'Surgeons' Hall riot'. She had then
practised medicine in Leeds and been elected president of the Medical
Women's Federation. Later, Edith sailed out to India and from 1883 ran the
Hospital for Women and Children in Bombay. On her return in 1905, Dr
Pechey-Phipson's Yorkshire links remained strong: she was invited to represent the Leeds suffrage society at the 1906 IWSA congress in Copenhagen,
while Huddersfield nominated her to the NUWSS Executive.

By 1907 in her early sixties and in poor health, this intrepid woman doctor made her last public appearance on the 'Mud March'. With local banners flying, 'we walked four abreast', Edith reported back to Huddersfield.[4] Long skirts might have trailed in the mud but touches of red and white splashed bright through the February gloom. The white NUWSS banner proclaimed a scarlet motto: 'The Franchise is the Keystone of our Liberty'. It all generated considerable press interest, with photographs of billowing wind-blown banners. And, given Horace Smith's magisterial homilies in court to Dora Thewlis about 'enticement' and the moral dangers of the London streets, this NUWSS procession was brave indeed.[5] It required enormous courage for eminent Edwardian suffragists like Dr Edith Pechey-Phipson to step off the safety of the pavement and down into the street.

The 'Mud March' was followed shortly by more suffragette imprisonments. Some suffragists, seeing tabloid front-page pictures of dishevelled girls like Dora, wondered how such wild antics were helping to persuade either the public or politicians. Certainly, such doubts were widely felt in areas like Huddersfield, stronghold of Liberalism, temperance and self-help.

Florence Lockwood, of Linthwaite up in the Colne Valley, was just one such well-connected Liberal woman who entertained grave reservations whether such undignified suffragette militancy really was the best way to sway crucial hearts and minds and win over the Liberal government. Florence was not only a talented painter like Emily Ford, but she also kept a regular daily diary. She later used these hand-written journals as the basis of her autobiography, *An Ordinary Life*. Now, a century on, suffrage historians reading this personal Edwardian testimony alongside the Huddersfield WSPU minutes book have a very rare opportunity to eavesdrop on the dialogue between Florence Lockwood, Liberal-suffragist of the Colne Valley on the one hand; and Edith Key, Huddersfield town-centre socialist and suffragette, on the other. The differences of personality and political perspective grew more marked during the high summer of 1907 when Victor Grayson, socialist firebrand orator turned by-election candidate, dashed over the Pennines from Manchester and into the constituency, here to be lionised by Emmeline Pankhurst and idolised by Colne Valley mill-girls. Florence was on the spot, a well-placed eye-witness to the drama — and wrote it all down as it occurred.

Born Florence Murray in October 1861 in Plymouth, she was the daughter of a sturdy snuff-taking Navy doctor. Her Victorian upbringing, though far more conventional than a Quaker's, was like an impoverished version of Isabella Ford's. There were two faithful family servants: Maria who cooked and cleaned, and Lucy the nursemaid who looked after Florence, her three brothers and two sisters. There were visits to wealthier relatives, endless piano practice and Church of England Sunday services. Of her elder brothers, one became a curate, another a lieutenant in the Navy, and the eldest a doctor – who tragically poisoned himself aged twenty-three. This plunged the household into lengthy black-robed mourning and social isolation: her dispirited mother never recovered from this family tragedy; her stoical father took off to his club.[6] Florence was nine years old.

Her adolescence, Florence's diary records, was shaped by loving relationships among the five surviving children, and by those endless hours of stupefying tedium, typically endured by mid-Victorian girls who were neither noticeably clever and motivated (like Edith Pechey-Phipson), nor visibly companionable conversationalists:

> Thus were the years of my young maidenhood maimed and my schooldays petered out . . . My diary habit became still more confirmed . . . I spent a desultory life, going much to Church, often picnicing, and visiting friends.

Florence and sisters Jess and Nell duly trooped off to local naval balls; yet without a more worldly mother to chaperone them, 'we were never properly in the swim' – and restlessly trooped back again. Languishing at home, Florence longed to make the most of her talents. She felt a rising discontent:

> I wanted something I did not find in society. An inclination for self-development stirred within me, but my mother was one of the old-school: eager that every effort should be made for the boys and their careers shaped; but, for us girls, she wished us to be content to sit by the fireside and do a bit of mending.[7]

In fact, Jess – following in the wake of Florence Nightingale, if not Edith Pechey-Phipson – decided to train as a hospital nurse. It was still an adventurous career for a respectable doctor's daughter. In 1885, she left home. Within five years, Jess had jumped on a train from King's Cross north to Huddersfield, a town unknown to her, and visited the doctors there, unfolding her plan to set up a nursing home. She put up her brass plate and advertised for nurses.

Florence, too, was blessed with one outstanding skill: she was a talented landscape painter. This began to open new directions. After leaving school, she took watercolour lessons from an old-fashioned local artist – even though unchaperoned sketching left Victorian young women prey to the advances of married men. Numbed by impoverished gentility, Florence felt aimless; she longed to leave home like Jess and obtain a training:

> It was not until I was twenty-six that I was able to renounce the dragging limitations of poverty; to throw off the inertia from which I suffered; the enervating influence of old parents; the unconscious repressions of home life; and to make the decision to study art in London . . .
>
> [A] friend . . . breathed a proposition into my ear that we should go to London together and study at the Slade School. I put the suggestion aside out of my mind as being too wild and not feasible, but suddenly, one hot Sunday evening in Church, the idea rose up before me and in an instant my decision was made. I whispered my resolve to my sister Nell, who sat beside me.[8]

The very next day, Florence broached the adventure to her mother – whose protestations were swept aside. Florence took off for London and, in September 1887, enrolled at the Slade, housed by University College in Bloomsbury, which, a decade after Emily Ford had studied there, remained a pioneer of women's art education. Here, a bewildered Florence found the teaching included a 'living model' posing 'in a very forceful attitude' in 'the life room'.

Long before Virginia Woolf and her sister Vanessa made the neighbourhood world-renowned, cosmopolitan Bloomsbury offered middle-class late-Victorian girls a new taste of freedom.[9] Florence moved into a bohemian boarding house where, at mealtimes, a good-looking actress was wedged between a missionary lady, two Indians between some German students. Here, at last, she made good friendships, took off on sketching expeditions – and returned home briefly in autumn 1888, just before her twenty-seventh birthday, 'Back to the same life, looking out on the same square, seeing the same people pass'. She tried to carry on painting, but 'I allowed small things to frustrate me. If my father entered the room where I was, and came forward to see what I was painting, I stiffened and shrivelled'.[10]

With most of her friends now married, Florence determined not to stagnate. She moved back up to London, enrolled at a Bloomsbury studio and took a room in another boarding house. Sketching expeditions even took her to Paris, with its new wonder, the Eiffel Tower. And the adoring friendship of an older woman painter led to commissions for landscape sketches of wealthy patrons' houses and estates. Her parents' deaths meant closing up the old family home with all its heavy Victorian furniture. But, by working as a sketching companion as well, Florence was beginning to earn her own living at last.

In 1895, after some bohemian drifting about, on the spur of the moment, Florence rented an empty attic studio of her own in Bloomsbury: 'The door was opened by an unprepossessing Frenchwoman in déshabille. As I entered, the well-known atmosphere of an old London lodging house greeted me and became thicker and thicker as we ascended storey after storey'. However, Florence furnished her studio in light new modern style with Eastern rugs and curtains; she put up her easel and displayed her sketches on the walls. Carrying coal and water up from the basement, she was able to make cups of tea and entertain friends; but Florence wrote ruefully, 'I certainly had no luck in lovers!'[11]

The 1901 census enumerator recorded Florence, aged thirty-eight, living as a self-employed 'Artist Painter', one of five lodgers in the French couple's house. This was indeed the most cosmopolitan of neighbourhoods, home to Italians working in the hotel trade, a German tailor, a Greek-born typewriter clerk and even a mural artist.[12] The household census might give the impression that Florence's metropolitan independence was permanent. It was not. That Christmas, she travelled up to Huddersfield to visit her sister Jess at her nursing home. And her life changed.

After Christmas, Jess had to visit an elderly housekeeper who had broken her leg up at Black Rock House, home of a Colne Valley woollen manufacturer. Florence agreed to accompany her sister, despite the damp fog. Together they found the right tram out of Huddersfield. Florence was a visitor travelling in foreign lands; with her painter's eye and diary writer's ear, few were better placed to capture the quaint idiosyncrasies of the rural-industrial Colne Valley landscape:

The great mills were all lighted up. The black smoke from their tall chimneys was blown into fantastic forms. The hills on either side of the valley – peppered with houses even to their top-most ridges – stood out gaunt and rugged in the evening light, and here in the tram car were specimens of these hill folk, our fellow passengers, bandying witticisms on our mode of transit, for electric trams were still a nine days' wonder in the valley.

Often their broad native dialect was unintelligible to us . . . 'You git out at Th' oyle 'ouse for Josiah's', they said in chorus . . .

As we turned out of the tram car it was cold and bleak, the wind and rain buffeted us, the steep granite-set hill before us looked uninviting. The drains by the roadside steamed and sent up a sheepy odour; a cart, coming down the hillside heavily laden with cloth, made quaint music with its brakes. Black Rock Mill was just 'loosing' [closing]; the workers came clattering along in their clogs; the women had each a basket on their arm and the men a little tin box.

We asked one of the women to direct us. 'Yon's the chimney and th' 'house is in t' yard'. The factory chimney she indicated seemed to be surrounded by a cluster of houses piled one on top of another. Into the labyrinth we penetrated by a little unsightly lane . . . Just inside was a little old-fashioned ivy-clad house sitting on its patch of lawn. The mill beyond was dimly lighted for the night work. As we stood on the doorstep, we could hear the pulse of the engine and the roar of the swollen stream. It all seemed so mysterious and quite reminiscent of a Brontë novel.[13]

16. *The approach to Black Rock House, Linthwaite, from a sketch by Florence Lockwood, 1903.*

The manufacturer, widowed Josiah Lockwood, was away with his grown son, and returned only later that evening. Having missed his visitors, he wrote to invite them to lunch on New Year's Eve. He even sent his carriage to the nursing home to collect them, and changed out of his blue work clothes into his best Sunday suit to greet them. While Jess tended to her patient, Josiah, a square-set man with dark beard and a diamond ring, showed a curious and enthusiastic Florence round Black Rock Mill, everything from:

> The greasy wool off the sheep's back, and at last the finished tweed cloth. On leaving the weaving sheds to get back to the little house . . . he asked 'Would you like to join at Black Rock Mill?' Regarding the proposal as a joke, I answered accordingly and said, 'Yes! It would just suit me!'[14]

In fact, neither was joking. The following evening, Josiah called at the nursing home and proposed. Florence accepted. Both her diaries and autobiography are undemonstratively terse at this point. But clearly, they both had close friendships and absorbing work (lucratively so, in Josiah's case); yet they were two lonely people and both grasped instinctively at this unforeseen opportunity. They walked together from Linthwaite back to Huddersfield along the top road with its stunning view of Colne Valley. 'Its lights were rivalling those of the heavens. It was an impressive walk', is all Florence wrote.

The whirlwind betrothal shocked Jess. Their father, after all, had been a doctor, while Josiah was just a self-made manufacturer, living cheek-by-jowl with his mill. Florence, the less conventional sister, waved away such snobbish scruples. Who wanted to live in an uninteresting new villa with a man speaking perfectly grammatically?

Back in her Bloomsbury studio, Florence soon introduced the West Riding 'rough lad' to her friends. Each of the two tribes, south and north, was mystified by the dialect of the other, her friends anxious that Florence was 'giving myself to a stranger in a strange land'. However, a grand lace-trimmed dress was laid out, and Josiah, with his kind face and keen eyes, quietly married Florence, upright and thin, before just a handful of friends and relations (including Josiah's son Sam) at St Giles' Church in London on 2 July 1902. After a brief honeymoon, they returned home to Black Rock. Here Florence soon found herself surrounded by Josiah's myriad relations. Half Linthwaite seemed to be cousins of one sort or another.

Like Lavena Saltonstall's Hebden Bridge, Colne Valley had a Methodist chapel or co-operative store on every other corner, a brass band for every occasion. Large wool mills crept up the hillsides towards the moors, weaving sheds encroached into small traditional fields, looms clattered near

17. Florence and Josiah Lockwood, 1902.

cows munching grass. With the late mechanisation of wool, the upland handloom-weavers' cottages had ceased work only within living memory.

Josiah Lockwood's family had long lived in Linthwaite: his father had woven by hand in the top storey of Black Rock House. He then took advantage of new machinery, set up as a small manufacturer, and before long was employing thirty men, eight boys and nine females – while still farming seven acres. Josiah had twelve brothers and sisters: the daughters baked, brewed and milked, while the sons followed their father into Black Rock Mills. The mills prospered and spread up the small clough and, aged twenty-four, Josiah married Mary, daughter of a well-to-do local dyer. They settled at Black Rock House, and in 1882 Sam was born. But within six years Mary fell ill and was sent to convalesce on the healthier Lancashire coast. Here she died, aged thirty-one, from peritonitis, inflammation of the abdomen.[15]

Sam was sent to a small boarding school nearby and widowed Josiah was looked after by housekeeper Martha (later joined, as the mill prospered, by a cook).[16] And there at Black Rock he stayed, increasingly affluent, for fourteen years, surrounded by his sprawling Lockwood family. As a widower, congenial Josiah socialised with other local manufacturers' families; male camaraderie focused on horses and hounds, the workings of the mill steam engine, commercial talk and, occasionally, Liberal politics.

It was an extremely close-knit community, everyone thoroughly familiar with everyone else's business: news travelled from one end of Linthwaite to the other faster than someone could walk. The place remained steeped in rural-industrial folklore and traditions: electric trams might run along the valley, but horses still strained to heave the coal up from railway to mills. The almost-present past lingered on in Linthwaite.

Leaving Bloomsbury behind, Florence Lockwood now plunged into life at Black Rock House. It was always going to be tricky. Sam, now aged nineteen and undoubtedly distanced from his father's new wife, had gone on a trip around the world the day after the wedding. Josiah's sister Sarah had come to stay to ensure that when the newly-weds returned, 'the white lace curtains and crochet antimacassars were extra white and stiff, the aspidistra plant in the window looked healthy, and the wedding presents laid out on an oval table', all of which Josiah pronounced a 'good do'.

Sarah then inducted Florence into housekeeping mysteries: instructions for polishing the handsome brass fender and fire-irons for half-an-hour every day figured prominently. However, Florence, with vivid memories of her airy Bloomsbury attic-studio with its Eastern rugs, had other ideas. Nothing evoked Victorian domestic heaviness more than aspidistras and antimacassars. And Josiah wanted his new wife to be happy; Florence and the servants began clearing out hoards of old furniture, much of it undoubtedly dating back to Josiah's first marriage:

> I had the heavy valances, curtains and flower pots removed from the windows. The red rep sofa and chairs were covered in chintz . . . I then made a place where I could write my letters, had some shelves made for my books, and Josiah gave me a new piano. The equestrian bronzes, beaded sofa cushions . . . were relegated to the attic, but the elaborate brass fender and fire-irons I gave right away! . . .
>
> Josiah often came in from the mill during the morning to see how we were getting on in the house. On finding us busy and happy and the prospect of a good dinner, he returned to the office soothed . . .
>
> One day, however, he happened to come in just as the sideboard was disappearing through the gates . . . He said, 'I am fair grieved. It cost many a pund!' I knew I had gone too far without his consent; I hated to hurt him . . . the subject of sideboards remains a delicate one.[17]

Florence sat and painted the Black Rock neighbourhood scenes, and converted the spacious attic into her studio. However, other aspects of Linthwaite life proved far harder to shift. Florence the Bloomsbury painter was now very definitely Mrs Josiah Lockwood, wife of the prosperous manufacturer. While Josiah escaped with the other local mill owners to smoke in a snug, Florence was expected to socialise with their wives, so proud of their spacious new villas – with grapes in the ceiling mouldings, new electric bell pulls and new gramophone:

> The manufacturers' wives who called on me had their stated 'at home' days once a month . . . To be aware of these days was quite a business. 'The first Thursday' or 'the last Tuesday' etc.
>
> Drawing rooms are mostly used occasionally, so I began to know the atmosphere of these rooms, a slight mustiness combined with the smell of cakes, etc, for these are landed in the room early in the afternoon . . . The admirable crochet-bordered tea cloths, d'oyleys and serviettes are not lost on me, nor the flowing strings of 'the girl' and the magnificence of my hostess as she rustles into the room with apologies for not being ready.
>
> Our conversation at these 'At Home' days is, however, very homely, mostly about our servants. I am asked if I am suited with a girl, and if I have washed my blankets yet . . .
>
> After a time I decided to receive a few friends in the attic [studio] instead of the tiny drawing room . . . I had a blazing fire and two sensible kettles singing on the hobs. I thought we should get to know each other better and we could talk more naturally if I gave my friends some occupation, so . . . I put tempting bits of mending all begun, with needles, cotton, thimble and scissors to hand . . . a stocking to mend, and I read aloud from my diary. But my efforts at friendly informality did not succeed and attendances dwindled.[18]

Linthwaite was not readily tempted away from its traditional ways. One of its strongest cultural habits was Liberalism. Naturally, the extensive Lockwood family played leading roles within local Liberal patrician networks, administering benign local paternalism. Josiah's elder brother, as chairman of Linthwaite Urban District Council (UDC), ran local government; his younger brother, a magistrate, upheld the law; while Josiah himself helped ensure that Linthwaite's traditional political culture remained convivially Liberal.[19]

Brought up a Tory, Florence now found herself afloat in a strange sea of Liberalism. At the 1906 General Election, the Colne Valley constituency did not even have a contest: Sir James Kitson MP, a major Leeds employer, had been returned unopposed. In Linthwaite, a Liberal Club and a Working Men's Club both thrived; but the nearest Labour Club was up at

Slaithwaite or down at Milnsbridge. Indeed, on Linthwaite UDC, it was not till 1906 that a Labour candidate stood for the first time; he lost by seven votes.[20]

About this time Josiah brought home the secretary of the Navvies' trade union, gold rings in his ears. John Ward MP now sat in the Commons as 'Independent Lib-Lab'. Josiah asked his guest's politics and, relieved that he was not entertaining a socialist MP, took him following hounds and hunters over the bleak moors. Returning to the Black Rock fireside, their visitor regaled Florence with his stories:

> And so I got my first lesson in politics.
>
> My Tory prejudices were strongly up against him at first as we talked, but I gradually began to see with other eyes. However, when Josiah ventured to take me to a Liberal meeting in Huddersfield Town Hall during the [1906] General Election, I was terribly disgusted; I hated the whole atmosphere of hoary-bearded old men, and the songs they sang before the speakers came.
>
> John Ward seemed surprised and disappointed that I took no leading part in the affairs of the valley. I explained that the dissipations of the Churches and Chapels were distasteful to me, I hated bazaars, and there seemed no other outlet. I tacitly accepted that politics were outside the range of woman's intellect.[21]

Had Florence and Josiah not read of the released suffragettes' arriving at the 1906 Huddersfield by-election; of the arrest and imprisonment of Dora Thewlis in spring 1907; or of the rowdiness at the Marsden open-air meeting? None of this appears in either Florence's printed diaries or in her *Ordinary Life* autobiography. This silence was surely not because they did not 'know' of these sensational local news items, but more because the Huddersfield suffragettes belonged to a separate tribe. The valley-bottom town-centre socialist-suffragettes had not so far really impinged upon the Lockwoods' traditional Linthwaite. Overnight, in July 1907, however, all this was shifted into a combustible combination. And so, for the sensational Victor Grayson by-election, we rejoin the urban world of Eliza Thewlis, Edith Key, Elizabeth Pinnance – plus Adela Pankhurst and her mother.

Born in Liverpool in 1881, Victor Grayson was the son of a Yorkshire carpenter. (Later, rumours flew about more exotic origins: Victor as the illegitimate son of an English aristocrat, possibly the Duke of Marlborough, and thus distantly related to Winston Churchill.[22]) He spent much of his boyhood enchanted by the ships in the Liverpool dockside, and ran away to sea when he was fourteen on a sailing ship bound for Australia. Stowaway Victor was discovered and, thrown off the ship at Tenby, tramped 200 miles home.

He joined a church mission, became an engineering apprentice, and began reading socialist pamphlets. He joined a men's dockside debating society, and before long was up on rickety soapboxes himself, a youthful orator. Meanwhile he read widely – mainly theology and economics, an unusual but powerful combination. Victor's talents were spotted by a Unitarian minister who (not unlike Orage's early patron) acted as an educational benefactor; this helped him to study for the Unitarian ministry at the Home Missionary College in Manchester, linked to the university. Here, Victor's inspiring speaking skills grabbed attention. 'If the word went round that Grayson was talking in the Common Room', one student recalled, we 'would flock down in crowds; what did he talk about? – oh, socialism, it was all socialism, it was a kind of religion with him'.[23] Before long, Victor was soap-boxing at Manchester's Tib Street and handling the hurly-burly.

Naturally, Victor joined the ILP branch in Manchester. This plunged him into the maelstrom of disputatious socialist-suffragette politics. It also introduced him to Emmeline, Adela and Christabel Pankhurst, plus other early WSPU members like Teresa Billington. Victor probably joined in late 1904; before long his oratorical flair (and impecunious student pocket) was noted by the branch: it accepted his offer to deliver three lectures on Socialism at Tib Street for 5/- [25p] fee.[24] At the same time, branch members, especially Adela, hurled themselves into feeding needy school children – and, of course, into women's suffrage.

Victor certainly knew the Pankhurst family well by October 1905 and the start of suffragette militancy (on which the branch formally congratulated comrades Christabel, and Annie Kenney). Victor and the suffragettes formed a congenial local youth wing, all impatient to overthrow the political system and enfranchise women *now*. Emmeline's suffrage oratory must have had a powerful effect on Grayson. On Emmeline's part, Grayson, the same age as Christabel and Sylvia, would have seemed almost like another son. The family was drawn to this good-looking impetuous rebel boy.[25]

However, from early 1906 when the WSPU moved down to London, criticism of some women branch members surfaced; and by the Cockermouth by-election that summer, internal strains grew so fierce that there were even calls for Christabel and Teresa Billington to resign. Victor, meanwhile, got caught up in local unemployment demonstrations, his studies increasingly neglected. Finally, in July 1906, he withdrew from his course to give himself to socialism and eked out a living with journalism and lecturing. Aged twenty-five, he moved into two tiny rooms in Manchester's smoky Ancoats slums, confident his oratory would keep him from starving.[26]

Meanwhile, the branch dispute – socialism or women's suffrage – grew bitter in the Manchester ILP. Women withdrew from branch meetings. The majority of members still supported the WSPU and the Pankhursts, but by spring 1907 the minority left to form a separate branch. Victor himself loyally remained with Adela and the suffragettes. Indeed, his commitment to Votes for Women was growing as passionate and fervent as his socialism.[27]

From now on, Grayson's rise within the labour movement was meteoric, despite the narrowness of his trade unionism experience. As a recent biographer put it, Victor:

> preferred the emotions of the platform to the humdrum tasks of political organisation. But in the circumstances of 1906–7, his revivalist socialism struck a telling chord among many activists of the ILP . . . For his sympathisers he represented the hope of a better world that owed more to moral conversion than to legislation.[28]

This was felt nowhere more keenly than in the Colne Valley. Grayson had agreed to substitute in December 1905 when a well-known Labour MP suddenly withdrew from speaking in Huddersfield. Aged twenty-four, Victor's dazzling oratory had made a tremendous impression. Before long, he was invited back to local ILP meetings along the Colne Valley.[29] His idealistic socialism found a highly receptive audience as he tracked up and down the valley. For his part, Grayson must have found the rural landscapes refreshing after Manchester. And in January 1907, despite his lack of labour movement experience, he was selected as Colne Valley Labour League parliamentary candidate.

Victor criss-crossed the valley-floor textile communities. So, too, did the suffragettes. It was just so easy to jump on a Manchester train and steam over the Pennines, as Hannah Mitchell recalled:

I must have worked the Colne Valley from end to end, often under the aus-
pices of the Colne Valley Labour [League]. Sometimes we just went . . . from
door to door to ask the women to come and listen, which the Colne Valley
women were usually willing to do.[30]

The suffragettes sold pamphlets as they went, to pay for their fares back
home. During 1906–7, these ties strengthened: the Colne Valley was natural
territory for the WSPU, away from bitter city-centre disputes. Adela
Pankhurst spoke at Marsden, Mary Gawthorpe at nearby Berry Brow.[31]
Nationally the WSPU's strategy might increasingly focus on Westminster and
cabinet ministers; but up in the Colne Valley, the early WSPU's close links to
an almost religious socialism still readily found sympathetic audiences.

Yet up towards Linthwaite clough, above the socialist and suffragette
rabble-rousers, a different order still prevailed. However, the old certainties
and familiar political landmarks of Josiah Lockwood were about to be
rudely awakened.

Created in 1885, the Colne Valley constituency sprawled right over the
Pennines – from Annie Kenney's Springhead right across to Milnsbridge
and over the hills to Honley. It was always traditional Liberal territory.
From 1892 the seat had been held by Liberal grandee Sir James Kitson MP,
the largest engineering employer in Leeds and friend of Herbert
Gladstone. His was a patrician *laissez-faire* Liberalism that had scant regard
for any labour movement. It was able to take advantage of the weak trade
union organisation among the Colne Valley wool mills, while reassuring
middle-class voters that traditional Liberalism remained safe with Kitson.
The Graysonites had it that the Liberal electoral machine was so well oiled
that Kitson need only visit his constituency once a year, to be met by a
posse of influential businessmen, escorted to the hall – where, as soon as he
entered, the crowd rose and cheered, and the meat tea and speeches could
begin.[32] Now aged seventy-one, Kitson was just waiting for the nod to ease
himself up into the House of Lords. This complacency was underpinned by
local wool mills' prosperity. Unknown tub orators and their rabble-filled
labour clubs could be happily ignored.

However, in mid-June, events suddenly accelerated. Rumours of a peerage flew. On 22 June Grayson was hurriedly adopted as Colne Valley
candidate. Within a week, Kitson's peerage was confirmed, and by-election
battle was joined. The cosy Liberals fielded an uninspiring candidate: Philip,
son of Victorian radical John Bright. By contrast, Grayson's strikingly bold

election address, offering himself 'as Labour and Socialist candidate', pulled no political punches:

> As a socialist my life will be spent in hastening the time when the land and other means of production will be the property of the whole people, and not a privileged class.
>
> For too long you have been represented in Parliament by the rich classes such as brewers, landlords, lawyers, employers, financiers and their numerous hangers-on . . .
>
> Should you put your trust in me, I shall add one more emphatic voice to the cry for a fuller and freer life for all.

Grayson attacked unemployment; he demanded old age pensions, the nationalisation of the railways and the abolition of the House of Lords. Amid these revolutionary promises was – equally uncompromisingly – suffrage:

> *Women and Votes*
> The placing of women in the same category, constitutionally, as infants, idiots and Peers, does not impress me as either manly or just. While thousands of women are compelled to slave in factories, etc., in order to earn a living; and others are ruined in body and soul by unjust economic laws created and sustained by men, I deem it the meanest tyranny to withhold from women the right to share in making the laws they have to obey. Should I be honoured with your support, I am prepared to give the most immediate and enthusiastic support to a measure giving women the vote *on the same terms as men*. This is as a step to the larger measure of complete Adult Suffrage.[33]

Grayson was fervent in his commitment. He now added his own challenge to Edwardian *men*: how could they claim to believe in fair play and justice, if their manliness was based upon the dishonourable subjection of women?

The campaign opened to cloudy and gloomy weather. The Grayson camp lacked a car and spectators huddled beneath umbrellas. Huddersfield WSPU had just held its meeting with Eliza Thewlis and Laura Wilson speaking at the town's Market Cross, the wet weather dampening its black-and-white banner. The branch now whirred into action.[34] As local secretary Edith Key would have telegraphed WSPU headquarters, urgently demanding national speakers.

There was no time to lose. On Saturday 29 June Emmeline Pankhurst arrived in Slaithwaite for a flying visit, accompanied by Edith Key. The pro-Liberal *Colne Valley Gazette* delighted in reporting how these unwelcome off-cumdens 'were engaged in a vain search for apartments' for a campaigning base; and it could not resist reporting how, when Emmeline seized the opportunity to hold an open-air meeting, she:

> approached several waggon owners of unquestioned Radical fidelity [Liberal faith] for a loan, but they point blank refused. A sympathetic tradesman proffered a chair, but Mrs Pankhurst slyly protested that there was not sufficient understanding on a chair. However, to make the best of a bad job, the chair was at length accepted, and Mrs Pankhurst began to address the meeting. A few lads – who were old enough to know better – started throwing peas and orange peel at the speaker.

But, despite this mocking hostility, the suffragettes refused to quit. The next evening they held a meeting at Milnsbridge; and Adela addressed a meeting in Honley market place to an audience of several hundred for over an hour. She had just had her twenty-second birthday, and had emerged a strong, if not succinct, tub speaker. Adela had also picked up the shift in WSPU tactics; while part of her speech concerned women's low wages and destitution, it also reflected a new and challenging directness:

> Women have learnt how to play the game of politics, and they are playing to win. If the Liberal candidate will get a pledge from the Government that they will enfranchise the women next session we – the Suffragettes – will pack our traps and leave the constituency.[35]

As the campaign ratcheted up into top gear, Adela raced round the constituency, speaking at Milnsbridge's fair-ground and at a Meltham mill-workers' meeting. (Yet it was difficult to gauge the suffragettes' impact, since both the pro-Liberal *Huddersfield Examiner* and *Colne Valley Guardian* exercised a virtual news blackout.) However, Grayson was at last lent a car – and the weather miraculously changed to sunshine, showing the Colne Valley countryside at its most fresh and glorious as the campaign reached its crescendo.

By Sunday evening 30 June, Victor Grayson had even reached up to Holyehouse in Linthwaite for one of his innumerable open-air meetings.

He brought his revolutionary message right to Josiah and Florence Lockwood's very doorstep. Liberal heavyweights spoke from the Linthwaite school yard, with a Lockwood brother among the prominent supporters. The suffragettes could not be far behind then in clambering up the hillside towards Black Rock.

Despite the conversations with John Ward MP, Florence Lockwood, with her loathing of hoary old men and their election songs, still felt alienated from electoral politics.[36] Yet, as the sunshine came out, Florence too found herself swept up in by-election fever. It was all a novelty, so she recorded the enthralling moment in her diary:

> One day . . . when I was coming though Linthwaite Fold, I stopped and helped to swell the crowd who were listening to Mrs Pankhurst – a woman speaker was something quite new. That was a psychological moment for me; I edged nearer and nearer to hear her. What she said was new and inspiring to me. Why should women be political nonentities indeed? It was women's duty to demand that they should be allowed to exercise a Parliamentary vote and to understand and take part in the affairs of the state side by side with men.
>
> As I walked slowly up the hill on my way home, deeply impressed, one of my sisters-in-law overtook me and touched me on the arm. I asked her if she had been listening to Mrs Pankhurst. 'No, indeed!' she indignantly replied. 'I believe woman's place is in the home'.
>
> This limitation of woman's sphere set my heart beating furiously and I took up the cudgels in defence of votes for women for the first time.

Florence's sister-in-law resisted this new-found faith, not just because she held to traditional gender distinctions but also because the suffragettes uncompromisingly urged opposing the government by voting against Bright. Florence went home to Black Rock and mentioned to Josiah her encounter among the crowd in Linthwaite Fold. Ever the practical man, he was busy with hay-making; the full implications of what his wife had heard from Mrs Pankhurst did not quite strike home yet. Josiah, loving husband, perhaps viewed his wife's new-fangled enthusiasm rather as he had accommodated her landscape painting; he remained unruffled:

> The next day we were peacefully haymaking in the fields behind the mill. I had just collected a few friends and brought out tea; we were just enjoying

our first mugfulls when two women entered the field. My friends remarked; 'They look like suffragettes!' The strangers made their way up to Josiah who was at a little distance directing the hay-makers. Soon he put up his hand and shouted, 'Some of your friends, love!' and he came with them across the field to our encampment.

Adela Pankhurst wore a little, dirty, limp print dress, her face was sun-burnt, freckled and perspiring, her voice already hoarse from over-use, though she told us the evening campaign was still before her. 'Well, tell us what it is you want', said Josiah, seating himself on a [hay]cock. They also dropped into the hay as if utterly fagged out. 'Well, we want to know if you will lend us a cart from which to speak in the Fold tonight?' 'Eh, yes! You have asked that already, but what is it you are here for?' Then she began to expound the demands of her Society [WSPU], ie, 'that the vote should be granted to women on the same terms as it is, or may be, granted to men.' It was the first time we had heard the formula which afterwards became so well-known. The three men of the party indulged in merriment at the bare idea of votes for women and began to chaff her and ask all sort of absurd questions which she answered with her croaking little voice, while chewing a whisp of hay. 'You will be wanting women to sit in Parliament next,' they said. 'Yes, why not?' she replied. Before the suffragettes left they seemed rested and refreshed with tea and comforted by having found a sympathiser in me.[37]

This incident dramatically indicates how, even by mid-1907, Votes for Women had scarcely penetrated ordinary Edwardians' lives beyond the cities, some large towns and a few northern industrial centres such as Hebden Bridge. In small tucked-away communities like Linthwaite, it remained perfectly possible for a busy manufacturer and his artist-wife not to have come across the suffragettes or their anti-government tactics of opposing Liberal candidates. All this despite the WSPU being so in evidence at the recent Huddersfield by-election, and despite the imprisonment of suffragettes like Dora Thewlis.[38] The local Liberal press news blackout meant that up in the Lockwoods' hamlet people remained unaware of the growing bond between dashing Grayson and the suffragettes.

The familiar political landscape was changing dramatically right before Florence and Josiah's very eyes. In the glorious summer weather and with the scent of new-mown hay rising from the fields, Grayson toured in the newly acquired car up and down Colne Valley's winding roads; at every stop, children swarmed around his car, men working on the roads cheered him as he went, and, legend has it, his supporters (wearing red ribbons and 'Grayson' buttons) carried him shoulder high.[39]

Last-minute press interest grew. The *Daily Mirror* dispatched a news photographer to track the wild enthusiasm crescendo of polling day, Thursday 18 July. Rather impishly, its photo-spread recorded two male speakers from the two main parties each addressing an audience – of a lone listener apiece. Alongside, suffragette speakers attracted a large and eager crowd, mainly women. The *Mirror* photo, confirming the balmy weather, showed a well-dressed speaker (possibly Emmeline Pankhurst) standing on a cart at Linthwaite Fold – probably the very same cart that Josiah had so casually lent Adela.

THREE CANDIDATES FOR ONE SEAT.

18. Daily Mirror, 19 July 1907, 'Polling in the Colne Valley Division Yesterday'.

Another picture, depicting enthusiastic Colne Valley mill girls, was captioned: 'many of them who cared nothing about votes before are now eager in their desire to enjoy the privileges of the franchise'. With suffragettes motoring around the valley, a final photo depicted Emmeline Pankhurst standing on the car in black skirt and white blouse, with a hatless girl, probably Adela Pankhurst, Nellie Martel posing in front, plus small boys – possibly Edith Key's sons, Lancelot and Archibald, now aged about thirteen and fifteen.[40]

Colne Valley's polling day was a historic moment which lived long in Graysonite legend and local memory:

> About noon the following day crowds began swarming along the streets to Slaithwaite Town Hall. There were several thousand there before long, mostly mill workers, in shawls, clogs and working clothes, red ribbons plentifully besprinkled on caps and coats . . . The Liberals among them were still confident, repeating the Liberal agent's prediction that 'Bright'll be in by 500'. Inside, at the count, the socialists watching with incredulity and anxiety the votes piling up were encouraged by the muffled strains of the *Red Flag* sung by the crowds outside.
>
> At the first signs of movement from the windows of the Town Hall the noise and chatter and banter stops. The High Sheriff came out first; then Grayson, pale as death. For a moment the crowd was stunned, listening as the Sheriff began reading the result. He got no further than Albert Victor Grayson . . . A great shout rose. The crowd of staid hard-headed Yorkshire folk went wild, cheering, laughing, then crying and weeping almost hysterically.[41]

Grayson's car was drawn through the streets by ecstatic supporters. When they halted by an inn, Grayson, still white-faced and with croaking voice, proclaimed to the crowd, 'This epoch-making victory has been won for pure revolutionary socialism. We have not trimmed our sails . . . We stand for equality, human equality, sexual equality – for the abolition of the sex ties, and I thank the women for what they have done to keep the Liberal out'.

Grayson's majority might be merely 153 but his unexpected and sensational victory exceeded his supporters' wildest dreams.[42] It made headline news. Saturday's *Daily Mirror* front page depicted an immaculate wing-collared Grayson portrait, above a delightful photograph of 'Colne Valley Mill Girls Wait for the Election Result', excited by the hubbub and all looking just like so many of Dora Thewlis's younger sisters. Indeed, the *Mirror* added, one of the most remarkable features 'was the great interest taken in the election by the young mill girls of the constituency. Not only made suffragettes by Mrs Pankhurst's eloquence, many of them wore the Socialist colours and helped the Labour candidate to win the seat'.[43] Voteless all, to be sure, but perhaps their infectious excitement persuaded their fathers or older brothers to vote for Grayson.

On the night of the election victory, back in Huddersfield Mrs Pankhurst addressed a celebration meeting in St George's Square.[44] On this occasion, it did seem that the suffragettes had swung the election. They

19. 'Colne Valley Mill Girls Wait for the Election Result', Daily Mirror, *Saturday 20 July, front page.*

now had their candidate, a compelling speaker, right at the very heart of power: the House of Commons. With a few more such victories, the WSPU would surely have the Liberal government on the run. It was certainly tempting for a tactician like Christabel to exaggerate the influence of such by-election losses on the Liberals. She wrote vindicating her tactics: 'By the defeat of the Government at Colne Valley, our movement is brought a stage nearer success . . . We have only to pursue with unflagging energy our by-election policy and victory is certain'.[45]

Local Liberals were dumbfounded. The *Huddersfield Examiner* and *Colne Valley Guardian* went very quiet in reporting the result, beyond alarmist corre-spondence about Grayson wanting to abolish marriage.[46] Few Liberal households can have been more shaken than Josiah Lockwood's. Husband and wife had now had time to mull soberly over the hayfield encounter with Adela in the cold light of electoral day:

> I think Josiah regretted having lent the cart on which they stood while they expounded to the crowd why they should vote against the Liberals . . . until it [the government] introduced a bill to bring in votes for women.
>
> The Liberals lost the bye-election! Victor Grayson got in. The anti-gov-ernment policy of the suffragettes left a very tender spot, and my 'votes for women' tendency had to be kept in abeyance for a time.[47]

While the Linthwaite Liberals disconsolately licked their electoral wounds, Florence could not discuss such delicate issues with her husband. Troublesome Adela and her mother may have departed, but John Ward MP still visited, and his conversations with Florence about women and politics continued. Gradually, perhaps during winter 1907–8, she grew more daring. Her suffrage convictions and confidence took shape, with 'slowly a small degree of power to express them'. She cast around her. Should she join the Huddersfield WSPU branch? Florence didn't think so. She had few interests in common with women like Edith Key or Dora Thewlis, beyond the refusal to accept women's votelessness. The differences largely hinged upon political style: in textile West Riding precious few manufacturers' wives were active suffragettes. Recent tactics of seizing the propaganda opportunity at industrial disputes, as at Halifax and Hebden Bridge, meant the WSPU represented a threat rather than an opportunity. And its determined opposition to all things Liberal further distanced women like Florence Lockwood. While she remained 'Mrs Josiah', she would need to find other ways to support suffrage: she did not relish the trip to the Linthwaite shops, for a chance encounter with a sister-in-law would be like running the gauntlet.

Instead, Florence joined the local NUWSS branch. This offered a more congenial home for her new suffrage convictions, without forcing her to betray Josiah and his family. This experience, she wrote, 'brought me into touch with the few women of the locality who were awake to the new order of things.'[48]

Six months had passed since the courageous 'Mud March'. The NUWSS, with its three dozen local societies – including the seven across Yorkshire – could feel proud of its Huddersfield branch. It was very active, very well-connected, very Liberal. For its Women's Franchise Declaration, several hundred signatures were handed into officers, based at Huddersfield Liberal Association rooms in Imperial Arcade; Huddersfield's MP, the Liberal Sherwood, was thanked for his support.[49] Dr Edith Pechey-Phipson gave generous donations.

Reflecting the world of a patrician elite, with its expectation of deference, branch members came less from the valley-floor textile communities than from Huddersfield's higher suburban slopes, notably residential Edgerton; or from country towns like Honley [see Map III, page 108]. The support of sympathisers such as union leader Alderman Allen Gee JP was valued. But it was Emily Siddon of Honley House, elected founding branch president (even in her absence), who was the local suffrage dowager. The real hard work, however, seemed to have been undertaken by branch secretary Helen Studdard, wife of a self-employed cabinet-maker, living in a modest town-centre street.[50] Both the WSPU and NUWSS branches shared similar democratic procedures; but the NUWSS branch could book the Town Hall or Temperance Hall for meetings, rather than holding them outdoors like the WSPU.

The arrests of spring 1907 and Grayson's subsequent Colne Valley victory over the Liberals were quietly glossed over in the world of Miss Siddon and Mrs Studdard.[51] To them, the local WSPU suffragettes seemed inconvenient political nobodies who merely disrupted local political harmony with its slow but sure progress.

The local Liberals cast around for another way of increasing the number of politically active women. Florence Lockwood happened to encounter a woman neighbour in Linthwaite village, who invited her to a meeting at the local Liberal Club that evening. Florence was loath to leave her Black Rock fireside, but having promised she set out. Inadvertently patronising, she wrote in her diary, 'I often think what a lot I should have missed in my life if I had stayed at home. At the Liberal Club I found a room full of women with shawls over their heads looking like a flock of penguins . . . There was a sigh of relief when Mrs Josiah sailed in to take the chair'.

The speaker that evening was Cicely Corbett, an NUWSS suffragist so caught up in hectic campaigning that she seldom slept in the same bed twice during the suffrage years. Cicely's father was a Liberal MP, her mother Marie Corbett was an active Poor Law Guardian in Sussex and rural district councillor, who had been on the 'Mud March'. Florence continued, 'The penguins listened apparently unmoved to the speaker's able pleading of the Woman's Cause. Only one ventured to remark at the end of the lecture, "There's naught wrang with men".' Florence offered Cicely hospitality that night and brought her back to Black Rock. She was the Lockwoods' first suffrage guest but certainly not their last. Indeed:

> Our house became a haven for organisers and speakers. Josiah enjoyed this type of woman, and seemed proud of my advanced feminist views, though he couldn't get there so quickly himself. At suffrage meetings, if I was speaking or presiding, he would wave his red pocket handkerchief from the audience as a signal of distress. 'Thou hast done well, love! Give up'.[52]

Votes for Women campaigning transformed Florence Lockwood's life. She was soon drawn into an active Liberal world similar to that of Marie

Corbett. One effect of the Grayson victory was that the Huddersfield NUWSS branch soon galvanised itself into greater political momentum. Women might not be able to vote at parliamentary elections but they could play an active part in local government. More women must be put forward for election to town councils and, in outlying areas like Linthwaite, urban district councils.[53] It seems likely that Florence Lockwood heard about plans to nominate more women for local election, and went along to a meeting.

A few months later, Helen Studdard came to drum up support and enrol new members: a small Linthwaite Women's Liberal Association was formed.[54] Florence joined – being persuaded that the association existed 'for the propagation of Liberal principals and to get just laws for women, including the Parliamentary vote'. And before long she became president of the larger Colne Valley Women Liberals. For local Liberals, keen to bounce back to power at the earliest electoral opportunity, Florence was indeed a valuable political catch. She realised that 'the Liberal community had decided I was a fitting person' to stand for election as one of the Poor Law Guardians, and she found herself sucked in further. Ever helpful, 'they drew up my election address and distributed leaflets to every household in the township'.

On election day the count was at nine o'clock in the evening. The socialist candidate came top of the poll, but Florence was second and so was elected too. Both new Guardians now met amicably together at Poor Law Union board meetings to assist Linthwaite's destitute; here they 'found we were not such ogres after all; we were both discontented with the existing conditions which create such human wrecks as were brought before us'.[55] Florence Lockwood's new civic career was broadening out beyond Josiah's traditional horizons.

Her artistic talents were also appreciated in the Huddersfield NUWSS branch. From 1908 onwards the Artists' Suffrage League, and the involvement of leading Slade-ians, notably its talented chair Mary Lowndes, inspired a wave of glorious banner-making. It was in this creative context that Florence 'embarked on making a great banner "Votes for Women – Huddersfield" for the members of the [NUWSS] branch to carry in demonstrations and processions'.[56] With her landscapist's design and traditional feminine embroidery skills, her work evokes Colne Valley. And fortunately, like the Huddersfield WSPU minutes book, it is one of the very few early northern suffrage banners to survive.[57]

*

20. *Huddersfield NUWSS banner embroidered by Florence Lockwood.*

Victor Grayson took his seat in the House of Commons; his maiden speech was an uncompromising attack on Lord Cromer, imperialist and anti-suffragist. But, scarcely identifying with the Labour Party, he was a tempestuously short-lived rebel MP. Victor Grayson was one of those shining meteors who sped across the Edwardian sky leaving behind a shower of smouldering stars. In the memories of Colne Valley socialists for years afterwards, the 1907 by-election summer and Grayson's light burned forever bright – even if subsequently he did fall to earth and disappear into mysterious obscurity.[58] And for WSPU strategists he proved an unreliable guide to routing the Liberals.

Meanwhile, Florence Lockwood's banner design points us forward to the glorious suffrage processions of June 1908 onwards. From the intense community involvement of Halifax, Hebden Bridge and the Colne Valley, the Votes for Women campaigns now widened out. They reached beyond their early industrial northern heartland and the community suffragettes, to capture the national imagination, and to lend the Edwardian suffrage narrative its most familiar images.[59]

PART THREE

Hearts and Minds
1907–1911

Votes for Women everywhere: Mary Murdoch
and the Coates clan

1907

While Florence Lockwood applied her embroidery needle in the Colne Valley and Victor Grayson confirmed himself as a brilliant if unreliable MP at Westminster, the Liberal government, despite all the signatures collected and prison sentences endured, obstinately refused to enfranchise one single Edwardian woman.

This provoked increasing anger and frustration, which fuelled an even broader suffrage campaign nationally. It now began to acquire the public contours familiar later from conventional suffrage histories. The movement, once limited to large cities like Manchester and London, plus the smaller Pennine textile communities, now began to widen out. By 1908–9 Votes for Women campaigning *everywhere* became a reality: networks of local branches mushroomed and converts popped up in unlikely locations. A rich range of specialist groups – an Actresses' Franchise League, Men's League for Women's Suffrage and even Lord Cromer's League for Opposing Women's Suffrage – also sprang into life. Alongside, brand new suffrage papers began publication, taking campaign news out to the further reaches of the kingdom and helping to recruit new members. No longer could suffragists be caricatured as 'just Liberals' or suffragettes as 'just socialists'.

A far broader cast of women now made dramatic entrances: the community suffragette 'rebel girls' were joined by more experienced women. These talented converts often found themselves living in a landscape where they felt slightly out-of-place, due to their careers, European identities or marriages; yet they were determined to make their voices heard on Votes for Women, citizenship and democracy. Florence Lockwood was one: a square Bloomsbury peg in a round Linthwaite hole. Bertha Lowenthal also stuck out among Huddersfield suffragists as daughter of a German-born wool merchant; then she alone defected from the Huddersfield NUWSS branch to join the local WSPU, where, as a well-to-do woman, she was unusual among the other suffragette activists.[1] In Middlesbrough, Marion Coates-Hanson was married to a naturalised Prussian and, with her sister-in-law Alice Schofield-Coates, ran the local suffragette campaign; similarly in Hull, pioneer woman doctor Mary Murdoch commanded the NUWSS branch.

Meanwhile, in the immediate wake of the Colne Valley by-election, internal tensions grew within the WSPU nationally. The issues at stake were partly political, and concerned the contentious question for ILP women of whether to support Labour candidates at by-elections. And they concerned most particularly WSPU internal democracy – or lack of it. At the heart of the matter was this question: who ran the organisation, and *should* Emmeline and Christabel Pankhurst (and intimates like Emmeline Pethick-Lawrence) hold full control? The autocratic style of leaders like Christabel might suit Annie Kenney but did not suit all. Those suffragettes, often in the ILP, who wanted the WSPU to be democratically run included Teresa Billington-Greig (now married), Charlotte Despard and Hannah Mitchell. They tried to argue for open communication channels so that, for instance, distant branches were not merely the butt of leadership edicts issued by the London headquarters, but could be democratically consulted about how money raised was spent, and on whom.

By autumn 1907, the relationship between local membership and national leadership grew increasingly disputatious. Of the sixty-nine WSPU branches, over a quarter were based in Lancashire and Yorkshire, with others further north in Scotland. As we know, the early northern suffragettes in branches such as Halifax and Huddersfield drew strongly from among ILP members like Laura Wilson or sympathisers like Lavena Saltonstall. Yet, with the WSPU headquarters now in London and its anti-government strategic sights set on Westminster, tensions inevitably brewed. It was almost as if the WSPU had developed two political styles: the community suffragettes flourished up in Halifax and Huddersfield, while in London's Kensington, Chelsea and the Home Counties, increasingly well-connected suffragettes put their minds to more lavish fund-raising.[2]

Teresa Billington-Greig and others aimed to raise the issue of internal democracy at the WSPU annual conference planned for 12 October 1907. Emmeline and Christabel, however, interpreted such questioning as arrant disloyalty. Anger grew insurmountable: the WSPU now split, and from this was born the Women's Freedom League.

As so often results from such frenzied internal conflict, arguments among the national leadership merely left grassroots members feeling bemused, confused, and just plain let down. The history of the WSPU has traditionally been that of leadership figures rather than of local suffragette experiences. Luckily, Edith Key's meticulous Huddersfield minutes book allows us to see vividly how these rifts were experienced locally: a branch tussling with the dilemma of democracy versus loyalty. After all, Emmeline Pankhurst had not only been Huddersfield's founding speaker, but had just recently worked for the Colne Valley victory with the local suffragettes. Members now went ahead and selected two branch delegates for the 12 October WSPU conference, and planned a branch picnic for August. But this, it turned out, could no longer be just a social event: branch members found they even had to take picnic minutes – including the passing of 'a vote of confidence in Mrs Pankhurst & helpers'. Huddersfield was indeed a loyal branch: despite straitened finances, it committed itself to sending its £1 subscription towards WSPU funds.[3]

Meanwhile, Emmeline and Christabel, demanding loyalty of WSPU members, cancelled the planned October conference. Fury flared during September. 'Disloyal' suffragette rebels decided to hold their own meeting anyway. Within days of Emmeline cancelling the conference, Huddersfield apprehensively held *its* branch meeting. Edith Key's minutes remained a masterpiece of clerical brevity, as members struggled to respond to bewilderingly contradictory WSPU appeals from both democrats and loyalists:

> Correspondence read from Mrs How Martyn and Mrs Despard, also correspondence from Mrs Pankhurst.
> Mrs Pankhurst explained her position & the following resolution was passed:
> That the members present express their confidence in Mrs Pankhurst and the women working with her; & pledge themselves to strive to secure Votes for Women by the methods laid down in the Constitution.[4]

Loyalty indeed. Shortly after, the branch invited Christabel and Mrs Pethick-Lawrence up to speak at its mass rally scheduled for November – and even decided that a framed portrait of Emmeline Pankhurst would be offered as a prize for the ten-table whist social planned. In the Colne Valley by-election afterglow, it seemed that no member wanted openly to question the Pankhursts' authority, nor entertain any yearning to disembark and join the new Freedom League.[5]

Unlike Huddersfield, the Halifax WSPU branch had had no dramatic by-elections, and had experienced less recent contact with the Pankhurst leadership. Its loyalties were tugged violently to and fro. When the rebels, led by Charlotte Despard and Teresa Billington-Greig, held their meeting on 12 October, Laura Wilson arrived from Halifax to tell a troubled tale. The bewildered branch had held frenzied and confused discussion:

> Our members decided the quarrel was a London quarrel, and that the people in the Provinces knew nothing about it. They wanted to know more, and they unanimously decided that they would be represented at the Conference [today] . . .
>
> I might tell you that our women are not women in politics, but they have just come along because of the women having been sent to prison [in spring]; they resent the indignities being heaped upon women.[6]

Laura's hectic account evokes the chaotic debate that must have erupted in other northern WSPU branches.

The rebel suffragettes attending the meeting claimed *they* were the WSPU mainstream, as they believed it was they who had been betrayed by the leadership. They reviewed the militant campaign over the last twelve months. So much had happened: the release of prisoners for the Huddersfield by-election, growing imprisonments (Laura Wilson and Jenny Baines, then Mary Taylor in February, followed by Lavena Saltonstall and Dora Thewlis in March). The rebels presented an authoritative summary, naturally stressing their democratic procedures and informed decision-making.

From this dissident meeting sprang the breakaway organisation led by Charlotte Despard and Teresa Billington-Greig. Perhaps about one in five suffragettes left the WSPU to join this new freedom-loving organisation.[7] In November, they voted to call it the 'Women's Freedom League', with Charlotte Despard as president. It lacked, however, control over either the WSPU's growing finances or its premises.

One particularly vocal critic of the WSPU's hollow democracy was Marion Coates-Hanson from Middlesbrough on Teesside, at the very northern tip of Yorkshire's North Riding, beyond the North York Moors (see Map I, p 6). In late-Victorian Middlesbrough, heavy dockside development offered plentiful job opportunities in the coal and coke, steel and chemical industries; and

Marion's father found work as a colliery weighman – literally, weighing coal. The large Coates family lived in Linthorpe, a residential suburb away from Teesside's towering chemical works, railway marshalling yards, and ship-building docks. Marion – like Adela Pankhurst and Mary Gawthorpe – became a pupil teacher, while her brothers worked as engine-fitter apprentices or as white-collar pay clerks in the iron works. For example, her elder brother, twenty-nine-year-old Charles, worked as a 'Coal Exporter Clerk' for a coal and coke merchant. At the turn of the century, prosperity spread in such northern industrial towns, and Charles grew affluent.

Marion then met Gottlieb Eric Hansen, a naturalised German, also with a well-paid respectable job as a clerk to an iron merchant. In 1898 they married and Marion, aged twenty-eight, gave up teaching. The couple opted for an anglicised name; and the Coates-Hansons, now employing a housekeeper, lived just two doors away from her brother Charles and family. This Coates dynasty became the dynamic powerhouse of Middlesbrough's suffrage campaign.[8]

Marion Coates-Hanson was an active member of both the ILP and the WSPU. At the 1906 General Election, she acted as election agent for Middlesbrough's independent socialist candidate, George Lansbury, persuading him to include votes for women in his manifesto; and the first WSPU Annual Report listed her name as the contact for the Middlesbrough branch.[9] But now, at the October conference, Marion was most forthright in her protest at the WSPU leadership, its disingenuous financial accounts and high-handed appointments. They had, she accused:

> Overstepped the mark entirely . . . and really a rumpus ought to have been made long before this . . .
>
> I think enormous sums of money have been spent rather recklessly . . . I would like to know how it is that money goes so rapidly, because very little of it, comparatively speaking, is spent in the provinces, rather than on headquarter's expenses and organisers' salaries.[10]

Unsurprisingly then, Marion Coates-Hanson joined the new Women's Freedom League (WFL), becoming a member of its national committee. The Middlesbrough branch was the key WFL group in Yorkshire, and it undoubtedly took most of the local suffragettes with it.[11] Broadly, the WFL provided a welcome home for those who relished neither NUWSS Liberal sedateness nor WSPU undemocratic perils. For ILP women like Marion, it provided a congenial yet empowering political space.

Sheffield and York followed suit later with WFL branches. However, unlike Scotland where Teresa Billington-Greig held sway, there were in Yorkshire no other defections from the Pankhursts' WSPU. Halifax, despite Laura Wilson's impetuous appearance at the conference, did not form a WFL branch. Such socialist-suffragettes may have entertained doubts about WSPU leadership; but most either remained with WSPU for the moment or moved into wider labour movement politics.

Nevertheless, this split within the WSPU signalled the growing vulnerability of early northern WSPU branches in Pennine textile communities like Halifax and Huddersfield. The community suffragettes' original fire was dampened, though not extinguished – as Lavena Saltonstall, Laura Wilson and Edith Key continued to show. The WSPU had boundless energy and flair; but the more democratic NUWSS's more cautious expansion might better prove sustainable in the longer term.

Mrs Fawcett's NUWSS was growing into an effective countrywide organisational network: increasingly strong on the ground, it could reach out to women almost everywhere. One particularly active NUWSS branch was in the large fishing port of Hull, across on the East Riding coast, where its founding president and suffrage dowager was the commanding Dr Mary Murdoch. A month after the Women's Freedom League conference, in November 1907, a by-election was called in Hull West. Both the WSPU and the NUWSS, each with its own election strategy, travelled east; and Mary Murdoch was well poised for a glittering by-election performance.

Scotswoman Mary, born in 1864, was the daughter of a Liberal solicitor. After an elite education, she returned to her family in Scotland to play the Victorian role of 'daughter-at-home'. Then, after her mother died, Mary decided to follow in the earlier pioneer footsteps of Edith Pechey-Phipson, though by now it was slightly easier: no 'Surgeons' Hall riot'. In 1888 Mary entered the London School of Medicine for Women in Bloomsbury, still a very daring career choice; and here she found herself drawn to women's suffrage. Once qualified, she was appointed in 1893 to the key post of house surgeon at the children's hospital in Hull. Then, three years later, she set up as a general practitioner there, Hull's first woman GP; and she was appointed senior physician at the children's hospital. She relished such a fulfilling vocation: 'From the day you put up your brass plate never refuse a piece of work'.[12] Mary's professional career was in contrast to the lives of so many other upper-middle-class women – Mrs Pankhurst thrown onto her own resources when widowed;

Isabella Ford, lacking training and feeling she had failed as a novelist; Florence Lockwood, with art training but patchy earnings. Mary Murdoch's was already a career golden with achievement, her professional status lending her limitless confidence.

21. Dr Murdoch in her writing room, Hull.

From Leeds, Hull was reached (by those who wanted to visit) only after a long train journey eastwards past Selby and East Riding's flat fields, as the Humber estuary widened out to the sea. This isolated city, cut off from more cosmopolitan West Riding, soon skipped to Dr Murdoch's rather imperious tune. She swept all before her. Mary's old friend, Mrs Fawcett, conjured up the doctor's household:

> In her home, surrounded by her beloved little dogs, adoring servants and friends, she was the very pulse of the machine, keeping everything sweet, strong, and wholesome . . .
>
> Sick children beamed with joy when the door opened and revealed the beloved physician. No wonder she was such a wonderful children's doctor. Burly policemen beamed on her when she asked them to do something for her – to go out, for instance, in icy rain to fetch her a cab.[13]

Mary's biographer added, 'Suffering called forth from her great compassion . . . Her answer to the call was a life of self-abnegation and devotion to work. She was a born combatant, the champion of the oppressed'. Being enthused with a sense of adventure – without which 'I should be dead' – Dr Murdoch did not suffer fools gladly, nor bores, and would defiantly sit in her car in her garage for nearly an hour to avoid such people.[14]

In the mid-1890s Mary was assisted in Hull by Dr Mabel Jones, who left to work in Brighton.[15] Then in 1900 Mary met dazzling Dr Louisa Martindale, who shortly afterwards also joined her in the busy Hull practice. 'The friendship and understanding which grew up between them', Mary's biographer noted discreetly, 'brought a new happiness into her life'. Mary, uninterested in conventional marriage, was very probably a lesbian.

If Mary Murdoch swept all before her in Hull, the wealthy Liberal Martindales of Sussex swept all before them across the globe. Mrs Martindale was ambitious for her daughters to have the magnificent careers her generation had been denied.[16] Louisa, born in 1872, was educated by English and German governesses. She, too, studied at the London School of Medicine for Women; and in 1899–1900, once she qualified, Louisa (Lulu, as she was known to her friends) received a letter from Dr Murdoch offering her the post of assistant at £1 a week (plus 2s 6d [25p] for her laundry). The Martindales looked up Hull on the map, and Lulu set off north. Yet this was not quite the glittering medical career that Mrs Martindale had in mind for her daughter.

About 1900 her mother and sister embarked on a world tour, and Louisa went, too, to study at first-hand hospitals in India, Australia and the US. Mary Murdoch travelled down from Hull to see them off and, Louisa added, 'to remind me that she wanted me to come back to her on my return'. A letter from Murdie (as she was called) awaited Lulu at every port, 'pressing me to join her in partnership', on return.[17]

Finally it was agreed: Lulu would become Murdie's salaried partner; she would share Murdie's house, and be paid a modest £120 a year. To work with such an outstanding woman GP was excellent medical experience, if demanding. If they ever went out in the evening, 'we left our phone numbers with our maids'. Their main diversion was 'public work', notably the campaign for the vote. Louisa inspired Mary. It became a shared crusade, and they set about rousing Hull. As Louisa recorded, 'We started a Women's Suffrage Society . . . holding all committee meetings in our house'. Indeed, in 1904 Mary became founding president of Hull's NUWSS branch. This was active and effective from the start: the branch held monthly discussion meetings which soon attracted 200 members, formed satellite branches in neighbouring towns like Beverley, and presented a petition from the women of Hull to the House of Commons.[18]

Lulu and Murdie's lesbian relationship seems to have been conducted with utmost discretion, further protected by professional propriety and class hauteur. However, the sharing of home-plus-practice seems to have suited Murdie more than Lulu who, in time, found it rather intense and claustrophobic. Mrs Martindale intervened to prise her daughter and her golden career prospects away from provincial Hull, and Louisa left the north in 1906, deeply missed by Mary, for Brighton (where she met the Hon. Ismay Fitzgerald: 'I invited her to come to me for a fortnight, with the result that she stayed thirty-five years').[19] Yet the two women doctors still kept in closest touch long afterwards; Lulu's influence on Murdie left its indelible mark, notably the passionate championing of improved status for women:

> I can't keep out of it. God planted the seed in me when I was born and I have watered it freely . . .
>
> Standing on an almost limitless shore, we can see coming slowly in the great rolling waves which go to make the inevitable high tide of women's progress, kept back often by seemingly impossible rocks and creeks, but still coming on. And no one can keep it back.[20]

Luckily, Mary's rather Whitmanesque prose was accompanied by considerable organising panache. After Louisa left, Mary continued to give priority to suffrage, inspiring others; ten local women stood for election as Poor Law Guardians, while another member (who had been to the International Woman Suffrage Alliance congress in Copenhagen) stood for election as city councillor.[21]

In all this activity, Mary Murdoch was pivotal. It was in her house on Beverley Road that the suffrage committee always met one evening each week. Mary often acted as NUWSS branch delegate, on trips down to London. She also squeezed in suffrage meetings after her hospital rounds: she would hurriedly prepare her talks and then, fortified only by swallowing three raw eggs, race off to local towns by train and speak until her voice gave out. Indeed, Dr Mary Murdoch *was* the suffrage inspiration locally: 'I can play upon their dull souls'.[22]

Initially, Mary clung to her family's Liberalism: she would drive Hull voters to the poll in an open carriage decorated with party colours. Now, thanks to Louisa, this was overtaken by suffrage. So, when in November 1907 the by-election was called, Mary grasped the opportunity for distinctive theatrical display, enlivened by the new suffragist colours of red, white and green. One letter captured her electoral panache:

> Tomorrow is the nomination day, when the candidates go to the Town Hall. I am going to drive through all the chief streets in a brake, with a pair of chestnut horses to show them women mean to be in it [the election]. My seat on the box is very high, like a Highland coach, right over the horses. They are carrying the colours; my whip, with streamers of red, white and green, advertising our big meeting [on Thursday], when I am taking the chair . . .
>
> Even the dogs are wearing the colours . . . We have invited all five [three] candidates to come and speak; all the members [of Parliament?] are watching us closely. The suffragettes have paid us the compliment of not holding a campaign here as they think we are doing it so well, and we never say one word against them.[23]

Mary did indeed drive through the midst of the crowd, to bursts of cheering. The NUWSS took an election committee room and set about advertising the public meeting that she would chair. But as for WSPU suffragettes leaving them a clear field in Hull West, Mary Murdoch had spoken too soon.

During all the WSPU tensions and the split that formed the Women's Freedom League, Mary Gawthorpe was among the witnesses of the divisions over autocratic leadership and the WSPU's growing distance from the ILP. However, as an itinerant organiser, her personal gratitude to the Pankhursts (perhaps increased by economic dependence after her long illness) probably strengthened her loyalty to the leadership. Mary was duly rewarded with a place on the WSPU's national committee, and by November was back on the campaign trail. Ever a popular speaker, she was an obvious choice for the WSPU to despatch off to Hull West.[24]

Mary Murdoch's NUWSS public meeting had billed as speakers both the Labour candidate and the Liberal, Guy Wilson, a patrician figure close to the local aristocracy. Such a Liberal was naturally a red rag to the WSPU bull. Emmeline Pankhurst, star speaker on the by-election circuit, arrived in the city. With victory over the Colne Valley Liberals still a glowing memory, Emmeline wrote to the *Hull Daily Mail* throwing down the suffrage gauntlet once again to the government. She challenged the Liberal candidate whether, 'If elected, will Mr Guy Wilson move an amendment to the King's

22. *Mary Gawthorpe*, centre, *Hull West by-election campaign, November 1907; other women unknown.*

Speech, if Women's Suffrage finds no place in it? . . . Will Mr Guy Wilson do all in his power to persuade the Government to introduce a Government measure', and if the Government refuses, 'is he prepared in that event to oppose the Government?' Unless he pledged to take these actions, Emmeline added menacingly, such a hypocrite, professing to be a friend of suffrage while actually supporting a government which taxes women and obstinately refuses to enfranchise them, must be opposed by 'women who really want votes'.[25] So the gloves were off – between the suffragettes and the Liberals, but also between the tactics of suffragists and suffragettes.

Mary Gawthorpe, along with Nellie Martel and others, arrived in Hull. Mary exuberantly promised the local reporter that she would form a WSPU branch; and that 3,000 type-written circulars would be dispatched to women householders reminding them that, although their names were on the municipal electoral register, they were unable to vote for their own MP simply because they were women. Reviving her old musical skills, Mary even began to rehearse a children's choir, teaching them a 'Votes for Women' song; she added she was planning for polling day a procession of women holding banners, and even a band. The *Hull Daily Mail* gave the suffragettes good coverage, both for being newsworthy and for not being Liberals.

Equally innovatively, a 'Suffragette' card game had been produced: the cards, depicting well-known suffragettes (as well as a 'haunted house' with the shadowy figure of a woman over the Houses of Parliament) were a merchandising novelty and bought by women 'as souvenirs, as well as for entertainment afforded'. Mary Murdoch's dashingly flamboyant carriage and Mary Gawthorpe's choir, the new card game, and the promise of banners were all new Votes for Women spectacle aiming to capture the public imagination. The theatrical display could reach people and places that the familiar appeals to reason might not. Hull West took suffrage by-election choreography to new heights.[26]

Soon, the *Hull Daily Mail* reported: 'The suffragettes take the badinage and the banter of the crowd and give back clever retorts' – always a speciality of Mary Gawthorpe's when addressing open-air street corner meetings.[27] So the scene was set for Hull Women's Suffrage Society's much publicised meeting on 26 November, with both Liberal and Labour candidates, chaired by Mary Murdoch. The hall was packed to standing. Suffragettes turned up in numbers to heckle Guy Wilson. Mary Gawthorpe managed to obtain a stategically positioned seat in the front row alongside the platform. Through Mary Murdoch in the chair, 'a youth' tried to ask Wilson a question which he had written out. The *Hull Daily Mail* reported the unfolding drama: Mary Murdoch was trying to control the meeting when a suffragette voice – undoubtedly Mary Gawthorpe's – rang out clearly:

> 'We may take it that Mr Wilson is here under false pretence. We want a question answering at a woman's meeting representing unenfranchised women'.
>
> 'Will you, if elected, move an amendment to the King's Speech in case woman's suffrage is not included in it?' asked Miss Gawthorpe . . . Her question non-plussed the candidate.
>
> There was considerable commotion, and it was clear that there were several sympathisers of the suffragettes present.
>
> 'I ought to have notice [of the question]', said Mr Wilson.
>
> There were several interjections, when, above the commotion, came another suffragette, clear and resonant. 'Mr Wilson knows his opinion, surely'.
>
> 'I am in favour of women's suffrage,' said Mr Wilson.
>
> 'That is not the answer to my question. If woman's suffrage is not in the King's Speech, then we shall not have it next session. Will you in that case move an amendment to show that you have a genuine belief in woman's suffrage?'
>
> The question was cheered from different parts of the meeting.
>
> Mr Wilson continued to be most courteous to the suffragettes, who appeared to be dotted about in all parts of the crowded seats.

Liberals, growing annoyed at Mary Gawthorpe's persistent heckling, retaliated with cheers when Wilson gave an unhelpfully evasive reply. Mary resumed her front-row seat. The suffragettes persisted; but their frustration grew, especially when Mary Murdoch ruled from the chair that no further questions be asked of Wilson – who had already picked up his hat 'ready for escaping'. Suffragettes began to leave too. However, Mary Gawthorpe managed to have the last word, declaring emphatically:

'Other ladies who are in Hull will know that Mr Wilson is not going to do anything for them. (Applause) We apologise to Miss Murdoch for interrupting. We came to see the representative of the Government in power which denies justice to women.'

At this point, Mary Murdoch explained that the NUWSS was non-political, supporting both Labour and Liberal candidates because both promised to support women's suffrage – unlike the Tory:

'who gave as a reason why he could not support women's suffrage that woman was too good and too gentle to mix up in the mire of politics, but it was a remarkable fact that Sir George Bartley had the assistance of a large number of ladies to do the nasty, dirty work of canvassing. I hope that women will set their face against such dirty work until they could themselves go to the polling station, and put their cross to a ballot paper'. (Applause)[28]

Mary Murdoch was an adroit and witty chair.[29] The by-election built to a climax. On Thursday 28 Adela Pankhurst, now aged twenty-two, hurried breathlessly across to Hull, spoke at no fewer than three meetings that evening, and then without a pause hastened back to the West Riding.

During the count, Mary Gawthorpe, Nellie Martel, and other suffragettes gathered among the crowd of women on the Town Hall balcony. In fact, despite all the barracking, Wilson won – though his Liberal vote was reduced by more than 3,000. Mary Gawthorpe told the *Hull Daily Mail* that, for his narrow defeat, the Tory had only himself to blame, once 'he declared himself dead against woman's suffrage'. Mary, much given to blithe promises, assured the reporter that the suffragette campaign in Hull was not at an end and she would stay and try to form a branch.

Indeed, the Hull West contest showed that the suffrage campaign now reached almost right across the kingdom, out even to the fishermen on the

North Sea docksides. No Liberal candidate was safe; suffragettes as fearless as Mary Gawthorpe would persist with heckling, even winning some sympathy from the election crowd. And the WSPU and NUWSS were both offering wider and more colourful campaigning, with flamboyant street-theatre spectacle, fun, and even card games.

However, Victor Grayson's Colne Valley victory had proved to be a false dawn: Liberals across Yorkshire were difficult to dislodge. And, once the election excitement subsided in isolated Hull, it appeared too difficult to sustain a WSPU presence there – compared to the more stable organisational credibility of the NUWSS branch.

Dr Mary Murdoch not only continued with suffrage, but also became caught up in public health campaigns. Louisa Martindale had earlier caused uproar by declaring forty per cent of Hull pupil teachers had lice; now indefatigable Mary railed against appalling local housing conditions, without which good doctoring was just a drop in a slum-lord's insanitary bucket; her outspokenness led to howls of protest from Hull property owners. All the while, Mary continued to 'descend "like a whirlwind" upon her friends in Brighton in the middle of the night', sitting and talking animatedly till dawn, sleeping an hour, then catching the morning train back to Hull, for her hospital round and GP's surgery.[30]

As the suffrage battle developed during 1908–9, Mary Murdoch, perhaps softened by suffragettes like Mary Gawthorpe, developed far greater sympathy for militancy than many other suffragists. Indeed, when the NUWSS publicly disassociated itself from suffragette militancy, Mary Murdoch threatened in a fiery letter that the Hull branch would fiercely protest:

> We shall whip up as many votes as possible, but London has so many branches it can always outvote us. However, if the resolution is carried . . . we shall publish our protest on the same day . . . Then our Committee will secede in a body from the Union [NUWSS] . . . I will not condemn them [suffragettes] in public, even if death comes.[31]

Mary Murdoch had lost her temper, and in the event Hull did not secede. But she sent in her personal resignation from the NUWSS (though retaining her close personal friendship with Mrs Fawcett). Indeed, Mary (like Bertha Lowenthal before her) even joined the WSPU, subscribing to its funds; however, she had little sympathy with its autocratic leadership style and increased militancy, and does not seem to have been active. She relished the 'indescribable freedom of having no party'.

Further north, Marion Coates-Hanson and her Middlesbrough Women's Freedom League [WFL] branch were joined by Alice Schofield. Alice, born in 1881, was a trained teacher who had come under the influence of Teresa Billington-Greig when they taught in the same Manchester school. Her interest in suffrage was aroused while walking through Manchester with her grandfather and hearing Emmeline Pankhurst speaking to a crowd about Votes for Women. Like both Teresa and Marion, Alice also joined the WSPU early on, and also then left in 1907 to join the new WFL. From spring 1908 she worked as a WFL organiser, sent to the north-east, and by 1909 this took her to Middlesbrough. Here, at a rowdy open-air meeting in nearby Guisborough, she was rescued from the violent mob throwing rotten eggs and tomatoes by Marion's elder brother Charles Coates, now a fairly wealthy coal exporter. They married, and Alice Schofield-Coates also settled in Middlesbrough's Linthorpe suburb; helped by servants (including governesses later for the children), she continued her League organising.[32]

Both Alice and her sister-in-law Marion remained key members of the small Middlesbrough WFL branch. While isolated, it prided itself on its democracy, friendships, and tolerance towards other groups. It also staged imaginative suffrage productions. From about 1908–9, the Actresses' Franchise League plays department enriched local campaigns by offering wonderful scripts. Middlesbrough was one of the WFL branches which was lent costumes and props so that it could put on performances of *A Pageant of Great Women* by Cicely Hamilton, herself an early WFL member and founder of the Women Writers' Suffrage League. This pageant was designed to encourage suffragettes locally to stage artistic propaganda with minimum professional support: Cicely Hamilton even came up to Middlesbrough to play the leading role, 'Woman'.[33]

Nationally the WFL always worked imaginatively with suffrage's cultural propaganda, often with stunning panache. It too now devised its own suffrage colours: green, white and gold. League branches in the North East planned a Green, Gold and White Fair, and Middlesbrough bought a branch banner. Such was the richness and variety of the growing suffrage campaign.[34] The Coates dynasty, through Alice and Marion, confirms how Votes for Women tentacles now reached even to isolated Middlesbrough. With novel playing cards and Mary Murdoch's dashing by-election carriage suffrage was brought centre-stage and registered it indelibly in the Edwardian popular imagination.

23. Alice Schofield, Women's Freedom League.

24. Women's Freedom League banner, 'Dare to be Free', with symbolism of wings of freedom rising from a beating heart, embroidered in green, white and gold.

CHAPTER 8

'Womanly endurance': Edith Key and Lavena Saltonstall
1908–1909

While Mary Murdoch fought the Hull West by-election and the Coates clan created Middlesbrough's Women's Freedom League, the rebel girls of the Pennine West Riding remained largely loyal to the Pankhursts. WSPU membership was no longer an easy option, as direct confrontation with Liberal politicians escalated. For instance, in November 1907, Home Secretary Herbert Gladstone speaking in his Leeds constituency was howled down and, the papers headlined the next morning, 'put to flight'.[1] Even suffragette propaganda meetings now demanded thoughtful planning and preparation.

By the end of 1907 Huddersfield branch members were beginning to feel the strain. WSPU leaders like Christabel Pankhurst and Emmeline Pethick-Lawrence who had earlier readily agreed to come up to speak now seemed rather more elusive. This made good tactical sense to WSPU headquarters: the Huddersfield area, having had two by-elections, was no longer a political priority. But to the local committee trying to pin down speakers, it felt like a vexing snub. Organising a mass meeting for November, Edith Key wrote again to Emmeline Pethick-Lawrence begging her to reconsider and adding 'we've been disappointed before'; failing her, they would book Mary Gawthorpe.

In fact, Huddersfield remained a vital northern outpost for the WSPU, and both Emmeline and Christabel *were* pinned down. However, with Bertha Lowenthal a lone well-to-do member in a predominantly working-class group, the branch had financial anxieties too, despite the fund-rising whist drives. Edith had to write to Christabel, requesting that the national 'Union will be responsible for expenses if Mass Meeting is a financial failure', believing that, like a trade union, the whole would support the local parts.[2] Eventually window bills advertising this December meeting were printed and 'girls for literature stall asked to sell postcards'. Then there was security to arrange, given the real fears that the tag of suffragette militancy would trigger crowd violence, condoned by the police. Edith Key's committee went to great lengths to ensure safety, carefully noting that the three policemen required initially were doubled to six, and that husbands (like Bob Pinnance) would act as stewards and doorkeepers.[3]

On the platform at the mass meeting in Huddersfield Town Hall sat local suffragettes, including some who had been imprisoned (probably Ellen Beever and Annie Sykes, Elizabeth Pinnance and Ellen Brooke). However, Laura Wilson, who was in the chair, had hardly begun speaking before the meeting was violently interrupted by hecklers at the back. The stewards and the half-dozen police threw out about twenty 'irresponsible youths'. Then, as soon as Emmeline Pethick-Lawrence stood up to speak there was immediately another disturbance at the back. Once the hecklers had been ejected, Christabel Pankhurst spoke without interruption. She gave a compelling address on how the Liberals were not liberal enough, explaining the WSPU's tactics of interrupting Liberal meetings like that of Herbert Gladstone.[4]

It was all growing rather edgy. Public safety could no longer be guaranteed, and this sense of real danger took its toll. By Christmas, the Huddersfield WSPU branch was beginning to feel rather fragile. So when Edith Key sat down at New Year 1908 to write her first annual report, she thought carefully about what to say. So much drama had erupted in just twelve months, with such transformations in the lives of many of those eighty women who had so readily signed up just a year earlier. Reading her report a century later, we can distinctly hear Edith Key's voice − slightly anxious, but unyielding in its commitment to the cause. Her heartfelt candour offers rare insight into the thinking of community suffragettes then. Regularly dipping her pen into the inkwell, Edith Key set down in neatly sloping handwriting the events since the branch's inauguration by Emmeline Pankhurst and Nellie Martel; she chronicled all its campaigns, and added:

> This year's record, though it has entailed much self-sacrifice on the part of our women, especially those who have suffered imprisonment, has demonstrated their determination to force upon the attention of the nation the fact that women must be recognised as citizens equally with men. In

those cases where our undertakings [i.e. events] have not paid their own
way, socials and whist drives have been arranged, the success of which have
[*sic*] enabled us to close the year with a small money balance to the Branch's
credit.

In addition to the work which the Branch has accomplished *as* a Branch
[i.e. locally], many of its members rendered useful service to the Cause as
anti-Government crusaders during the Colne Valley by-election; and at
Batley, Leeds and Huddersfield, and other places where Cabinet Ministers
have been advertised to speak, have gained admission to their meetings, and
aided in putting such Ministers to confusion.

There is one regrettable feature in connection with our Branch, which I
am aware, is common experience in every kind of movement. It is, that
though we have so large a number of names on our books, the whole of the
sacrifice, and the brunt of the work is left to be borne by a small band of
determined spirits.

I would therefore urge all women that it is their duty to strengthen
the hands of our members in order that justice may be secured for our
sex.

In conclusion, it is my duty on behalf of the Branch, to thank our
numerous male friends who have in any way rendered service to the
Branch, either as door-keepers, stewards, suppressors of disorder,
protectors, speakers, or press correspondents; and to hope in the coming
year which will undoubtedly be an eventful one, we may count on a
continuance of their sympathy and practical assistance.

Signed, Edith A Key
Hon Sec[5]

Strikingly, Edith's language of personal 'sacrifice' is almost religious in
tone. The moral burden, despite all the impressive branch activity, was
almost impossible to sustain. There was a sense of personal exhaustion
among these plucky Huddersfield suffragettes. However, more still was
demanded of them in the onslaught on the Liberal government.[6]

The WSPU escalated the campaign with exciting publicity coups. In
January 1908, Flora Drummond led a group of suffragettes into Downing
Street while a cabinet meeting was in progress and chained herself to the
railings, an action rewarded by three weeks in prison — and subsequently
immortalised in suffrage history books.

However, campaigning grew increasingly dangerous. Laura Wilson and

Jennie Baines tracked Herbert Asquith, Chancellor of the Exchequer, across to Lancaster. Laura tried to enter Asquith's meeting, but after she was ejected, both women spoke from a 'lurry'. The anti-suffrage crowd tried to topple it right over a six-foot parapet, though sympathisers managed to prevent this. Their lurry was still dragged some distance, to the cry of 'Rush them into the canal'. Police had to form a bodyguard, and Jennie Baines and her husband managed to escape. However, the crowd caught hold of Laura Wilson and tore her dress. It was only the intervention of two burly attendants from the local asylum that allowed her to flee into a backyard and, through a clever police ruse, eventually to make her escape.[7] The peril now had an edge of violence.

More broadly, WSPU demands upon local suffragettes grew. Annie Kenney and Adela Pankhurst were back in Huddersfield in February – urging members once again to go down to London and take part in the third WSPU Women's Parliament, timed again for the King's Speech. Branch members wanted to avoid any repetition of Dora Thewlis being pilloried before the nation's newspaper-reading eyes, her adolescent isolation in Holloway paraded before the public. They knew this time that the action needed careful thought and planning. The threat of arrest and imprisonment loomed large.

Inevitably, the number of suffragettes prepared to go down from branches like Huddersfield and Halifax was smaller than the previous year. Young, single and living in lodgings, Lavena Saltonstall had less to risk than others. Although still a shadowy figure, Lavena was emerging as a particularly quixotic suffragette, and was the only woman to venture down from Halifax (she might have already given up her weaving job, predicting another spell in prison would put it at risk).

The WSPU Women's Parliament started on Tuesday 11 February, 1908. According to Lavena's own rather idiosyncratic account of events, she went – or so she claimed – at the head of a small deputation to present a petition to the Prime Minister. (In fact, she was probably among a group of suffragettes determined to march to Parliament, then rush with the petition into the House of Commons lobby.) Security was tight. 'The police on duty outside were having the sharpest tussle they have ever had with the suffragettes, who came from all parts of the country', reported the *Daily Mirror*. By the end of the day there were over fifty arrests.[8]

These suffragettes were taken to Cannon Row police station where they were charged. Twenty-six-year-old Lavena gave her address as Haugh

Shaw Road, Halifax and was listed as 'of no occupation'. Perhaps due to unforeseen overcrowding, the women were allocated unusual accommodation – whence Lavena wrote a defiantly witty letter to the *Halifax Courier*, published the next day:

Cannon-row Police Station billiard-room
Feb 11, 10 p.m.

Sir,
According to everybody's expectations, I am writing to you at the above address. There is a sort of 'no-place-like-home' feeling among the 50 of us. There are more [suffragette arrests] to follow. I don't suppose editors or reporters or the majority of Halifax natives will ever possess the necessary qualifications for a peep inside Cannon-row Police Station . . . so I will let you know how we have spent the time.

First of all, as head of a small deputation, I went towards the House [of Commons] where the police resisted me in the performance of my duty – namely, presenting a resolution to C-B [Campbell-Bannerman]. I got arrested. Unfortunately I lost my followers in the crowd.

After we were charged, we went up into the billiard-room, where tea was sent in; the officers off duty 'shopped' for us. I procured stamps, and postcards, and writing paper. We are not to go out till the House rises – so say the officials. I wonder how far it has to rise. We whiled away the time singing and reciting, and the gentlemen in blue enjoyed it as much as we did. I shall conclude in wishing success to the police concert. I had intended going, but fate decreed otherwise.

Yours sincerely,
Lavena Saltonstall

and on the back of this bizarrely carefree letter she added laconically, 'I got my arm hurt in the struggle'.[9]

The following day, Wednesday 12th, Lavena and the others appeared in court, charged with insulting behaviour and obstructing the police. Prosecuting once again, Mr Muskett questioned a constable – who told the court how at 4.40 p.m. he had been on duty in Parliament Square 'when I saw Saltonstall make several attempts to get into the House of Commons', pushing up against the line of police guarding the building. Twice, he stated, he asked her to move away but on both occasions she refused; indeed she tried to rescue another arrested woman by grabbing hold of the constable's belt. So he arrested her. Asked in court if she had anything to say in her defence, Lavena merely replied, 'I have nothing to say except he [the constable] resisted me in the execution of my duty'. Significantly Lavena was borrowing the language of citizens' rights and duties, playing pompous Liberals' hypocrisies back to them in court. The magistrate bound Lavena over to keep the peace; but she insouciantly refused – and was dispatched to prison. From here, ever the news journalist, she immediately despatched another telegraphic postcard to the *Halifax Courier*:

> Rochester-row Police Cells
> February 12, 1908
>
> To Editor of 'Courier',
> Sentenced to six weeks in second division, or keep the peace for twelve months. Have chosen the least of two evils – six weeks – LAVENA SALTONSTALL.[10]

If she served her full term, Lavena would not be released till the end of March.

Not all those arrested seemed so carefree. In Huddersfield, the WSPU branch waited anxiously during Tuesday for news of the Women's Parliament. They heard that Ellen Brooke and Ann Older, both from the Honley area, had indeed been arrested. At the branch meeting that evening, their fate was naturally the main topic. The branch stood firmly behind them both, passing two resolutions, one congratulating Ellen and Ann and the other congratulating the Women's Parliament. However, the members' mood changed somewhat when the length of the prison sentences sunk in. Keenly aware of what six weeks in Holloway meant, Edith Key again sat down five days later to write to the two women who were locked up:

> Dear Friends
> The members of the Huddersfield Women's Social and Political Union desire me to convey to you an expression of their appreciation of your action and to hope that your health and strength and womanly endurance may enable you to complete your sentences, so neither Government or that part of the public still hostile to the just claims of

our sex, shall find satisfaction in having broken the spirits of our sisters
in Holloway Gaol.

> With best wishes, I am
> Yours in the cause,
> Edith A. Key
> Hon. Sec.[11]

It was a moving letter to receive in gaol – where every prison regulation
felt as if purposefully designed to break the spirit of even the most steadfast
suffragette held behind bars. The letter was inspired by the ideal of personal
sacrifice to the great, glorious Cause.

Emmeline Pankhurst was arrested on 13 February, the last day of the
Women's Parliament, and was also sentenced to six weeks. Her first spell in
prison, it was a harsh experience which she never forgot. She was released
on 19 March, as was Lavena Saltonstall. Next morning the released prisoners were entertained to a welcome breakfast, after which they rushed off
to Peckham in south London where another by-election had been called.
The women paraded through the streets in open brakes, dressed in close
reproductions of their prison clothes.[12]

Lavena then returned home to Halifax. That evening, local suffragettes
mounted a welcome meeting in the town. Laura Wilson had, however,
hardly begun speaking before a howl went up 'Goa hooam an' mend yer
husband's socks', and she was drowned out by youths breaking into song.
'Ugly scrimmages were indulged in', despite pleading from male sympathisers. Pandemonium erupted when Lavena herself tried to explain her
aim of reaching the Houses of Parliament. Yet she gave as good as she got:
'A lot of you may sneer at women but you aren't brave enough to go to
prison'. The crowd grew threatening, one rush nearly toppling Laura and
another trampling several suffragettes underfoot. Lavena herself was
severely kicked. As the crowd began to throw missiles, Laura had to close
the meeting. Afterwards, suffragettes were chased through the town-
centre streets by a crowd of hundreds.[13] In a close-knit local community
like Halifax, life as a known suffragette was no longer a comfortable option.

In Huddersfield, the WSPU branch carefully took stock of the emerging
situation, and continued business-as-usual, running a ninepenny fund-
raising dance while selling the new suffragette weekly *Votes for Women* paper
and badges.[14]

Then, in April, prospects for women's enfranchisement began to look

even grimmer. Campbell-Bannerman was replaced as Prime Minister by
Herbert Asquith. Asquith combined the Liberals' political fear that enfran-
chising women would benefit the Conservatives electorally, with personal
elite male anti-suffrage prejudice. In addition, when Asquith had been
Home Secretary in the 1890s, he had had to deal with the political violence
threatened by both European anarchists and Irish protesters. He had taken
a tough line with political disorder and law-breaking, refusing to distinguish between 'political' and 'non-political' offenders. The conflict between
suffragettes and Liberal politicians now sharpened.[15]

The cabinet reshuffle triggered ministerial by-elections. Among those
involved was Winston Churchill. A by-election was called in North West
Manchester, with Churchill standing as the Liberal candidate. It promised
to be a flamboyant contest: Eva Gore-Booth's sister, Constance Markiewicz,
arrived from Ireland and lent panache to the proceedings by driving a
coach, drawn by four white horses, through the city to publicise the radical suffragists' cause. Christabel Pankhurst set up WSPU shop in her home
city, too.

Lavena Saltonstall was one of the suffragettes who agreed to campaign
in Manchester. Once more, she wrote a spirited account of the contest
which captured both the escalating danger and the suffragettes' sense of
impish fun. After her years in the clothing factory, Lavena was now having
the time of her life. In North-West Manchester, she wrote:

No party has expended more time or energy than we suffragettes have.
Every day we have chalked all the pavements with the times of our meetings, also the names of the speakers. Personally, I find these expeditions full
of adventure, which is just what I enjoy. Sometimes I have to leave off
chalking to head a meeting in the streets in order to answer questions.

Canvassing also I have found full of incident. I absolutely love the
Ancoats people, and especially those who live in the darkest and poorest districts . . . The open-air meetings are the best for propagating our cause. The
most curious thing happens whenever we appear on the scene.

The Conservative may be holding forth . . . The Liberal may be making
a thousand promises . . . the Socialist may be banging one fist on top of
another . . . but whenever we make our appearance every orator loses his
crowd and they all come around us . . .

There is an element in the city who make it their business to attend our
principal meetings and try to overturn the waggon . . . To-night three of us
went to Stevenson Square . . . There were in the crowd hundreds of lads

ranging up to 16 or 17 years of age who made it their business to throw missiles . . .

The Manchester police have put forth every effort to save us from these hooligans . . . After the police got us from the crowd they escorted us back to the hotel where we meet every night to recount our adventures . . .

Each night we [also] repair to a certain café where reporters join us. Uninterested spectators would . . . never imagine we are plotting the downfall of Mr Churchill. On Friday we are putting forth every effort to smite the Government. Each one of us is to be in charge of a polling booth. Mine is St Matthew's school, Byron-street. Our business will be to 'keep the Liberal out'.[16]

In fact, Churchill was defeated and the Conservative elected (though this may have been due more to the constituency's natural Toryism than to Lavena's campaigning).

Another by-election was triggered in April for Dewsbury. Here the Labour candidate was Ben Turner who, like his fellow trade unionist Allen Gee, was specially sympathetic to the WSPU. Suffragettes, among them Lavena and Laura Wilson, went to help this loyal suffrage supporter, sharing a waggon with Christabel Pankhurst. Ben Turner recalled how, in his area of the constituency, his own family offered them shelter after crowd trouble:

When the militant suffragettes came to Batley they got thrown out of the public hall just for interjecting observations. Young Liberals and young Tories delighted in pushing them about. About ten of the folks finished up in the Market Place with a great meeting in sympathy with them and then dined at our house and slept as best they could on the floors and couches and beds we had.[17]

Meanwhile, the WSPU was planning a great demonstration in Hyde Park for June. Well beforehand, branches were encouraged to commit themselves to it. Huddersfield members resolved they would try to attend and ordered two dozen tickets. Yet there remained nagging anxieties about the cost, despite the whist drives and dances.[18] This became a worry because, following the NUWSS's innovative colours (red, white and green), Emmeline Pethick-Lawrence decided to use Hyde Park to launch the WSPU's own colours: purple, white and green. The WSPU leadership saw this made good campaigning sense: co-ordinated imagery would make a far more magnificent splash. Unfortunately for Huddersfield, the branch had just ordered special members' scarves with white lettering printed on black. So, the following week Edith Key had to enquire about the price of new scarves, badges and rosettes for Hyde Park, though no order seems to have been placed. Members felt increasingly put-upon. Sensing that enthusiasm in this key northern outpost was flagging, Annie Kenney's sister, Nell Kenney, also a WSPU organiser, was sent to ginger them up to send large numbers to Hyde Park.[19]

As the next chapter shows, the Hyde Park demonstration was a tremendous success, but the cost to local members was considerable. The Huddersfield branch, usually so active, went strangely quiet for the next six weeks. Regular branch business was suspended while a big demonstration was planned for September, and members had to work under Adela Pankhurst's direction to ensure its success. Success it was, with Emmeline Pankhurst and Mary Gawthorpe speaking.

Nevertheless, the steam seemed to be gradually ebbing out of the branch. By February 1909, when Edith Key's minutes book ends, branch energies were focused on survival. Weekly meetings had been replaced by monthly discussion classes (on, for instance, the position of married women). Bertha Lowenthal offered a cake as first prize for a fund-raising whist drive, with refreshments bought out of 'Union Funds', (six white bread rolls, a jar of potted beef, 1 lb butter).[20] The WSPU branch minutes seem to end abruptly on this note of catering pathos; the initial energy of so many women was hard to sustain in the face of so many difficulties.

However, individual campaigning certainly continued in Huddersfield even though, with no further branch records, it is more difficult to track local activities. Edith Key's papers throw sudden shafts of light: they include typescript memoirs by her sons, Lancelot then aged about seventeen, and Archibald two years younger. Archie recalled the impact his mother's continuing suffragette role had on their home. In addition to their ILP father:

Mother was also on the political road, making trips to Manchester to confer with suffragettes Emmeline Pankhurst and her three daughters. Simultaneously then the music room became unofficial headquarters for the ILP and plotting room for suffragette militancy . . .

[WSPU] regional administration was strictly a pay-as-you-go [i.e. voluntary] service . . . Our home became regional headquarters where skullduggery, illegal acts and conspiracies were continually hatched.[21]

Archie confessed himself to be 'desperately in love' with Adela even though she was some nine years older than he was. Lancelot also recalled the Pankhursts: 'I got to know the inner workings [of the WSPU branch] because most of their meetings were held at Bradford Road', the family home: he and his brother 'had to turn out' when their parents offered hospitality to visiting speakers.[22] The two boys were also now old enough to act as bodyguards for their mother's courageous suffragette friends; and independent businesswoman Edith Key was strong enough and unusual enough to raise her voice bravely and persistently about suffrage in her own home town.[23]

It is more difficult to track Lavena Saltonstall's own thinking at this time. Even after her kicking by the local crowd, Lavena retained her suffragette exuberance. She had glimpsed new freedoms and these had transformed her life. There could be no turning back. Laura Wilson and other friends in the local labour movement seem to have helped Lavena to find employment and become involved in trade union organising.[24] Yet even Lavena, after enduring two imprisonments, was really beginning to wonder about the value of militancy as a tactic, and whether it might not be more effective to take a longer view of how to win votes for women.

Soon after her release from Holloway and after the Manchester by-election, Lavena decided her life should take off in a fresh direction. In early May 1908 she and Laura Wilson went 'on the tramp' – from Halifax to Wakefield, a distance of about twenty-five miles; they intended to gain admittance to a workhouse casual ward. Lavena, never a woman to let a journalistic opportunity slide, was soon writing a regular weekly column for the new *Halifax Labour News* on suffrage, religion and politics – including 'Suffragettes on Tramp':

> It was during my enforced stay as one of His Majesty's guests in Holloway Gaol this year that I fell to wondering what sort of life tramps enjoyed. I had ample time for making resolutions during my five weeks' imprisonment, and one of the resolutions I made was to go on 'tramp' as soon as an opportunity presented itself. Being a Suffragette, the moment the opportunity came I seized it . . .
>
> We collected old clothes . . . We decided to warble some soul-stirring tunes if we had hard times . . . Finally all arrangements were made for a week on the tramp, and accordingly on the 5th of May, clad in garments of an antiquated design, with print aprons to cover our dresses, we sallied forth . . .

We tried to comfort ourselves with the thought that at any rate it was our choice to be on tramp, but even this did not make us feel less tired, less hungry or more cheerful . . . The word 'dinner' roused tender memories . . .

A deadly feeling of faintness came over me, gripping me from head to foot. But I fought against it. I had only once in all my life experienced that same feeling, and that was in Holloway Gaol, towards the end of my sentence. Suffragettes have not to give in to every passing feeling of faintness they may experience.

We passed through Dewsbury. We passed the Market Place where, at the commencement of the election, we had stood on a waggon with Miss Pankhurst . . . We kept steadily on tramp till 3 p.m., by which time we had arrived at Ossett . . . We had now been nine hours without food.

Eventually, Lavena and Laura reached the station at Wakefield; here, assisted by local police, Laura telegraphed home for the train fare back and these two women managed to make their way back to Halifax.[25]

This was a post-imprisonment springtime escapade. Lavena never lost her suffragette faith; but for the longer term, she now seized wider opportunities – to continue her education which had been so abruptly halted half a lifetime earlier.[26] Luckily, a new self-organising Workers' Education Association (WEA) was now in existence and in 1909 a branch was formed in Halifax. Lavena was soon caught up in a WEA tutorial class on economics.[27] She also contributed a 'WEA Corner' column to the local paper, her subjects ranging from votes for women to social inter-dependency. The latter, inspired by her economics tutor, even managed a side-swipe at Asquith:

Among other lectures we have had was one wherein we learned that, with all our vain talk about individual and British independence, all of us – from the gravedigger and gas inspector down to the mere politicians who are talking twaddle about manhood suffrage – all are dependent upon hosts of people for all our blessings and miseries.

It seems we can neither eat nor be merry without the help of thousands of other people. Shirtmakers, bootmakers, butchers, bakers and candlestick workers, dyers, . . . weavers, dockyard labourers . . . each have to contribute their share before any of us can call ourselves civilised. Even the Prime Minister has to be indebted to his laundress, charwoman, cook, housemaid and mother before he can – with any dignity – voice his humble and elementary opinion of woman's qualification for a vote.[28]

Adult education certainly gave Lavena's drive an additional fillip. From this sprang her sharpest journalism, now reaching a broader readership. Lavena's 'Letters of a Tailoress' for the WEA magazine drew upon her memory of growing up a rebel girl in claustrophobic Hebden Bridge:

> If girls develop any craving for a different life or wider ideas, their mothers fear that they are going to become Socialists or Suffragettes – a Socialist being a person with lax views about other people's watches and purses, and a Suffragette a person whose house is always untidy.

Life remained a journey, an adventure, Lavena added:

> I only pass through this world once, and I don't intend to pass through, as a bird flies through the air, leaving no track behind. There are plenty of people plodding along beaten tracks without my joining the company. There are miles and miles of little-frequented paths on life's highway and faintly marked pathways always attracted me more than the beaten road.[29]

Life for rebel girls like Lavena would never be the same again. Even though she now avoided further arrest and imprisonment, she never lost her original anger – nor did her new confidence dull her incisiveness. As an adult student, she took on a socialist novelist, Ethel Carnie, who attacked the WEA for 'chloroforming the workers' by not offering revolutionary political education. Lavena resented such condescension. She demanded for WEA students like herself as wide a cultural curriculum as the well-to-do had always been able to enjoy: 'Greek art will never keep the workers from claiming their world; in fact, it will help them realise what a stunted life they have hitherto led. Nothing that is beautiful will harm the workers'. She added,

> The members of the [WEA] tutorial classes are quite as able as herself to hear a lecture on industrial history, or economics, or Robert Browning, and remain quite sane. As a Socialist, as a trade unionist, as a suffragist – or a suffragette, if you like – I resent Miss Carnie's suggestion that the WEA educational policy can ever make me forget the painful history of Labour, or chloroform my senses to the miseries I see around me.

By 1909 the mass community suffragette uprisings in Halifax and Huddersfield had had their day; their passing symbolised the end of an era for those early WSPU branches based in Pennine mills and workshops.[30] Rather, WSPU militancy began to be shaped by individual suffragette mavericks – both by some familiar names, such as Adela Pankhurst, and those newly sprung up. At the same time, the sustained 'hearts and minds' campaigning of constitutional NUWSS suffragists took Votes for Women imaginatively out, not just to distant cities like Hull and Middlesbrough, but now right out into the furthest Yorkshire dales, wolds and most remote fishing harbours.

CHAPTER 9

Banners and vanners: Isabella Ford and her sisters
1908–1909

Centrally positioned, Leeds remained *the* first city of Yorkshire. With its population of half a million, it was matched only by industrial Sheffield to the south. Bradford immediately to the west and Hull to the east were both half its size, while Huddersfield and Middlesbrough were smaller still.[1] Its Irish and Jewish immigrant communities helped ensure Leeds remained the most cosmopolitan of Yorkshire cities. While Alfred Orage might have left for London to launch the *New Age*, Leeds Arts Club continued with lectures on 'What do we mean by "Ideas?"' and 'Art and Democracy', providing a sympathetic *pied-à-terre* for suffrage. Mary Gawthorpe, who worked in the Leeds-Bradford area during 1908, would drop into its enticing *conversaziones*.[2]

Leeds' pattern of Edwardian suffrage campaigning in many ways followed that of other industrial West Riding communities. Its NUWSS branch collected signatures on the Franchise Declaration and sold badges. Yet for all Isabella Ford's ILP links, it remained resolutely middle-class, largely rooted in the drawing rooms of Headingley and the northern suburbs; fluctuated, probably with liberal-leaning members now feeling constrained about pressurising the government beyond its levels of activity.[3]

Leeds' WSPU, however, attracted a new and different group of women, many of them working-class 'rebel girls'; they lived in the city itself or its inner suburbs, so familiar to Mary Gawthorpe from childhood.[4] During the Women's Parliament in February 1907, Leeds suffragettes who were arrested and imprisoned included two teenagers, both from the congested city streets depicted so graphically by Orage. Elsie May Stevenson was a twenty-one-year-old typist. Alice Noble worked as a domestic servant; her age was given in court as eighteen, but she was more probably sixteen like

Dora Thewlis. Of the others, forty-year-old Blanche Stevenson was a housekeeper, looking after the children of a twine-and-thread manufacturer; as he lived further out, this was probably a fairly isolating job. Mary Titterington aged fifty was a draper married to a bootmaker-shopkeeper; the family lived down near the River Aire and had at least four children, of whom two daughters helped sew the boots.[5]

Sadly, most of these Leeds suffragettes remain fleeting figures, with just a brief newspaper reference of an arrest to help track an address. But there the detective trail stops, for no WSPU minutes book, lying hidden for a century, has come to light. After Mary Gawthorpe left, Leeds has no intimate written suffragette record – until Leonora Cohen becomes active a few years later. For the suffragists, there is no Florence Lockwood with her diaries, or Edith Key with her minutes book. The suffrage history of this great city remains tantalisingly unrecorded, even within its own local histories.

However, Leeds stood out among the other large Yorkshire towns and cities in one important way: not only was it represented in the Commons by *five* MPs (four Liberals, one Labour), but the Leeds West MP was none other than the Home Secretary himself, Herbert Gladstone. No surname evoked Liberal values more vividly than 'Gladstone'. Indeed, Herbert himself was actually born in Downing Street (when his father was Chancellor of the Exchequer), and became only the second prime minister's son to reach the cabinet since William Pitt the younger.

Herbert Gladstone had been a Leeds MP since 1880 and had risen comfortably through the Liberal ranks, as chief party whip. He was then Home Secretary for five crucial years, 1905–10, introducing some of the progressive domestic legislation (e.g. the Eight Hours Act) upon which the Liberal government so prided itself. Now he found himself in a tricky situation: unlike Asquith he was not an instinctive opponent of women's enfranchisement; yet he was responsible for public order, the prison service and the security of ministers, notably Asquith himself. Gladstone's cautious balancing act grew trickier from 1907–8 onwards as suffragette militancy mushroomed.[6]

With the Home Secretary as MP for West Leeds, the city acted as a political magnet for itinerant Votes for Women organisers and speakers: Mary Gawthorpe, Emmeline and Adela Pankhurst and others congregated in Leeds for militant actions. Drama frequently followed. When Gladstone spoke in his West Leeds constituency, headlines the next morning proclaimed that 'Suffragettes wreck a West Leeds meeting'.[7]

Then, on 11 February 1908, Leeds suffragettes took part in the WSPU's third Women's Parliament. Along with Lavena Saltonstall, Ann Older and Ellen Brooke from the Honley area, three Leeds suffragettes were arrested – including Mary Titterington again, and her daughter Amy, now aged about twenty-one and working as a milliner. As it was Mary's second time in court, she was given forty shillings or two months; the others were sentenced either to be bound over to keep the peace for a year, or six weeks in prison. They, of course, chose the latter, and were dispatched to Holloway in special vans.[8]

At the same time, a by-election campaign in Liberal-held South Leeds was gathering pace. This drew the WSPU into the city: not only Mary Gawthorpe but also Emmeline and Adela Pankhurst. Mary's anti-Liberal electioneering was emphatic: 'If you vote for the Government, you will plump for [i.e. support] the imprisonment of women, and if you vote against Mr Middlebrook [Liberal] you will give the Government the biggest slap it has had yet'.[9] The campaign culminated in a torchlight procession led by a band, with a rally on Hunslet Moor. Speakers included Emmeline and Adela, Jennie Baines and Nellie Martel, plus Elizabeth Pinnance and Ellen Brooke from Huddersfield. In her autobiography Mrs Pankhurst evoked how 'The throngs of mill women kept up the chorus in broad Yorkshire: "Shall us win? Shall us have the vote? We shall!"' The Hunslet Moor rally was indeed fairly boisterous by-election fare; of the heckling, the *Yorkshire Post* noted laconically, 'At all the platforms there were interruptions, but the suffragettes managed to say a good deal in the three-quarters of an hour they were able to stick to their waggons'.[10]

Of the three candidates, only Labour supported women's suffrage. However, during the by-election, the NUWSS did only general non-party propaganda work – which was acutely frustrating for ILP suffragists like Isabella Ford; she felt hemmed in by NUWSS policy, 'longed to "go for" the Liberal and had to hold myself down' for the present. But ever conciliatory, Isabella reported enthusiastically to her good friend Mrs Fawcett, 'The WSPU behaved splendidly – and there were no rows. I see more and more their policy is far more workable than ours: but we never clashed . . . Mrs Pankhurst's procession was fine and we cheered and waved as they passed our rooms – and they did too'. She added that some women Liberals, feeling growing disaffection for the government, were actually refusing to work for Middlebrook – who, in the event, won. In the longer-term, however, the Leeds suffragettes kept Gladstone and his Liberal cabinet colleagues firmly in their sights.

Such a strategically positioned city was of course the ideal venue for broader suffragette propaganda to win local hearts and minds. To help fund-raising, Emmeline Pethick-Lawrence designated 15–22 February 1908 as Self-Denial Week, the proceeds of doing without luxuries like coffee or tea to be donated to the WSPU. After the by-election, Mary Gawthorpe remained in her home town, probably staying with her mother or married sister. With Jennie Baines she set up a committee room and proceeded to take South Leeds by storm. They obtained a piano-organ:

> One turned the handle and the other, armed with a tambourine, received contributions, and two or three other suffragettes temporarily hauled the machine about pending the arrival of a man, who, it was said, had been engaged for the shafts.
>
> Miss Mary Gawthorpe assisted in the opening of this novel campaign and provided with a green cloth bag on the end of a cane, she very effectively scooped in not merely coppers, but many silver coins.

The site was near Elland Road football ground, so Mary adroitly exploited this novel possibility, attracting favourable publicity in the local papers; she explained she was arranging 'a suffragette benefit match for them [the Leeds team], at which she would kick off'. A few days later the women toured Hunslet, not far from Beeston Hill where Mary, her mother and brother had once fled years earlier. Indeed, the campaign became quite a family affair. The press reported how Mary was assisted by her five-year-old nephew 'who carried a bag such as church wardens use at the end of a stout stick. He stuck to the work quite gamely.'[11] Luckily, the photograph of Mary and young Sidney campaigning has survived, as have her nephew's tiny leather gloves, 'worn by Sidney when helping Auntie['s] Suffragette Work', along with Mary's simple little bag, appliquéd, 'Votes for Women' and on the reverse 'Self Denial', visible in the photograph.[12]

So the general Leeds suffragette pattern emerges: considerable action and itinerant stirrers-up, but with less sense of a strong WSPU branch. Possibly the daunting imprisonment of Mary and Amy Titterington had had a sobering effect on local women. There seemed to be no local Edith Key figure to steady their nerves and introduce the WSPU leaders round the constituency, nor a Bertha Lowenthal to provide some financial stability.

*25. Self Denial Week 15–22 February 1908, Leeds. Mary Gawthorpe, with Self Denial sash and bag.
In foreground, holding a tambourine and wearing a Votes for Women sash, probably nephew Sidney.*

Indeed, the suffragettes dispersed from Leeds after the 1908 by-election, and the work of keeping the Votes for Women campaign alive in the city fell mainly to the more patient suffragists in the local NUWSS branch. Among these, none played a more crucial role than Isabella Ford and her sisters, Emily and Bessie. Bessie especially undertook much of the thankless political drudgery of ensuring the franchise demand did not die between high profile events. Yet, again, we strain to hear the individual voices of the modest Ford sisters, catching it only occasionally.

One of the 'great families' of suffrage, the Ford sisters, now in their fifties, still lived at Adel Grange – along with their five indoor servants, coachman and gardener. Of the three, Emily was the most conservative. She had not joined her sisters in the labour movement; rather, she had converted from Quakerism to Anglicanism, painting several altar panels for churches in Leeds and London. However, women's suffrage brought her back to working with them in this common cause. Emily had a *pied-à-terre* cottage and studio in Chelsea, described as a 'meeting ground for artists, suffragists, people who <u>did</u> things'.[13] Indeed, she was vice-chairman of the Artists' Suffrage League, and her best-known poster design illustrates the hypocrisy of denying working women the vote.

Isabella was closer in her affections to Bessie. Bessie was treasurer of the Leeds Suffrage Society and both sisters were vice-presidents. Isabella was

They have a cheek, I've never been asked!

26. Designed by Emily Ford, 'Factory Acts', 1908, published by the Artists' Suffrage League.

not only a key branch speaker, but also somehow took on the presidency of nearby Bradford Society; and the Fords also hosted garden parties, meetings and fund-raising events at Adel Grange.[14] The three sisters running the Leeds Suffrage Society almost on their own had advantages (sustaining it during lean years), but some very distinct disadvantages (deterring the growth of a next generation to pass the baton to). One gets a sense of the Fords no longer feeling able to conjure up much inspiration: it took all their energy to keep things going. They did not need to offer political chaperonage, as there were no young suffragists needing it: in Leeds, as across Liberal Yorkshire, the NUWSS never really drew recruits from the next generation who had great impact.[15]

Kindly Isabella, caricatured by some as a plain English spinster, was seen by others as a witty and inspiring speaker. She was certainly active on the national suffrage stage: a long-serving member of the NUWSS executive, who represented the NUWSS at the International Woman Suffrage Alliance congresses – a useful choice as she 'had' languages, being fluent in both French and German.

From 1908, the unwitting agents for ratcheting up NUWSS campaigns into a more imaginative and effective gear were Liberal politicians themselves. Their obduracy in the face of growing franchise demands provoked increasingly deep frustration. Out of this anger grew not only the well-known spiralling of suffragette militancy, but also the NUWSS's reaching out imaginatively to new publics. Isabella Ford and her sisters were centrally involved in this, both with the new banners and also as intrepid 'vanners'.

Herbert Asquith, long-standing opponent of enfranchisement, argued that women did not care about the vote. Shortly before becoming Prime Minister in April 1908 he had offered to lift his opposition 'the moment I am satisfied of two things, but not before, namely, first, that the majority of women desire to have a Parliamentary vote, and next, that the conferring of a vote upon them would be advantageous to their sex and the community at large.[16]

This was a challenge. Subsequently, Herbert Gladstone, recalling his political youth, had thrown down an even more specific gauntlet to suffrage organisations:

> There comes a time when political dynamics are far more important than political argument . . . Men have learnt this lesson, and know the necessity of demonstrating the greatness of their movements . . . Looking back at the political crises of the 'thirties, the 'sixties and the 'eighties [1832, 1867, 1884 reforms acts] it will be found that people . . . assembled in their tens of thousands all over the country . . . Of course it cannot be expected that women can assemble in such masses, but power belongs to the masses, and through this power a Government can be influenced.[17]

If this pair of Herberts required visible evidence of women's 'desire' and their power of mass assembly, then this is indeed what they would get. In spring 1908, the WSPU, as we know, began organising for its great demonstration in Hyde Park scheduled for 21 June. The NUWSS was equally quick off the mark with theirs on 13 June. Building upon the success of the 'Mud March' a year earlier, it planned even more magnificent pageantry. The NUWSS set up a special Procession Committee, and the Artists' Suffrage League provided an inspiring 'Bugler Girl' poster, with advance publicity displayed on hoardings across the country in the weeks leading up to the event.

Such political symbolism and visual novelty was crucial if the march was to have the public impact the organisers desired. As the historian of 'suffrage spectacle', Lisa Tickner, notes:

27. 'The Bugler Girl', poster designed by Caroline Watts and published by the Artists' Suffrage League, advertised the 13 June 1908 procession and other NUWSS events. In her symbolic armoury, the bugler girl sounds her wakening call.

The impact of the Mud March had been enhanced by the dignity and determination of its participants, the gaiety of their red and white favours . . . But above all else it derived from the novelty of the spectacle, which rested on the impropriety, by conventional standards, of women demonstrating on the public streets at all.

That card was a risky one, and it could not be played twice. The 1908 procession had to be made to surpass the Mud March by means other than by the courting of notoriety. The solution was to 'embroider' the precedent of 1907: symbolically . . . through the production of an unprecedented series of art-needlework banners.[18]

If any one woman could claim credit for the beauty of the 13 June spectacle, it was Slade-trained Mary Lowndes, chair of that creative powerhouse, the Artists' Suffrage League. Florence Lockwood was, of course, another such artist determined to design and embroider Huddersfield's demand for the vote as beautifully and evocatively as she could.[19] In Leeds, Emily Ford was involved in local banner-making; Isabella recorded how:

The Artists' League are working most beautiful banners for the various societies. Our Leeds Women's suffrage society has a banner in blue and gold,
with the Leeds arms and the words 'Leeds for Liberty' . . . Every banner will
be gorgeous and beautiful in colour and design.

Although the WSPU demonstration and the NUWSS procession were
being organised separately, the ever-conciliatory Isabella Ford urged ILP
women to attend both if they possibly could, so that Leeds was well represented in London.[20]

Special trains were laid on to enable thousands of suffragists to travel
down to London from cities such as Leeds, Sheffield and Hull. Mary
Murdoch's Hull branch even opened a committee room a month before
the procession and over a hundred pounds was subscribed by local members towards the travel costs, with a special Women's Suffrage train
provided from Hull and back; afterwards the branch bullishly claimed that
'our contingent was the largest of those sent by the provincial Societies'.[21]

Even before the day itself, it was clear that the staging of the NUWSS
procession was going to be a triumph of public pageantry. In advance,
Oxford Street shops began selling elegant lace blouses – with 'Votes for
Women' woven delicately round the yoke, to catch the unaware admirer.[22]
From eleven o'clock on the day itself, suffragists on the special trains from
all over England pouring into London stations were met by NUWSS stewards, each distinctively recognisable in red and white scarves; the northern
arrivals were hurried off to restaurants on the Strand for a quick lunch.
Robing Rooms were set up for university and medical women (like Mary
Murdoch or Louisa Martindale) near the Embankment; here, by two
o'clock, suffragists assembled six abreast. Within half-an-hour, crowds grew
so large that tram traffic had to be halted; the orderly procession stretched
for two miles right past Westminster and up Whitehall.

Then, on the chime of three and at the signal of a drum roll, the procession led off to the music of a silver band. Banners fluttered in the wind.
At the head was the NUWSS banner with its motto, 'The Franchise is the
Keystone of Our Liberties'. Beneath it marched Mrs Fawcett, resplendent in
her honorary doctorate robes of blue and scarlet. The first eight blocks of
marchers comprised local NUWSS societies with their banners, arranged
alphabetically. Leeds was well represented, with its own 'Leeds for Liberty'
positioned in the middle. The International Woman Suffrage Alliance contingent marched alongside almost 140 women doctors in a blaze of scarlet.
Business and professional groups followed – among them the Writers'

Suffrage League, its banners commemorating authors including Charlotte and Emily Brontë. Other groups included the Women's Co-operative Guild, an organisation of married working-class women, who were followed by the Women's Freedom League; bringing up the rear rode Countess Markiewicz in a four-in-hand carriage. Altogether, between ten and fifteen thousand women took part in this procession. The *Daily Mirror* offered its readers a panoramic bird's-eye-view of the densely packed two-mile long procession on its way to the Albert Hall. However, it was the dignified pageantry and medieval banners that captured the public imagination in an unprecedented way. One press reporter confessed:

> I have seen many processions. But they were all processions of men. On Saturday I saw a procession of women. It was more stately and more splendid and more beautiful than any procession I ever saw . . . The women have done what the men failed to do. They have revived the pomp and glory of the procession. They have created the beauty of blown silk and tossing embroidery . . . It was like a medieval festival, vivid with simple grandeur, alive with ancient dignity . . .[23]

28. *Banners carried on the NUWSS procession, 13 June 1908.*
A. *'Leeds for Liberty', watercolour design, Mary Lowndes [purple].*
B. *'Charlotte Brontë, Emily Brontë' banner, unidentified designer. [green, white]*
C. *'Edith Pechey-Phipson MD', banner designed by Mary Lowndes. [died 1908.]*

Bessie Ford was in the throng of the procession. The repetitive nature of her work as Leeds Society treasurer had made it easy to lose sight of the beauty behind the aim of the cause, but marching in this procession through London with so many thousands of others was a thrilling experience. A letter she wrote captured this exhilaration: 'Those women's faces are beautiful – it was quite glorious to see them, they seemed to shine . . . No, nothing can push it back, women are stirring and rising up everywhere, it's like a great flood'. The procession was just what suffragists needed. Also excited by the spectacle was Isabella Ford – who set off the next day by boat for Amsterdam and the International Woman Suffrage Alliance Congress.[24]

The striking public triumph of the NUWSS procession was matched a week later by the WSPU's 'Woman's Sunday' demonstration on 21 June in Hyde Park, on an even larger scale. For this the WSPU, as we know, had invested careful planning, co-ordinating its colours and drumming up local support. Adela had spoken for an hour from a soap box in Halifax, before being rescued from the crowd by three constables and six plain-clothes police.[25] In Bradford, Mary Gawthorpe worked hard for a good suffragette turnout; a special 'Suffrage Sunday: Excursion to London' was advertised, leaving Bradford at 8.25 a.m. and returning from King's Cross on the 7.30 p.m., offered a 11/- [55p] return train fare.[26] By such means, Yorkshire contingents set off from Leeds and Bradford, Halifax and York, Sheffield, Hull and Dewsbury.

In all, there were seven WSPU processions, each with a chief marshal. Mary Gawthorpe was at the head of one contingent, as the Amalgamated Musicians' Union struck up a march. Ethel Snowden and Keir Hardie carried the ILP banner: 'The World for the Workers'. According to the press, the procession may have lacked the previous weekend's dignified graduates in their caps and gowns, but certainly made up for this with 'dash and go' and flair. The *Daily Mirror* headlined its photograph 'World's Greatest Demonstration of Women', estimating fifty thousand people in Hyde Park. Some of the vast crowd might have come just out of idle curiosity – for Emmeline and Christabel Pankhurst were now Edwardian celebrities; but the WSPU had aimed for a quarter of a million attendance and may even have exceeded this.[27]

Afterwards, Christabel hurried away to the WSPU headquarters to send the Prime Minister, by special messenger, the Hyde Park resolution calling upon his Government to enfranchise women without delay.

Two such vast and magnificent demonstrations may not exactly have been what obdurate Asquith or Gladstone had in mind. Surely even Asquith's government could no longer deny that hundreds of thousands of women did indeed feel sufficiently strongly to take their demand for the vote on to the streets of London? However, Asquith's cool response, relayed formally through his private secretary, remained an evasive statement; he still hedged about his commitment to women's suffrage with insultingly vague references to some 'remote and speculative future'.[28]

This was provocation in the extreme. It was nigh impossible to organise larger or more impressive public street pageantry. Yet Westminster and Whitehall would not listen. Asquith remained aloof, deaf to suffrage appeals. In frustration, two suffragettes arrived in Downing Street with a bag full of stones – which they proceeded to throw at the windows of Number 10. This was an individual initiative, rather than part of WSPU strategy. It was non-verbal direct action, born out of growing anger; and unlike interrupting Liberal meetings, harassing cabinet ministers or heckling election candidates, attacks on government premises represented an escalation. Stone-throwing was a distinctly new form of suffragette militancy, prefiguring violence aimed at property that was to come.

After Hyde Park, Emmeline Pankhurst announced that similar demonstrations would be held in great cities: Nottingham, Manchester and Leeds. Mary Gawthorpe organised the Leeds event on Sunday 26 July. Her handbill announced: 'If you believe in JUSTICE, join the Women's Procession . . . Come and march with the women who are fighting in the Cause of Liberty'. The WSPU again went to every length to ensure success. The long procession was led by Emmeline, Adela and Christabel Pankhurst, Emmeline Pethick-Lawrence, Annie Kenney, Jennie Baines and Mary Gawthorpe. They sat in ten decorated waggons. Accompanied by brass bands, local WSPU members marched under their own banners. The procession wound up from the city centre to Woodhouse Moor, where a crowd estimated at 100,000 waited. First speaker was Adela – never the briefest of orators, but obviously an effective crowd-warmer: she spoke for an hour and a quarter. The resolution was passed supporting suffragettes incarcerated in Holloway and pressing the government to extend the franchise to women. Some undoubtedly came along to the rally hoping for exciting tussles; but the local press reported that, if so, the crowd was disappointed, for the proceedings were 'remarkably orderly'.[29]

The mid-summer processions had most certainly alerted a far wider newspaper-reading public to Votes for Women. The franchise demand was now out proudly on the streets. Yet if it was impossible to convince Asquith and

Gladstone directly by sheer force of numbers and pageantry, then still more imaginative actions were needed to reach more Edwardians in more places. From this realisation sprang one of the suffrage movement's most inventive initiatives.

That summer, both the Women's Freedom League [WFL] and the NUWSS organised special caravan tours which adventurously zigzagged across the country. They took the precedent of political caravanning from, for instance, the *Clarion* newspaper. The WFL was particularly quick off the mark, with a specially built van pulled by a horse named 'Asquith' which toured the home counties. (However enticing the prospect of goading an arrestingly-named cart-horse, vanning did not fit with the WSPU's tactical priorities.)

The NUWSS tour was even more adventurous, helped by its recent expansion. By summer 1908 it could proudly announce that it employed three permanent organisers, two of whom now became vanners. Margaret Robertson, with a literature degree and a small edition of Keats to her name, was a talented open-air speaker with valuable political skills; she had resigned her teaching post to become a regional organiser. Emilie Gardner, recently graduated from Cambridge in history, lent the tour a certain effusive enthusiasm.[30]

From August 1908 the horse-drawn NUWSS caravan toured right through the sprawling Yorkshire countryside. Fortunately, the development of news photography and the popular explosion of the Edwardian picture-postcard craze has bequeathed historians a series of richly evocative cards. At the time, these were still a merchandising novelty, often sent to other suffragists. Preserved a century later, this poignant postcard sequence offers a running visual commentary on the rigours of 'vanning it'; and it also allows us to track the exact route of the horse-drawn van as it wended its way out to the coastline of the rural North Riding.

The NUWSS van set off in late August for its first stop, Whitby. At this isolated little fishing port, Margaret Robertson managed to park the caravan right by the water's edge. The first postcard, dated 21 August 1908, depicts Whitby harbourside with its fair booths. Gathered around the caravan is the curious Edwardian crowd: a boy in a sailor hat, mothers pushing babies in elaborate perambulators, a fisherwoman in an apron with a basket on her head.

The NUWSS caravan was sturdily constructed, with attractive side windows, white-painted and shuttered, a small chimney, and front porch-roof to protect the speaker from the inevitable Yorkshire rain. From Whitby, the

29. Whitby, 21 August 1908, suffragists speaking from the front of the van.

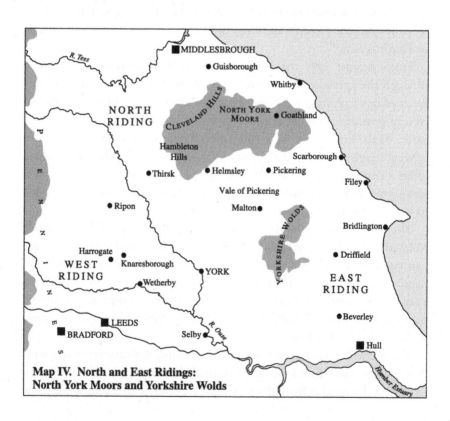

**Map IV. North and East Ridings:
North York Moors and Yorkshire Wolds**

cart-horse plodded its way up Glen Esk, hauling the caravan into the high North York Moors. After about ten miles, it reached the small village of Goathland. Here, before the premises of William Pearson, Grocer and Post Office, one suffragist stood upon a chair to speak – facing a loyal handful of committed supporters seated immediately before her – then a large and visible gap, with a straggling circle of wavering bystanders and non-committal men leaning with sticks. Most Goathland women kept a safe distance.

30. Goathland, probably 1908.

This postcard was probably sent by Margaret Robertson (the signature is unclear) and is addressed to Mary Fielden, another suffragist who became a full-time NUWSS organiser and joined the tour. The message simply said: 'sending this card as a little memento of your meeting at Goathland.'[31]

From here, the route led south over the high North York Moors and down into the broad Vale of Pickering, and then across to the coast. The caravan progressed eastwards, where the seaside resorts of Scarborough and, further south, Bridlington, had developed to cater for affluent Edwardian holiday-makers. Here, Margaret Robertson on the top caravan step engaged with a small seaside crowd: a girl with her bicycle, men in summer boaters, curious children listening, a newsboy with *his* bicycle.

31. Bridlington, Margaret Robertson speaking, September 1908.

The rigours of travel demanded practical clothes and permitted new identities. Greatcoats, white shirts and ties suggest that vanning, like women-only colleges at university, created a liberating space. Vanning offered a transforming experience: hatlessness allowed Edwardian suffragists to embrace all the masculine freeedoms evoked by Rebecca West's open road.

From Bridlington, Emilie Gardner sent a postcard a younger schoolgirl sister or niece, anxious about her examinations and hoping to follow Emilie's academic success. The artless scribbled message reads breathlessly:

> Good child – it's jolly fine [news] & I'm awfully glad [about your exam results]. It showed that all your dismals was in vain & now you will be allowed up to go on to Newnham [college, Cambridge] eulogium [praise]. Hurrah. Give my love and congratulations to Polly.
>
> It is ripping you have passed in everything & good luck. I am going to be in Hull over weekend C/o Dr Mary Murdoch, 102 Beverley Road. After that I may have to go to Newcastle by-election. I do not want to but probably must. Em G[32]

The meandering caravan, its horse cared for by an invaluable male supporter, McArthur, reached Beverley by 9 September, doubling back up to Driffield on 12 September. This vanning schedule of travelling, speaking,

32. Probably Emilie Gardner (left) wearing a greatcoat and tie; Margaret Robertson, seated, with white decorated hat, probably 1908. The vanners sold books, leaflets, badges and advertised their meetings — on the Market Square, Old Bridlington at 3.30 or '6.30 By the lamp-post near Britannia Hotel'.

sleeping was punishing. The message on the back of one postcard, probably from Margaret Robertson, reads:

> I did my 3 changes [of horse] very well & got here at 2.30. Went straight to meeting & spoke from the van. There were plenty of people & very attentive. Tonight we have indoor mtg [meeting] at 7.30. Tomorrow we go to Malton.

Send me a p.c. on Tuesday morning to P.O. Pickering. I shall be with van till Sat. Only Miss Gardner and McArthur are here.[33]

As the caravan backtracked to Pickering, this voyage had succeeded in reaching fresh rural communities, previously untouched, with the suffrage demand.

33. Rural caravan scene, probably late Aug 1908. McArthur in soft hat is seated reading on the van steps. A jug suggests fetching milk from a nearby farm, and the bucket hanging below fetching water from a stream.

This Yorkshire tour ended around late September as the weather grew colder and a by-election in Newcastle beckoned. Though lasting only a month, it had proved very effective, penetrating remote rural communities across North and East Ridings with Votes for Women – to the delight of Isabella Ford as she heard of its success in traversing her own Yorkshire backyard.

During the winter of 1908–9, WSPU frustration and anger with Asquith and his Liberal government grew. Suffragette militancy escalated, reported in *Votes for Women*. WSPU stone-throwing and window-breaking grew more commonplace, and the NUWSS became more openly critical of the use of violence.

At the same time the NUWSS became more efficiently run. By 1909 its membership reached over 13,000. Money poured in and the NUWSS began to organise its local societies into great regional federations. Then, from April 1909, the NUWSS also started publishing its own weekly paper, *Common Cause*.[34] This enabled local societies to keep in touch with the NUWSS executive and with each other. It made not only for a widened readership but also now allows suffrage historians to plot the route of the 1909 caravan tour with greater narrative accuracy than for the previous summer.

By early spring 1909, Isabella Ford was working closely with Mary Fielden. Publicity methods included mock debates, garden parties and collecting petition signatures; but progress could be dishearteningly slow. So in June, Isabella and Mary decided to repeat the success of the previous summer and organise another regional caravan tour – also through rural Yorkshire. Isabella, now in her mid-fifties, decided to go vanning too. It was an admirably courageous decision for a woman accustomed to a bevy of servants and who might never have shopped and cooked a meal in her life. Mary, on the other hand, may well have been in awe of her, since Isabella had the ear of the leadership, her employers.

Luckily, the picture postcard sequence continued. The tour organisation was now put on a slicker footing, with *Common Cause* running a 'Yorkshire Caravan' series. The tour started with three meetings in Whitby on 7 June, then pulled up to Goathland again, *Common Cause* appealing urgently for funds 'as the expense of horse-hire in this hilly district is a very heavy item'. Isabella joined Mary at Pickering between the moors and the wolds. Here, Isabella reported 'some delightful visitors at the inn there took us in to supper after hearing our speeches – the supper included the most delicious cream – and next morning photographed us and escorted us some half mile on our way. The cows in the field at Helmsley where our van was placed (free of charge!) were delighted with us, and rubbed themselves against our wheels all night in spite of our remonstrances'. Here, a decidedly rare, if faded, photograph of Isabella, dated 11 June 1909, shows seated by the cart-horse shafts an older woman – undoubtedly Isabella – alongside a young woman standing, presumably Mary.[35]

Vanning was hectic. To help with the hard work, Isabella and Mary were joined by Ray Costelloe, an energetic suffragist also just graduated from Newnham (who, as Ray Strachey, became best known later as author of *The Cause*). The three suffragists tried to skirt along the edge of the

34. Pickering, Isabella Ford, probably with Mary Fielden, June 1909.

Hambleton Hills – a rather over-ambitious undertaking, perhaps, as a rather flustered Isabella reported in the *Common Cause*:

> The Thirsk route was impossible, owing to steep hills. Two people in a van cannot easily manage the work. Of Miss Fielden's energy, care, and unselfish kindness and economy I cannot speak too highly, but she needs helpers. Nice as vanning is, it is extremely tiring when you have to earn your living as you go along and make all arrangements for horses, men etc. It is too hard work for only two people, if daily travelling is necessary. All the way through beautiful old villages we distributed leaflets and did house to house visiting, so that we were constantly on the go, constantly talking and arguing. We found Miss Costelloe invaluable, a very excellent collector [of donations] (and cook).[36]

The van was now travelling from Malton via York to Ripon. McArthur seems to have been swapped for a more flamboyant horsewoman. The Hon. Mrs Evelina Haverfield was an adept rider who habitually rode astride rather than side-saddle. She had recently transferred her allegiances from the NUWSS to the WSPU; however, her horsemanship had been cannily secured by the NUWSS, which proved invaluable as 'two steeds were necessary on account of the hilly country, but we had to dismiss them' and obtain other horses.[37]

The caravan then headed west for the spa resort of Harrogate. Here, Evelina Haverfield reported, they were warmly welcomed by local ILP members and Isabella gave a talk in an ILP hall. Evelina then managed to hire a stronger cart-horse and off they all set for Wetherby and on to Selby for 27 June – where they were able to exchange their 'Anti-Suffragist' horse ('obliging, but considered that politics were a man's sphere') for a skewbald pony (a 'lamb') in the Selby horse show. However, outside political events kept intruding on the delights of rural vanning. Evelina Haverfield returned to London, took part in another WSPU deputation to Westminster on 29 June, found herself arrested on a WSPU deputation and became preoccupied with her lengthy high-profile trial. Mary Fielden had to leave to travel north to work at the Cleveland by-election; and the suffragists left the caravan in Selby.[38]

By late July, Isabella, too, had left the tour and gone home to Leeds for a local suffrage society fund-raising garden party. Here, Ethel Snowden, just back from America, gave a talk on how political equality would improve women's industrial conditions; and this was followed by an entertaining mock debate between a suffragist and an 'anti', a favourite staple of such occasions. With name-play reminiscent of Lavena Saltonstall's 'Pankson Baines', Isabella agreed to play the part of the 'anti', a 'Miss Ford-Cromer'. Mary Fielden reported, tongue-in-cheek, how Isabella 'with particular delicacy drew the attention of the audience to that most touching and pathetic line of Mr Austen Chamberlain, [a leading Conservative 'Anti'] – "Men are men and women are women!"' At the close of the debate the suffrage resolution was carried, 'Miss Ford-Cromer's two hands being the only dissentient ones'.

By now even the middle-class Leeds Society members acknowledged that it could not limit its appeal to suburban garden parties: it had to challenge the government in its own backyard – Herbert Gladstone's West Leeds constituency. As a result of meetings held in Liberal clubs, working men's clubs and local parks, Gladstone received almost fifty resolutions, signed largely by men i.e. voters.[39] The Leeds branch had come a long way.

By winter 1909–10, then, upper-middle-class women, who had never knowingly got up in the morning without a maid to light the bedroom fire, help them dress and serve breakfast, were undertaking actions previously undreamt of. Emily Ford chaired a meeting. Bessie and Emily even walked as 'sandwich women' displaying a suffrage poster in the street. And

Isabella had braved caravanning. If they were not 'rebel girls', the Ford sisters had nonetheless pushed the boundaries.

By then WSPU stone-throwing and window-breaking had grown routine. As a Quaker, committed to anti-militarism and non-violence, Isabella could not condone such tactics – however tempting it might seem. (Another Quaker suffragist confessed, 'I rather long to go and break some windows. I am not sure whose but I think any liberal offices would answer the purpose'.[40]) The NUWSS however grew critical. Peaceable Isabella was hard-pressed to tread an amicable line between hostile and sympathetic suffragists. The conciliatory twinkle in her eye would be needed over the next few years.

Meanwhile, suffragists like Isabella Ford and her sisters helped win Edwardian hearts and minds. Alice Schofield-Coates's pageants in Middlesbrough and Mary Gawthorpe's tambourine-rattling in south Leeds had all helped to ensure that, by the General Election of January 1910, every single Edwardian – except perhaps the most curmudgeonly hill farmer living at the head of the remotest Yorkshire dale – had heard of the suffrage demand. Votes for Women now indeed reached everywhere. The NUWSS, with its regional federations, beautiful banners and intrepid 'vanners', was even beginning to recruit a new generation of activists who would begin to take it in imaginative new directions – as Part Four tells.

CHAPTER 10

'A genius for revolt': Adela and Mary again
1909–1911

Rebecca West's fiction, inspired by Mary Gawthorpe and Adela Pankhurst, captured the WSPU's love affair with impetuous beautiful youth. It disdained the tired, the old and the compromised. In her novel *Adela*, West's eponymous heroine 'was not only a beauty: she was also that seething whirlpool of primitive passions, that destructive centre of intellectual unrest, that shy shameless savage, a girl of seventeen'. In contrast, Adela's poor relations, waiting upon her wealthy uncle Tom Motley, were 'drab women in the most miserable fag end of middle-age ... Their backs were ... bent with toil and bony across the shoulder-blades with the ridge of cheap corsets'.[1] Rebecca West's Adela feared to identify with them and with Uncle Tom's values. His pompous mahogany furniture:

> seemed a symbol of mean and drear Eternity . . . The gross companionship of torpid middle-aged people obviously incapable of passion – flashed before her and sent the virgin blood protesting through her veins . . . Adela's youth and the violence of her hatred betrayed her . . . she suddenly thirsted for life and beauty and joy. Visions passed by her: of blue seas sleeping silently at the feet of golden mountains . . .[2]

By the time Rebecca West began writing *Adela*, about 1910–11, she had just left Edinburgh for London, where she moved into freelance journalism, her writing gaining a fluency her earlier fiction lacked. West had earlier worked as a teenage dogsbody in the WSPU, probably in Manchester where her sister lived, and she now took a broad critical swipe at the way the WSPU:

wasted a wonderful opportunity when it encouraged its working-class members with a genius for revolt to leave their mills and go to south coast watering-places to convert retired Anglo-Indian colonels. If the mill-girls had stuck to their mills, the teachers to their schools . . . and had preached revolt in their own circle, England might have been covered by now by a network of disaffected industries, clamouring for political and economic emancipation. As it is England is merely starred with groups of sympathis-ers too heterogeneous for effective action and too largely composed of middle-class women to organise industrial revolt.[3]

Well, yes and no. West was arguably right about Annie Kenney, whom the WSPU had indeed dispatched south. But West, now whirled away in London's literary *Les Jeunes* circle, had few links with the industrial north. She failed to grasp that the early suffrage success with the cotton trade unions did not translate easily beyond Lancashire – not even to Yorkshire. West also glossed over Mary Gawthorpe's continued WSPU organising in Lancashire and the West Riding; here Mary, though recovering from an operation after she was kicked in the stomach, remained an exceptionally popular speaker.[4] And West also missed Adela Pankhurst's sustained campaigning in Sheffield.

However, West was right to identify its organisers as increasingly the powerhouse of the WSPU. For changes were taking place in the organisa-tion. Some local branches – like Huddersfield – flagged under the strain. Over a dozen Yorkshire branches were listed in late 1907, but by 1908 this had shrunk to half, and soon individual branches were no longer even recorded. Instead, the WSPU focused its efforts on those few larger cen-tres – especially Leeds, Bradford and Sheffield – where an organiser was active.[5] Donations from well-to-do sympathisers now poured in to fund the salaries of organisers, whose direct links to WSPU headquarters lent dynamism, energy and action to a local campaign.

Adela Pankhurst was fast becoming *the* Yorkshire organiser. She raced between Huddersfield and Keighley, Halifax and Bradford, though she was increasingly based in Sheffield.[6] Nevertheless Adela, with her socialism and her complex relationship with her elder sisters and mother, was not typical of WSPU organisers. Nor was Sheffield, foremost of Yorkshire's heavy indus-trial cities, a typical WSPU base. However, this political marriage of industry and organiser was made in heaven – not an Anglo-Indian colonel in sight.

Tucked into the southern corner of West Riding, Sheffield was traditionally England's cutlery capital, and was now also dominated by Yorkshire's coal and steel industries. The city itself was surrounded by hills, with large new factories strung along the River Don. People flocked to jobs clustered in smoky factory communities. In *Adela*, Rebecca West's melodramatic adolescent imagination talked up the industrial misery of such a city:

> A mass of darkness patched with greasy roofs, a network of narrow alleys overhung by the livid fumes of the factories, a squalid undergrowth of hovels spiked with tall chimneys . . . A distant furnace sighed tragically, trains softly rattled away on their mysterious traffics. Slowly, as the sun died majestically on the skyline, the town awoke . . . and began to proclaim the secrets of her heart under the cover of night. She . . . vehemently confessed her burning lusts in the undying furnace-flames . . . she pretended to luxury, for the red and green signals on the railway-line that sundered her straightly from North to South gleamed richly like jewels on the ribbon of darkness.[7]

In reality, Sheffield was a mixed community, with strong business and residential areas, usually loyally Conservative. So Liberals had to work hard, regularly sending up ministers hoping to persuade voters of the rightness of Lloyd George's ambitious economic reforms.

Sheffield's long-established NUWSS branch was dominated by Dr Helen Wilson. Like Mary Murdoch, she had trained at the London School of Medicine for Women and shared Mary's professional confidence, though she lacked her more *outré* flourishes. Helen's father was Liberal MP for nearby Holmfirth and Helen, very much her father's daughter, voiced the highly respectable Liberal suffragism so prevalent across Yorkshire.[8] There was now also a WSPU branch. To the shock of respectable Sheffield, who thought it disgraceful, three local suffragettes were among those arrested in spring 1907. One was the WSPU branch secretary Edith Whitworth.[9]

During autumn 1907, the WSPU had kept up its attacks on Liberal cabinet ministers whenever they ventured out. On 20 November Lord Haldane, Secretary of State for War, was to speak in Sheffield for the local Liberals. Adela hurried over from Leeds and, to headlines 'Suffragette Heroine in Sheffield', planned an intensive anti-Liberal propaganda campaign. A score of suffragettes, including Adela and Annie Kenney, met Haldane's train as it drew in that afternoon. They displayed large placards and presented him with a petition. However Haldane stated he would not be mentioning suffrage in his speech that evening. He may have regretted this: as he left, his car was plastered with 'Votes for Women' posters.[10]

Admission to the hall was tightly controlled, with no woman permitted to purchase a ticket unless proven *not* to be a suffragette. Even these women were restricted just to the balcony, so that any trouble erupting would be confined to the upper reaches of the hall. Yet somehow or other, Adela, Annie, Mary Gawthorpe and others gained access to the hall's entrance, with tickets obtained by male sympathisers. Predictably, they were refused entry when they tried to make a dash into the hall itself, and fighting broke out with the police on duty.

WSPU male supporters were always less detectable. As the meeting began, one man stood up and shouted to Haldane, 'Are you in favour of votes for women?' The huge Liberal crowd bayed, 'Put him out', and the Liberal stewards did just that. Since they had failed to gain entry, Adela, Mary, and the others resigned themselves to holding a rival meeting outside the hall, despite the November chill. Adela even climbed a drain-pipe and, clinging on precariously, addressed the crowd. The following day, Haldane rashly visited Sheffield University – only to encounter suf-fragettes again. Mary wickedly presented him with a fistful of suffrage handbills. Already, the Liberal government could see Sheffield spelt trouble.[11]

From here, Adela sped up to Leeds to harass Herbert Gladstone. She met with more success than at Sheffield: Adela stood on her seat and asked the Home Secretary a question, though she was drowned out in the hubbub.[12] She then, as we know, hurried across to Hull for the by-election there.

Certainly Adela, while politically fearless and full of derring-do, still harboured a memory of emotional neglect as a child. Her feeling of being pushed to the unloved margins remained, while not only Christabel but also Annie Kenney seemed to take the significant place in Emmeline's affections. During summer 1908, Adela joined Annie near Bristol, staying with a colonel's daughters (they described Adela as 'a dear little thing of 23 and except when she speaks looks like a timid child').[13] And for the great Hyde Park rally in June, Adela was presented dressed in white, and spoke from Platform Ten. But certainly by autumn, she was firmly pushed back into Yorkshire, staying in cheap lodgings or with local sym-pathisers, working tirelessly across Leeds and Bradford. Mary Gawthorpe occasionally visited, but otherwise Adela held together the Yorkshire cam-paign virtually single-handed.[14] Dedication seldom comes stronger than Adela's.

*

During winter 1908–9, WSPU anger at the Liberal government grew and with this militancy escalated. The new parliamentary session was to begin on Monday 12 October; Emmeline Pankhurst wrote to Asquith asking for the women's enfranchisement bill to be included in the government's autumn programme. On Friday she received his negative reply. Conflict immediately flared, and a series of set-piece street confrontations between suffragettes and the police erupted.

The following day, Saturday 10, both Asquith and Gladstone were to address a Liberal meeting in Leeds. Once again suffragettes descended on the city. At the hall, mounted police were well prepared and the Liberals kept careful control of tickets, many over-stamped 'Men Only'. As the ministers arrived in Leeds by train, they were greeted by Jennie Baines addressing the crowd – which swarmed around as the procession made its way to the hall. Local press recorded that Baines cried 'Break down the barricades and compel a hearing', though later she denied incitement. A rush of people stormed the doors, demanding entry. The police closed in: Baines and five other suffragettes were arrested. The press headlines, 'Wild Street Scenes in Leeds', reflected local hostility, with an effigy of Mrs Pankhurst being burnt at Holbeck Feast.[15]

In London, conflict between the WSPU and the police escalated further when Christabel organised suffragettes to 'Rush' the House of Commons. Both she and Emmeline were arrested for incitement and given lengthy sentences in Holloway. Alarmed at this development, Adela wrote to the Home Office for permission to visit her mother and elder sister in prison.[16]

Later in October, Adela chaired a meeting in Bradford for Emmeline Pethick-Lawrence, and then rushed off down to Sheffield. Here on Thursday 29 Reginald McKenna, first Lord of the Admiralty, was scheduled to speak in the city's historic Cutlers' Hall. Britain then was keeping a wary eye on the German navy and on German battleship-building, with a popular 'We want eight and we won't wait' cry for British Dreadnoughts – a hot issue, given local unemployment. This was therefore a set-piece meeting, with McKenna dangling the carrot of naval procurement before local industrialists; invited city dignitaries loaded with naval and military medals all assembled for his heavy-metal speech. A torchlight procession of unemployed 'hunger marchers' massed outside, with a strong police cordon to separate the two.

Into the midst of this throng dashed madcap Adela Pankhurst. By now she knew that she would be recognised by the Sheffield police if she tried to brave an entrance. So she devised a plan: she acquired a disguise and, with Edith Whitworth and just a few others, stepped forward. The *Sheffield Independent* reported sardonically that the chief excitement that evening 'was created by Miss Adela Pankhurst', who came:

> in disguise, and her first ruse was to try and get into Cutlers' Hall by posing as a kitchen maid, but finding wily policemen on guard even there, she recognised that other methods would have to be adopted, and promptly moved off.
>
> She went to the Town Hall, where, from the steps, she began to 'hold forth', and soon a crowd of 800 or 900 people congregated. But two police-men promptly hauled her off the pedestal, and so she took refuge at the Monument. There she was the darling of the crowd, and her declaration of war in favour of votes for women was freely interspersed with boisterous cheering. When she announced, 'I am going to the Cutlers' Hall now to see Mr McKenna' the crowd yelled 'And we are going with you', and almost irresistibly a move was made in that direction.

Adela tried to disentangle herself from the crowd, but it was not read-ily directed by a kitchen-maid. Events were getting out of hand. Adela and Edith, followed by the cheering crowd, went towards the hall. The police were on the alert, and there was a struggle to rush the cordon:

> 'I want to see Mr McKenna, I am going in. Now, I shall. We want votes for women', she declared . . .
>
> 'No, you are not going, Miss Pankhurst', Chief Inspector Hollis urged respectfully, but firmly.
>
> The campaigners were not to be put off . . . There were some ugly rushes, as the crowd surged heavily and did its best to help the women . . .
>
> For something like ten minutes there was a hot encounter between con-tending forces, and the rushing and crushing was such as to almost squeeze the life out of the 'Votes for Women' champions.
>
> In one skirmish, Miss Pankhurst was separated from her friends . . . For some 90 minutes the contest was maintained, and that in no drawing room fashion . . .
>
> Miss Pankhurst and the others were roughly handled. Eventually, exhausted and perspiring, the leading lady was accompanied to the front of the Town Hall by a cheering crowd – but not to give in, as she put it.
>
> The crush hampered all her movements, and so she boarded a tramcar

and later drove to her apartment, there to get rid of the kitchen girl disguise. The police were wondering what had happened to her, when, about an hour later, a cab drew up near the hall. Its occupant was Miss Pankhurst, who jumped out and made a dash to gain the hall door, but she was captured before she could get to the red baize [carpet?] at the entrance. That meant her being escorted [away] again . . . and the decision, finally, that she had done her share in upholding the women's cause against tremendous odds.

She was very much exhausted as the result of the buffeting and rough handling she had been subjected to, and, while she spoke well of the Sheffield police, she stated she was hurt more than usual in the scuffle.[17]

From such frenzied incidents, the implications of WSPU tactics become crystal clear. In the wake of Christabel's 'rushing' the House of Commons, confrontation now grew to near-violence. This meant sympathisers had to choose: remain a WSPU militant and risk imprisonment, or become an arm's-length donor – or join another suffrage organisation. Inevitably, the number of women who could risk prison diminished. In Sheffield, Adela increasingly had to operate virtually on her own. Even Edith Whitworth, married to a postal telegraphist and with two young children, began to have doubts about the value of scuffling with police on the streets. Adela remained willing to lay down almost life itself for the cause, as she hurled herself heroically into the fray, oblivious to the bruising of her own body. After all, her mother and elder sister were spending the winter in Holloway.

With WSPU window-breaking becoming routine and Jennie Baines standing trial in Leeds, tensions mounted within the broader suffrage movement. In Sheffield, local NUWSS suffragists like Dr Helen Wilson were outraged at Adela's undignified kitchen-maid antics with the 'Out-o'-Works' unemployed. Such suffragists, strongly anti-militant, attended a peaceful rally in Manchester, along with nearly 2,000 other North of England women. Towards the front of the procession, they held aloft their banner, red serge embroidered in silk: 'Sheffield demands Vote for Women'. Helen Wilson marched, resplendent in the brilliant scarlet and purple cap and gown of a Doctor of Medicine.

Sheffield was indeed a city of extremes: either starched Liberal respectability or the rough-and-tumble of the crowd. Readers will have their own suffrage sympathies – Helen Wilson's red banner, Isabella Ford's caravanning, Adela's heroics. The smaller, breakaway Women's Freedom

League meanwhile opted for a third way. A small Sheffield branch of the
League was now formed, probably in the aftermath of the McKenna scrimmage and in reaction to the WSPU's consorting with violence. This must
have been a tremendous blow for Adela, not least because one early defec-
tion was Edith Whitworth, WSPU branch secretary.[18]

In spring 1909, amid political crisis with the rejection of Lloyd George's
'People's Budget', a by-election was announced, triggered by the death of
the Liberal MP for Sheffield Attercliffe. Suffrage organisations whirred into
action. Helen Wilson led a NUWSS non-party 'propaganda only' campaign,
with Mary Fielden, the Yorkshire organiser, campaigning to persuade
voters to sign an 'Electors' Petition' – with copies displayed at polling stations on election day. Meanwhile, Adela led the WSPU's campaign against
the Liberal candidate, arranging dozens of outdoor meetings. Her mother
arrived, driving round the constituency in an open carriage. Indeed, the
Liberals were denounced with such fierceness that they hit back with a
leaflet:

> Working men do not be fooled by Mrs Pankhurst,
> Suffragette and Tory lies nailed to the counter.

35. Sheffield Daily Independent, *23 April 1909, Adela Pankhurst in full voice addressing factory
workers at Attercliffe.*

Alongside, the new Women's Freedom League branch ran its own meetings, with 'election postcards' signed by 2,300 pro-suffrage voters and dispatched to Asquith. In the event, the Labour candidate wrested Attercliffe from the Liberals. This new MP left for Westminster carrying the NUWSS petition of over 5,000 voters' signatures, to be presented to Parliament when he took his seat. All excellent propaganda, though perhaps such a rich variety of suffrage tactics, plus the growing association with public violence, offered ammunition to the Anti-Suffragists.[19]

From mid-summer, direct confrontation between the state and the suffragettes, already fairly brutal, intensified. In July 1909 one imprisoned suffragette initiated a new and devastating tactic, subsequently adopted by many in the WSPU: the hunger strike. The prospect of a woman starving herself to death merely for demanding the right to vote so sobered the government that it responded in the autumn with its own chilling new tactic: the forcible feeding of suffragettes refusing prison food. This was a major turning point in the militant campaign. Indeed, the Home Office now stepped up its surveillance by Special Branch officers to report on leading WSPU members and monitor their activities across the country.[20]

As well as in Yorkshire, Adela also campaigned up in Scotland. On one visit north, she was met by Helen Fraser, four years older than Adela and WSPU's Scottish organiser. Helen remembered later how shocked she was by how ill Adela looked:

> As I met her at the train I could hear her breathing. Horrified, I said, 'Did your mother see you when you left last night?' I thought she said 'Yes'. Anyhow, I took her to the room I had booked, and sent for a very well-known woman doctor whose comments on her travelling like that were acid, but she secured a nurse and Adela successfully got rid of her pneumonia.[21]

While in Scotland, Adela was arrested, charged with window-breaking and sentenced. In prison she too began hunger-striking and so was now liable for forcible feeding. Examined by the prison doctor, Adela was described, with memorable clinical precision, as 'a slender under-sized girl five feet in height and (in health) seven stones in weight'. The doctor added that the local Criminal Lunatic Department superintendent 'was impressed by her extraordinary appearance and bearing and did not hesitate to say she was of a "degenerate type".' Being deemed unfit to endure

forcible feeding, Adela was released. However, the brutality of such buffeting in Scotland certainly struck Rebecca West forcibly: she wrote of how
a young Liberal supporter in Dundee demonstrated his enthusiasm for
reform 'by winding Miss Adela Pankhurst's scarf round and round her
throat' until he nearly strangled her.[22]

The friendship with Helen Fraser was a happy bonus for Adela and
would last a lifetime. Both women were affected by the shocking violence
they experienced in Scotland. About this time Helen, who disagreed with
stone-throwing tactics, resigned from the WSPU and was quickly snapped
up by the NUWSS. Adela, she recalled, also began to have doubts about the
rightness of the WSPU's escalation of militancy, but held on for a little
longer. She remained enthralled by – and perhaps in thrall to – her
mother and elder sister, despite the emotional battering that entailed.
Helen quoted one critic's view of this: 'Mrs Pankhurst would walk over the
dead bodies of all her children except Christabel and say, "See what I have
given for the cause."' Indeed, when Emmeline was in America on a lecture
tour, twenty-year-old Harry Pankhurst grew very seriously ill; on 5 January
1910 he died, to Emmeline's immense sorrow. Her brother's death shocked
Adela: she felt ill and very tired.[23]

There was scarcely time to grieve. A General Election was called in January
1910, to confirm the Liberal government's determination to push budget
reforms through Parliament by curbing the obstructionist power of the
House of Lords. The WSPU produced compellingly shocking cartoons
highlighting Liberal hypocrisy on forcible feeding titled 'Modern
Inquisition'. The NUWSS, with so many members still staunch Liberals,
opposed only those candidates unfavourable to suffrage, successfully
organising election petitions in constituencies such as Barnsley.[24]
However, with the all-male electorate, Asquith's government was able to
keep the electoral agenda focused on its reforms, marginalising voteless
women's demand for citizenship.

For the election campaign, Adela, still mourning, went to Scarborough.
After the hurly-burly of Sheffield and Scotland, this picturesque coastal
resort offered a refreshing contrast. The train journey from York [see Map
IV, p 206] curved along the River Derwent, skirting along the Yorkshire
Wolds. Scarborough's main street sloped down from the station to the harbour, broad sands and two piers. Beyond stretched South Bay with its
grandly sweeping Esplanade, sedate hotels, and a stunning coastline running north to Whitby. Scarborough provided a respectably enjoyable

holiday resort for affluent Edwardian visitors. However, with few of them registered as electors, the town was traditionally Liberal; and all the women boarding house keepers, however significantly they contributed to its prosperity, had no right to cast a vote.

Though isolated, Scarborough had a long-standing NUWSS presence. Now Adela arrived, aiming to wipe out the Liberal majority; she set up a WSPU committee room in a shopping street. Three local suffragettes bravely walked through the town as sandwich-board women to advertise meetings, including a crowded one addressed by Emmeline. But to find a space in the electoral chatter was uphill work; the local press, trumpetting its Liberal free-trade faith, bracketed Tories and suffragettes together as the common enemy – and crowed when the Liberals held the seat.

After the Election had confirmed Asquith's government in power, Adela stayed on in Scarborough, helping to form a WSPU branch there. That spring, she worked in the area with Helen Archdale. Helen, married and with children, was an experienced suffragette whom Adela had met in Scotland, and who was now also a WSPU organiser. Within a year, Scarborough opened a well-placed WSPU shop, its broad window displaying purple, green and white posters, brooches, scarves and 'all kinds of other pretty things'.[25] Before long the WSPU would find it extremely useful to have a nest of suffragettes strategically placed out near Scarborough harbour.

Adela also travelled inland to the conservative agricultural constituencies like Ripon and Skipton. Exactly when this panoramic photograph [on p. 226] was taken is unclear; but the speaker looks distinctly like Adela and the market place closely resembles that of Grassington. It certainly evokes the expectant crowds that Adela's oratory drew around spring 1910, ensuring the suffrage message reached any remaining dales farmers.

That spring, Adela still had to stretch herself all along the east coast; she moved her base back to Sheffield, initially with Helen Archdale. They made Sheffield the regional headquarters and both lived in the city, helping form WSPU branches in nearby Rotherham, Doncaster and Barnsley. Sheffield WSPU even opened its own city-centre suffrage shop in Chapel Walk, which also doubled as the WSPU office. A rare surviving letter from Adela captured her hard-working organiser's dedication. Writing to a local sympathiser who had volunteered for the local committee, Adela thanked her, adding that 'if you cannot come to the meetings you can help us by giving us your views'.[26] The perfect politician's encouraging letter. However,

36. 'Miss Pankhurst at Grassington', probably spring 1910.

when Helen fell ill, Adela was on her own; and by autumn 1911, she had not only left Sheffield but, more significantly, had cut adrift from the WSPU.

The reasons why are intertwined. Partly it was a result of Adela's failing health, not helped by Harry's tragic death. As early as the Colne Valley by-election, her voice had begun to weaken and now became very hoarse. As the stress caused by militancy grew more intolerable, her voice failed completely by mid-1911. In the end, Adela and Helen Archdale retreated to a health resort in Scotland in an attempt to recuperate.

Adela's doubts about the effectiveness of militancy now grew, and this had family repercussions. Christabel had already seen rebellious Teresa Billington-Greig split off to help form the Women's Freedom League. She feared that Adela with her base in the north would do the same and separate to form a rival organisation. However, Adela could not have been more different from Teresa Billington-Greig: slighter, more vulnerable, loyally devoted to the WSPU for over seven years. And she was *family*. Nevertheless, her work was viewed with increasing suspicion by the WSPU leadership and placed under unwelcome scrutiny. Sylvia Pankhurst wrote later of how Christabel regarded Adela 'as a very black sheep among organisers, because the warmth of her Socialism did not always permit her to comply with [the] requirement' that, whatever your own politics, you did not offend well-to-do conservative sympathisers.[27] Along with Sylvia's own personal coolness towards her, this all took Adela almost to breaking point. Much later, she recalled how she then felt:

> I cannot say how any difference with Christabel arose. I remember thinking that special favour was shown to Annie Kenney . . . yet we others were reprimanded because our districts were not as flourishing as Annie's . . .
>
> Christabel grew suspicious of rivals. Someone said I was the best speaker in the family and this remark was repeated several times. Christabel, I think, took it into her head that I would use my talent to form some faction against her . . . Mrs Pethick-Lawrence was severe with me about my accounts. I never could raise enough money but then I had very poor districts to work and held many open air meetings that were not financial.[28]

For the past eight years, since her mother had formed the WSPU in the family parlour in Manchester, Adela had given it her all: her youth, her health, and – nearly – her life. All this was drawing to a close. By the end of 1911, Adela had moved to London with Helen Archdale, finding odd jobs there. Certainly by 1912 Adela's involvement in the WSPU had ended.[29]

Helen Fraser, Adela's steadfast friend, recalled later how 'they – Mrs P and Christabel – were quite ruthless in getting "rid" of Adela'. Adela's own account is that it was Annie Kenney who, suddenly out of the blue and apparently on her own initiative, wrote to Adela and 'asked me to promise not to speak in England again'. Sylvia's version is that Adela, suffering from pleurisy, conceived the idea of becoming a gardener, and Emmeline offered to pay for her horticultural training 'but exacted a promise that she would never speak in public again in this country'. Certainly, Adela wrote to Helen Fraser later of how, in mid-1912, her mother gave her £200; and as this was not enough to find herself a profession, she went to Studley horticultural college, where: 'it just got me as far as a Diploma . . . And then I had to find work in a world absolutely hostile to militancy . . . I discovered I was absolutely friendless . . . I was like the old soldiers who return from the wars & are then turned out to beg in the streets!'

It was a profound shock. Adela's critics might suggest that she reached for the martyr's crown too readily; but she now had a mighty lot to feel martyred about. Certainly, Emmeline, too busy to see her youngest daughter, would now write to Helen Archdale about Adela: 'she ought to think herself a very fortunate girl'. What Adela dubbed: 'the family attitude –

Cause First and human relations – nowhere', had marginalised her most decisively.[30]

In autumn 1910, Mary Gawthorpe, after lengthy sick leave, also retired from being a WSPU organiser due to her continued ill-health. She referred later to 'all the complications of that wretched period', when 'I was so utterly crushed at my failure to keep going, the inability to rally'.[31] But of course, because she was not 'retiring' from her own family, the process was less of a profound wrench than it was for Adela. After a year, Mary resigned from the WSPU itself: by about the end of 1911 both Adela and Mary had, after their long campaigning years, cut themselves adrift from the WSPU.

By then, Mary had grown closer to a new group of feminist thinkers. In November 1911 they launched a new journal, the *Freewoman*, to explore issues far wider than just suffrage: free love and homosexuality, celibacy and women's economic independence. Mary was a useful editorial addition, introducing journalists like Rebecca West to the paper; and the *Freewoman* gave Mary the opportunity at last to write, taking a longer view. She also now contributed a powerful rebuttal of suffrage movement critics in Orage's *New Age* journal, confronting head-on the Nietzschean male supremacist rhetoric she had encountered at the Leeds Arts Club. Mary wrote imaginatively, angrily and eloquently:

> Who are You? You are Man, the Thinker. And who am I? I am Wo-man, the Thinker . . . who carries the Womb . . .
>
> It is not that I rebel against Nature but that your new variation on the old theme, he for God and she for God through him, promises continued outrage upon her. It represents for me the great conspiracy, the repeated folly of the ages . . . Your thought for Woman is too little. It is too *cheap* . . .
>
> This civilisation might have, today, the glorious confident outpouring of a free and radiant womanhood . . . The new Eve stands already at the door. Can it really be that you do not know her?[32]

Rebecca West had captured this love affair with impetuous beautiful youth; and as Adela and Mary bowed out of the WSPU, a new – if smaller – group of maverick rebel girls sprang impetuously forward, their uncompromising militancy separating them yet further from the democratic suffragists.

PART FOUR

Mavericks and Democrats
1911–1914

CHAPTER 11

Such smashing girls: Leonora Cohen
1911–1912

Both General Elections, January and December 1910, had confirmed the authority of Asquith's Liberal government. The power of the Conservative-dominated House of Lords to block Lloyd George's 'People's Budget' was curbed. In summer 1911 a Parliament Act resolved this constitutional crisis, and progressive reforms such as national insurance legislation were enacted. However, in the three remaining peacetime years the government remained dogged by successive waves of increasingly violent political conflict. Home Rule for Ireland was resisted with growing ferocity by Unionists – both the Conservative Party and Ulster Protestants – some of whom even began military drilling. Within the labour movement, trade union militancy sometimes turned violent: Home Secretary Winston Churchill ordered troops to fire on strikers at Tonypandy in south Wales: Labour MPs found themselves uncomfortably torn between supporting Liberal reforms and defending trade unionists. Troops were also dispatched to the East End, for a siege in Sidney Street where Russian anarchists had taken refuge.[1] Week in week out, Ulster refuseniks and syndicalist workers shared the newspaper headlines with Votes for Women.

During 1911 a spirit of optimism infused the suffrage campaign. A new Conciliation Bill, carefully designed to satisfy all parties, had just passed its second reading, with the government promising parliamentary time for its third reading. In this positive atmosphere, the WSPU planned a 'Women's Coronation Procession' for mid-June. The Women's Freedom League agreed to take part, as did the NUWSS. However, some suffragists remained extremely unhappy about dancing to the tune of the window-breaking WSPU; Mary Lowndes, queen of the banner-makers, was one. In the end, conciliatory Emily Ford, also in the Artists' League, offered to make shield-shaped banners, each inscribed with the name of local town councils which had passed resolutions supporting the Conciliation Bill – and 'so made as to show no possible relation to the WSPU'.

Echoing George V's coronation, the theme of the procession was proudly imperial. There was an 'Empire Car' and a Historical Pageant; Scottish pipers, Welsh choirs, and Irish harps; for the NUWSS, there were Emily Ford's eighty newly designed banners. The Women's Freedom League contingent, led by now elderly Charlotte Despard, included the Middlesbrough delegation with a new banner for which the branch had rustled up 8/6d [42.5p]. There was a contingent of 700 suffragette prisoners (or their proxies) all dressed in white, plus supportive Men's Leagues. Altogether, there were 40,000 women walking in seven miles of 'gold and glitter and sparkling pageantry'. The impact of this universal spectacle, representing *all* suffrage groups, was acknowledged by extensive press acclaim of its greatness, dignity and beauty.[2]

However, in November 1911, despite this propaganda coup and despite all the NUWSS's skilful lobbying, Asquith casually announced a new government-backed Reform Bill for the next parliamentary session. Provocatively, this bill would include manhood suffrage-giving the vote to *all* men; and, Asquith graciously added, suffragists might, if they wished, attach an amendment for women. Few announcements could have unleashed greater fury. Legislation to enfranchise all men but not a single woman had been the campaigners' greatest fear. Great Tory ladies took as a personal affront the extension of the vote to their gardener's boy but not to them. The small Independent Labour Party (ILP), still largely the equality conscience of the Labour Party, sprang into action with a brave 'Political Equality Campaign' and began lobbying Labour leaders prior to January's Party conference. This historic initiative did not go unnoticed by the NUWSS, which began to rethink its own strategy: democratic suffragists, as Sandra Holton helpfully calls them, now worked hard to forge an innovative electoral pact with Labour.[3]

In the WSPU, fury was intense. A wave of window-smashing followed, with heckling of cabinet ministers and even setting fire to pillar-boxes, destroying the mail within. Indeed, November 1911 drew a line marking the final stage of the campaign. This crisis galvanised a fresh cohort of rebel girls, suffragettes prepared to take on the government even at the risk of imprisonment and forcible feeding. Into this titanic struggle sprang a handful of young women across Yorkshire, largely based in cities – Leeds and Sheffield, Doncaster and York – individual mavericks or recent recruits to local WSPU activity. No longer did they spring from the mainstream – the mills and workshops within textile communities – and no longer could they speak for a mass movement. Rather, they were a mixed group of individualists, some recently left school, working as milliners or in shops, others married with young children. Some had been brought up by impoverished widowed mothers, others came from immigrant communities, and – in one case – even from the landed gentry. Appalled by Asquith's betrayal, they felt they no longer had much to hold them back. In the spirit of youthful daring, they used their guile and imagination to pitch themselves headlong into battle against the Liberal government. They pitted their wits against the security forces responsible for law and order: the police and prison authorities. Amid fears for public safety, over the next three years plain-clothes detectives gave chase to the suffragettes in almost Keystone Cops style.

Anti-militant critics would say this strategy was counter-productive in that the crucial constitutional demand for citizenship got lost as the Home Office was forced to grapple with public security issues. However, this argument failed to cut the mustard with Leonora Cohen and Molly Morris, Lilian Lenton and Violet Key-Jones, who sped across the region, goading the authorities wherever they went.

Leonora was born in Hunslet, Leeds, in June 1873, daughter of Jane and Canova Throp. Canova, listed as a stone carver on Leonora's birth certificate, was an artist and sculptor whose carved panels still stand in Leeds. Canova developed tuberculosis of the spine: Leonora remembered him bedridden, turning out pot-boiler paintings. When she was five, he died, aged only thirty. Widowed at twenty-nine, Jane was left to struggle. She moved to the city centre and returned to working as a seamstress, using the earnings from her needle to raise Leonora and her two younger brothers.

As a child, Leonora also suffered from TB and, because she was fragile, was taught by her mother at home. She only attended school briefly – and not very happily: fatherless pupils were stigmatised as socially second-rate, teased by more well-to-do girls. Soon Leonora was helping her mother with garment-finishing at home. With their skilled needlework, mother and daughter stitched mass-produced sleeves (which Leonora went to collect from the factory) into boys' sailor-suits, finishing them by sewing on anchor and crown badges.[4]

It was a childhood of genteel impoverishment. Jane employed a daily maid for heavy housework so as to preserve her hands for fine embroidery. She stressed healthy food to combat the recurrence of TB, and the household became vegetarian, often happily engaged in bread-making. Like so many others, the family was also in constant migration round Leeds city streets, moving in search of better rented accommodation. Treats and trips were rare; Leonora was twenty before she went to the theatre.

When Leonora left school about 1887 she was apprenticed to a fashionable city-centre milliner. Here she worked a year without pay before becoming a probationer on 2/6d [12½p] a week. Leonora and the others would work into the night to finish the elegant hand-tucked hats in time for Edwardian garden parties. Leonora soon proved skilled and efficient; when she was sixteen she graduated to head milliner and her weekly wage went up to 16/- [80p] though her position still involved sitting up all night to finish an order.[5] Eventually she was paid £80 a year [£1.50 per week]. By the turn of the century, when she was in her mid-twenties, Leonora became a millinery buyer at Bridlington, the Yorkshire seaside resort near Scarborough, doubtless providing hats for the holiday trade. By this time she had met Henry Cohen.

The Cohen family was among the earliest wave of Jewish immigrants to Leeds. Henry's father, Abraham, a hawker, was born in Warsaw and his mother, Rosetta, in Prussia. They married in 1852 in one of Leeds' first synagogues. Abraham became a watchmaker and, after Rosetta died, a jeweller and silversmith. One of at least nine children, Henry became an apprentice watchmaker too. By the time he was in his twenties, he was a jeweller's assistant, probably helping in the family city-centre business and living above the shop. The Cohens were a hard-working family, who never closely identified with later Jewish arrivals in Leeds fleeing Eastern Europe and congregating in a Yiddish-speaking ghetto. Indeed, by the turn of the century, Henry had moved further out to a residential area beyond the university.[6]

When she was fifteen, Leonora was invited to a children's party where she first met Henry Cohen. They met again a few years later and were strongly attracted. It was a daring, even foolhardy courtship, yet they decided to marry. This caused consternation all round: 'marrying out' was unthinkable in Jewish communities. Henry was cut off by his family, while Leonora's mother did not want her daughter to marry at all, believing that she 'should do something for women' to prevent future generations from having to go through what she, an impoverished widow with no political voice, had had to endure. Despite these fierce misgivings, in March 1900, thirty-two-year-old Henry Cohen, watchmaker and jeweller, did indeed marry twenty-six-year-old Leonora Throp, millinery buyer (and possibly pregnant), at the register office in Bridlington, a safe distance from Leeds; neither family acted as witnesses at the ceremony.

Leonora recalled that she could not mention Henry to her mother for years; but these 'family troubles only pushed us closer together'. Back in Leeds, the couple moved into Harehills, a northern redbrick terraced suburb. As befitting a businessman's wife, Leonora retired from millinery. In November, their daughter Rosetta (named after Henry's mother) was born; sadly, just one day short of her first birthday, she died of tubercular meningitis. Henry and Leonora moved to a fresh house nearby; and the following November, Reginald Cohen was born. Reg survived.

For the next nine years, evidence of Leonora's life is sadly lacking. Leonora and Henry, devoted to each other, determined to live a tranquil domestic married life, unlike her over-worked mother and his congested family. For Leonora, her home became a sanctuary. She immersed herself in bringing up Reg, baking bread, making marmalade; and in due course her mother became reconciled to the marriage. Henry's business prospered and Reg was eventually sent to boarding school. As a respectable businessman, Henry became a staunch Liberal, even joining the redoubtable Leeds and County Liberal Club.

Leonora grew interested in the sweated industries campaign, particularly over women's low pay. And she had retained some of her mother's grievance about women's unfair disenfranchisement. Her mother, though, had never joined the Leeds Women's Suffrage Society, believing that it was not for women like her. Leonora later recalled:

> My mother was a wonderful woman and I can always remember something she said to me as a child. You know how children say they belong to this party or that, depending on how their parents vote?
>
> Well, my mother said it was no use me pretending to belong to any party because I would never have the vote. It seemed to me so wrong and I always wanted to do something about it.[7]

Certainly, Leonora insisted that it was the harshness of her mother's life and votelessness that turned *her* into a suffragette: 'When I saw the kind of people who had votes and my mother had none – it didn't seem fair, to say the least'. She added that she would put her capable mother beside incapable men she saw going to the polling booth, and who were not worth her salt.[8]

Leonora's two brothers were also interested in suffrage, and when some well-known suffragettes were imprisoned, they challenged her with, 'What are you going to do?' In fact, at some point, Leonora did join the Leeds WSPU branch, probably having observed the arrests of local women like Mary and Amy Titterington. Later Leonora reminisced: 'I simply joined, when [it] started in Leeds . . . Oh, I was in everything!' (This recollection is rather fuzzy: there is no evidence that she was involved during the Mary Gawthorpe years, or indeed that they even knew each other.)

Leonora began to play a supportive role around 1909–10, selling papers and fund-raising, her speciality being marmalade-making. Certainly by 1911 she was WSPU branch secretary.[9] And then suddenly, in November, when Asquith broke his suffrage commitment by announcing a manhood suffrage bill, Leonora was almost overnight seized by Votes for Women passion. Appalled by the Prime Minister's betrayal, she now determined she would never give up the fight with the government for the vote – to the death, if need be. A fearless woman, her personal militancy soon amazed the newspaper-reading public. Luckily, the collection of Leonora's papers, sadly scanty for the first thirty-eight years of her life, is extremely rich for late 1911 to 1914 – the period when she plunged full-throttle into militancy.

Leeds was fortunate to have the services of the WSPU Yorkshire organiser, Mary Phillips. Another of the experienced Scottish suffragettes, she did for the Leeds-Bradford area what Adela had done for the Sheffield-Scarborough stretch. Leeds WSPU had also secured an office right in the city centre; and, like Scarborough and Sheffield, it too had opened a shop, its large window decorated in 'the colours', with cartoons drawn by a local member.[10]

Immediately after Asquith's announcement, the WSPU circulated local branches, asking members to volunteer for a deputation to Westminster on Tuesday 21 November. Leonora was among those who volunteered to go, along with other local Leeds women, including a May Boyd-Dodgson.[11] This was Leonora's first visit to the capital, and she would have discussed this dangerous venture with Henry – who had his beloved wife's safety at heart. A day or so before she set off for London, the WSPU issued detailed guidance, so that the 400 women who had volunteered knew what was involved and came fully prepared:

On Tuesday [21] evening, when coming to the Demonstration, it is advisable not to bring more money than is absolutely necessary, nor to wear jewellery, furs, nor to carry umbrellas.

In the event of arrest, you will be taken to Cannon Row or another police station and charged, when it is advisable *to make no statement* . . .

Bring with you to the police court the next morning a HANDBAG containing night things and a change of clothing, brush and comb, etc., *also do not forget to come provided with food sufficient to keep you going for the day* . . .

You will receive full instructions from Mr Pethick-Lawrence on Wednesday morning. You need not worry, as everything has been foreseen.[12]

37. Daily Sketch, *22 November 1911, 'Leaders of the Suffragist Rioting before the furious onslaught last night'. Leonora Cohen: probably the arrowed figure.*

WSPU militancy was certainly about to change Leonora's life. 'I lost every friend I had', she recalled, but said, 'Oh, well, I've joined these people . . . and what's more, I'm intending going to London'.[13] Afterwards she remembered that, when facing a militant action, she nearly died of fright and had to steel herself to the crowds beforehand. As an experienced milliner, Leonora always dressed with becoming elegance, now enhanced by the services of a professional dressmaker. It might be the depths of winter, but she selected her coat and hat with care; she could see the risks were high. She bade farewell to Henry (Reg would have been away at school) and set off down to London with May Boyd-Dodgson and the others. Here Leonora made her way to Caxton Hall for a WSPU meeting.

As she was undoubtedly quite a catch for the WSPU, she was allocated a seat on the platform, behind Christabel Pankhurst who chaired the meeting; above her hung a backdrop of WSPU banners – recorded in the first surviving photo of Leonora.

Emmeline Pethick-Lawrence then led the deputation of four dozen women from Caxton Hall to Parliament Square, with a resolution demanding equal franchise rights for men and women.

The *Yorkshire Post* parliamentary correspondent took up the story. As Leonora and the others stepped forward, he caught the drama and filed a sardonic report:

> All the roads adjacent to the Houses of Parliament were blocked by sturdy men in blue, who stood in steady lines waiting for the feminine onslaught . . . Plain clothes men hung about furtively about under lamp-posts; ambulance men paraded with self-importance . . . We found little to suggest that the peace of Westminster was about to be disturbed . . .
>
> But a sudden change came over the scene. The flash-light of the photographer announced the approach of the enemy from Caxton Hall . . . The Scotland Yard officers had the pale set faces of men who knew they would have to go through with it. The men in blue stamped their feet and slapped their chests with desperate determination – they did not like the impending job, but duty was duty . . . From the Clock Tower the hour of eight was boomed out by Big Ben . . .
>
> Little groups of Members of Parliament were gathered within the police lines opposite St Margaret's Church waiting to see the battle. This was my place too. It was the most obvious point for the militant ladies to strike at on their way from Caxton Hall to the Palace of Westminster. We did not know of their arrival until the outbreak of hostilities. The police were between us and them. Suddenly dashes were made at various parts of the line, and we could hear little hysterical cries and see serviceable suffragette hats bobbing about. 'Pass on, please; pass on,' was the quiet exhortation of the mounted police, as they wheeled about here and there, keeping back the more desperate. That pacifying and persuasive 'Pass on!' was one of the most ironical things I have ever heard.
>
> But it was soon to be shown that official irony is an indifferent weapon against the enraged suffragette. When a mounted policeman backs his horse into an ordinary crowd the crowd give[s] way. The fighting females did not give way. They seized the bridles of the horses, and clung on like grim death . . .

It was not pleasant to see those women carried off by the police . . .

The battle varied, and from time to time reinforcements of police would be called up to strengthen some point where the attack was being pressed with particular energy. The men in blue would swing out from Palace Yard, their breath smoking in the frosty air, and would grimly bear down upon the place where their manly services were needed.[14]

Police officers paraded in pairs in front of public buildings (such as the Local Government Board offices) along Whitehall, where more reporters were stationed. They provided a second view on the unfolding tumult. For a second — separate and unpublicised — group of suffragettes, armed with bags of stones and hammers, set forth on a surprise attack to smash windows of government offices and commercial premises. About eight o'clock two well-dressed women and 'four harmless-looking girls' suddenly threw stones at Treasury and Home Office windows. Before long, there was scarcely a ground-floor window left along that part of Whitehall. Cheers from the crowd were punctuated by the crash of stones through plate-glass windows, followed by shattering panes, then police whistles. The startled reporter added, 'the window smashers were quite methodical in their work, the stones they used being enclosed in little cloth bags, which by the aid of long linen tapes were used as slings'. Shop fronts and newspaper offices in the nearby Strand and Charing Cross were also attacked.

By her own account Leonora was in the middle of the scrimmage as it grew increasingly dangerous. The evidence is somewhat confusing about exactly what happened as the crowd swirled around her in Parliament Square that evening. She said she 'was thumped on the jaw with [the] clenched fist of [a] policeman, and knocked down under a mounted policeman's horse', that she was sprayed with foam from the horse's mouth and her clothing torn. Claiming she had been in danger of being trampled underfoot, she threw a stone only as a last resort to save her life (elsewhere she said as a protest), smashing a window in the Local Government Board building. She had carefully written out her statement in green ink:

Votes for women
This is my Protest against the Liberal Government for its treachery and torture of the Suffragettes of Great Britain who claim the right to have the Vote and become recognised Citizens.
Signed, Leonora Cohen
Leeds[15]

There were mass arrests: by midnight, the number had risen to 223. Among them were Leonora Cohen and May Boyd-Dodgson from Leeds.[16] That evening Leonora was taken to Cannon Row station, charged with malicious damage, and at two a.m. was bailed (for £2) to appear the next morning at Bow Street police court nearby in Covent Garden. Since Henry was expecting her home, she sent him an urgent telegram.[17]

On Wednesday 22nd, Leonora duly appeared in court, along with over a hundred other cases, all attracting large crowds outside; she was again bailed (this time for £10) to appear in court again the next day, Thursday. Eventually Leonora reappeared at Bow Street police court on Monday 27th at 10 a.m.; however, perhaps because the court system was growing exhausted by its daunting backlog of window-smashers, her charge sheet now merely stated 'police'.[18] In the confusion, newspapers, bulging with arrests and court hearings, could no longer log the details of one Leeds offender.

The next day, Tuesday 28th, the wearied Bow Street magistrate, Marsham, dealt with fifty more cases, Muskett once again prosecuting. When it was her turn to step into the dock, Leonora made a defiant speech: she denied that breaking a government window was 'malicious', claiming she threw the stone only as a last resort to save her life, as she was in danger of being trampled underfoot. This did not persuade Marsham, who sentenced Leonora to seven days. May Boyd-Dodgson received five days, and together they were all taken off in a Black Maria to Holloway. Here Leonora became just another prison number, labelled 'Reg. No. 11474'.[19]

The experience of arrest and imprisonment was indeed a transformative moment for Leonora. As *Votes for Women* suggested of this batch of arrests: 'The police court is not a court of justice, but a court of injustice . . . The lessons of the police court have burned themselves into the souls of the Suffragettes.'[20] Ever afterwards Leonora carefully preserved her police charge sheets and even the small Holloway Prison label. How she endured that week in prison and the anxiety felt by Henry are not known.

Back home, Leonora and Henry could now reassess the new situation. Henry adored his wife and remained supportive. Believing in the dignity of motherhood, he held that wives of propertied men should be able to vote. He was, however, worried about Leonora addressing open-air meetings which could so easily turn violent. And as a member of the elite Leeds and County Liberal Club, he found other clubmen had views about his wife becoming a gaol-bird. They admonished Henry that he should 'tie her to the table leg' to stop her leaving home again on nefarious escapades. Yet

38. Leonora: 'After my release from Holloway Prison wearing the prison badge, Portcullis with broad arrows in purple, green & white.' Rosemont Studio, Bond Street, Leeds.

Henry's loyalty was unshakeable. 'He stuck all that for my sake', she said. Indeed, Leonora needed to count upon that solidarity at home. 'I lost every friend I had . . . My name was mud'. Both husband and son staunchly stuck by Leonora in her new career as suffragette militant.[21]

For the WSPU, smashing the windows of buildings unconnected with the Liberal government represented a new departure, one requiring speed, co-ordination, a decoy deputation. There were quick arrests, to keep struggles on the street to a minimum. Christabel, familiar with the history of reform movements, hastily defended this new direction militancy had taken, arguing that men had won the vote by riot and rebellion. Others still needed convincing: vigorous correspondence on 'window smashing and the suffrage' raged in the *Yorkshire Post* between the editor and Mary Phillips as WSPU organiser in Leeds – Mary echoing Christabel's line.[22]

It was war between the WSPU and the government. Suffragette militancy continued to spiral during 1912. Not only were there further window-smashing raids on West End plate-glass shop windows, but freelance militants also widened their attacks on property even to arson. The government continued forcibly feeding hunger-striking prisoners, both women and their male sympathisers. In February, one man's horrendous case came to public attention. William Ball, imprisoned after protesting against the forcible feeding of male supporters, went on hunger strike and was himself forcibly fed. He claimed he was given electric shocks while strapped down for feeding – testimony dismissed by the investigating medical experts. However, this inhuman treatment so affected Ball that he lost his sanity, was certified as a lunatic and sent to Colney Hatch Asylum. The government robustly defended its actions.[23]

Suffragettes remained unconvinced. In a protest at Ball's mistreatment, they broke Home Office windows. Among them was Mary Gawthorpe, although still not fully recovered in health and no longer a WSPU member. Mary was arrested and taken to Holloway; here, she too embarked upon not only hunger strike but the much more terrifying thirst strike. Due to her chronic illness, she was released after just thirty-six hours to recuperate. Mary remained a fierce opponent of this brutal gaol regime, organising a protest petition against forcible feeding in Dublin's Mountjoy Prison. But her own fragile health now meant she took no further active part in the suffrage campaign. It also provided a pretext to withdraw from her joint editorship of the individualist *Freewoman*, which had distressed her by its attacks on Pankhurst suffragette militancy.[24]

For Leonora Cohen, the government's hypocrisy left her in no doubt of the rightness of window-smashing. She became increasingly active in the Leeds WSPU branch, taking responsibility for publicising a Christabel Pankhurst meeting. There were also meetings in local schools, a speakers' class to build women's confidence, and close links to the Leeds labour movement; all this suited Leonora and her concern with women's low pay.[25]

In early March the WSPU issued another invitation to Parliament Square to coincide with a Commons' debate, and Leonora apparently decided to take part again. The press reported how:

some hundreds of women sallied forth carrying large muffs in which hammers were concealed, and at a given moment, according, it is believed, to a pre-concerted signal, they went up to the plate-glass windows of various shops and deliberately smashed them with the hammers.[26]

This simultaneous destruction reached right along the Strand, up into Bond Street and even to Harrods in Knightsbridge. A clerk working inside the Home Office had a narrow escape from a flying stone and broken glass. There were over a hundred arrests, including May Boyd-Dodgson again, but somehow Leonora – presumably also muffed and hammered – managed to evade the police this time. Henry would have heaved a sigh of relief.[27]

Ever defiant, Christabel now turned the miners' strike against the government too. 'The fact that the miners are going to get legislation because they have made themselves a nuisance is a direct incitement to women to endeavour to obtain a similar privilege'. *The Times* described how 'bands of zealots summoned from the country wandered about the West-end of London', with these provincial women smashing windows with hammers and stones, leading to further arrests. Leonora's exact involvement may be hazy, but the broader impact is clear: London was now in uproar. The Royal Academy decided to close its exhibition of Old Masters and the British Museum shut. Window-breaking certainly remained the greatest controversy, with Mary Phillips and the *Yorkshire Post* editor still slugging out the rights and wrongs. There were widespread fears for the public safety of innocent bystanders; and one MP demanded legislation to allow firms whose plate-glass windows had been smashed to claim damages against the WSPU.[28]

Certainly, that spring Home Office files began to bulge with lists of suffragette prisoners in Holloway being forcibly fed, and with letters of protest over forcible feeding – including protests from doctors objecting to this grisly practice.[29]

As the window-smashing battle raged, other suffrage groups questioned the effectiveness of these seemingly dangerous tactics. Sympathy for the WSPU began to leak away. The NUWSS expressed its indignation at harmful WSPU behaviour, while the Women's Freedom League (WFL) preferred its own non-violent tactics of tax-resistance and census evasion.[30]

We can catch this ambivalent tone by listening to members' voices in the League's Middlesbrough branch, far removed from West End plate-glass smashing raids. These North Riding women provide a commentary on the internal suffragette tensions triggered by the tumultuous militant actions, and personal costs paid.

This small League branch in Middlesbrough was still run by the Coates clan: Alice Schofield-Coates and her sister-in-law Marion Coates-Hanson. They had been joined by two sisters, Lottie Mahony in her early twenties and teenager Amy, daughters of an engine-stoker. The branch's campaigns remained broad: getting women elected as Guardians and ridding child health provision of 'the taint of pauperism'; these were leavened with discussion about Ibsen and 'Women and the New Philosophy'. There was support for an Edinburgh–London Women's March, plus merchandising of WFL tea, chocolate, and candy tied in white, gold and green, the WFL colours.[31]

The branch was tolerant and democratic, and all proceeded amicably until April 1912, shortly after the window-smashing raids. Lottie Mahony challenged militancy, proposing that the League should not 'be incapacitated through the imprisonment of its leaders'. However, her younger sister, Amy, encouraged WFL members to participate in 'well-thought out schemes whether involving imprisonment or not which do not unnecessarily expend our forces'. There was also tension about planning in case of the arrest of the national leaders – especially Charlotte Despard, a celebrity suffrage figure. These were difficult times for militant groups, stretched to breaking point.

At this point, Marion Coates-Hanson and six others resigned from the WFL national executive because, in the words of the branch minutes, 'the majority of delegates put conf[idence] in Mrs Despard and gave her power to rule, and Mrs Coates-Hanson would not submit to the ruling of one person'. Marion shortly after resigned from the branch itself; the secretary wrote, with genuine sorrow at losing the founder member, asking that she reconsider. Marion disliked the cult of leadership, feeling more at home in the democratic ILP. It was a bitter parting: she even asked for her 13/6 [67.5p] affiliation fee back. As well as a political squabble, this was also a family affair, with rumours circulated 'about private matters of the Branch'. Alice Schofield-Coates remained in control, and Charles Coates (Marion's brother) became president, and took part in a public debate, speaking for the League against anti-suffragists.[32]

However, nationally, Charlotte Despard remained president and the League bravely continued, despite such everyday tensions. But, by 1913, the League was feeling the anti-suffragette backlash, whipped up by those who utterly distrusted the WSPU and felt alienated by its increased militancy. In the Middlesbrough branch, discussion continued on about militant tactics, and in early 1913, it was finally decided to support the

League policy of 'constant defiance of the law', protesting against a harsh sentence passed upon Mrs Despard 'under laws which women have no hand in framing'.[33]

The WSPU now entered its final, desperate phase. Christabel Pankhurst was exiled in Paris. In autumn 1912 the Pethick-Lawrences were expelled from the WSPU they had loyally supported for so long. A new paper, the *Suffragette*, edited with defiantly imperious panache by Christabel, began immediate publication as the WSPU's official – and very militant – voice. With stridently belligerent cartoons on its cover, the paper declared war on that three-headed giant, the 'coalition government'. It decreed that even Labour candidates should be opposed at elections. It was now war on the Labour Party too. The WSPU had long disparaged the NUWSS, and had no patience for the electoral alliance with Labour that the democratic suffragists were systematically building.

Some experienced suffragettes grew sick at heart: that the years of WSPU campaigning were all just for this authoritarian militia-like cell? Yet certain newer converts to militancy – like Leonora Cohen – entertained no doubts. Her loyalty to Emmeline and Christabel Pankhurst remained absolute. She was soon addressing Sunday evening open-air meetings in Leeds, speaking outside chapels, and standing on a plinth right outside the Town Hall, catching the crowds as chapels came out, with Reg loyally selling Christabel's *Suffragette* newspaper:

> Every Sunday night, I used to hold a meeting and take the [banner] and unfold it as the chapel [congregation] was leaving, and I used to take him with me, and he had to sell the *Suffragette* paper and if he couldn't sell any [he] used to say, 'Buy a paper' – which someone would, and used to talk to him – until I came off the plinth. He was so loyal to the suffragettes.

'We had a dreadful time of it in Leeds', she added, 'You've no idea of the abuse we got. The women used to shout they'd like to hang me with the green scarf I was wearing.'[34] However, the unquestioning loyalty of Reg and Henry to their adored Leonora remaining absolute, she placed herself resolutely in the firing line again and again.

CHAPTER 12

Pillar-boxes and beefeaters: Molly Morris and Leonora
1912–1913

When the WSPU reflected back and asked 'Why the Union is Strong' it significantly identified spiritual values and:

> the inspiration given to all connected with the Union by the heroic women in the fighting line who are risking health, and life itself, in order to gain the enfranchisement of women of their own time and of future generations. The Government's persecution, which in the past year [1913] has increased in its cruelty, has stirred the women of the Union to the very depth of their soul. The WSPU has come through this fire of persecution like tempered steel . . . Those individuals who, despite the passing of years and long service of the cause, possess the quality of perpetual youth, and are able constantly to receive new inspiration, cleave to the Union more closely than ever – while those fall away who started with a limited stock of faith, and have grown, as it were, spiritually old and infirm. And thus, just as the tree freed of its dead wood flourishes exceedingly, even so the Union flourishes because it retains that which is vital and loses only that which is no longer vital.[1]

This rhetoric of personal sacrifice allowed those expelled, or leaving to join other suffrage organisations, to be dismissed as 'dead wood'. The contrasting of 'the spiritually old and infirm' and 'the quality of perpetual youth' was the heady stuff to inspire idealistic girls to throw everything up and commit themselves to the WSPU. Molly Morris did just that. In winter 1912–13 she became a WSPU organiser and, most helpfully for suffrage historians, afterwards wrote her own life story.

*

Molly Morris had been brought up on rather vague stories about her family history: that her father's family may have been German-Jewish and that her mother's family was descended from a long line of Irish kings. If Molly sounded imprecise, well she might. Of all the rebel girls, she had the most wandering raggle-taggle ancestors.

Molly's father Julius was born in London's East End; here his father, German-born Isaac Moritz, was an india-rubber-coatmaker. Moritz became Morris, the first of many family name changes. Teenage Julius moved north, working as a general labourer in the Manchester-Salford area.[2] Here Molly's mother Clara lived, Clara's father had been a cattle drover who was imprisoned at one point; his wife, Molly's grandmother, surviving as a street hawker during his absence. Later the grandmother worked as an earthenware dealer, claiming to be a widow (though in fact her erring husband was living nearby in a vast lodging house, probably a doss house, still giving his occupation as cattle drover – an increasingly arduous way to earn a living in urban Salford).[3] So Molly grew up on the romanticised tales of two key late-Victorian communities of the dispossessed: Jewish and Irish.

Julius (who anglicised his name to Alfred) and Clara married in 1886 in Salford, and moved out into Lancashire. He got work as foreman cutter in a rubber-manufacturing factory, and their daughter Ethel (as Molly was called prior to *her* name change) was born in June 1890, one of seven children. Her happy rural childhood was somehow disrupted. Molly's father Alfred, politically a radical, had rather recklessly thrown up his job to support a workers' wage claim. Clara was furious. There were scenes at home. The family had to move back to the Salford slums. At this point Clara got a job as the 'lady manager' of a dairy shop further out of the city.[4] Alfred lost his job again, Clara became the breadwinner, and bitter quarrels between Molly's parents persisted. Clara walked out, then returned; eventually Alfred went to Birmingham – and never returned. To keep her beleaguered family afloat, Clara, a clever needlewoman, turned to making and selling children's clothes.

Molly entertained one fierce ambition when she was young: to become a nurse. But as the eldest daughter, she had to leave school and go out to work as an assistant in a bakery and confectioner's shop, as well as take on much of the housework. Resourceful Clara, helped by local philanthropic women, even got a job as a local health officer. But, as Molly's adolescent years passed, her own fierce yearning to become a probationary nurse had to be put on long-term hold – though she attended general education evening classes.[5]

Molly's was a home where socialist ideas were discussed. Clara, now working in public service, warmed to the rising socialist and labour movements. Thus mother and fifteen-year-old daughter came to hear of Christabel Pankhurst and Annie Kenney's arrest after the 1905 Free Trade Hall meeting. This, Molly reminisced later:

> had shocked me and offended my sense of fairness. My mother was indignant and held forth to her daughters on the matter, and we were very much in agreement with her. Quick to act as always when deeply stirred, she at once made enquiries as to where the Manchester group of supporters of the WSPU met together, and joined them . . .
>
> At the first meeting she attended they appealed for helpers to carry through a publicity campaign they were planning. My mother promptly said she could bring her daughter along. That of course meant me. I willingly responded . . . I was still only about sixteen years of age. So my dreams of a nursing career were superseded for a time.[6]

Molly knew nothing of politics; but to her, women's claim to the vote seemed plain common sense: as in Leonora Cohen's family, her mother 'had for years been the mainstay of all of us', and Molly, too, had borne adult responsibilities at home. So she threw herself into this exhilarating life: overnight she met new people and made new friendships:

> I began distributing leaflets and going around with my mother and other adult speakers to their meetings, and I chalked the walls and pavements with the slogans 'Votes for Women', sold pamphlets at meetings

and, later, copies of *Votes for Women*. On one occasion, Molly reported, she was arrested for chalking the pavements to advertise a meeting at which Emmeline Pethick-Lawrence and Adela Pankhurst were to speak; but the Manchester police chief seemingly took a benign view of these escapades ('Miss Morris, you girls give me a lot of worry') and she was quickly released.[7] Her mother, Molly recalled, became a good speaker, and together they would find themselves after an enthralling meeting, the trams stopped, miles away, walking all the way home.

Over the next few years, the Morris family circumstances gradually eased. Among Molly's closest suffrage friends was – of course – popular, merry Mary Gawthorpe, WSPU organiser for the Manchester-Lancashire area 1908–10. Nine years older than Molly, and considerably more experienced at dealing good-humouredly with hecklers, Mary took the younger woman under her wing, while Molly helped Mary organise for the WSPU in Manchester. Probably through Mary, Molly met Alfred Orage, Victor Grayson, and other socialist intellectuals – Molly's own Leeds Arts Club. Possibly it was Mary who advised the name change from 'Ethel' to 'Molly', during discussion of errant fathers. Certainly it was all an exhilarating contrast to her shop-assistant world, introducing Molly to the wealthy sympathisers out in the suburbs, upon whose largesse the WSPU depended for funds.[8]

Despite the social chasms within the WSPU, Molly greatly admired the Pankhursts. Beautiful Emmeline, radiating passionate sincerity, 'could hold any meeting in rapt attention', while Christabel was compared with the great orators of her time. So, although she had admired the Pethick-Lawrences too, when they were ousted from the WSPU in autumn 1912, Molly – like Leonora – remained firmly a Pankhurst loyalist. Though sad that differences had arisen, Molly certainly believed 'there were no divisions in the ranks of local organisations'. She read Christabel's new *Suffragette* with its lurid declaration of 'war' between the WSPU and the 'coalition government'. Molly referred to it as 'our paper'; and in late 1912, still working in the shop, she saw in the *Suffragette* a job advertisement that caught her eye: 'Wanted. An organiser for the Sheffield branch of the WSPU':

> Mary Gawthorpe urged me to apply for the post. I was in a dilemma. I seemed to be pulled in so many directions at once . . . I was now a young woman of twenty-two and had no doubts whatever that I could do the job, nor had Mary . . .
>
> Certainly there were not the same ties as hitherto, to hold me firmly at home . . . [Yet I was not] sure how my mother would react to the proposition, for a year or two earlier she had most vigorously opposed any suggestion of making application to become a probationary nurse . . . When however I consulted her about this job, to my great surprise she agreed that I should apply and rejoiced with the rest of us when I was appointed. Whether this was due to the influence of Mary Gawthorpe or enthusiasm for the WSPU I don't know, but she agreed.[9]

And so Molly said all her goodbyes to family and friends and boarded a train in Manchester, heading through the Pennines and the Peak District to Sheffield:

I sat back in the railway carriage and the train steamed out of Victoria Station and I breathed a sigh. I didn't like leaving Manchester and everything and everyone I associated with it. As the train rolled along I wondered what the future held . . . I pondered over that question a long time until I received a reminder that Sheffield was near at hand and Votes for Women had not yet been won.[10]

Sheffield WSPU was mightily relieved to see Molly Morris. Adela Pankhurst and Helen Archdale had left the city over a year before. The branch was run almost single-handedly by its secretary-cum-treasurer Elsa Schuster. She co-ordinated the city-centre shop in Chapel Walk, with its fund-raising 'self-denial efforts', 'At Home's' and exhortations for paper-selling.[11]

Elsa Schuster, something of a shadowy figure, had been born in Leipzig, Germany, and seems to have had an independent income. In November 1910, the WSPU's attempt to 'rush' the House of Commons had met with such widespread brutality that it became dubbed 'Black Friday'. Elsa Schuster had taken part in the 'Black Friday' deputation; she was later arrested for stone-throwing and sentenced to fourteen days in prison. After her release, this valuable WSPU recruit was somehow despatched north to sustain Sheffield after Adela's departure.[12]

Without a salaried WSPU organiser, however, the city lacked the pizzazz of, say, Mary Phillips' Leeds branch. So naturally, when Molly arrived in blackened industrial Sheffield, Elsa met her at the station and took the new organiser under her wing. To Molly, Miss Schuster appeared an older 'very quiet refined person . . . rather spinsterish in appearance, she was always well dressed, always kind and helpful'. Elsa took Molly to stay with a WSPU member out in the suburbs until she found digs with sympathisers nearer the WSPU office. The unlikely pair soon became firm friends.

Beyond loyalty to the Pankhursts, however, Molly remained fairly naïve about suffrage politics. With only her shop-work experience, she wondered how she would cope with her new 'organising' role, but she soon discovered she had *just* the right experience for the job because:

The term 'organiser' as applied to the post to which I had been appointed in Sheffield was a misnomer. I found myself in charge of a small shop selling from one counter the literature of the movement, and from another the handiwork, needlecraft goods etc, made by women members to be sold to raise funds for the organisation, organising sales of the *Suffragette* at meetings, indoor and outdoor, helping the Hon. Secretary in the arranging of social gatherings of women in well-to-do houses . . . Most of my days were fully occupied in the shop.[13]

Nights were different. Elsa and Molly 'spent many a night on chalking excursions in the outlying districts, as far away sometimes as Doncaster, returning in the morning hours as the workers were pouring into the factories', about 6 a.m. 'We kept this up for a long time' – until Molly's neighbours grew suspicious that the nights away were *not* chalking expeditions. Indeed, in contrast to Adela, eventually worn down by years of tub-thumping and street scrimmages, Molly paints WSPU life as exhilarating fun. She was new to it, younger, and in good health. It was all a ripping adventure.

Sheffield reflected the narrowing *Suffragette* focus of the national WSPU: small groups, surprise *attentats* (as anarchists called their propaganda by deed). From late 1912 there were minor arson attacks, using dark liquid poured into pillar boxes – though little damage done to the mail inside. (These attacks stiffened the resolve of local suffragists, who vigorously condemned such violent tactics and argued the constitutional case.)[14] As the WSPU war with the government grew fiercer, Molly became part of the postbox-firing squad; later she reminisced about this escalating militancy as 'the most exciting experience', referring in rather a debonair tone to 'bombs' (when she probably meant inflammable liquid). In her autobiography, she described how the London office would direct the assaults on pillar-boxes:

Miss Schuster and I first visited London and it was from headquarters we got the bombs for the job. How many boxes we fired in and around the Sheffield district I could not tell. But the occasion on which I fired the big letter box outside the Town Hall is best remembered. It was one afternoon when I got someone to take charge of the shop. I slipped several into this box as if posting letters. Contrary to expectations (in that some time was supposed to elapse before they were fired) I had walked only a few yards away when smoke belched out of the box. At the same time a car backfired in the street and the people thought a bomb had exploded. The fire brigade came dashing up and a crowd gathered round. I mixed with the crowd and looked on. Of course the police and detectives came too. A detective standing beside me remarked most sympathetically, 'We know it's the London lot who do

this kind of thing, Miss Morris, and not you young ladies . . .' How fortunate
I was he thought like that. I had quite a number of these little trouble-
makers in my handbag ready for posting![15]

Generally, little damage was actually done to the mail in the pillar
boxes. However, when a box at Sheffield's General Post Office was emp-
tied, a packet containing some explosive mixture burst open in the
postman's hands, and he only narrowly escaped injury. Ten days later,
after suburban postbox raids, some mail *was* destroyed. In one box was
found the remains of a glass tube which had contained some explosive
mixture; it was labelled 'Mackenna', a reference to the new Home
Secretary Reginald McKenna.[16] We can almost plot Molly Morris's organising period in Sheffield by the pillar-box outrages.

Even WSPU organisers had Sundays free. Molly joined a ramblers' club,
escaping the city to spend wonderful days exploring the nearby dales, talking and singing together (and on one occasion calling in upon Edward
Carpenter). Back in Sheffield, the ramblers often returned early enough to
find the open-air political meetings still buzzing:

> Several of us would make for our shop nearby, collect what copies of the
> *Suffragette* were available and circle around the crowd until they were all
> sold . . . [One] Sunday evening . . . I was moving around the edge of [the]
> crowd selling *Suffragette*, I asked a rather serious looking shy young man who
> was just about to join the crowd to buy a copy of the paper. He did.

Molly acted as a magnet to such politically-minded workers, so this:

> meant adding another to the list of young men who regularly found their
> way to our shop in Chapel Walk, most of them socialist working men who
> were active in one or other phase of the Labour Movement. That they were
> interested in Votes for Women I have no doubt . . . and . . . could always be
> relied on without asking to act as bodyguards . . . It was great fun.

This particular man was Jack Murphy – who proposed. Molly, caught
up in suffrage thrills and with her nursing ambition still unfulfilled, replied
she was uninterested in marriage, though Jack persisted. However:

> the visits of our working men supporters, unknown to them, created a
> problem. The ladies from Fulwood [outer suburbs] and district began to take

objection to finding men in the shop and to hold me responsible for their presence. Of course I resented this and finally resigned from the paid job.[17]

Molly left the WSPU shop, and soon found an assistant's post with a medical supply association, continuing with suffrage on just a voluntary basis. One more rebel girl had had her life totally transformed by the Votes for Women campaign. Although we leave Molly here, her autobiography throws a bright – if narrow – spotlight on the thrilling world of the twenty-two-year-old WSPU organiser.

By then, the Votes for Women campaign was set to escalate into its final pre-war frenzy. In January 1913 the Reform Bill, announced earlier by Asquith, was proceeding slowly through Parliament. It had reached the committee stage, and here pro-suffrage MPs planned to add clauses to widen the franchise to wives of voters. To gather support, Emmeline Pankhurst wrote on 10 January to WSPU members, making an emotional appeal: 'There are degrees of militancy . . . To be militant in some way or other is, however, a moral obligation. It is a duty which every woman will owe to her own conscience and self-respect, . . . to all those who are to come after her'.[18]

The WSPU also organised a deputation of working women to Lloyd George at the Treasury for Thursday 23 January; it aimed to kill 'the convenient fiction that the demand for the vote is confined to a small section of the leisured and well-to-do'. Leonora Cohen, representing local tailoresses, agreed to join this lobbying. She arranged for her mother to look after her home while she was away, and packed her bag. So, on Wednesday 22nd, among the Leeds suffragettes setting off were Leonora, and draper Mary Titterington carrying their banner: 'WSPU Leeds Representatives–Working Women Deputation. Is It Peace?' On Leeds station, as the train guard waved his flag, one woman told a reporter that on industrial issues, compared to enfranchised men, women were not listened to; and that working-class suffragettes 'who have hitherto been quiet, are going to resort to militancy'.

Leonora and the others stayed overnight in London; then to vigorous cheering they drove down Whitehall in carriages decked with flags.[19] A strong police cordon was again drawn across Whitehall. Leonora, well wrapped up but still elegant, posed on the Treasury steps alongside Scottish fisherwomen and Yorkshire textile workers, teachers and nurses. On behalf of the Leeds tailoresses, Leonora informed Lloyd George:

The average wage of girls is 7s [35p] a week. It is impossible for girls to live on that wage. It is a season[al] trade, and there are good times and bad times, and when a girl goes round morning after morning and receives no work and has no pay up to the weekend, that makes her very often lead a life of shame . . .

Leeds is known to be one of the most immoral cities of England and the reason is that young girls are literally driven on to the street for their livelihood in times of slackness . . . I therefore appeal to you on behalf of these working women. If you could see them you would see that they have got a haunted look.[20]

Leonora's persuasive argument about the 'haunted look' apparently made a deep impression upon Lloyd George who, she recalled, said 'I only wish I could place it on the floor of the House'. Certainly the deputation also impressed the tabloid press.[21]

39. 'Fisherwives and Pit Brow Lasses on Deputation to Chancellor', Treasury, Leonora Cohen (arrowed) far left, Daily Sketch, 24 January 1913.

Later that day, Thursday 23, the debate began on the Reform Bill. It received a sudden legalistic buffeting. The Speaker of the House of Commons ruled that no women's suffrage amendment *could* after all be added to it. Worse still, on Monday 27 Asquith announced that, regretfully, the bill would be dropped. This setback shocked all campaigners. Emmeline Pankhurst believed the government's treachery only proved her suspicions. NUWSS Liberals felt bitterly betrayed; and at the Labour Party conference that Thursday, it was easy for suffragists to persuade the delegates that the suffrage-labour pact must be further strengthened.

Leonora Cohen was among those absolutely incensed at the government's shabby treatment of working women. It made a nonsense of Lloyd George's show of sympathy. She wondered what to do. The exact sequence of events is difficult to track: a suffragette does not readily divulge her plotting, and Leonora's memories sixty years later seldom form an exact chronology. She seems to have decided to stay on in London for the week. On Thursday 30 she probably attended a WSPU meeting addressed by Emmeline Pankhurst, who exhorted suffragettes to further acts of militancy, saying she took full responsibility for all such acts.[22]

The WSPU now responded with guerilla fighting. Arson attacks were now targeted at not only public buildings, but also at masculine pleasure-places, notably golf courses. In a York pillar-box, letters addressed to Asquith, containing two tubes of liquid, ignited when exposed to air.[23] It was war. With arson went hunger strikes and further furore over forcible feeding of suffragettes in prison.

Leonora recalled that when volunteers were called for a window-smashing raid on Bond Street shops, she stepped forward. She decided, however, to sleep on it, and that night had second thoughts about destroying private premises. Instead, her favoured target would remain government property. She vowed, 'I will not return to Leeds without making my own protest in my own way'.[24] Thinking it out carefully, despite her hostess's misgivings, she determined that:

> I did not want to let Mrs Pankhurst down so I said I would do something else. I didn't know just what, but something dramatic.
>
> I went out into London and bought a guide book. I searched through it looking at art galleries and goodness knows what. Then I got to the 'T's. The Tower of London. I thought, that's the place. They've never had a woman there before causing trouble.
>
> Three of us got hold of an iron bar from a [house] fire grate. Then I

wrapped a piece of paper round it saying 'This is my protest against the Government's treachery to the working women of Great Britain'.[25]

On Saturday 1 February, Leonora once again dressed with deliberate care: she looked the acme of elegant respectability. She filed down the iron bar, along with a second one, and packed them into two small parcels, concealing them under her coat. (Visitors to the Tower had to give up bags and parcels before entering.) She caught the underground, 'But I was so frightened I could not get out. I had to go round again. I got out the second time and staggered up to the Tower.' On Saturdays the public was admitted free, and she nervously hovered among the crowds at the literature stall, buying picture postcards and a guide to the Tower, then standing around pretending to read them. Finally she summoned up her courage and strode inside. 'I was fortunate to see a crocodile line of schoolboys weaving its way into the Tower. I joined them at the back making people think I was a teacher. Then we got to the Jewel House'.

Leonora was a tall woman. At about 10.30 a.m., she fixed on her plan of action. She waited till the two beefeaters patrolling the room were a distance away. Then she snatched one iron bar from beneath her coat and flung it with all her might, right over the heads of the schoolboys clustered round the glass cabinet.

There was a sudden crash. A gasp ran round the chamber. Instantly the beefeaters, plus a police sergeant especially employed at the Tower on Saturdays, were on top of Leonora and she was arrested. They saw at once the smashed glass case and the piece of iron wrapped in brown paper. The room was cleared. Their examination revealed Leonora had tied round her waist a bag containing other implements; from her skirt pockets she handed the sergeant the second iron bar wrapped in paper, with a green label attached by a purple velvet ribbon: 'Votes for Women – 100 Years of Constitutional Petition[s] Resolutions Meetings & Processions have failed'. He demanded 'Have you anything else?' She produced a hammer from the same pocket and these were all taken from her. 'What have you done this for?' they demanded. 'It is my protest against the treachery of the government against the working women of Great Britain,' she declared.[26]

The law wasted no time. The full panoply of legal formalities was now set in motion. The Lord Chamberlain's office was called; Leonora was marched off in the custody of the beefeaters and police to what she took to be the dungeons, and then to the police station – collecting, as it was a Saturday, a crowd of gaping followers by the time she got there. She recalled she was put into a filthy cell; in protest she kicked the door until they moved her to the matron's room.

At this point luck was on Leonora's side. Although it was Saturday midday, the superintendent discovered by telephoning round that Thames Police Court was still sitting. Here, Leonora appeared before a stipendiary magistrate. The charge against her read: 'That she within the County of London unlawfully and maliciously did commit damage to certain public property to wit did break a glass show case at the Tower of London the damage being to an amount exceeding £5 to wit £7'. Witness statements were taken, not only from the beefeater and police sergeant, but also from the Lord Chamberlain's Chief Clerk – as well as a compliant glass-case-maker who conveniently put a price of £7 on the damage. As the prisoner, Leonora herself dramatically made her statement again: 'I have no witnesses to call. I should like to say I have made my protest against the government for their late treachery to the working women of Great Britain who have been promised votes to the number of millions and they have been disappointed. Therefore my protest.' She was then bailed at £40 to appear in court on Tuesday 4 February. The magistrate, undoubtedly aiming to make Leonora's case a strong deterrent to other suffragettes, decided that, as damage conveniently exceeded £5, her case would go for a full trial before a judge.[27] He had just made a very bad mistake.

Even as she returned through central London, Leonora found she was not only in the newspapers, but also on its billboards. They proclaimed: 'Suffragette's Raid on the Tower of London'. Indeed, Leonora, who so far had been reported in the press only as one suffragette among many, now truly hit the national headlines:

Woman's Outrage at the Tower. Glass Case Broken in Room of Crown Jewels. Royal Palaces shut. Alarming Development in Suffragette War.

A fashionably-dressed, well-spoken woman gained admission to the Tower by ticket. She was seen to be gazing intently at the Crown Regalia, which are kept behind iron bars, and then turned her attention to the unguarded glass cases which are ranged round the room, each containing valuables of a historic nature. Suddenly she produced what looked like a short bar of iron, and the crash of glass startled the few people in the room.

Yeoman Warder Ellis made a dash for the spot, and found the glass casing upon the insignia of the Order of Merit (created by King Edward VII) in fragments. The beefeater seized the woman and gave her into custody.[28]

The Times added that this and other attacks, such as cutting telephone wires, meant the closure of royal palaces; ladies were now banned from even entering Hampton Court Palace galleries 'until they had given up their muffs', and all visitors had to hand over their umbrellas and walking sticks. There were serious fears over priceless treasures in the British Museum. Another paper, prompted by 'the audacity of the new school of lawlessness', ran an alarmist headline 'Is the King's Crown Safe?' (The answer was yes: the Crown Jewels, then valued at about six million pounds, were now being protected by a powerful electric current.)[29]

Back in Leeds, Henry Cohen learnt from the papers of his wife's action; he apparently collapsed, exclaiming, 'Oh, my God! What next?' Luckily, while Henry protested 'Not again', Leonora's mother thought the action was wonderful.

Leonora's case on Tuesday 4 February was trial by jury. She had been informed beforehand of the formal procedure: the clerk of the court would read out the charge and the defendant would then plead guilty or not guilty. She certainly talked to Henry – who offered his wife some extremely canny advice and invaluable contacts.

First, the judge, Robert Wallace QC, heard the cases of other suffra-gettes, each pleading not guilty to window-breaking damage at West End shops. They were found guilty and were sentenced, one to five months, four to three months, and one was bound over.

Then it was Leonora's turn. She conducted her own defence. Judiciously giving her address as that of the Leeds WSPU office, Leonora also emphatically pleaded not guilty. Her trial proceeded. The prosecuting counsel stated his case and called his witnesses. Beefeater Ellis, yeoman warder, told the court how on Saturday he had suddenly heard a crash and found inside the smashed glass case a piece of iron; attached to it was a label with the words, 'My protest against the government's treachery to the working women of Great Britain'. On the second lump of iron were attached the words 'Rebellion against tyrants is obedience to God'.[30] The police witness added that when Leonora was apprehended, she stated, 'It is quite true, it was intentional'.

Leonora had jotted hand-written notes beforehand, probably after dis-cussion with Henry: 'Ask all witnesses if I was Hysterical? Rub it in!!' The trial then moved to the crucial technical question of the precise cost of repairing the smashed case, which the compliant case-maker had estimated at £7. Leonora, coming from a craft family and with her husband a skilled watchmaker, rejected this. Her hand-written notes indicate how she would fearlessly cross-question this witness:

> Ask expert how he makes out the price at £7. 'How did you arrive at the value of the case, when you had never even looked at it?' I say, if the State pay £7 for that case it is money wasted by the Government. Such fancy price. Women would not pay it. What is the size? How much per foot? What is the thickness of the Glass?[31]

Leonora duly summoned her own expert witness: the manager of a firm supplying glass show-cases to the jewellery trade. Indeed, the hearing was postponed while he went to inspect the damage to the case at the Tower. The following day, Wednesday 5 February, he presented his technical report to the jury. He estimated the cost to the trade of replacing the glass at only £3, adding:

> I have supplied an estimate to repair the damage for £4.10/- [£4.50]. This would leave a good profit. I should be prepared to do a job of this sort on these terms any day. I say the damage does not exceed £5 at the outside,

and that indeed he 'would do the work for £4 18s'. After her invaluable witness had stepped down, Leonora submitted to the court that 'the Damage does not exceed £5 at the very outside. Therefore it is for the Prosecution to prove my case. I submit this court has no jurisdiction on my case', and indeed she should never have been indicted for the offence.[32]

At this dramatic juncture, the judge told the jury to decide whether the value of the glass case was under or over £5. They retired and deliberated for a long time. Eventually, he instructed them, 'If you have any doubt about the matter, you must give the prisoner the benefit of the doubt.' The juror foreman replied, 'We are in doubt about the value'. The jurors therefore returned a verdict of 'not guilty' – and acquitted the accused. As she was discharged, Leonora said, 'I am much obliged to your Lordship for your kind attention and', she added smiling, 'for their decision, to the jury'. She could at last return home to Leeds.

The press duly reported this amazing verdict. 'Leeds Suffragette: Acquittal follows Smashing of Tower Show Case' ran one headline, and another marvelled at 'A Leeds Woman's Escape'.[33] So a combination of Leonora's peerless poise plus Henry's astute technical advice succeeded in persuading both judge and jury. Even in 1913 twelve men were still prepared to acquit a woman who got as near as dammit to smashing the Crown Jewels in the Tower of London. The considerable power of the state to control the suffragettes was here apparently limited by a public sense of fairness and even sympathy. Certainly Leonora's acquittal was a victory for the WSPU over the government's security forces.

In February and March 1913, greater suffragette violence erupted. There was an attack on the orchid house at Kew Gardens, then on Lloyd George's house, and another on the refreshment pavilion at Kew. Bulging Home Office files recorded the surveillance of suffragettes by plain-clothes police and detectives; prison files told of photographing and finger-printing of suffragettes. Into this law-and-order frenzy about how to contain hunger-striking martyrs, the Home Secretary introduced the government's most controversial piece of legislation: the Prisoners' Temporary Discharge for Ill-health Bill. On 25 April it finally became law, and soon became known as the Cat and Mouse Act. It allowed women out of prison to recuperate for a specified number of days; when the licence expired, the security forces could pursue them again.[34] Which they now did.

CHAPTER 13

Pilgrims and fugitives
Florence Lockwood and Lilian Lenton

SUMMER 1913

In spring 1913, when the Home Secretary was rushing the 'Cat and Mouse' legislation through Parliament, a second very different suffrage narrative was unfolding. In early 1912 Mrs Fawcett's NUWSS had forged its electoral alliance with the growing Labour Party, as the only political party which really supported women's suffrage. It soon strengthened that alliance, setting up a special Election Fighting Fund (EFF) in May-June so that the NUWSS could help Labour candidates more effectively at by-elections.

Its by-election strategy and the cross-country propaganda pilgrimages it now put in place were far less theatrically dramatic than surprise suffragette arson attacks or defiant court-room speeches to judge and jury. However, a newer and more energetic generation of suffragists now steered national NUWSS policy, drawing in impressive numbers of women: by 1913 there were over 50,000 members, with local societies steadily mushrooming and now nearing 500.[1] By reaching out to so many across the nation, the NUWSS campaigns achieved similar political significance, albeit less sensationally, as those of the WSPU.

In the light of all the many pressures for suffrage exerted by the NUWSS, the WFL and the WSPU, we need to understand *how* the Liberal government could for so very long get away with denying women the vote (and indeed imprisoning and forcible-feeding them merely for demanding it). We need to look away from the big cities; for out in the country across great regions like Yorkshire, there was a rather different – and more complex – story.

A growing number of women, now ready to demand full citizenship, felt comfortable joining the NUWSS. With rising membership its organisation on the ground grew; its local societies were divided into sixteen regional federations, two of which covered the three Yorkshire ridings; and the NUWSS likened itself symbolically to a great oak tree, growing from its mid-Victorian acorn.

40. *NUWSS Acorn.*

Likewise, the Labour Party, which was now strengthened by key union affiliations, notably the Miners, represented the big battalions of organised working people. The key labour leaders were not short-lived socialist meteors like Victor Grayson; nor untypical pro-WSPU maverick free-speech champions such as George Lansbury.[2] Rather, they spoke with an increasingly influential voice at Westminster and beyond. The Liberal government had to listen to men like Philip Snowden MP or miners' leader Robert Smillie.

Across the country, however, the strengths of the Liberals and the labour movement varied. In Lancashire, trade unions were well organised; while much of Yorkshire remained a Liberal stronghold, with trade union- ism weak outside of skilled male workers like the engineers and miners. Certainly West Riding women workers in wool and worsted mills were still poorly organised. So those few active women trade unionists who were involved in suffrage campaigns were less likely to join the NUWSS (with its closeness to Liberal employers) and far more likely to join the WSPU. For instance in Leeds, Bertha Quinn, organiser for the clothing workers' union, had already appeared in court for suffragette militancy.[3]

Across this region, the long-established strength of the NUWSS still lay with the traditional local Liberal elite, such as manufacturer's wife Florence Lockwood in Colne Valley or Dr Helen Wilson in Sheffield. Regional lead- ership was held by the great and the good, often members of the landed gentry; this was particularly so in the North and East Riding Federation, whose president, Almyra Gray of the York Suffrage Society, was married to the Under Sheriff of Yorkshire.[4]

Thus, campaigners like Isabella Ford gained new energy from EFF work, but must have felt isolated. However much ILP-ers like Isabella might cajole, old-hand Liberal suffragists did not take too kindly to the NUWSS's new-fangled national policy directives, however democratically arrived at, telling them they ought to work to support Labour candidates. There was agonised hand-wringing and foot-dragging among Liberal suffragists across Yorkshire.[5] Certainly, the Election Fighting Fund, now employing special EFF organisers, was always stronger in Lancashire. The big Manchester Federation could supply EFF organisers, such as radical suffragist Selina Cooper, and the West Riding Federation gratefully accepted them. Their task was now to win over working-class voters; such men had to be con- vinced that women's citizenship was a democratic right, that it was a political priority, *and* – in 1913 – that it was not just a law-and-order issue about arson attacks and forcible feeding.

This was a mighty challenge. By now, little of the earlier fluidity between different organisations remained. Mrs Fawcett argued that physical force was a solution neither for suffragettes nor for the government, and in pri- vate expressed her objection to co-operating with the WSPU, which is 'guilty of . . . outrages' and encouraged 'similar crimes'. Even tolerant Isabella now admitted that 'we disassociate ourselves from the militants'.[6]

Shortly after the Election Fighting Fund was set up, the enormity and com- plexity of this challenge was vividly illustrated when a by-election was called in Holmfirth just south of Huddersfield. A scattered rural constituency combining agriculture with textiles and coal mining, this was traditionally a safe Liberal seat, held by Helen Wilson's father. EFF organisers set their sights on the miners and their powerful trade union (which had nominally switched allegiance from Liberal to Labour three years earlier, though most local miners failed to notice this). Isabella travelled across to Holmfirth for the campaign, and was joined by organisers from the other side of the Pennines, like Selina Cooper. But even with the loan of a Manchester Federation motor car to reach isolated villages, the EFF strategy of persuading rural miners that women's suffrage was of any concern to them proved hard work. The local Labour Party was reluctant even to share committee rooms with NUWSS organisers. Although the Labour vote increased, the Liberals still held the seat. It was all going to be very difficult.

In January 1913, with the surprise ruling by the Speaker of the House of Commons followed by Asquith's announcement, the EFF commitment was strengthened. At the Labour Party conference just three days later, a women's suffrage amendment was debated – to which the ILP added a controversial amendment that Labour MPs should oppose *any* franchise bill which did not include women. A Miners' delegate protested: this would not help the working man. Whereupon Philip Snowden, always a persuasive orator, sprang to his feet, accusing the delegate of allowing Labour 'to steal more votes for men at the expense of women'. The ILP amendment was passed (the Miners remained neutral) and there was jubilant clapping and cheering from suffragists in the conference gallery.[7]

In spring 1913, however, the correspondence of the NUWSS West Riding Federation's organiser, Helena Renton, reveals her problems with EFF. She wrote asking to have Selina Cooper for as long as the Manchester Federation could spare her, for work in Leeds and Bradford, Doncaster and Dewsbury; with so many miners' lodges to be skilfully lobbied across coalfield constituencies, Renton added rather desperately, 'We really could keep Mrs Cooper going for some time in this Fed'. The priority was a big Miners' trade union conference scheduled in Scarborough for September, and Selina set to work, skilfully cajoling.[8]

Everyone loves a thrilling tale, often preferring it to the everyday political complexities of the suffrage campaign on the ground. With no dramatic newspaper headlines of the latest arson attack or set-piece court confrontation, it is easy to lose sight of the quieter suffragist story. Personal eye-witness evidence remains scanty. Luckily, in Florence Lockwood's diaries we can, by reading between the lines, discern clearly the timeless yet complex world of Liberal suffragists in these last few Edwardian peacetime months.[9]

The Colne Valley constituency, after its brief Grayson socialist-suffragette aberration, had lapsed back comfortably into traditional Liberalism: Labour did not even field a candidate at the last election. Here, Florence Lockwood remained not only president of the Colne Valley Women Liberals but also a Liberal Poor Law Guardian for Linthwaite. After a decade of married life with old-fashioned Josiah at Black Rock, she had settled into comfortable mid-life.

Florence, still feeling a fairly recent convert, wore her new suffrage faith with a naïve keenness. However, among her bourgeois social set, any per-suading fell on stony ground. One afternoon Florence attended a progressive whist party on the other side of Colne Valley. Guests rolled up punctually in carriages and motor cars:

> We took off our wraps in a grand bedroom, displaying our diamonds, satins, and crêpe-de-chine . . . The daughter in pink satin poured out the tea . . . The lady I sat next to asked me if I rinked [skated], and I said 'No! I have become interested in "Votes for Women" and politics generally' . . .
>
> Having only arrived there lately myself I was unduly disgusted with women who were ignorant of national affairs. She said she had no time to bother with it and she turned to her more intimate friend on her right and I heard her say 'Shall you wear it on the 12th?'[10]

Florence went home by tram, like Josiah feeling more at ease with local mill-workers' banter than with the satins of their employers' wives. In such discouraging circles, she could hardly strike out on a lone political limb and embrace the new NUWSS suffrage–labour alliance. Josiah and the rest of the Lockwoods would have felt very uneasy had she done so. Indeed, even though the Holmfirth constituency was only a hillside away, Florence says nothing about the new strategy. Her diaries convey just a sense of strain within her marriage, only partly explained by poor health: 'Josiah and I were both out of sorts and life was becoming burdensome'.[11] Florence was possibly turning a conveniently unseeing eye on this upstart alliance, laps-ing back into what felt most comfortable: traditional Liberal arguments for enfranchisement familiar to John Stuart Mill half-a-century earlier. These were, she believed, arguments that might persuade others: so about late 1912 Florence bravely wrote a pamphlet, *The Enfranchisement of Women*. She had it printed locally, and its cover bore her pleasant portrait. Almost taking the words out of Mill's mouth, Florence wrote that:

> Every free man should be recognised as having a right to a say in making the laws he has to obey.
>
> It is only slaves who have to obey laws without being consulted, and women are in that sense still in the position of slaves . . .
>
> If the present Reform Bill . . . becomes law, without amending it in favour of women, we shall be face to face with the political enslavement of women in its most acute form. Every young man of 21 years of age will be the political master of his mother . . . It is hoped that every self-respecting woman will turn with anger against such an insult.

However, Florence's voice of reason grew angry when she listed all the suffrage organisations. Of the WSPU's window-smashing tactics she declared, 'Everyone has heard and been shocked by the excesses of this extreme wing'. As a suffragist, 'we acknowledge the heroism of the "extreme wing", but at the same time the Old Society [NUWSS] realises that the same arguments which would justify stone-throwing would also justify all sorts of crimes for political ends, and we do not approve'.[12]

Florence might sound pompous, alongside daring Leonora Cohen or Molly Morris – contemporary readers now feel tolerant towards suffragette window-smashers and attackers of pillar-boxes – but that is partly because the women's franchise demand ended in victory, and partly because they cost no Edwardian lives, whether postmen, Whitehall clerks or schoolboys visiting the Tower. It was the strong fear that spiralling WSPU militancy *might* endanger innocent bystanders that Florence tapped into. She wrote her pamphlet to help persuade wary members of the public – like the whist-playing socialites.

The cautious NUWSS retained its strong links with the International Woman Suffrage Alliance (IWSA) and this introduced Florence to the wider suffrage world. In May 1913 a handbill arrived through the post about an IWSA congress to be held shortly in Budapest. Well-rooted at Black Rock, she had no desire to respond. However, the invitation caught Josiah's eyes and he said, 'Why not go?' Florence found journeys exhausting: travelling without a maid to help her dress was flustering. She definitely would not attend as an official delegate; but perhaps if she went just as an observer she would enjoy it. She made a hasty dash into Huddersfield to buy suitable clothes, then gauchely greeted friends with the news that tomorrow she was off to Budapest for an international women's suffrage congress. 'Oh, indeed', they replied – and promptly changed the subject. To find exactly where she was heading, Florence got out a map, looked up the city, and felt very superior telling people that it was the capital of Hungary on the River Danube.[13]

Budapest was an eye-opening experience. At the congress, Florence encountered well-known suffragists and writers from America and Germany, France and Holland. 'I felt a sense of ease to be a dwarf among these women, instead of standing out as something exceptional and eccentric, as I appear at home'. Two themes stood out. The first was the IWSA attitude to WSPU militants. At the 1906 congress the WSPU's membership application had been opposed by Mrs Fawcett, IWSA vice-president. Now, the president, an American, argued that it was *suffragette* sufferings that had roused world-wide interest in the vote, and a special resolution was agreed supporting the Pankhursts, despite the misgivings of Florence, Mrs Fawcett and others. The second concerned what women should do when they won the vote – notably over war and peace. One French delegate made an impassioned appeal for waging '*La guerre contre la guerre*'. Apart from Quakers like Isabella Ford, English delegates such as Florence were taken by surprise: there would surely never be another European war.[14]

But even before Florence set off for Budapest, the suffrage campaign had – in her eyes – swung yet further into the shocking 'excesses of the extremist wing'. The Cat and Mouse Act now spawned suffragette fugitives. Amongst them few 'mice' were more successfully elusive than dancer Lilian Lenton who stood trial in London then Doncaster. Behind her was a conspiratorial web spun by suffragettes like Violet Key-Jones of York. Florence and Isabella, Lilian and Violet all shared the same enfranchisement aims; yet, across a shared Yorkshire landscape, they pursued such utterly divergent campaigning tactics in the last Edwardian peacetime months.

Lilian Lenton was the most flamboyant of the rebel girls and the youngest: she was just a three-month-old baby when the census enumerator came in 1891. Lilian Ida Lenton was born in Leicester, daughter of a carpenter and joiner (probably a skilled craftsman), in January 1891. The eldest of at least five children, she grew up amid Leicester's shoemakers and hosiery workers.[15] Lilian was slim, lithe and striking; and, with what must have needed considerable determination for a working-class girl, she avoided dressmaking or shop-work. Instead she trained for a career as a dancer.

Winter 1911–12, triggered by Asquith's Reform Bill announcement, was a time of widespread window-smashing, pulling in recruits like Leonora Cohen. Lilian recalled later that she had been to a WSPU meeting and was so inspired by hearing Mrs Pankhurst speak that 'I made up my mind that night that as soon as I was twenty-one and my own boss and that I'd got through these examinations I would volunteer'. Lilian's twenty-first birthday fell in January 1912. Her first act of militancy 'was breaking a window in connection with a big window smash'; she met at the agreed London rendezvous – where 'somebody said, "We're doing post offices tonight, but I think there's only one left"'.[16]

In March 1912 Lilian, using her middle name and going under the pseudonym of 'Miss Ida Inkley', took part in the WSPU's window-smashing raids, along with Leonora Cohen. Lilian was among those arrested and was given a particularly harsh sentence: two months in prison – though without the additional hard labour penalty given to certain suffragettes then.[17]

Lilian had so far been merely a name in the long lists of suffragettes arrested. Then, in the wake of the Commons' Speaker's ruling against a women's suffrage amendment, in February 1913, just days after Leonora's Tower of London attack, Lilian apparently visited WSPU headquarters and 'announced that I didn't want to break any more windows but that I did want to burn some buildings', so long as 'it did not endanger human life other than our own'. She was told of another girl who 'had just been in saying the same thing, so we two met, and the real serious fires in this country started'.[18]

Details recalled fifty years later may be hazy but, clearly, once Lilian became a militant suffragette she was unstoppable. She was in and out of prison (six times, she believed), and:

> whenever I was out of prison my object was to burn two buildings a week . . . The object was to create an absolutely impossible condition of affairs in the country, to prove it was impossible to govern without the consent of the governed . . . No one could ignore arson, nor could they ignore young women who went about saying what I said – that whenever we saw an empty building we would burn it. And, as I say, after that I did burn an empty building whenever I saw one.[19]

Determined on arson, she struck out on a series of terrorist acts on a destructive scale quite distinct from Leonora's closely-targeted aims.[20]

Lilian was apparently arrested with her co-arsonist on suspicion of having set fire to (and indeed burnt to the ground) the Kew Gardens refreshment pavilion on Thursday 20 February. She appeared at Richmond police court, was remanded in custody and denied bail. In protest at this, Lilian refused food in Holloway. She began her prison sentence in good spirits 'making light of her two days' fast'. Then, on Sunday 23rd, at the first attempt to forcibly feed Lilian – tied down to a chair by half-a-dozen wardresses in the presence of two doctors – the tube was accidentally passed into her trachea (windpipe). Sloppy prison 'food' poured straight into her left lung, causing septic pneumonia. Lilian collapsed. Bovril and brandy were hastily administered; the prison governor rushed in; frantic phone calls followed. Lilian was critically ill. She was hurriedly released that Sunday evening, carried on a chair to a waiting taxi and, accompanied by the prison doctor, taken to a friend's house to recover.[21]

As Home Secretary, Reginald McKenna followed Lilian Lenton's collapse in prison extremely closely – as well he might. Protest at the brutality of forcible feeding poured into the Home Office. To one correspondent, McKenna replied that as Lilian had been 'in imminent danger of death' in prison and given the undesirable alternative, her release had to be authorised.

Lilian eventually recovered, disappeared and somehow managed to evade re-capture. Her case grew into a political *cause célèbre* however. Sir Victor Horsley FRS and other eminent medical specialists protested at the grave risks of feeding a prisoner who resisted. In the Commons McKenna faced accusation that forcible feeding was 'most barbaric and cruel'.[22] All the while the Temporary Discharge legislation was under discussion in Parliament. Passions ran high. The Bill finally received Royal Assent on 25 April – and much of the ensuing narrative is of course shaped by the repercussions of this, the Cat and Mouse Act, allowing a woman out of prison to recuperate on a temporary licence of so many days; when the licence expired, the security forces were empowered to detain her again.

Suffragettes greeted this notorious outcome of a national law-and-order crisis with outrage. In Bradford pillar-boxes were fired; golf greens were daubed with 'No Votes, No Golf!' slogans. The plate-glass windows of a Huddersfield golf clubhouse were mysteriously smashed and suffragettes suspected.[23]

The Cat and Mouse Act now meant that the police had to be extra sure they were pursuing and re-arresting the *right* suffragette 'mouse'. Surveillance techniques therefore tightened – in prison with finger-printing, and even covert photographing of suffragettes' faces using new camera lenses, operated by a professional photographer concealed in a van in the prison yard while the women had their exercise period.[24]

Leonora Cohen was naturally among those who reacted with forthright anger to this escalation of the government's war on unenfranchised women. In this increasingly inflammatory atmosphere, and with a strengthened police presence, she must surely have suspected by now that she was being shadowed by plain-clothes police, following her every footstep, noting down her every word. As indeed she was.

On 20 April, Leonora gave a strong speech on suffrage at a Miners' Institute meeting in East Leeds. According to the shorthand notes taken by a detective, she allegedly said:

> It is only when we make the situation intolerable that we shall get the vote. I shall never go on a deputation to the House of Commons again, and suffer my body to ill-treatment. I am going for property . . .
>
> Threepennyworth of paraffin will do more, a great deal more than all the [fund-raising] collections. One good building burnt down does more good than all the meetings. I urge you women, every one of you, who think we ought to have better conditions, to come and take part in this great fight.[25]

Then, on Friday 2 May, Leonora took part in a WSPU free-speech visit to the Ceylon café in Leeds. Here it seems, Leonora 'suddenly left her seat, threw aside her coat, displaying a sash with the letters "WSPU" upon it', and attempted to address the crowd from the balcony. Apparently the café management had got wind of the plan beforehand and police officers were to hand; within minutes the suffragettes were escorted off the premises.

On Sunday 4 May the Leeds WSPU organised an open-air procession to Woodhouse Moor on the city outskirts. Here was a chance to display banners and sell the *Suffragette*. It was also an occasion for well-choreographed elegance and modish millinery: nothing must detract from the dignified seriousness of women's claims to citizenship.[26] At this meeting Leonora allegedly told the crowd:

> The time has gone by for constitutional work. We women are outside the constitution. We are outlaws. I say here that women have not done enough.
>
> We are not going to get six weeks [imprisonment] for asking questions. I would rather have five years for burning down a mansion . . .

41. WSPU Procession to Woodhouse Moor, Leeds, 4 May 1913.

Our local branches are self-supporting, and it certainly does not cost much for threepennyworth of paraffin and threepennyworth of fire-lighters.

This was the final provocative straw for the Leeds police. The Deputy Chief Constable of Leeds now reached back into his dusty statute books. On Friday 9th he pounced, swearing before a stipendiary magistrate a floridly formal statement, that:

One Leonora Cohen is a disturber of the peace of Our Lord the King and is an inciter of others to commit divers crimes and misdemeanours against the peace . . . and . . . is likely to persevere in such unlawful conduct . . . that . . . further disturbances of the peace of Our Lord the King and further crimes and misdemeanours against the peace . . . are likely to be done and com-mitted by divers people being women, and he . . . therefore prays that she the said Leonora Cohen should be caused to appear before me or some other justice of the peace . . . that she be ordered . . . to abstain hereafter from conduct and language likely and calculated to bring about a violation of the law and of the public peace.

No compromise here. At the instigation of the Director of Public Prosecutions (DPP), Leonora was arrested by a detective inspector on Sunday 11.[27] She was presented with a lengthy hand-written list of accusations, citing the 1861 Malicious Damages Act. These included damaging letters posted in pillar-boxes in Leeds using 'various fluids', and general crimes committed by WSPU members 'of which Union one Leonora Cohen is a supporter she being Honorary Secretary of the Leeds Branch'. However, in Leonora Cohen, now well-known locally since her courtroom victory post-Tower of London, the Leeds police had met their match.[28]

Henry Cohen's steadfast support of his wife's actions was now unshakeable: he had already anxiously consulted his solicitor for advice. The Cat and Mouse Act had stiffened his resolve. Henry might be a Liberal clubman, but he now saw his wife as a victim of unreasonable state persecution. Together the Cohens made copious hand-written notes in preparation for the court case.[29]

Leonora duly appeared before a stipendiary magistrate on Wednesday 14 May. The room was crowded, including several suffragettes and male sympathisers. A buzz of excitement rippled round the court as Leonora entered:

> She wore a black serge tailor-made costume, with a white lace blouse, a green straw hat trimmed with green and mauve silk and a black spotted veil. A bunch of lilac and white flowers reposed on the table in front of her seat, and she frequently consulted a formidable batch of manuscript. She was accompanied by her husband, who throughout the proceedings took frequent notes and handed her messages.

Smiling, Leonora took her seat with Henry in the well of the court. Then, at the magistrate's suggestion, she moved forward to sit immediately behind the DPP lawyer from London, so she might hear better the case against her. As she moved forward Henry, carefully carrying the posy of violets in WSPU colours, followed and sat beside his wife, frequently prompting her during her cross-examination of the witnesses.

The DPP lawyer alleged that Leonora had disturbed the peace with speeches at the Miners' Institute and Woodhouse Moor. He submitted that these speeches:

> amount to incitements to other persons to commit crime. I will not go into the details ... but it is sufficient for the moment to indicate that they

contained such remarks as 'We must have property' . . . and 'Every woman in the [WSPU] Union is ready for anything, namely, arson and pillar boxes'.

Handley, Deputy Chief Constable of Leeds, stepped into the witness box. He too alleged that 'certain damage has been done by persons who are supporters or sympathisers of this society', the WSPU. Leonora then cross-questioned him:

Leonora: How many militant actions followed my speeches?
Handley: That I cannot say.
Leonora: Have you any evidence to prove that any damage can be attributed to the members of the WSPU?
Handley: We have no evidence.
Leonora: Thank you.[30]

Then the detective inspector quoted from his shorthand notes on what he held were the most incriminating parts of Leonora's speeches at both the Miners' Institute and Woodhouse Moor meetings. Leonora then called *her* first witness, a former Leeds Labour councillor present at Woodhouse Moor. He stated that no part of her speech suggested inciting her audience to commit malicious damage. Her next witness, present at the Miners' Institute said – rather less plausibly – that he did not think Leonora 'wanted anybody to take part in the militant propaganda'.

At the end of all this, Leonora read her prepared speech to the magistrate, challenging him: 'How can you sit in judgement on a woman on this trumped up charge of incitement?' She said the distorting jumbling of various parts of her speech, making them appear to have a different meaning than that intended, was most unfair and that no case had been made against her. However, the magistrate, Atkinson, said he believed her words did make her guilty of incitement, and asked her to undertake to refrain from such actions in future:

Leonora (dramatically): No. That is asking me to forego my principles. If I have to sacrifice anything I will sacrifice life itself.
Woman in public gallery: Hooray. (Slight applause.)
Atkinson: You have been asked to give an undertaking that you will not commit crime against the law of England.
Leonora: (indignantly) I shall give no undertaking, because it would be sacrificing the principles I have at heart. I tell you I could not do it.

Atkinson: Well, if you do not give an undertaking it confirms my impression very strongly that you meant to do so [incite] when you were addressing the mob. Are you prepared to enter into the same recognisances . . . to be of good behaviour?

After some hesitation, Leonora did agree to be bound over, to be of good behaviour, and to take no part in the militant movement. Henry Cohen, traveller and importer, agreed to a surety of £50, as did a second local man. As the court rose, a woman in the gallery shouted out 'Votes for Women'.[31]

Leonora and Henry left. Certainly it was not the full acquittal of the Tower trial, yet it was arguably a symbolic victory. If the Home Office had planned this to be a warning shot fired over the WSPU's northern bows, then it was disappointed. Suffragettes as impeccably dressed and articulate as Leonora could fearlessly cross-question police witnesses and magistrates, giving as good as they got.[32] This was one of the court cases McKenna could have well done without.

The Cat and Mouse Act had intensified covert state surveillance. With the police now pursuing suffragettes, and prison authorities deploying hidden cameras, the chase became a surreal combination of comic melodrama and something more sinister. There are problems about the survival of evidence of this shadowy underworld of police chase and suffragette evasion. However, among those offering shelter to fugitives in Yorkshire was Edith Key. In the wake of the nearby golf course attack, her Huddersfield house had, according to her two sons' memoirs, 'become regional headquarters where skulduggery, illegal acts and conspiracies were continually hatched.'[33] They also remembered that, once the Cat and Mouse Act released hunger-striking prisoners out on licence, 'our house became a refuge and a hiding place for any woman who violated her parole'. Both their parents now 'ran the risk of being charged with harbouring fugitives from justice'.[34] And Edith Key's great-granddaughter, who grew up in the very same Huddersfield house as a young child, remembers its deceptively long rambling corridors, attic rooms with small rooms leading off other rooms, and a cellar, all offering ideal cubby-holes for secreting suffragette 'mice'.[35]

Fugitive suffragettes could count on certain well-placed sympathisers around the county. But with this heroic resistance there was also a mounting sense of powerlessness. As one male supporter put it, 'the last two years before the war were a nightmare . . . It had then become literally a fight to the death'.[36] No suffragette epitomised this war waged against women more iconically than Emmeline Pankhurst, now subjected to repeated arrests and imprisonments, hunger strikes and, weakened, released under Cat and Mouse licence. News of her death was expected daily by suffragettes. It was in protest at this that, on Wednesday 4 June, Emily Wilding Davison memorably ran in front of the King's horse at the Derby at Epsom, an act caught dramatically on film. Her injuries proved fatal and led to her death that weekend. The well-orchestrated funeral procession of this celebrated suffragette martyr was staged a week later. Suffrage groups, like Middlesbrough WFL branch, sent strongly worded protests to the government, which they held responsible for her death.[37]

In the emotional frenzy of summer 1913, Emily Wilding Davison was not alone in being inspired to historic heroism. The narrative now moves to Balby, an unassuming suburb of Doncaster about twenty miles east of Sheffield – and to Lilian Lenton again. If Leonora's court case in May had attracted only local press interest, a month later Lilian's hit the national newspapers jackpot – assisted by her shadowy neighbourhood co-conspirator, Violet Key-Jones.[38]

Violet Key-Jones was born in Ireland about 1883. Her father John Jones was a surgeon major in the army, a posting which took him around Britain. Her mother, Harriet Key, came from a wealthy gentry family long based at Water Fulford Hall on the banks of the meandering River Ouse outside York: the manor had been the Key ancestors' since the sixteenth century. Violet's uncle still lived there with his children, assisted by half-a-dozen domestic servants; he offered his occupation to successive census enumerators as 'Lord of the Manor', 'Justice of the Peace', 'Esquire' or just plain 'Landowner'. By the turn of the century Violet's mother was widowed and returned to live near York's impressive railway station. Here, too, lived eighteen-year-old Violet, possibly still at school – plus an elder brother usefully employed as a locomotive engineer and probably destined for higher things within the railways, and two other children.[39]

When the WSPU militant campaign touched Violet it gripped her with a passion – whatever the personal cost. Just weeks after the first suffragette hunger strike in 1909, Violet Key-Jones was in prison and also refused food, and did so again a few months later.[40] Such a well-positioned activist, with an independent income and impeccable dynastic credentials, was a tremendous catch for the WSPU, and should be fully used. Certainly by 1911 Violet, now in her late twenties, was working as an energetic organiser, based at the WSPU York office right in the city centre, including staging "Suffragette amateur theatricals" like 'How the Vote was won'.[41]

However, as Rebecca West had observed, the WSPU liked its organisers to move around to where they might be most effective: by early summer 1913 Violet Key-Jones had boarded a train heading south from York, and travelled straight to that other great Yorkshire railway centre, Doncaster, to make a base there.

Doncaster, a railway and coal town, was safe Liberal territory, its politics enlivened by rumbustious horse-racing – and some noisy campaigning. Adela Pankhurst had spoken in the market place to rowdy hooting; and Molly Morris and Elsa Schuster had made forays there. How convenient a communications centre for the WSPU to base Violet so that she might organise that ambitious eastern stretch: Doncaster, Scarborough and York. She rented an unremarkable suburban house, 15 Osborne Road, between the town centre and the race-course. Here, with the Cat and Mouse Act in force, Violet could quietly plot and scheme.

Doncaster was, however, somewhere that suffragettes were well advised to have bodyguards. On 22 May at a town-centre meeting, the rowdy crowd subjected Violet and her male bodyguards to a battery of rotten eggs and orange peel; lads snatched away their leaflets. Seeking refuge from the missiles in a nearby Catholic Club, Violet said defiantly, 'This sort of rowdyism can only help the cause . . . I would have spoken had I been able to make my voice heard above the noise'.[42]

The following Saturday, suffragettes apparently responded – with an unsuccessful attempt to blow up a local uninhabited mansion. Police reported suffragette leaflets soaked in paraffin (though others reported a bomb whose fuse had fizzled out). A heavy iron bar holding the shutters in place had been wrenched away, suggesting to the *Doncaster Chronicle* 'some male assistance'. Violet told the paper the 'outrage' was a direct result of the government's treatment of suffrage; she vehemently denied it was retaliation for the previous week's 'scenes' and remained evasive about the involvement of local suffragettes. A few days later, there was an attack on Doncaster golf club, with corrosive acid poured onto the turf: suffragettes were believed to be responsible for this 'outrage'.[43]

If Doncaster police were so far foiled, their luck now turned. The sequence of events can be pieced together from the prosecution's evidence at the ensuing court case.

Number 15 Osborne Road, it transpired, was a veritable hive of suffragettes. Violet Key-Jones rented the house with Kathleen Brown, a well-known local suffragette who had been imprisoned three times. They apparently had a domestic servant, twenty-year-old Augusta Winship. Violet was conveniently away on holiday; but staying as a visitor was a mysterious 'May Dennis'. A frequent visitor to the menage was eighteen-year-old apprentice reporter with the *Chronicle,* Harry Johnson, who lived nearby with his parents; he and Kathleen would lend each other interesting novels by writers such as Balzac.

Harry had recently been spotted buying a quart of paraffin. Then on Monday 2 June just before midnight, two people left the house carrying a two-gallon tin of paraffin, cotton wool and newspapers, plus a bag containing fire lighters.[44] They entered the large empty-looking Westfield House in suburban Balby, getting in by breaking a window. They planned to set fire to the house, believing it to be empty. However, a caretaker, seventy-two-year-old Mary Beecroft was asleep upstairs and was awoken by breaking glass. She lit a candle and bravely went to top of the stairs, calling out 'Who is there?' The couple replied, 'We are only Suffrag[ettes] and doing no harm'; they apologised for disturbing her, having thought the house unoccupied. Beecroft ordered them out and they dutifully filed out of the back door, depositing their equipment in the Westfield shrubbery as they left. Beecroft blew a whistle to summon help but it was too feeble. She eventually got hold of the police at 6 a.m. A sergeant came round, searched the shrubbery and found the equipment – sticky stuff, newspapers, and a piece of paper with 'Miss Key Jones' written on it.

The following evening, Johnson apparently hurried round to Violet's house, saying there was a warrant out for him. He was indeed arrested, and stated that if he was refused bail he would go on hunger strike. His mother apparently brought him in a shilling dinner but he would not touch it. She also permitted the police to search his belongings – which turned up manuscript in his writing, a life of a militant suffragette. Meanwhile servant Augusta Winship was summoned for an identity parade 'with eight shop girls'; Beecroft decisively picked *her* out as Harry's accomplice.

On Monday 9 June, Doncaster police court was unusually full. On the bench sat no fewer than eight magistrates, presided over by the mayor. Every seat was occupied; on a public bench sat the local suffragettes, including Violet Key-Jones, who had now returned, wearing her WSPU colours and a Votes for Women badge. A girl with hair down her back sat nearby; the lawyers' section was crowded with barristers and solicitors. A thrill of excitement ran through court as the two accused took their places in the dock. Harry Johnson looked pale and ill, while confident Augusta was laughing frequently.

The prosecution was in the hands of the Town Clerk, traditionally a lawyer, who carefully presented his case. The defence, presented by Johnson's lawyer, hinged on the unconvincing identification by Beecroft, an elderly lady without her spectacles on, in a darkened hall lit only by one candle. Beecroft insisted it was Johnson. Augusta Winship robustly denied ever being near the hall; she was at home in bed, and said Beecroft was quite mistaken in picking her out.

Then a thrill rippled round the court. Augusta's defence lawyer called upon a 'May Dennis' to stand up. The slim girl with hair tumbling down her back immediately rose. May Dennis, 'a rather good-looking girl, who, having her hair loose down her back, had a youthful appearance' (apparently 'not above 16'), stepped into the witness box to give evidence. Slowly and deliberately, she told the court *she* was the woman whom Beecroft had seen. May Dennis even admitted to breaking into the house, accepting responsibility for the action.[45] When asked why she had entered the house, she replied without any hesitation at all, 'To burn it'. A long-drawn 'Oh!' arose from the public gallery. However, when questioned as to whether her real name was 'May Dennis' or indeed 'Lilian Lenton', and who her male companion had been on the expedition – she resolutely declined to be forthcoming – despite the Town Clerk's appeal to the magistrates that she should answer. She just laughed.

The magistrates retired at length to consider their verdict. In the end, Augusta Winship was fully acquitted and released. Harry Johnson was committed to the Assizes and bailed. The town clerk immediately asked for a warrant to arrest 'May Dennis' there and then. And the loose-haired woman, booed by some in court, was conducted into the now-vacated dock, smiling at everyone. She was identified merely as May Dennis, a friend of Violet Key-Jones, who was staying in her house for a few days. She was remanded till the next day. From the gallery there was lusty cheering and even clapping. Outside the court, the crowd booed the suffragettes, who had to be protected by police.[46]

Newspapers like the *Daily Mail* and *Daily Mirror* suggested sensationally that the girl was indeed Lilian Lenton (not sixteen as supposed, but twenty-two). The accused, they claimed, was the suffragette awaiting her trial for the Kew Gardens firing hunger striker, whose forcible feeding in Holloway had so endangered her health that the Home Secretary had ordered her release – since when nothing had been heard of her. The press was certain that Doncaster's May Dennis was indeed Lilian Lenton, the arsonist.[47]

On Tuesday 10th, the court was again crowded. There were three magistrates, Violet Key-Jones and other supporters in the public gallery, plus a detective from Scotland Yard there to arrest 'May Dennis', if she was bailed, for 'the Kew Garden outrage'.[48] Harry Johnson and May Dennis stood together in the dock, guarded by a wardress. Alongside, leaning on the edge of the dock, was the plain-clothes detective sergeant who had arrested Dennis in court, and further back, the police sergeant who found equipment in the shrubbery. Harry and May were now jointly charged with entering Westfield House with intent to commit a felony. Johnson pleaded not guilty. More frustrating for the Scotland Yard detective, May Dennis, still totally defiant, refused to plead because, she stated, she did not acknowledge the authority of the court. Questioned again, Beecroft said she saw the man with a box, the girl with a bag. The mayor committed both prisoners to trial at the Assizes in Leeds.

42. *'Caught at Last: Lilian Lenton is sent for trial'*, Daily Mirror, *11 June 1913*.

Harry Johnson was granted bail. He was subsequently sentenced to twelve months' hard labour in Wakefield Gaol; here he too went on hunger strike and was released under the Cat and Mouse Act, after which he evaded the police, prompting a chase around the country.[49]

However, the defence lawyer for May Dennis said he was instructed by her not to request bail. Both prisoners were led down to the cells. Lilian Lenton (for it was generally understood by now that it *was* she who had adopted the 'May Dennis' alias, even if this could not be proved) was transported to Leeds to await trial. She was locked up in Armley – where she immediately began a hunger strike, despite having tempting food placed before her. The Home Office needed to keep the closest watch on this prisoner. The Armley authorities despatched a telegram on 13 June, anxiously asking about 'May Dennis' whether 'in the Event of Liberation on Bail should photo and fingerprints be taken?' Without hesitation, the answer came back: 'Yes'. It is probable this was the moment when the memorable covert photograph of Lilian was taken unawares, using a hidden camera. For the Prison Commission now stipulated:

> Photographs should be taken in every case. As, however, photographs cannot be taken by force, you should instruct the officer who takes photographs at your Prison to endeavour to take a photograph without the knowledge of the prisoner.[50]

43. *Lilian Lenton alias 'May Dennis', convicted of arson, photographed covertly in prison, probably Armley gaol, Leeds, June 1913.*

This prison spy-camera drama, coupled with another letter-box 'outrage' at Doncaster for which suffragettes were suspected, ran in tandem with agonies unfolding elsewhere: Emily Wilding Davison's martyr's funeral on 14 June, and Mrs Pankhurst's re-arrest and subsequent release due to illness.

In this fervid political atmosphere, Lilian Lenton (though the press still could not prove her real identity) continued her hunger strike in Armley. Then, on Tuesday 17th, after seven days without food, she had been so 'reduced to state of prostration' that the prison doctor signed the certificate for her release. Shortly before noon Lilian left Armley in a taxi-cab for a private suburban house. The Leeds police, alerted to her release, had plain-clothes officers follow her taxi to its destination, Chapel Allerton, and keep a watch there.[51] This was the home of Frank Rutter, Director of Leeds Art Gallery, active at that site of suffragette sympathy, the Leeds Arts Club, and secretary of the Men's Political Union for Women's Enfranchisement Leeds branch.

Lilian Lenton, a very weakened invalid, sheltered behind the Rutters' domestic doors: she ate a little bread and milk. Here, the plot was hatched for spiriting her away before her Cat and Mouse licence expired. It was planned in most careful detail, with each person knowing only the part they themselves would play in the conspiratorial melodrama. Leonora Cohen probably played a key role, even if rank-and-file members of Leeds WSPU knew nothing.[52] The Rutters were kept in the dark – not difficult as Frank was extremely busy with his daring post-Impressionist exhibition, and both he and his wife had arranged to be away from home. (Lilian had probably been kept in the dark too, and just knew she was going to 'friends'.)

The plot ran like clockwork. A young man was ordered to take a delivery van and an errand 'boy' with a basket to the Rutters' house: all he knew was that he had to pick up a WSPU member. 'She' knew merely that she had to impersonate an errand boy. So the bogus errand 'boy', a young member of Leeds WSPU, was driven up to the Rutters', eating an apple, 'his' head buried in a copy of *Comic Cuts*. When the van arrived, the driver was instructed to call out 'Groceries' and to wait. The door opened, a woman called out 'all right, it's here'. The 'boy' entered via the back door, still reading his comic and munching his apple, and, walked inside with his grocery basket.

A few moments later, Lilian, looking identical, head buried in *Comic Cuts* and munching the apple, walked out carrying the now empty basket. She got into the van, threw her basket inside and the van drove away. It proceeded about a mile. Then Lilian switched to a waiting taxi; accompanied by her friends she was driven off to Harrogate, the sedate spa town about eight miles away from Leeds' hurly-burly.[53]

The taxi arrived about 10 p.m. Here, a Harrogate taxi-driver – who must not have believed his luck – picked up 'two persons in men's clothes' and took them off to Scarborough, a distance of some forty miles [See Map IV,

p. 206]. Scarborough might be an equally sedate seaside resort but, as we know, it was another nest of suffragettes, with its own suffrage shop and Violet Key-Jones holding meetings on the Esplanade.[54] Here, suspicion at such an extravagant taxi fare was aroused: a local person who heard the pair talking and was sure one had a woman's voice, remarked to the taxi-driver, 'I'll bet 20 to 1 that they are not both men'. However this clue was never followed up as Lilian Lenton was, of course, still believed to be under police surveillance at the Rutters' suburban home in Leeds.

So, from Scarborough Lilian Lenton escaped. Some thought she had boarded a private yacht; suffragettes stressed she *had* reached the Continent, though the harbour authorities argued such a departure would have been noticed. (Lilian had opposed leaving England, but her physical weakness from her hunger strike had been intensified by all the strain of her escape, and this made it easier for her friends to persuade her to flee abroad, as she could not be concealed in England for very long.) The Home Office remained particularly keen on the re-arrest of Lilian Lenton, 'one of the most daring of the younger band of militants'. However, the suffragettes had stolen a march on the detectives in Leeds for two crucial days.

On Friday 20, Lilian's Cat and Mouse licence formally expired; plain-clothes officers, still watching the Rutters' house, attempted to pounce. But their 'mouse' had escaped – apparently in male clothing in a motor car. The police made desperate attempts to catch up with her; local forces at last communicated (perhaps even passing on copies of the spy portrait) and Harrogate police passed on clues to Scarborough. But there was no sign of Lilian. The police were foxed. The yacht story was discounted after a rumour of a sighting on York station, but this too fizzled out. In the end the police admitted they believed she had gone to the Continent. Lilian was presumed to be at 'one of the watering places on the Dutch coast'.[55]

The furore over her fugitive disappearance was further stirred when the correspondence between the Home Office and Royal College of Surgeons on Lilian's forcible feeding after the Kew pavilion incident was published. Eminent doctors stated that food had been poured into her lungs, and only her youth and good health saved her from extremely serious conse-quences.[56] Lilian's case had proved a *cause célèbre*, highlighting both the medical barbarity of feeding a resisting prisoner and the fact that a fugitive 'mouse' could evade recapture by the 'cats'. Thanks to the spider-web net-work of Violet Key-Jones and others, Lilian had – for a few months at least – outwitted the surveillance state, even though it was now equipped with the newest telecentric lenses for covertly capturing good photographic likenesses of prisoners.[57] Suffragettes were fast becoming McKenna's worst public security headache, with all the potential to cause maximum political embarrassment to Asquith. It was into this inflamed political atmosphere that the NUWSS Suffrage Pilgrimage marched in July 1913.

Despite all the tensions surrounding the Election Fighting Fund – yelps of pain from Liberal suffragists, general uneasiness within the Labour Party and trade unions – the NUWSS still held firm that demanding votes for women could only be effective if the majority of women were *seen* to back that demand. The NUWSS believed that for its behind-the-scenes lobbying of miners' unions and key politicians to be effective, it must demonstrate widespread and visible public support.[58] This would be hampered if its key constitutional demand was overshadowed by distracting public safety controversies over security services and police, prisons and doctors, aliases and errand boys. The NUWSS would not let its patient propaganda be drowned out by the sound of shattering glass. Like its earlier caravanning tours, it would take the campaign out to local communities; here, surely people could distinguish more clearly between suffragists and militants. And, given the labour–suffrage pact, the NUWSS's national priority was now to widen support among working-class communities.

And so, to coincide with its international presence in Budapest, the NUWSS planned its great national pilgrimage. Setting off on 18 June, pilgrims with banners marched along a network of routes, converging in Hyde Park on 26 July. On the north-east route, they started off from Newcastle-on-Tyne. When they marched into Leeds, pilgrims were greeted by Isabella and Bessie Ford. They reached Wakefield on 2 July on their way to the mining villages of south Yorkshire.

However, with the EFF enthusiasm weak in Yorkshire, hard work was required. The NUWSS in Sheffield increased its membership to nearly 200, while a branch was hastily formed in Doncaster, still mesmerised by fugitive Lilian Lenton.[59]

Into the midst of this marched the steady NUWSS pilgrims from Wakefield. Accompanied by local branch members, they reached Barnsley on Thursday 3 July; here a huge crowd greeted them on May Day Green, and they stayed overnight. They then marched on down to Rotherham on Friday 4, holding meetings in small mining communities, with Helena Renton for the West Riding Federation speaking. At 7 p.m. the pilgrimage reached Rotherham, where they were welcomed by another large crowd and given tea in a local Congregational church; they held another large meeting in the Market Square, to wide interest from miners and their wives.[60]

The next day, the pilgrims set off for Sheffield. Here they were piped into the city by the Recreation Prize Band; a large crowd of 5,000 assembled for a meeting which, despite the presence of plain-clothes police, remained peaceful. After a weekend in Sheffield, they regrouped on Monday morning and departed for Chesterfield.[61]

44. Suffrage pilgrims leaving Sheffield along Pinstone Street. Sheffield Daily Independent, *8 July 1913.*

With its national routes, local supporters and finally its Hyde Park rally, the NUWSS pilgrimage successfully distanced itself from arsonists and fugitive suffragettes. It was a magnificent propaganda victory, convincing both Asquith and McKenna to open their doors to suffrage delegations.

Other NUWSS initiatives now included Friends of Women's Suffrage, to build working-class support by visiting women in their homes. The Active Service League, helping to win over new women as Friends of Women's Suffrage, was another open-air propaganda scheme that sprang from the pilgrimage. This was all coupled with some deft NUWSS bending of ears of trade union leaders, notably Robert Smillie of the Miners. Thus at the

Miners' Conference in Scarborough in October, Isabella Ford even chaired the key eve-of-conference suffrage meeting.[62]

A final arm of the NUWSS strategy continued to be its Election Fighting Fund. In November a by-election was called at Keighley, where the Liberal MP had to stand for re-election. This textile manufacturing constituency on the Lancashire border included idyllic hilltop villages like Haworth. The NUWSS despatched Selina Cooper, and, despite bitter cold, Isabella and Selina spoke at one of the largest election meetings. But such an ambitious political strategy as the suffrage–labour alliance still experienced creaking tensions. ILP suffragists who were enthusiastic about the EFF became angry that the NUWSS still could not bring itself to support the Labour candidate, since that would mean opposing the Liberal, an old 'friend' of suffrage. At all levels of the NUWSS, traditional Liberal loyalties kept reasserting themselves in Yorkshire, despite the continued provocations thrown down by the Asquith government.[63]

The regional NUWSS default position often remained conservative caution. One local example illustrates this. The minutes book of the Barnsley Women's Suffrage Society reveals a cautiously respectable branch: it even decided against making Friends of Women's Suffrage a definite campaign; and it drew particular attention to the ruling that no one who was a member of a militant society should also be a member of the NUWSS. Of the Active Service League 'nothing definite was decided', while muted sympathy was expressed for old-style critics of the EFF policy.[64] Clearly the labour-suffrage alliance, despite the dynamic new activists at a national level, remained a struggle in such regions as Yorkshire.

In Huddersfield, however, the energetic NUWSS branch ran an effective Active Service League. Florence Lockwood, inspired by her visit to Budapest, was one of those recruiting new Friends of Women's Suffrage. She would meet up with fellow suffragists and set off up the valley or over the hills to a nearby village. They would fly their red, white and green colours, explaining the importance of women's suffrage wherever they could get a hearing.[65] By such means, well over 45,000 Friends were enrolled nationally. Florence and others like her trusted that the patient, rational wooing of women through pilgrimages and 'Friends' schemes was as effective a suffrage tactic as firing empty buildings and fleeing the police. In summer 1913 both tactics ran in tandem.

CHAPTER 14

Unsafe City: Leonora, Lilian, and Florence again
1913–1914

By the end of 1913, the Women's Freedom League branch in Middlesbrough was gearing itself up for what people saw was the coming general election, planning its own suffrage shop and a giant poster campaign in the election run-up.[1] For the WSPU centres, news in the *Suffragette* reported how Violet Key-Jones sped between Doncaster and York, stirring up both. In Sheffield, Elsa Schuster organised a jumble sale and *Suffragette* sellers. Scarborough ran a cake and sweets stall at its WSPU shop. The Leeds branch mounted protest meetings outside Armley gaol every Sunday for as long as a prisoner remained inside.[2]

Yet there were also tremendous strains within the WSPU nationally. On the one hand, Sylvia Pankhurst now led an independent East London Federation of Suffragettes; on the other, Christabel used the pages of the *Suffragette* to promote her book, *The Great Scourge*, about the threat to women of venereal disease carried by men: her Manichaean world was increasingly divided into good and bad.

Despite such tensions, suffragettes like Leonora Cohen remained fervent WSPU loyalists. To her, everything paled into insignificance beside the fight against a treacherous and brutal government. She would go to any lengths, short of direct violence. An opportunity to bring this fight to her own doorstep came in November 1913 when Asquith braved a visit to her home town.

Leeds was no longer a safe city. There was an attempt to fire the football stand in Headingley. Security measures were tightened. Almost every member of the Leeds police force had to be ready to protect the Prime Minister, strengthened by reinforcements drafted in. For some days before Asquith's arrival, Leeds suffragettes believed they were being shadowed by detectives. He was to stay in the rural outskirts, at Gledhow Hall. Police guarding the building stumbled upon a handful of women scaling the high walls and gave chase; but the women jumped down from the wall and escaped in the darkness.

On Friday evening 28 November, the Coliseum hall was surrounded by 800 police. The crowd grew so dense that mounted police had difficulty keeping lines clear for tramcars. Ladies' tickets were limited just to wives of MPs and parliamentary candidates, and to bona fide Women's Liberal Federation delegates. Any woman seen loitering nearby was regarded with suspicion and immediately asked to move on.[3] Not far away, suffragettes took to the streets in a procession, at the head their banner, white letters on green: 'Strong reasons make strong actions'.

As indeed they did. At 9.15 p.m., Leonora and another woman threw stones to smash the plate-glass windows of the nearby city-centre Labour Exchange. Later that evening, a large plate-glass window of the *Yorkshire Evening Post* office was also smashed by a brick – wrapped in paper with the message: 'The Government torture women. Carson and Larkin go free' – a comparison with how Irish protesters who, enfranchised, were treated.

Leonora was caught by a constable just as she raised her arm to throw a stone through the Labour Exchange window. The next day, Saturday 29th, Leonora (and the second woman, who refused to give her name) were charged at Leeds Police Court with wilful damage to three plate-glass windows. This time repair was costed at £26. The stipendiary magistrate said, as the damage was over £5, they would need to go for a full jury – again – and he remanded them till Wednesday 3 December. Leonora stated they would both go, not just on hunger strike, but also on more terrifying thirst strike. The magistrate refused to register any concern about this; at which Leonora protested hotly that her treatment by the police 'is worse than in Russia'.[4]

In Armley, Leonora was one of four suffragettes who refused food, and she refused drink as well. She was released on health grounds on Monday 1 December, out on licence for seven days under the Cat and Mouse Act. Her friends were extremely worried about her as she was too weak even to have her temperature taken, let alone appear in court.[5]

The 'Headingley two' accused of the football fire did appear, one a dark-haired woman of about twenty-five, the other 'a girlish figure in green cap and sports jacket'. Evidence against them included postcards with messages: 'No Vote, No Sport, No Peace – Fire, Destruction, Devastation', and another, addressed to Asquith: 'We are Burning for "Votes for Women."' They made complaints against several Armley warders for using violence to obtain fingerprints. The magistrate, not usually moved by prisoners' oratory, seemed to accept that their complaints carried weight: they would be conveyed to the Home Secretary and the Prison Visiting Committee.[6]

Leonora was too ill to appear in court. With her life hanging by a thread, it was a battle to the death. Henry and Leonora Cohen had more desperate, urgent discussions. Both were united in their contempt for the government's washing its hands of its actions and the barbarity of the consequences. On Monday 8 December Henry posted a scorching letter, pointedly written on the headed notepaper of the Leeds and County Liberal Club. Addressed to the Home Secretary himself, Henry's hand-written draft survives:

My wife Leonora Cohen was released a week since today from Armley Prison under your cat & mouse act.

She was in a state of utter collapse & was considered in serious danger of losing her life by her medical advisers & also I believe by the prison doctor.

I am told now, that her licence has expired, she is liable to re-arrest at any moment.

If this step is taken, I tell you seriously that I shall immediately close my house and leave her on the hands of the prison authorities.

I do not propose to be the scapegoat & bear the burden & consequences following as the result of you carrying out this barbarous & iniquitous measure.

If her life has to be taken as a requital for the offence of breaking a pane of glass, well & good, but it shall not be done piece-meal with my connivance.

Therefore please understand fully that without in any way writing this letter in the way of intimidation, I am absolutely determined I will not again receive her back from [Armley? page ends][7]

The Home Office hastily acknowledged this, and on 10 December a Home Office civil servant dispatched this curt reply to Henry at the Leeds and County Liberal Club:

Leeds

Sir,
In reply to your letter of the 8th instant regarding the health of your wife, Leonora Cohen, I am directed by the Secretary of State to say that you appear

to misunderstand the position. Your wife's condition was due entirely to her voluntary refusal to take food while she was remanded to Prison on a criminal charge and she was released in order that she might be prevented from committing suicide or doing further injury to her health.

I am, Sir,

Your obedient Servant,

C. Blackwell.[8]

Henry remained totally dissatisfied with this dismissal, as the draft of his reply makes clear:

In reply to yours, please inform the S of S from me that I understand the position perfectly.

My object in writing to him is apparently misunderstood by him.

As you say my wife was released in order to prevent her committing suicide, I take it that her re-arrest would mean that the government would be simply providing another opportunity for her [to die].

However the only point I wish to make is this, that in the event of her re-arrest (which she will not attempt to evade) in whatsoever condition she is released she will not be taken off the hands of the prison authorities by me, & she will herself refuse to be taken elsewhere.

And by making this plain to the Home Office & the Prison authorities I am claiming for myself all relief from possible <u>consequences</u>.[9]

Henry had bravely decided, given his limited room for manoeuvre, he would refuse to receive Leonora, should the injuries she sustained through a further prison sentence prove fatal; and thus responsibility for her death would lie with the Home Office – and not with him. Just six months after Emily Wilding Davison's martyrdom, Henry was playing for the highest political stakes: his wife's very life.

In fact, someone in authority (possibly the police) seems to have whispered a word of advice in Henry's ear: leave Leeds and take your wife out of the city somewhere safer. Once Leonora was away, Leeds would be quieter for the police.[10] More hurried discussion ensued. Henry had lived all his life in Leeds and built up his local business. In the end, the Cohens decided to pack up and move to that most sedate of Yorkshire towns: Harrogate. Here Leonora enterprisingly turned her hand to a small boarding house and, given her vegetarian experience, advertised in the *Suffragette* classified columns:

Harrogate – Reform Food Boarding Establishment situated in healthiest part facing moors . . . Excellent catering by specialist in Reform diets. Late dinner, separate Tables . . . Stamp for booklet – Mrs LEONORA COHEN, WSPU, 'Pomona', Harlow Moor Drive, Harrogate.

Leonora certainly joined the WSPU branch there; members, she recalled, welcomed her with open arms.[11] Harrogate might be safer than Leeds, but Leonora had by no means relinquished her militant sympathies.

The final eight peacetime months continued with frenzied dialogue between suffragettes and the Home Office. On 9 March 1914, at a packed public meeting in Glasgow, Emmeline Pankhurst was arrested by truncheon-wielding police. The following day, Mary Richardson slashed Velásquez's *Rokeby Venus* in the National Gallery. Other major protest acts of arson followed. That same day, 10 March, a confidential Home Office memorandum to all prisons tightened state surveillance with spy photography. Portraits, it confirmed, were to be taken without force, and, the memo stressed, 'without the knowledge of the prisoner' (though with comical reference to borrowing a camera from local police or if necessary hiring one). There was no new technological trickery to help with finger-printing, and guidance was that three fingers was acceptable – with the cautious proviso that the Medical Officer be present to offer advice 'in the event of serious resistance being offered by the prisoner'; also, a hot-line in emergencies to the Criminal Record Office, New Scotland Yard, 'who would send an expert officer to the prison to superintend the repetition of the process in the presence of the Medical Officer'.[12] Fatal strain on the hearts of weakened suffragette prisoners could still cause considerable political embarrassment.

By April, photographs of suffragettes in prison, caught by the long-lens camera, were circulated in narrow strips to anxious art galleries. These portraits now grab our attention as all look so strikingly relaxed. None looks more poignantly informal than the photo of 'May Dennis' alias Lilian Lenton, imprisoned for arson. Though perhaps slightly gaunt, her dark hair hangs down her back – rather as it had in the Doncaster court earlier. The hidden camera caught the elegant cut of her two-button coat, Lilian's slim figure suggesting her earlier career as a professional dancer. Haunting images indeed, not least when reproduced in a crude photographic strip – evidence of how Asquith's Liberal government secretly spied on such women, imprisoned merely for demanding the basic democratic right to vote.[13]

45. *Lilian Lenton and other suffragettes photographed unawares in prison, 1913. Photographs were then circulated in narrow strips.*

In this frenzied spring, amid fears of insurrection and fears for the safety of cabinet ministers, the offices of the *Suffragette* were raided. The WSPU expelled Sylvia's East London Federation of Suffragettes. There were further attacks on pillar-boxes in Bradford and York, Scarborough and Rotherham; when postmen unlocked the boxes, phosphorus burst into flames; someone hurried to fetch sand, saving some letters. Mrs Pankhurst was arrested on a deputation to Buckingham Palace, an incident captured in one of the best-known suffragette photographs. Throughout, the WSPU kept up its constant comparison between the government's leniency towards rebellious Ulstermen and its harsh treatment of voteless women.[14]

On 4 May the elusive Lilian Lenton was tracked down to Liverpool, re-arrested, and taken to Leeds to be tried for the Doncaster charge. She too went on hunger and thirst strike. On 8 May at Leeds Assizes Lilian, though ill and weak, appeared in court. As soon as she entered the dock, she turned to the jury and stated: 'I want to ask you to refuse to have anything further to do with this case. Not for my sake, but for the sake of your own honour', that is, colluding with a system of trying voteless women with man-made laws. The prosecuting lawyer attempted to put his case: that Lilian's actions in the 'empty' Doncaster house might have resulted in the death of the elderly housekeeper. Lilian retorted, 'This is absolutely ridiculous, because we always look first to see if anyone is there'. Throughout her trial, she continued to address the jury, thus, according to the *Suffragette*, 'rendering the legal proceedings inaudible'. Eventually the judge intervened: 'Miss Lenton, listen to me. Don't you think you have made enough protest?' She retaliated, 'No, I shan't stop protesting as long as this court sits', and she continued to speak right through the judge's summing up, telling him 'I don't want to hear anything you have to say'. In the end, the jury retired briefly and returned a verdict of guilty. The judge, matching Harry Johnson's punishment, sentenced Lilian to twelve months. As she was led out of court, pandemonium broke out in the ladies' gallery. Several women jumped to their feet, one crying out loudly: 'My lord and fellow members, this is a gross injustice. You have no right to sentence this woman. She is not fit to be sentenced. How can you, sir, as the judge, allow this sort of thing? I do not know how you can sit on that bench—' at which point the heckler was seized by police, thrown out of court and taken to Armley.[15]

On Sunday 10 May, Leonora and others organised a meeting outside the gaol to protest against this torture.[16] Lilian, having embarked on a hunger and thirst strike, was released. She was taken by police in a car to Harrogate. Leonora recalled later that she gave this fugitive 'mouse' shelter for eight days, helping to nurse her back to health. Reg Cohen, his mother recalled, was 'so loyal to the suffragettes when I housed them'. He even lent his Norfolk suit and cap so that Lilian might disguise herself – once again – as a boy. The Reform guesthouse conveniently faced a large common; here, Lilian reminisced:

> the house was surrounded by detectives whose job it was to arrest me if they saw me go out . . . The next day [the common] was covered with people, knitting, and with their babies . . . watching the house, because the police were all round it, and they wanted to see what happened when I tried to get out.
>
> Well, they not only had police all round it, but they erected a light in the garden next door . . . and the light was trained on to the [Cohens'] windows so it was impossible to get out of an upstairs window or the downstairs window without being seen, because you would get out into the middle of this light. However, I went down into a coal cellar. I was dressed in the suit of the small son, a schoolboy, of my hostess.[17]

Lilian's own memories of how she once more outwitted the police involve crawling up the coal chute, creeping across the neighbouring back gardens and over walls. With breathless melodrama, she was spirited away again under the detectives' very noses.

After this escape, the police continued to keep watch on the Cohens' house where, inside, Leonora busied herself with fund-raising marmalade-making. Harrogate's sedateness was no guarantee against violence: in June, Leonora, now joined by her mother, was injured by a mob of roughs who smashed up their suffrage platform.[18]

By the outbreak of war, police still had not caught up with fugitive Lilian Lenton.[19] Leonora and Lilian, like Violet Key-Jones and Edith Key, remained part of the shadowy underworld which grew in the wake of the Cat and Mouse Act.

The WSPU had certainly changed almost out of recognition since its for-mation eleven years earlier. Then it had been succoured by the ILP; small yet vibrant Pennine WSPU branches had been packed with community suf-fragettes, textile workers and wives of engineering trade unionists. But by 1913–14 it was all very different. The WSPU now turned its anger not just on Liberal and Labour but barracked even old ILP allies like Keir Hardie.

The politics had changed, and so had the danger. In tightened, belea-guered cells, handfuls of Emmeline's suffragettes remained active in a few key areas.[20] Sheffield WSPU advertised a garden party and a parasol parade. In Doncaster, intrepid Violet Key-Jones, still operating from her town-centre office, ran a market stall and interviewed the Bishop of Knaresborough on the wickedness of forcible feeding. And York WSPU offered suffragette bicycling trips and a *café chantant*. Violet Key-Jones was located centrally here, though she also had a base in Darlington (presum-ably making her one of the railway's most regular travellers). Scarborough sold the *Suffragette* at hotels on the Esplanade, and still ran meetings on the West Pier; its shop reported that Christabel's *Great Scourge* was selling well.[21]

However, given how much Christabel talked up WSPU successes in the pages of the *Suffragette*, it is very difficult to get a clear impression of how much a parasol parade or *café chantant* really played with the public any longer. Certainly, some suffrage historians argue that, by August 1914, the position of the semi-clandestine WSPU, its leaders either expelled, in prison or abroad, and lacking an office, was far more precarious than later suffra-gette commemorations try to suggest.[22]

*

The contrast with the NUWSS could not be starker. It had succeeded in shifting itself away over much of the country from its top-down Liberal elitism of a decade ago; now it was running the labour–suffrage pact through its Election Fighting Fund, and had enrolled about 45,000 Friends of Women's Suffrage – even if in some places this remained patchy.

In June, Florence Lockwood, actively out campaigning and enrolling 'Friends', invited Anna, a new Hungarian friend she had met in Budapest, to visit Black Rock. Anna arrived and Josiah declared he was 'fair pleased' with her. The two women threw themselves into the campaign. Florence's health meant she had missed the great 1913 NUWSS pilgrimage. However, there was now a smaller pilgrimage organised in the Skipton constituency around Wharfedale. Wearing the pilgrims' red, white and green cockle-shells, the two women set off. Anna wanted to linger at Bolton Abbey's romantic ruins, but was briskly admonished by Florence:

> That was not what we were there for. We had to waylay everyone we met, and offer them leaflets – reasons why woman's suffrage should be granted – and wake up the inhabitants of the little villages through which we passed, and hold meetings on the greens with the same object. At Grassington we lost the last train home. I was very cross about it at the time, being tired and mazy in my head with the heat and fatigue. However, the evening meeting was memorable, and I am glad we didn't miss it. Being chairman, I was up in a cart with the speakers, and I looked down upon a vast attentive crowd assembled in the broad cobble-paved market-place. They listened till the sun went down, and, when questions came, we had a sparkling time.
>
> We found a lodging in the village street, and woke up to a very hot summer's morning. A neighbour was playing on his fiddle . . . The old-world ditty breathed of peace and contentment, and remoteness from the world of strife.

Not for long. In the middle of Anna's visit, Germany declared war on Russia and France: it would invade France through Belgium. Josiah anxiously read the newspaper headlines: 'British Naval Reserves Mobilised'. Luggage was hastily packed and Anna set off forlornly from Huddersfield station on 4 August; she hoped to reach Budapest and her family. Florence had arranged to spend that day, 4 August, in a nearby village with other members of the local Active Service League. Feeling bleak, she thought that it would be comforting to meet fellow suffragists and share her sense of opposition to war as the means of settling international differences, and perhaps to hold a peace demonstration. So Florence set off, again flying her red, white and green colours. How wrong she was. Only a few Quaker suffragists shared her views about warfare.

However, back at Black Rock that evening, tired though she was, Florence:

> put the finishing touches to the [new] Women's Suffrage banner which I had been embroidering with such high hopes. Little remained to be done, only a few stitches to the lettering: 'A New Age demands new Responsibilities for Women'. The motto assumed a new significance. All reform and progress must wait now. War will not help human liberty, I thought, as I folded up the banner and put it away.[23]

The world had changed.

PART FIVE

Afterwards
1914–2005

CHAPTER 15

Living with the memory

1914–2005

Afterwards, long afterwards, once the War had ended, the demand for which the suffragettes and suffragists had campaigned so persistently was finally won. The Representation of the People Bill, with its women's suffrage clause, passed through even the House of Lords, finally received the Royal Assent in February 1918, and became law. Women over the age of thirty gained the right to vote. Victory, even if not yet complete, could be celebrated. At a rally at the Queen's Hall, when she stepped onto the platform, Mrs Fawcett was greeted with a 'lively uproar of joy', the audience singing Blake's 'Jerusalem'. Another celebratory rally at the Albert Hall, attended by Mrs Pankhurst, sang 'Oh God Our Help in Ages Past'.[1]

At the December 1918 General Election, the first at which any woman could choose her MP, all suffragettes and suffragists (except the very youngest, like Lilian Lenton) were over thirty and could cast their votes. Women could now also stand as parliamentary candidates. Christabel and Emmeline Pankhurst and Emmeline Pethick-Lawrence all stood: none was elected. A few, however, did win. The first woman elected was Eva Gore-Booth's sister, Constance Markiewicz – who, as a Sinn Feiner, refused to take her seat. Nancy Astor, who took over her husband's former constituency after a by-election in 1919, became the first woman to sit in Parliament.

Eventually, on 2 July 1928, ten years after the first partial victory, all women over twenty-one were enfranchised – the so-called 'flapper voters'. Women at long last shared equal suffrage rights with men; and adult suffragist Margaret Bondfield MP became the first woman cabinet minister in 1929.

Rather than this parliamentary route however, the lives of the rebel girls took different directions – sometimes surprisingly unexpected. Of the stories told here, the most dramatic journeys were of those who had emigrated, usually to the farthest ends of the earth – taking with them their suffrage memories.

Adela Pankhurst had never settled to gardening, for which her punishing years of open-air WSPU oratory scarcely fitted her. Like her sister Sylvia, whose own East London Federation of Suffragettes was expelled from the WSPU, Adela no longer fitted in to Emmeline's army. Their mother was by then facing three years' imprisonment; and tensions between mother and youngest daughter mounted. As in any family dissension, there are two distinct versions, and luckily we can now read both accounts.

Adela was friends with Helen Archdale, who still worked closely with Christabel and the WSPU; indeed, Emmeline even seems to have used Helen as a intermediary, writing to her about Adela. 'How sorry I am that our naughty child is giving you so much trouble', Emmeline confided to Helen in autumn 1913; she had spent money on her daughter's horticultural training, so 'the best thing for A just now is that she be made to feel a sense of responsibility'. Adela's years of total commitment to the WSPU, including imprisonment and forcible feeding, were erased, reduced as she was to a vexatious small child. Emmeline soon found a convenient solution: Australia. 'I hope A. will take the right attitude about all this', Emmeline wrote to Helen. 'I have written to . . . Miss Goldstein announcing her probable arrival'. Australian suffragist Vida Goldstein, visiting Britain, persuaded Adela, as she herself put it, 'that my banishment from the Movement did not extend to Australia'.[2]

Emmeline paid for her daughter's fare to this farthest country, and Adela set sail in February 1914. Emmeline wrote again to Helen Archdale: 'After she had really gone I felt very sad & yet I know it is the only way for her to realise that she is really grown up. We have all treated her like a little girl'.[3] Aged twenty-seven, Adela had been 'banished' by her mother. This was the most painful of rejections. She never saw Emmeline, either of her sisters or England again. Later, Adela wrote philosophically about it – in terms of what had suited her beloved mother, then facing long imprisonment:

> It appeared to me that the best thing I could do for her was to make myself independent of the Movement and of her. I was very miserable, but down in the bottom of my heart, hope was stirring. I felt that I was not such a fool or a knave as I had been made out and that in another country I should find my feet and happiness, perhaps . . .

She gave me what money she could spare — it was very little — and I often wondered what she thought I should do in Australia when it was spent. I knew nothing of the country and neither did she.[4]

Adela's Australian biographer, however, probably comes closer to Adela's raw emotions around the time of the banishment. Verna Coleman quotes Adela's play *Betrayed* (1917), depicting an imperious mother addressing her rebellious socialist younger son:

We have been forbearing with you for a long time. I have excused you because you were young and because you were given a responsible position too early. But I tell you neither Spencer [Christabel-like elder son] nor I will tolerate open insubordination. As to money, I will give you none until you leave your present associates, and consent to take up a position in . . . the colonies.[5]

She arrived with absolutely no possessions; yet Australia turned out to be the making of Adela. Here, freed from wounding comparisons with her sisters and Annie Kenney, she obtained a job with the Women's Political Association and became a popular speaker. When war broke out, Emmeline and Christabel might back the fighting: Adela, like Sylvia, opposed militarism and campaigned against conscription. In 1917 she married widower Tom Walsh, socialist and seamen's union organiser. After the war, they both joined the Australian Communist Party; but this did not last long and politically they edged further and further to the right.

46. *Adela Pankhurst Walsh, 1929, journalist and mother.*

In addition to Tom's three children, Adela had five of her own; she was fully occupied and at her most joyful. Photographs clearly show her face radiating contentment, after years of stress and sorrow. Her daughter Ursula recalled how, as children, 'One of our earliest impressions is of mother, ready for an outing in a suit and hat giving a last minute poke to a copper full of washing', holding forth while absent-mindedly 'trying to take her apron off over a large brimmed hat'. Adela also still found time to scratch a living from journalism, including, in the late 1920s, writing her own brief memoirs for a conservative monthly.[6]

Mary Gawthorpe, too, emigrated, though for far less complex family reasons. In January 1916, she and her mother sailed to America, where Mary's married sister lived. She too thrived in her new country. She worked for suffrage and trade union organisations for about six years till continued ill-health forced her to give it up. In 1921, Mary married an American, John Sanders. Her life, more comfortable than Adela's in Australia, also lacked the latter's tendency to political extremes. Photographs show Mary and John (they had no children) enjoying their spacious garden together in Queens, New York.

47. Mary Gawthorpe, passport photograph, 1915.

The third rebel girl who left Britain, Dora Thewlis, also emigrated to Australia. Unlike Adela and Mary, Dora's flash of suffragette militancy and tabloid notoriety was now well behind her. She had just to get on with earning a living. Dora, like so many other Edwardians, was primarily an economic migrant. Some time before 1914, along with her elder sister and about twenty other Huddersfield girls, she left in search of a better life than that offered by the long hours in the Yorkshire textile mills. Dora went to Warrnambool in the Melbourne region, where she worked in blanket-weaving. She too loved Australia and never regretted emigrating; in 1918 she married Jack Dow, a second-generation Australian, and they had two children.[7]

48. Dora and Jack Dow, 1920.

The stories of the other rebel girls took a less global turn. Lavena Saltonstall – last heard of springing to defend the broad WEA curriculum against attacks about 'chloroforming the workers' – remained active in the Halifax WEA until 1916. Then, in June 1917 in Halifax Unitarian Chapel, thirty-four-year-old Lavena, now working as an electrical engineeer's clerk, married George Baker of Bradford, a forty-year-old private in the Duke of Wellington's regiment, and they went to live in Bradford. But after the War, this talented self-taught feminist journalist, happy to take on anti-suffra-gists, sadly disappears from view.[8]

Violet Key-Jones, in her mid-thirties when she could vote at the 1918 Election, remained as elusive after the war as she had as a WSPU impresa-rio.[9] Molly Morris, on the other hand, in the end achieved her lifelong ambition. During the War she trained to become a qualified nurse and worked at the West London Hospital. Persistent Jack Murphy visited her in

1920, regaling her with his exploits of travelling across Europe to revolutionary Russia and meeting Lenin. They got married, and set off to Moscow in 1921. After her son Gordon was born, Molly spent the next decade immersed in motherhood and the newly-formed Communist Party.[10]

Lilian Lenton saw no contradiction between her aim of burning two buildings a week and, when war broke out, patriotically binding up soldiers' wounds: she worked in Serbia with the Scottish Women's Hospitals Unit. Afterwards, Lilian became a speaker for the Save the Children Fund and, from 1924, for the Women's Freedom League; she often stayed with Alice Schofield-Coates in Middlesbrough.[11]

Alice, herself with three children, remained an active League member; in the 1920s, she and her husband Charles opened a vegetarian health-food restaurant-cum-shop, with the League offices above. There were, however, few regular customers in this unhelpfully suburban location, and this fund-losing venture had to be subsidised by Charles – until he lost his money in 1924. Alice became Middlesbrough's first woman councillor, a magistrate and chair of her constituency Labour Party. Along with her sister-in-law Marion Coates-Hanson she championed slum clearance and better housing, seeing the vote for women as the 'key to the door' for social and economic equality.[12]

The remaining women featured in this book, more established campaigners, often with professional lives or married with young children, may be tracked more briefly. Of the mid-Victorian suffragists born between the 1850s and mid-60s, Dr Mary Murdoch, having been taken ill while attending an emergency call out in the snow to a patient, died in Hull in 1916 aged fifty-one.

The War had divided NUWSS members just as it had the suffragettes. Quaker Isabella Ford had, like Florence Lockwood, opposed the fighting. Aged seventy, she died in her sleep at Adel near Leeds in 1924. In the Colne Valley, Florence had had no easy time supporting peace during the war. Josiah did not share her views, and would take his tea at the local Liberal Club. Restless, Florence began working on having her diaries printed – to discouraging response. When Josiah died in 1924, within days of his funeral Florence realised that there was little any longer to hold her in Linthwaite and moved south: 'I uprooted quickly; it was too sad. I came to London.'[13]

Leonora Cohen worked in munitions during the War. Like Alice Schofield-Coates, she became – with delicious irony – a magistrate, and was awarded an OBE in 1928 for her public work, becoming a well-known and honoured figure in her hometown of Leeds.

And there the story might have rested: everyone scattered far and wide, growing older quietly. But into the early 1930s sprang a new factor – which provided the framework for subsequent suffrage memories.

The history of suffrage had already begun to be written. Sylvia Pankhurst's initial chronicle was serialised in 1907 by *Votes for Women*. Then, in 1911, she published *The Suffragette: the history of the Women's Militant Suffrage Movement 1905–1910*, with a preface by Emmeline. Sylvia's book had significant long-term repercussions. It marginalised Fawcett's NUWSS, relegating it to a dowdy off-stage role, whence it made 'bitter reproaches and disdainful glances' at glittering centre-stage WSPU actors. In a sense this was merely Sylvia's journalistic enthusiasm, talking up a good militant story. However, the book also leached Adela almost entirely from its pages: while Annie Kenney is presented fully in a romanticised picture, Adela and Harry are erased from the early family, compared to 'we two children'. Although there are occasional references to 'provincial campaigns', great swathes of the country receive short shrift if Sylvia herself was not present. A dry and detailed chronicle, Sylvia's first book was, however, never going to be a best-seller.[14]

Emmeline's *My Own Story*, published in 1914, likewise erased Adela's childhood, just noting airily that 'two other children followed'.[15] The war then put paid to history-writing. Afterwards, Annie Kenney's romantic autobiography, *Memories of a Militant*, was published in 1924, vividly evoking her childlike faith in Christabel, yet frustratingly vague on the bigger picture.[16]

The final 1928 victory of *all* women winning the vote naturally triggered reviews of suffrage achievements. Ray Strachey, the NUWSS caravanner and friend of Mrs Fawcett, put the finishing touches to her history of the women's movement just as the bill was going through the House of Lords. *The Cause* (1928) offered a wonderfully wide sweep, but participants found it left out as much as it put in.[17]

The bill winning the vote finally became law on 2 July 1928 – timed, sadly, just after the death of Emmeline Pankhurst on 14 June. Both Sylvia and Christabel attended the funeral, though of course Adela could not. Among the many tributes paid to this heroic suffragette was a life-sized statue erected near Parliament, unveiled at a ceremony in spring 1930. As Pankhurst biographer Martin Pugh summarised, 'Emmeline's death had raised the stakes by transforming votes for women into history, thereby making the interested parties keenly aware of the need to defend their reputations and their ideas'.[18] When the 1929 Wall Street Crash ushered in an economic depression, making earning a wage harder than ever for one-time suffragettes and their husbands, it became even more tempting to scratch a living by writing a suffrage history.

In Australia, Tom Walsh had moved further right in his politics; he and Adela scraped along with bits of journalism. Understandably, Adela was among the first with her memoirs. Shortly before her mother's death, she wrote a brief typescript, 'The Story of My Life'.[19] This straight autobiographical narrative, reflecting Adela's growing conservatism, rails not only against later WSPU violence but also against its 'extreme Feminism', turning later recruits into 'very often uncompromising man-haters', and so swamping 'the finer ideals of the pioneers'. Adela's account ends abruptly: 'Before I could do anything in the Labour Movement, it was necessary for me to leave England, unless I wished to enter into open warfare with my mother'.[20]

Emmeline's death prompted more poignant reminiscence. Adela began a more ambitious memoir, 'Looking Backwards'. She now stressed her isolation as a child, her leaving school 'to enable my sister Christabel to take her law course at university'. Her history of the WSPU goes from the Free Trade Hall incident, through her savage pummelling at Boggart Hole Clough, to a very abrupt end in autumn 1906, waving 'good-bye to my dear tall brother' at the railway station and her 'wonderful arrival in London in the early dawn of a summer morning'.[21]

It was hard for Adela to take the family narrative further; luckily for her, she now found welcome employment with the Women's Guild of Empire, a patriotic organisation formed by former suffragette Flora Drummond. Adela founded the Australian Guild, and went round Sydney haranguing businessmen at lunchtime open-air meetings – on the evils of Communism and the virtues, in an Empire untarnished by industrial strikes, of respectable family life.[22]

Nothing could be further from Sylvia Pankhurst's politics and household: her son Richard was born in 1927, out of wedlock – and very publicly so. Sylvia's own very powerfully written and moving memoir, *The Suffragette Movement*, was published in 1931; it was publicised as *the* suffrage history and set the seal on how future generations saw the campaign. If you were in, you became famous; if you were out, you grew forgotten. Subtitled 'An intimate account of persons and ideals', it again dismissed the 'old' suffragists;

and, once Sylvia moved from Manchester to London, her account sweeps down with it: the Victor Grayson campaign gets only a few lines, while Sylvia's own East End role commands four chapters. Her account is a narrative of radicalism, from her own father's politics through to the War, with Emmeline and Christabel painted as betraying the movement with their military recruitment campaign.[23] But the erasing of Adela's organising role in northern cities like Sheffield is surely explicable only in terms of Sylvia's wish to wear the radical crown.

Adela was understandably hurt and angry. She defended Emmeline against any slight from Sylvia, writing 'My Mother: An Explanation and Vindication' in 1933; even Adela's banishment ('She gave me what money she could spare') is softened and Emmeline's devotion to the cause understood.[24] And in 1934 Adela's 'The Philosophy of the Suffragette Movement' contrasted 'the present Feminist movement' which sought to destroy the family with Emmeline's broader perspective. Adela was determined to vindicate her mother:

> It is said, particularly by my sister Sylvia in her book, that at the end she [Emmeline] forgot her children. I do not think that is really true. From her point of view, she was always devoted to her family, but she thought in helping the world she was making it better for us, too. She had not developed her gift for individual maternity, but merged it into a larger feeling for all homes and all children.
>
> When my children read in their school history that 'Grannie' got the vote for women, it means as much to them as would the memory of a 'Grannie' who knitted them socks and bound up wounded knees. When my daughters visit the Motherland, as full citizens ... they may well feel that their Grandmother gave them as much as if she had left a fortune to spend.[25]

In America, Mary Gawthorpe developed a warm relationship with Sylvia Pankhurst, generously showering gifts on baby Richard, the son she had never had. Sylvia meanwhile updated Mary on her financial problems and the progress of her suffrage book: 'I wanted to write simply my memoirs – Publisher wants a general title'. When she read *The Suffragette Movement*, Mary was hurt that she had been reduced just to a small walk-on part, and told Sylvia she was particularly cross that her story had been summarised in one brisk footnote.[26] But Mary still generously helped Sylvia promote her book in the US, though she became less selfless when she saw advertising for *The Suffragette Movement* popular edition, with a French translation loom-ing too. She demanded that the offending footnote be rewritten more accurately, warning she might go to a solicitor.

Sylvia's cry of poverty also irked Mary: with Sylvia's Pankhurst heritage and Richard's birth, she wrote, 'I believe you are one of the richest women in the world today in all that makes Life worth while'. And she was furious with Sylvia's vague promises about making the correction in a new edition: by 1935, the battle of the footnote still festered. Sylvia protested, 'You are simply attempting to stop people from buying the only history of our Movement there is'. Mary retaliated: 'A dictatorship of any sort could easily . . . cause names to disappear altogether from the record. They wouldn't even be written in water!' – as under German Nazism.[27] And there this sadly rancorous correspondence ended: Sylvia felt misunder-stood about publishers' commercial realities, and Mary remained incensed by the personal slight to her own credibility in the US. More positively, this helped convince Mary that the best way to set the suffragette record straight was for her to consider writing her own autobiography.[28]

This transatlantic controversy certainly revealed clearly how very dearly held were the personal memories of the Edwardian Votes for Women cam-paigners. Suffragettes like Adela Pankhurst and Mary Gawthorpe wanted to ensure that their own stories were not just 'written in water' and for-gotten. And help was at hand. If Sylvia's 1931 history provided the narrative structure for future readers, then a new Suffragette Fellowship provided organisational continuity between present and past. Formed in 1926 by former members of the WSPU and WFL, it aimed 'to perpetuate the memory of the pioneers . . . and thus keep alive the suffragette spirit'. For the Fellowship, 'inclusion in the community of militant suffragettes rested upon the defining act of imprisonment'. It preserved archival material and personal relics, and as a commemorative network organised regular cele-brations. In 1929 it sent out questionnaires to record suffragettes' memories. So even before Sylvia's book was published, the Suffragette Fellowship had opened the floodgates of memory.[29]

Among those who responded was Mary Gawthorpe. After Sylvia's his-tory, this encouragement at last to reflect back on her past was most welcome. Mary's answers to the questionnaire offered an illuminating and honest account, familiar to readers of *Rebel Girls*; for this helped prompt Mary to write her full-length autobiography, *Up Hill to Holloway*, eventually published by a tiny American press in 1962.[30]

By about 1933–4 Adela was also in close touch with the Suffragette Fellowship and with Elsa Gye, its secretary, who was obviously delighted to hear from the least-known of the Pankhursts. Elsa noted that Sylvia's book 'has created rather a bad feeling & most of us were terribly disappointed'; she added that, unlike Emmeline, 'Sylvia isn't great – and never will be – but she is a clever writer'. The Fellowship had had an 'Adela Pankhurst tea', and Elsa passed on news of Mary Gawthorpe – who 'is just the same merry little person – but not very strong'. Elsa, writing from depression-hit middle England, wanted to return to safer Edwardian days; hers was the voice of an old lady. When Elsa's sons saw a photograph of the 1934 Fellowship dinner, she told Adela how:

> they exclaimed 'Phew! What a lot'. So I hastened to explain that 27 years ago we were all young and lovely & full of pep and fire. I must say that we do not look a very dangerous lot.[31]

By the 1930s, two distinct commemorative styles had emerged. While the mementos and memories of former WSPU and WFL prisoners were preserved by the Suffragette Fellowship, the NUWSS had transformed itself into an equal rights campaigning organisation, the National Union of Societies for Equal Citizenship (NUSEC).[32] Alongside this, London suffragists acquired a major book collection in the mid-1920s: a library was established, later named after Mrs Fawcett herself and run by the Fawcett Society. Like the Suffragette Fellowship, the Fawcett Library survived thanks to voluntary support; and it also provided a repository for archival records, and encouragement for elderly suffragists to record their Edwardian memories of the constitutional campaign for the vote.

Having earlier rolled up their banners and stored their fragile photographs away in the attic, elderly suffrage campaigners now sat down to write – to set the record straight in the best way they could by telling their own stories. As early as 1919, a biography of Mary Murdoch, *A Woman Doctor*, was published, but is too hagiographical to offer a usefully candid portrait.[33] Self-effacing even in death, Isabella Ford, sadly, left behind scant personal trace of her suffrage days, having closed her scrapbook with the dampening down of her early novelist ambitions.

The only Yorkshire suffragist autobiography is, indeed, Florence Lockwood's. In 1932 she self-published *An Ordinary Life*, based upon her diaries (drawn upon in Chapter 6); but even this limited edition soon fell out of print.

Few people wanted to know the story of the women who never joined the Pankhursts. Florence herself died in 1937 in London aged seventy-five and was cremated at Golders Green, probably with very few people present. Huddersfield itself did not however forget Florence. In 1933 she had presented two beautiful landscapes (see page 9) to Huddersfield art gallery, and her suffrage banner to the town museum.[34] Yet the NUWSS and Fawcett Library story remained overshadowed by the more dramatic militant suffragette narrative, heightened by Sylvia's 1931 history and the Suffragette Fellowship.

After the 1939–45 War, frail campaigners felt increasingly like the last drying leaves on the Edwardian suffrage tree: Sylvia Pankhurst died in 1960, Adela the following year.[35] The Suffragette Fellowship published a newsletter, *Calling All Women*, to sustain contact between the survivors: it helped Lilian Lenton, the Fellowship treasurer, to keep in touch with Leonora Cohen JP in Leeds. On 14 July 1962, Mrs Pankhurst's birthday, when flowers were laid at her statue, Leonora was the main speaker at the Fellowship's public meeting in Caxton Hall. And in 1970, ninety-seven-year-old Leonora, and Lilian, again travelled to gardens near Caxton Hall for an unveiling by the Speaker of the House of Commons of the memorial to all suffrage campaigners.[36]

Lilian Lenton died in 1972, Mary Gawthorpe in 1973. Only the longest-lived suffragettes remained alive: sprightly Leonora Cohen celebrated her century in 1973. And by then professional journalists and historians were growing increasingly alert to the significance of the suffrage campaign: the Fellowship and Sylvia's 1931 book provided the ideal short-cut to the disappearing Edwardian past for busy writers, radio, film producers.[37] A stream of suffrage histories began to be produced. Roger Fulford's *Votes for Women* (1957) traced the story from the 1820s; David Mitchell's *Fighting Pankhursts* (1967) tracked the family's histories (including Adela's) from the war right through to their deaths; while Antonia Raeburn's *The Militant Suffragettes* (1973) included an interview with Leonora Cohen and, more briefly, with Lilian Lenton.[38]

Yet it was Sylvia Pankhurst's *The Suffragette Movement* that retained its canonical status as encapsulating *the* history of Votes for Women. Its centrality and popularity as the standard text was further assured after BBC TV relied upon Sylvia's book for its memorable *Shoulder to Shoulder* (1974) suffragette drama series. This was shown, and repeated, not only in Britain but also world-wide. In the US, Dame Rebecca West provided background information for the *TV Guide*.[39]

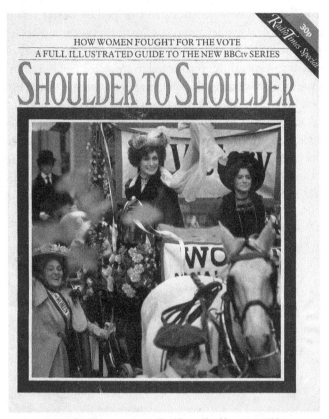

49. Radio Times *Special,* Shoulder to Shoulder, *cover, 1974.*

Shoulder to Shoulder told a dramatic story. Watching the series around the globe were the descendants of the rebel girls. In America, the nieces and great-nieces of Mary Gawthorpe watched; in Australia, the children and grandchildren of Adela Pankhurst Walsh watched; and in Britain so did the descendants of suffragettes such as Elizabeth Pinnance of Huddersfield. Also watching was a new generation of suffrage enthusiasts – including myself. Graphic scenes of forcible feeding in prison were absolutely gripping; but some of us wondered what *else* there was to suffrage history . . .

This celebratory television drama coincided with a renewal of interest in women's history, inspiring many of us to look again at the suffrage past. Since *Shoulder to Shoulder* (1974), Sylvia's classic history, with its focus on her London-centred campaigns, has been increasingly challenged by critics; and it has begun to be recognised for the regional – rather than national –

history it is.[40] Asking new questions and helped by newer research techniques, including oral history interviews with survivors and descendants, it became possible for Jill Norris and myself to uncover the history of the radical suffragists in Lancashire, recounted in *One Hand Tied Behind Us* (1978).

For almost a further three decades, however, the surprising history told in this book lay unrecorded. When I moved to Yorkshire in 1980, I became fascinated and wanted to uncover more of what had taken place. But so little seemed known; and feeling rather frustrated I went off and did other things. Only very recently has it become possible to recount the individual stories of the Yorkshire rebel girls narrated here. The sleuthing this entailed is recorded in 'Suffrage detective: tracking the evidence' (appendix 1).

CHAPTER 16

Rebel Girls: writing narrative history

The regional evidence I began to gather gradually took stronger shape (see 'Suffrage detective' appendix 1), with the rebel girls profiled here emerging particularly strongly. I decided to structure the writing of this book around an Edwardian group biography. My criteria for inclusion and omission became clear. The boundaries of the old three Yorkshire ridings provided a precise geographical frame: campaigns outside this region would be omitted.[1] The chronological narrative would be framed by the 1902 Yorkshire textile workers' suffrage petition (and especially the 1906 Huddersfield by-election) and by the outbreak of war in 1914. I would, however, set this regional Edwardian history within its broad suffrage context by sketching in the late-Victorian background, plus national political framework reference points – Asquith becoming Prime Minister, the start of forcible feeding, the constitutional crisis, the death of Emily Wilding Davison. These decisions both provided a firm focus for this story and set it within its wider historical context. I also decided to structure the book as a narrative organised around individual biographies, rather than around a thematic framework.

During the writing, I have been asked some searching questions about this book's title and its meaning. This final analytical chapter therefore suggests answers to these wider questions on the significance of the rebel girls to broader suffrage history.

Readers familiar with *One Hand Tied Behind Us* (1978) will want to know: have I changed my mind on militancy? In Lancashire, radical suffragists like Esther Roper and Selina Cooper grew highly critical of WSPU actions, preferring the NUWSS constitutional tactics. In *Rebel Girls*, I now appear to write far more sympathetically about suffragette militancy – such as Leonora Cohen's attack in the Tower of London and even Lilian Lenton's aim of burning two buildings a week until the Government gave women the vote.

The answer is: no, I have not changed my mind. I still sympathise with the radical suffragists' reluctance to go down the violence road. The WSPU pledged to endanger no life; but window-smashing and arson were tactics which could hit innocent bystanders: the WSPU was fortunate that no Whitehall clerk, suburban postman or Doncaster housekeeper was seriously injured. Additionally, NUWSS suffragists felt that escalating militancy became politically diversionary. It permitted Asquith's government to treat suffrage not as a democratic demand for women's citizenship, but as a law-and-order issue about public safety. A constitutional reform became a Home Office problem dealt with by police tactics and prison regimes. Then developments such as the Cat and Mouse Act let the government off the democracy hook, with sensation-seeking tabloid newspapers following every move of fugitive 'mice' instead of demanding enfranchisement for women.

Rather than changing my mind over three decades, I have moved house – from Lancashire, across the Pennines to Yorkshire. As the 'Suffrage detective' appendix records, I have tracked the history of Edwardian suffrage across this different region. The research process entailed reading different evidence, seeing new patterns and arriving at rather different conclusions. A distinct group of campaigners swam forcefully into view. So, by looking at this particular region, in *Rebel Girls* I present a different picture from that of *One Hand*.

I have also been asked whether the rebel girls formed 'a group'. The answer is both yes and no. Key actors certainly shared strong formative characteristics. Of the central eight rebel girls, all were born within the same decade: Mary Gawthorpe, Lavena Saltonstall and Alice Schofield in 1881; Violet Key-Jones about 1883, Adela Pankhurst in 1885, Dora Thewlis and Molly Morris in 1890, and the youngest, Lilian Lenton, in 1891. They all came of age at the new century's dawn. They were between fifteen and twenty-five years old in 1906 when this narrative takes off. The Edwardian suffrage campaign *was* their growing up. It transformed their lives – from isolated and confined adolescence, to envisioning novel freedoms and opportunities. Their demand for political rights suddenly offered them far broader experiences – amongst the most startling being arrest, court appearance and prison.[2]

Alongside the rebel girls campaigned more experienced women: Laura Wilson in Halifax, Edith Key in Huddersfield and Leonora Cohen in Leeds. Born in the 1870s, recently married and with young children, their hands were tied by family responsibilities – though Laura and Leonora were both imprisoned more than once.[3]

Born a generation earlier than the rebel girls, Isabella Ford and her sister Emily, Florence Lockwood and Dr Mary Murdoch all had their adult identities firmly established before the Edwardian campaign took off. Growing up with access to secondary education, they could seize new training opportunities – to become painters or even doctors. Rooted in family Liberalism (or married into it like Florence), these pioneer suffragists adhered to constitutional tactics, yet showed great daring – Isabella's caravanning, Florence's pamphlet, Mary Murdoch's discreet lesbian relationships. They must often have felt like round pegs in square local holes – whether Bloomsburyite Florence plunged into Linthwaite, or those with links to northern Europe (notably Germany) such as Bertha Lowenthal or Elsa Schuster.[4]

Analysing the key eight rebel girls, strong common personal experiences bound them together. Idealistic fathers left mothers labouring to hold the family together; daughters forged close bonds with mothers. Rebel girls developed strong personal ambitions which, even when economic realities forced them to defer or rethink, they refused to abandon. Adela's father had neglected to make a will; she forfeited her chance of university, instead becoming a pupil teacher. John Gawthorpe's political work took him away from home and into various pubs, triggering disputes with Mary's mother. Mary also had to forgo higher education, becoming another pupil teacher; she longed for the day when she would be twenty-one. With that independence, she could rent her own house and so be entitled to vote at local elections. Molly Morris too was saddled with a father whose political enthusiasms cost the family his wage; Molly also had to set aside her dreams and go out to work as shop assistant; and she, too, was close to her hard-working mother – who introduced her daughter to suffrage. Lilian Lenton likewise set store on reaching twenty-one: *then* she could take on the government. Slightly older, Leonora Cohen's artist-father died when she was a child; Leonora always maintained it was her hard-pressed mother's experience that convinced her of the importance of winning women the vote.[5] For Adela Pankhurst, of course, the mother-daughter-suffrage relationship always was far more complex and difficult.

These rebel girls shared a dream-time adolescence, full of romantic longings and yearning ambitions – Adela to write the novel 'which would shake the capitalist system to its foundations'; Mary to see more of life beyond her Leeds elementary schools; Molly to become a nurse. In fact, it was the Votes for Women campaign that helped fulfil some of those dreams by opening up new political horizons. It allowed Lavena to discover her razor-sharp writing skills; it took Molly out from behind her shop-counter and across the Pennines to Sheffield and its pillar-boxes. It even encouraged name changes for Mary and Molly. Suffrage memorably provided both the motive and the opportunity.

The rebel girls all shared the same suffrage aims. The vote was a crucial instrument for helping powerless women improve their working conditions – as Leonora told Lloyd George. The vote also symbolised their own personal conflicts and struggles. For them, its repeated denial by Asquith's seemingly uncaring Liberal government became the motivating force for rebellion. For Adela and Mary, this meant propaganda assaults on politicians, arrest and imprisonment; then, on becoming WSPU organisers, their political passion became their paid work. For community suffragettes like Lavena and Dora, demanding the vote meant participating in mass uprisings – followed by mass imprisonment. For later maverick militants like Leonora and Lilian, it meant doing the unthinkable: smashing a glass-case in the Tower of London, deciding to fire two buildings a week, fleeing police pursuit by sailing away in a yacht.

The rebel girls campaigned across a shared Yorkshire landscape. For Lavena, Dora and Leonora, this was determined by the region's economic activity: textiles and clothing. For Adela and Molly in Sheffield, it was the landscape of heavy industry, vividly evoked by Rebecca West. And for Violet Key-Jones, it was shaped by the Edwardian rail network, allowing her easily to reach cities, villages and seaside harbours up and down her east Yorkshire stretch.

The shared personal pressures of imprisonment made the lives of Lavena and Dora almost unbearable on return to their own communities. For Adela and Mary, their health suffered very seriously, Mary receiving a savage kick in the stomach. The danger of exhaustion and burn-out was very real. With hunger-striking and forcible feeding, Lilian and Leonora hung between life and death. This powerful bond of suffering, forged in the heat of the Edwardian militant campaign, later became the firm bonds of friendship, sustained by the Suffragette Fellowship and other campaigning networks. Evidence of this abounds: Elsa Gye's long letters to Adela in

Australia, Mary's promotion of Sylvia's book, Leonora and Lilian joining together at the 1970 suffrage memorial unveiling.[6]

Bound by all these common experiences and themes, this book is constructed as a collective biography.[7] Within this, three distinct groups emerge. First, of course, and lending the book its title, are the rebel girls themselves – militant campaigners born 1881–91. (Part One records the initial conversions of Adela and Mary; Part Two tells how Lavena and Dora became what I have characterised as community suffragettes; Part Three takes further the story of Adela, Mary and Lavena. In Part Four, the later group of suffragettes – Molly Morris, Lilian Lenton and Violet Key-Jones – I have distinguished as maverick militants.) Second, there was the more experienced group of suffragettes like Laura Wilson, Edith Key and Leonora Cohen. The final group comprises pioneer suffragists: Isabella Ford and her sisters Bessie and Emily, Dr Mary Murdoch and later convert Florence Lockwood.

The follow-up question frequently put to me is: to what extent did the rebel girls know each other and work together – in other words, did they literally comprise 'a group'? Again the answer is mixed. Yes, some did work closely together. Of course, as early WSPU organisers, Adela and Mary worked with a wide number of suffragettes (before ill-health and doubts about the escalating militancy meant they left the WSPU). Within Yorkshire, Adela arrived in strike-riven Hebden Bridge, then appeared at the Colne Valley by-election; she raced across to Hull West, then down to Sheffield. As a result of her key regional role, Adela knew more people than most, and may be seen as pivotal.[8] Of the early community suffragettes, Lavena Saltonstall (and certainly Laura Wilson) knew Huddersfield WSPU members like Edith Key. And in March 1907, Lavena and Laura, Elizabeth Pinnance and Dora Thewlis all shared arrest and its consequence: the experience of confinement in prison encourages friendships.

Also, no. While they were growing up, the rebel girls were separated by hill and dale across the sprawling Yorkshire landscape. Working-class girls like Lavena, Dora and Molly Morris led isolated lives: opportunities to see beyond their family, neighbourhood and workplace remained very limited. Their parents had been economic migrants, but once the Saltonstall and Thewlis families settled, they stayed more or less in one small textile community. Until Lavena and Dora adventured down to London in March 1907, their growing up was bounded by very narrow horizons: probably neither had travelled as far away as Leeds. Even with new-fangled electric trams, the next valley remained virtually inaccessible. They would not have had the opportunity to 'know each other'.

The rebel girls were further isolated by the social chasm of Edwardian class inequalities. Working-class girls leaving school expected to become weavers or tailoresses, and had little in common with girls in a well-servanted home, fortunate enough to train as artists or even doctors. The Edwardian suffragette experience increasingly changed that. Certainly from about 1911, as the campaign accelerated ever faster, rigid class divisions began to dissolve in the face of the cruel common enemy: Asquith and McKenna. Elsa Schuster befriended Molly Morris when she arrived in Sheffield. Carpenter's daughter Lilian Lenton was sheltered by Violet Key-Jones, from the landed gentry. Later, fugitive Lilian was offered refuge by Leonora Cohen, who helped her escape, even lending her son's clothes. A small tightening cell of arsonists on the run from the police was protected by a slightly larger band of loyal sympathisers like Edith Key. In the shadowy world of co-conspirators and plain-clothes detectives, old rigid hierarchies of class had to melt away.

Within the NUWSS, suffragists in Yorkshire still occupied more traditional worlds within which they maintained their established identities: Florence as an artist and Liberal Poor Law Guardian, Mary Murdoch as a respected GP, socialist Isabella as an ILP member. Arrest and prison never threatened, nor did peril and frenzy: the suffragists were each able to sustain their patient constitutional campaign for far longer, right up to August 1914.[9] Not only were their campaigning tactics diametrically different, but also they inhabited social worlds estranged from so many of the rebel girls: there is no evidence that Florence 'knew' of either Edith Key or 'baby suffragette' Dora Thewlis, both living just down the road.

Broader comparative questions remain. Readers will want to know: why did the Yorkshire and Lancashire suffrage campaigns take such different shapes, and why did local women make such different choices? For there were no radical suffragists like Esther Roper or Selina Cooper in Yorkshire; and in the Lancashire cotton towns, such rebel girls were of less significance.[10]

Part of the explanation lies in the distinct economic and employment structures of the two textile regions. Lancashire's strong trade union organisation among women cotton workers was never replicated in the West Riding. Here working women – whether in wool and worsted mills or in clothing factories – remained poorly paid. Rebel voices could be easily silenced by fear of victimisation. Yorkshire produced no textile workers like

Selina Cooper, with years of labour movement experience, nor like Ada Nield Chew, tailoress turned trade union organiser who later also became a radical suffragist. Indeed, the vast number of signatures on the 1902 Yorkshire textile workers' suffrage petition did not act as a springboard for women to become active NUWSS suffragists – which must have grieved Isabella Ford. Where economically active women workers were converted to the Votes for Women campaign, they invariably joined the WSPU – as did Lavena, Dora and Lilian Cobbe.[11] Unlike Lancashire, the 1902 petition energy never fed into the NUWSS.

The marked differences between the Yorkshire and Lancashire campaigns also stem from political personalities – notably the Pankhursts. The actions of Christabel especially left bruising divisions behind in the Manchester area, stoking radical suffragists' distaste for militant rhetoric. Additionally, Yorkshire universities produced no one like Esther Roper, energetic working-class Manchester graduate who seized the moment and made something of it. Although Mary Gawthorpe was involved in Leeds University extension classes, neither Leeds nor Sheffield universities played the same catalyst role as Manchester. Also, Isabella Ford, for all her support for women trade unionists and her ILP networks, seems not to have inspired significant numbers of Edwardian working women into NUWSS activity. The campaign probably needed Esther's fresh eye and youthful energy. Despite Isabella's vanning, the 1913 pilgrimage, and Florence's 'Friends' propaganda, the NUWSS in Yorkshire did not apparently recruit active younger women in any number. It largely remained run by the Liberal elite, as angry with suffragette tactics (in the case of Dr Helen Wilson in Sheffield) as with the government.[12]

These differences prompt the next question: how does the suffrage profile of Yorkshire compare with that of other great English regions. Since *One Hand* was published, there has been time to reappraise the radical suffragists of Lancashire as a unique phenomenon or as part of pattern. Suffrage historians have recently argued that:

> in many respects the position of the well-organised Lancashire working woman was a unique one. It is difficult to find such active and widespread support for the women's suffrage movement from working-class women in other regions, and certainly not within the NUWSS.[13]

No and yes. No, in that the early chapters of *Rebel Girls* tell the story of the community suffragettes and their wide-scale uprising among clothing and mill workers c.1906–8. Yes, in that they did not align themselves with the NUWSS, still associated with elite women and the Liberal Party of their employers. Rather, they joined the WSPU, then rooted in ILP socialism, and they formed dynamic local branches in winter 1906–7, as in Halifax and Huddersfield (even though those branches were seemingly not sustained much beyond 1908–9).[14]

This West Riding pattern is similar to another English region, Merseyside. Here working-class women, socialists and bohemian feminists joined the Liverpool WSPU branch – rather than the more decorous NUWSS led by city councillor Eleanor Rathbone, daughter of a Liberal MP.[15] However, in the North-East region around Newcastle the pattern seems nearer to Lancashire. Here NUWSS suffragists often had close ILP links and strong labour movement loyalties.[16]

Once the NUWSS introduced its Election Fighting Fund (EFF) in 1912, the differences grow more marked between Lancashire and the North-East on the one hand, and Yorkshire and Merseyside on the other. Lancashire offered real support to the EFF, with its radical suffragists in great demand elsewhere. The North-East, with grassroots suffrage–labour co-operation, demonstrated strong EFF commitment. On Merseyside, however, Eleanor Rathbone and the Liverpool NUWSS branch were outraged by this new political strategy, becoming diehard opponents of the EFF.[17]

Finally, if you thought that in 2006 there was nothing fresh left to know about women's suffrage – think again! In *Rebel Girls,* new actors – Lavena, Dora, Violet and others – move centre-stage and into the spotlight. Well-known household names (like Sylvia Pankhurst) retire to the shadowy wings or beyond, making just a fleeting appearance as designer of the WSPU early membership card and later as author of the 1931 history. After 1906, Christabel also becomes an off-stage voice, an unseen legal brain devising cunning strategies to tie the Liberal government in complex knots. Emmeline, naturally, makes inspiring entrances as star speaker on the by-election circuit or when Adela's campaign needs a boost. Centre-stage is undeniably commanded by forgotten daughter Adela, as WSPU organiser for Yorkshire, and we follow her from Manchester to Hebden Bridge, then up and down her daunting eastern stretch from Sheffield to Scarborough.

The standard scenery, so familiar from Sylvia's 1931 history and from *Shoulder to Shoulder*, is moved out towards the wings. Freshly painted backdrops are shifted into place – depicting Hebden Bridge's fustian factory chimneys and the large worsted mills crammed along Huddersfield's canal-banks. In front of this new scenery appear unknown actors: Lavena, Dora, Edith Key. Later, maverick suffragettes, some already glimpsed as fleeting figures on the traditional suffrage stage, now have the spotlight shone full on them.

We see all these campaigners clearly as never before. The light-beam swoops down to the Colne Valley and Florence's encounter with Emmeline and Adela in her by-election hayfield; to Sheffield and Adela disguised as a kitchen-maid; to the Tower of London with Leonora entering, iron bars wrapped around; to the Doncaster courtroom, where Lilian Lenton dramatically steps forward into the dock; back to Huddersfield, with Edith Key hiding fleeing suffragette 'mice' up in her attic; and across to Harrogate where Leonora aids fugitive Lilian to escape.

There is also a fresh play-script. The drama opens on the crucible years 1905–8, with Adela addressing community suffragettes in the textile and clothing communities of Hebden Bridge, Huddersfield and the Colne Valley. We listen to these actors' previously unheard lines: Lavena in her newspaper columns; sixteen-year-old Dora attempting to hold her own in court; Edith Key writing her poignant annual report; Leonora and Lilian eloquently lambasting the hypocrisies of Liberal politicians whose legal system forcibly fed women but would not give them the vote.

This wealth of spanking fresh evidence allows a brand new suffrage cast of actors to speak their new lines in front of fresh scenery. The world of the community suffragettes has been virtually unknown, most especially that of Lavena Saltonstall and Laura Wilson, who had disappeared without trace. To a few readers certain of the material presented here may be familiar: Adela Pankhurst and Mary Gawthorpe, Isabella Ford and Mary Murdoch all now appear in the 2004 *Oxford Dictionary of National Biography*. Some suffrage historians will already have heard of Leonora Cohen and Lilian Lenton. Yet even here, by reading local and regional newspaper reports, new cross-Yorkshire campaigns and connections spring into view – notably Adela's suffrage organising and Violet Key-Jones' conspiratorial networks.

By focusing on the Yorkshire region, fresh patterns emerge – sometimes confirming earlier suspicions, sometimes throwing up new interpretations. The suffragette drama familiar from Sylvia's history and *Shoulder to Shoulder* is confirmed as just a partial account. Her marginalisation of the NUWSS distorts the suffrage past: its well-oiled organisational machinery recruited members, set up new branches and won fresh 'Friends' to suffrage.[18] The notion that it was Sylvia who was 'the prime mover in making working women aware of the Suffragette Cause' is exposed as misleading, credible only if organisers like Adela are airbrushed out.[19]

And the standard account of WSPU continuities begins to fracture; by about 1911, the earlier generation of suffragettes – Adela and Mary, Lavena and Dora – had grown exhausted and decided to take the longer view. A different, smaller group of militants – Leonora and Lilian, Molly and Violet – stepped forward, prepared to risk all, even life itself.[20] The WSPU campaign had changed almost out of recognition: Asquith's government now got away with handling suffragettes as a law-and-order and public security issue (though McKenna must have held his breath every time a feeding tube was thrust down a suffragette's throat, or a 'mouse' out on licence escaped – hence the government's use of spy cameras in prison). The number of WSPU militants dwindled to a hardened band, yet there remained a wellspring of broader support – as Leonora's photograph of elegant Leeds suffragettes suggests – at a time when every woman continued to be denied the franchise.

More broadly, this fresh Yorkshire evidence, suggesting a new chronology and narrative, begins to shift suffrage historiography. And it reminds us how the Votes for Women campaign impacted on young Edwardian lives; that we are the inheritors of the rebel girls and their like. Their fight was for a basic constitutional entitlement, now built into the fabric of any modern democracy.

Appendices

Appendixes

Suffrage detective: tracking the evidence

The evidence which triggered the writing of this book unfolded itself only slowly. The story of my detective chase, hinted at occasionally throughout this book, is told here in its own right. This offers an account of my research methods, framework for selection, writing and interpretation; it also aims to place this Yorkshire history into the broader suffrage historiography and to inspire similar regional explorations elsewhere.

When Jill Norris and I wrote *One Hand* in the mid-1970s, I was living in Springhead, near Oldham in Lancashire – and was delighted to discover I lived next door to the mill in which suffragette Annie Kenney had worked.[1] Such sleuthing told me that Votes for Women campaigners, even household names like Annie Kenney, came from somewhere. They had local roots, they inhabited a local landscape.

Then in 1980 I moved across the Pennines to West Yorkshire. I wanted immediately to uncover its suffrage narrative. But there seemed precious little to go on, beyond a few unconnected biographical fragments. Friends were interested in Leeds suffragist Isabella Ford; but she seemed to have left no personal papers.[2] They were also fascinated by suffragette Leonora Cohen, who reputedly did something terribly daring, and was then still alive and well over 100. But, with Yorkshire such a vast patchwork of intensely-felt local identities, the research task was far too daunting to an incomer. I went off and did other things.

My fascination never left me. In the mid-1980s, I stumbled across an out-of-print autobiography of Florence Lockwood – who had unexpectedly encountered the Pankhursts at a fiery by-election on her own doorstep. Most intriguing – but how to place it? I let it lie. Then in 1988 in Halifax, I taught a New Opportunities for Women course; students' local research threw up a whole raft of forgotten Edwardian suffragettes, imprisoned in Holloway who – when they returned home to Halifax – were pushed to the margins, even in local histories. Some had unlikely names – like Lavena Saltonstall. One student even introduced into the class a leading local suffragette's elderly daughter. She entranced us all with Dinah Connelly's Holloway gaol stories: hard straw mattresses and a prison number – D2, 16. However, in the pressure of teaching, I foolishly omitted to tape-record this oral evidence. I was busy with other things; anyway, these Yorkshire suffrage fragments all seemed rather vague and disjointed.

Since the publication of *One Hand*, new perspectives have enriched and widened our understanding of women's history and of the suffrage past.[3] Lisa Tickner's wonderful *The Spectacle of Women* (1987) analysed the visual imagery of the Edwardian campaign, introducing readers to the work of suffragist artists like Mary Lowndes and Emily Ford. Doyen suffrage historian Sandra Holton wrote of Suffrage and the 'Average Woman'; like the radical suffragists, Holton's campaigners were ordinary women with ordinary lives, not 'a caste apart'; even women as deeply committed to the cause as Mary Gawthorpe of Leeds 'had lives apart from the movement'. She contrasted this to certain suffrage historians who, by focusing on the extraordinary personalities, have implied a separateness from political significance of the average woman's intimate, domestic family life and marriage.[4] Then Holton's richly researched *Suffrage Days: stories from the Women's Suffrage Movement* (1996) wove together the stories of seven campaigners, including Mary Gawthorpe. Lucidly exploring 'the entwining of formal politics and the politics of personal life', Holton's title was chosen to convey 'the golden aura of nostalgia' so often wreathing the memories of Edwardian campaigners, recalling years later their suffrage youth as *the* transformative experience of their lives.[5]

Elizabeth Crawford also left all suffrage historians in her debt with her encyclopaedic *The Women's Suffrage Movement: a reference guide* (1999) which, as well as biographies, listed local branches – from Aberdeen NUWSS to York WSPU. Alongside, local historians told us more about the Votes for Women campaigns in regions across the country: no longer just Lancashire, but also north-east England and Merseyside. These important new area histories challenged or even overturned conventional London-centred narratives: 'national figures retire to the margins, diminished in stature, or do not appear at all' – to be replaced by fresh new protagonists.[6]

However, parallel with these rich new perspectives, there has much more recently been a sense of a narrowing down again to the traditional suffragette narratives with a return to 'celebrity suffrage'. Competing

Pankhurst biographical tomes were published: Pankhurst loyalist June Purvis' *Emmeline Pankhurst: a biography* (2002) was matched by a family history *The Pankhursts* (2001) by political historian Martin Pugh, a Pankhurst critic. Could any two books be more different? A bitter spat between biographers seemed inevitable. Battle was joined: one paper even ran a double-page 'The Pankhursts – politics and passion', the two authors slugging it out. With 'Pankhurst' one of the twentieth-century household names, further biographies of individual daughters inevitably followed.[7]

Knowing only of Isabella Ford and Florence Lockwood, two women growing up in middle-class households, I felt the story lacked coherence and conviction. I was spurred on, however, by the publication of Holton's *Suffrage Days* with its chapter on Mary Gawthorpe. I even tracked down one forlorn copy of her vivid autobiography, *Up Hill to Holloway* (1962), long fallen out of print. Then in 1998, I agreed (though rather wished I had not) to give a talk in Bradford about women's suffrage in West Yorkshire. I padded out my rather skimpy research on the Halifax suffragettes and Isabella Ford with extensive quotation from Mary Gawthorpe's reminiscences.

There I would have left it. The fragments seemed more gaps than substance. It did not seem very likely that any new archival evidence would surface, and direct suffrage testimony had long since slipped from living memory. Leonora Cohen herself had now died – in 1978 aged a remarkable 105; and so also had the very last suffragette – in 1992 aged 102.[8]

Then I suddenly began to hear of startling new discoveries. These spurred me on and helped me join together these odd, disconnected jigsaw pieces I had long assembled. I had begun to teach suffrage history once again, and in 1999 offered a course in Huddersfield, at which a student called Margaret Pinnance turned up – who mentioned that her grandmother had been a local suffragette imprisoned in Holloway. Then, again in Huddersfield, on a wind-swept International Woman's Day walk in 2000, I learnt of the town's veritable hive of Edwardian suffragettes. The granddaughter of one, Edith Key, who had kept the Huddersfield WSPU minutes-book in her sideboard, had even recently deposited her papers locally – including this extremely rare minutes book, along with the typescript reminiscences of Edith's two sons. These offered a tantalising glimpse into early suffragette branch life in the north of England – so helping bring to life again the Huddersfield WSPU.[9] Thank heavens for family hoarding habits.

By 2003, although Edith's granddaughter had by then died, I was however able to interview *her* daughter, Julia Mitchell – about how her great-grandmother Edith Key had hidden fugitive suffragette 'mice', escaping the Cat and Mouse Act 1913–14, up in the attic of the very house in which Julia had grown up. Julia never knew her great-grandmother but felt really proud that she had been a suffragette, and after her own mother's death, donated the WSPU minutes book to the archives.[10]

By dint of such lucky detective work, I was also even able to track Huddersfield's most notorious suffragette: sixteen-year-old 'baby' Dora Thewlis, who had emigrated to Australia a little over ninety years earlier.[11] I despaired of ever making contact with her descendants – if they were still alive. After countless false leads, I traced Dora's daughter, Mabel Carey, to a suburb of Melbourne – where I recorded an interview in 2003. Herself now elderly, Mabel's memories of her mother's suffrage drama were understandably overlaid by more recent memories of Australia during the Depression; and were, since *Shoulder to Shoulder*, somewhat embellished (e.g. including forcible feeding), reminding me of the distance between now and our Edwardian ancestors.[12]

Along with this fresh Huddersfield evidence, news also blew in unexpectedly of an important cache of Mary Gawthorpe papers – recently deposited in a New York library by her three great-nieces. As Mary had died in 1973, the deposit had waited a full three decades. It was well worth the delay. This extensive personal archive now revealed how Mary, labouring away as a pupil teacher, reinvented herself as an Edwardian 'new woman' – partly by joining Alfred Orage's exhilarating Leeds Arts Club (and encountering Isabella Ford) and partly by joining the infant WSPU. For the years after *Up Hill to Holloway* ends, the Gawthorpe collection includes leaflets and pledge cards from Mary's organising in Bradford in 1908, as well as the angry 1930s correspondence with Sylvia Pankhurst.[13] Newly available photographs show that Mary changed completely in just a few years – from a pleasant yet uncertain eighteen-year-old in 1899 to a fearless suffragette.

I was luckily able to complement this fresh archival evidence with an interview with Mary's great-niece, living in Boston. Betty Meissner, born in 1931, recalled that her grandmother was always proud of sister Mary. Although her great-aunt was rather a distant figure, Betty and her two sisters 'grew up with Votes for Women, we grew up with Mary Gawthorpe'. After Mary died, the papers were stored up in Betty's attic in New England. Knowing about her great-aunt's marginalisation in Sylvia Pankhurst's book, she decided that Mary too 'had a place in history, and I just wanted that to be recognised'.[14] Betty's own daughter, Mary's great-great-niece, born in 1956 and a second-wave feminist, likewise recalled watching *Shoulder to Shoulder* and, fascinated by great-great-aunt Mary, remembered how, 'I was disgusted by the series . . . I thought, "Well, we have all the information about her in our attic"'.[15] So urged on, Mary's three great-nieces eventually deposited the Gawthorpe archive in the New York library. In March 2004, to honour this treasure trove, the Library organised a panel of women historians to commemorate Mary Gawthorpe, Leeds suffragette.[16]

The third surprise discovery concerned Adela Pankhurst. Since her 'banishment' to Australia in 1914, Adela's airbrushing out of the historical record had, until very recently, been almost complete and most systematic. A biography of Adela was published by Melbourne University Press in 1996: it was naturally stronger on Adela's later Australian years, leaving much of her Edwardian suffrage story still untold; and even this brief biography is now out of print.[17] Unlike Mary Gawthorpe, Adela had fled England carrying with her virtually no possessions. However, since Adela's death, her daughter had deposited the papers in the National Library in Canberra in 1968.

Though eerily silent on the Edwardian years, the collection does include Adela's later journalism; this tells us a great deal about how she reflected back upon the early years of that most charismatic yet disputatious of political families, the Pankhursts.[18] Adela's typescripts need to be read alongside Yorkshire newspaper accounts of her WSPU organising; tracking her campaigns from Hebden Bridge to Colne Valley, from Sheffield to Scarborough, they reveal Adela's own lesser-known version of events – compared to Sylvia's canonical account. While in Australia, I eventually traced Adela's granddaughter and was fortunate enough to meet her.[19] Susan Pankhurst Hogan was born in 1943, and as a child had grown up with elderly Adela: 'Yes, when I was very young Adela lived with us, and when I started school she took me to school, my first day at school'. A delightfully loving grandma, Adela recalled for her small grandchildren some idiosyncratic advice from Edwardian campaigning:

'You never got up to address a crowd, but you weren't standing in front of a plate-glass window because people wouldn't throw stones at you'. And she said, 'You always take an umbrella to a protest'. Words of wisdom.[20]

Other final pieces of the jigsaw also began to slip into place. In 2001, I was working with the Fawcett Library in London, preparing a suffrage display for its re-launch exhibition as the magnificent new Women's Library.

Here I was given access to its invaluable suffrage postcard collection –
including poignant photographs of the NUWSS's horse-drawn caravan
tour across rural Yorkshire, enticing in even intrepid Isabella Ford in
summer 1909.

A visit to the Abbey House Museum in Leeds which houses the Leonora
Cohen papers immediately made it clear that her recklessly daring
'smashing' suffragette deed actually took place in the Tower of London,
no less – as chapter 12 recounts. Leonora had kept not only her police-sta-
tion charge sheets but even the *aides-memoires* she used when defending
herself so eloquently in court, both for the Tower of London attack and
her subsequent trials. Equally methodically, Leonora had pasted into a
scrapbook the press-cuttings which recorded her daring deeds, from 1911
right through to 1966 – when, aged ninety-two, she opened a suffragette
exhibition at Abbey House Museum.[21] When *Shoulder to Shoulder* was broad-

50. Radio Times, *1974* – centre: *Leonora Cohen, aged 100.*

cast, Leonora, now aged a hundred, even appeared on the front cover of the *Radio Times*.

Other discoveries tumbled rapidly upon one another. I came across a copy of *Molly Murphy: Suffragette and Socialist* (1998). Then Molly Morris, aged twenty-two, she replaced Adela Pankhurst in Sheffield as regional WSPU organiser. Her autobiography conjured up the rebel girls' dare-devilry and the final suffragette years of firing pillar-boxes.[22]

In Huddersfield, a strong WSPU branch had fostered the survival of documentary materials, however fragmentary, from which local suffrage history could be written. Another example, in addition to the Key and Thewlis families, is Elizabeth Pinnance, born about 1879. Her son, aged about eight when his mother went to prison, did not like to talk much afterwards about what his mother had got up to; but Elizabeth's daughter Irene passed down family legend of suffragette daring. Irene's daughters both still live in Huddersfield and remember clearly their well-dressed and corseted grandmother. In 2003, on my visit to one daughter's extremely neat suburban house (just a stone's throw from where her grandmother was born about 125 years earlier), I was absolutely stunned to walk in and see, framed and displayed on the sitting-room wall, an illuminated testimonial, signed by Emmeline Pankhurst on behalf of the WSPU, and presented:

To Elizabeth Pinnance,

On behalf of all women, who will win freedom by the bondage which you have endured for their sake, and dignity by the humiliation which you have gladly suffered for the uplifting of our sex, We, the members of the Women's Social and Political Union, herewith express our deep sense of admiration for your courage in enduring the long period of privation and solitary confinement in prison for the Votes for Women's Cause; also our thanks to you for the great service that you have hereby rendered to the Women's movement.

Inspired by your passion for freedom and right, may we and the women who come after us be ever ready to follow your example of self-forgetfulness and self-conquest, ever ready to obey the call of duty and to answer to the appeal of the oppressed.

Signed on behalf of the Women's Social and Political Union

Emmeline Pankhurst.[23]

*

Other sleuthing was not always so productive. The Suffragette Fellowship questionnaires might have meant that all rebel girls were contacted. However, the Fellowship does not retain any record of, say, Lavena Saltonstall and Dora Thewlis. It reflected London and the south rather than the north; and, by focusing on the later rather than earlier WSPU, it omitted the community suffragettes.[24] About 1955, however, the Fellowship compiled a 'Roll of Honour: Suffragette Prisoners 1905–14'. Here are not only the well-known figures like Emmeline, Christabel and Sylvia Pankhurst and Annie Kenney, but also less celebrated names listed alphabetically: Helen Archdale and Jennie Baines; Ellen Beever, Ellen Brooke and Elizabeth Berkley; Lilian Cobbe, Leonora Cohen and Dinah Connelly; Mary Gawthorpe, Harry Johnson and Lilian Lenton; Hannah Mitchell and Adela Pankhurst; Elizabeth Pinnance, Lavena Saltonstall and Mary Taylor; Dora Thewlis and Amy Titterington; Edith Whitworth and Laura Wilson. Although no more than just a stark list, it provided corroborative evidence of suffragettes whose names otherwise appear in small-print Edwardian newspapers listed just as the 'also arrested'.[25]

Particularly unexpected new evidence, buried for ninety years among the official Home Office papers lodged at the National Archives, was uncovered only in late 2003, during preparations for celebrating the WSPU centenary. It revealed the full (and very sobering) extent of the Liberal government's secret surveillance of suffragettes. Unaware of being photographed, prisoners' portraits were officially recorded using the newest Edwardian technology: the telecentric lens. Suffragettes included not only those in Holloway, but also some detained in Armley gaol: thus we have the photograph of Lilian Lenton, maverick militant 'mouse' who evaded the Yorkshire authorities and became a fugitive. This unexpected archival discovery attracted considerable media attention, with wide public interest in images taken covertly as 'spy pictures', arguably making the suffragettes into the first such organisation subjected to secret state photography in the UK.[26]

Yet the passage of time – three generations – also inevitably heightened certain evidence problems. Suffrage had now moved beyond living memory. While some descendants – of Mary Gawthorpe or Elizabeth Pinnance – remembered their ancestors' daring deeds, other family memories had apparently disappeared without trace.

Jonathan Rose, historian of *The Intellectual Life of the British Working Classes* (2001), highlighted the Edwardian journalism of tailoress Lavena Saltonstall; but, by focusing on her later WEA writings, he leaves her biography dangling, without her suffragette history or local roots. My reading through that most unfashionable but invaluable of sources, local newspapers, confirmed that Lavena was indeed a leading Halifax suffragette. Yet, of all the stories told here, hers had been the most totally obliterated. What happened to her headful of memories: where would this most elusive community suffragette with a story to tell go? Local newspaper appeal for memories or photographs of Lavena Saltonstall, Dinah Connelly and the other Halifax suffragettes met with silence.[27] They remain 'the disappeared'.

Such feisty women as Lavena Saltonstall, Dora Thewlis and Elizabeth Pinnance still remained hidden from historians' view. They had clearly become militant suffragettes when they were very young. How could I find out about them *before* Votes for Women changed their lives, about the ordinary growing-up of the rebel girls?

To help me, an additional powerful research tool now became available: the hand-written household census of 1901. Detailed personal data of each individual is recorded in the census once a decade and is then released to public view 101 years later. So on 2 January 2002, the census taken on Sunday 31 March, 1901, just weeks after Queen Victoria's death, was duly made available to family and local historians. What made the release of the 1901 census data especially exciting was that the National Archives also made all the 1901 information accessible electronically through internet search. Post-millennium and almost overnight, family history changed. What critics had previously dismissed as the quaintly obsessive hobby of genealogy 'anoraks' was suddenly transformed into a hugely popular quest for roots and identities. This was complemented by the development of electronically searchable databases of birth, marriage and death certificates; and further digitalisation of late-Victorian censuses followed.

Reflecting this new popularity, BBC2 ran a major television series in 2004, *Who Do You Think You Are?* with celebrity genealogy detectives tracing their ancestral roots. Alongside, the archive film of *The Lost World of Mitchell and Kenyon* revealed the forgotten vibrancy of Edwardian street life, thronged with young workers pouring in their thousands out of northern mills.[28] People's history indeed.

This post-2002 electronic research revolution arguably compensates for the impossibility of direct oral testimony of Edwardian campaigners. The census and birth, marriage and death web-sites can be searched, both to track the utterly 'disappeared' like Lavena Saltonstall, as well as to trace the ancestry of, say, the families of Dora Thewlis and Edith Key who moved around so frequently. Molly Morris's raggle-taggle ancestry and Violet Key-Jones's dynastic immutability suddenly jump from the census pages. They can also confirm hunches: I had always suspected Annie Kenney of Springhead came from the edge of the West Riding; and both her birth certificate and the household censuses readily confirm this, bursting the marketing stereotype of 'Lancashire mill girl'. No suffrage campaigner was too humble to fall through the official recording net of the late-Victorian and Edwardian state: their biographical outlines could now be accessed at the click of an electronic mouse. If in 1963 E. P. Thompson's *The Making of the English Working Class* memorably rescued 'the poor stockinger, the Luddite cropper, the "obsolete" hand-loom weaver . . . from the enormous condescension of posterity'; and in the 1970s oral history pioneers similarly helped democratise historians' approach to the almost present past (as in recording direct oral testimony of daughters of radical suffragists in Lancashire), then surely the family history electronic revolution of the 2000s has the same potential research impact for rescuing forgotten Edwardians.[29]

By mid-2003 I was growing excited about the new sources that now tumbled forward one after another: the Huddersfield WSPU minutes book; the Gawthorpe papers and the Saltonstall writings; tracking the suffrage diaspora out to Australia and meeting descendants; the Home Office 'spy photograph' discoveries buried for ninety years; the Pinnance testimonial framed in a granddaughter's house. All this added up. As the detective trail revealed this unexpected evidence, and as my research was being completed, in winter 2003–4 I pondered the shape this book should take.

It was always going to be about Yorkshire.[30] With the information already available about Isabella Ford and Florence Lockwood, Mary Gawthorpe and Leonora Cohen, my original focus was the West Riding, especially Leeds and the Colne Valley. Then my research on the Pennine textile communities threw up figures like Lavena Saltonstall and Dora Thewlis. Research on the later period then took me further afield. The more I visited Sheffield and Doncaster, Scarborough and York, the more I realised that Part Four, the story of the maverick militants – Molly Morris, Lilian Lenton, Violet Key-Jones – was as important, and much of it completely unknown.

To understand the rebel girls I needed to place them in their landscapes. Armed with the 1901 census pages plus large-scale Edwardian maps, I set off across Yorkshire. I paced the streets they had inhabited, photographed their houses, and pressed my nose to their windowpanes. My journeys took me around Leeds – to Leonora Cohen's homes and to the town hall steps where she sold the *Suffragette*. I worked my way round Lavena Saltonstall's Hebden Bridge, pausing particularly at her house at the end of Unity Street. I revisited Huddersfield and took more note of the Thewlis mid-terrace home. I walked up the Colne Valley along the canal, peering into Florence Lockwood's Black Rock House, sad at its neglect. In Doncaster I walked from the station to respectably suburban 15 Osborne Road, the hidey-hole of Violet Key-Jones and her conspiratorial network; and I crossed to the other side of town, to try to trace the 'empty' house into which Lilian Lenton and Harry Johnson intruded one night. I travelled out to the coast to photograph Scarborough WSPU's suffrage shop, and then climbed down to the seashore to imagine whether Lilian Lenton had set sail to the Continent from there. And thence back to York, to visit Violet Key-Jones's WSPU offices there.

I sought corroborative evidence in the suffrage journals; in newspapers, whether local (both dailies and weeklies), regional (notably the *Yorkshire Post*) or national (particularly *The Times* and *Daily Mirror*). Such an unmod-ish research procedure as trawling through newspapers led to the dramatic Doncaster courtroom photograph of Lilian Lenton and Harry Johnson, first in the local press and then in the *Daily Mirror*. With Adela emigrating to Australia apparently without any personal papers, the best way to track her WSPU campaigns remained local newspapers. The press also provided an invaluable means of hearing the voice of an embattled lone suffragette – whether in Lavena's letters to the papers, or for the defiant repartee of Dora and Leonora when defending themselves in court.[31]

As research was completed and the book planned, certain central figures clearly emerged – Adela and Mary, Lavena and Dora, Florence, Leonora and Lilian. Enthusing to Lennie Goodings at Virago about these original stories, it became clear that those of the Edwardian rebel girls stood out compellingly – and we picked our title. It was not too tricky deciding which figures to select to drive the narrative, though on occasion it was frustrating that scant personal information was forthcoming – for Isabella Ford or for the Coates clan.[32]

Within the criteria for inclusion and omission described in chapter 16, this narrative history tracks those who campaigned wholly or mainly in Yorkshire. Where their actions took them down to London, we follow their story – such as Leonora's attack at the Tower of London. Those who were born elsewhere but who campaigned in Yorkshire are included: Molly's work in Sheffield, Lilian's appearances in Doncaster and Leeds. Otherwise, they are not.

Adhering to regional boundaries within a tight chronological framework offers historians a wonderful discipline. Digging a deep yet clear cross-section down through the layers within recognised geographical perimeters brings to light a significant new perspective, prompting a new suffrage history – so much of it hidden for a full century.

Rebel girls: biographies

For national suffrage figures, only brief biographical details are given, except when they played a significant role in the region. For suffrage campaigners such as Emmeline and Christabel Pankhurst or Mrs Fawcett, full biographies have been published. For book titles (including auto-biographies), please see Bibliography as well as entries in:

Suff Ann:	A.J. R. (editor), *The Suffrage Annual and Women's Who's Who*, Stanley Paul, 1913.
EC:	Elizabeth, Crawford, *The Women's Suffrage Movement: a reference guide 1866–1928*, UCL, 1999 and Routledge, 2001.
DNB:	*Dictionary of National Biography*, Oxford University Press, Oxford, 2004.
D Lab B:	*Dictionary of Labour Biography*, vols I–XI, 1972 onwards.

Notes:

xx	denotes mother marked birth certificate with a cross (father: x).
1891, 1901	women for whom there is little other information, census data is included.
	Place of imprisonment is Holloway Gaol, London, unless otherwise noted.

Annakin, Ethel (Snowden)

1880	born Harrogate, daughter of well-to-do builder.
c. 1894	pupil teacher (*see* Mary Gawthorpe); goes to teacher training college.
1905	marries Philip Snowden, ILP chairman (and from 1906, MP for Blackburn).
1906–7	invites ILP women members to sign *Manifesto* to WSPU.
1951	death.
EC.	

Archdale, Helen

1876	born Helen Russel, daughter of *Scotsman* editor.
1910	works with Adela Pankhurst in Scarborough and Sheffield.
c. 1912–14	Emmeline Pankhurst corresponds with Helen about Adela.
EC.	

Baines, Jennie

1866	born Birmingham; joins WSPU.
1907 Feb	imprisoned Armley gaol, Leeds, during Hebden Bridge fustian weavers' strike.
1908 Feb	South Leeds by-election; WSPU Self-Denial Week, Leeds.
1908 Oct	arrested Leeds outside Asquith and Gladstone meeting.
1913–4	escapes to Australia.
EC, DNB.	

Bauer, Nellie

1869	born Manchester; educated Cheltenham [Ladies] College.
1894	marries Carl Bauer.
from 1904	Hon. Sec., Bradford branch NUWSS.
by 1913	Secretary, NUWSS West Riding Federation.
Suff Ann.	

Beever, Ellen

1907	member, Huddersfield WSPU branch; aunt of Annie Sykes.
1907 Feb	housekeeper aged 35; at Women's Parliament, sentenced to 7 days.

Berkley, Lizzie

1883 Jun	born Hebden Bridge, father a schoolmaster.
1901	aged 17, fustian clothing machinist, Hebden Bridge.
1907	joint secretary, Hebden Bridge WSPU branch.
1907 Mar	at Caxton Hall, Westminster, aged 23, sentenced to 14 days.

Boyd-Dodgson, May

	lives in Leeds.
1911 Nov	WSPU deputation to Westminster; sentenced to 5 days.
1912 Mar	WSPU window-smashing, arrested.

Brooke, Ellen

1901	probably living in Wooldale, near Huddersfield.
1907	member, Huddersfield WSPU.
1907 Mar	aged 22, Women's Parliament, London; arrested and remanded.
1908 Feb	Women's Parliament, probably arrested; South Leeds by-election, speaks Hunslet Moor rally.

Coates-Hanson, Marion

1870	born York, where father was house porter at the asylum.
	family moves from York to Middlesbrough; becomes pupil teacher.
1898	marries Gottlieb Hansen; uses anglicised name, Coates-Hanson.
1906 Nov	Huddersfield by-election, campaigns for WSPU.
1907	leaves WSPU to join new WFL.
	active member Middlesbrough WFL branch.

| 1912 | resigns from WFL national executive and from Middlesbrough WFL branch. |

Cobbe, Lilian

	born Wakefield, father a maltster.
1901	Hebden Bridge: aged 32; joins clothing union, AUCO.
1907 Feb	chairs Mrs Pankhurst meeting, Hebden Bridge fustian weavers' strike.
1907 Mar	Westminster: tailoress, sentenced to 14 days, age given in court as 28.

Cobbe, Louie

1871 Mar	born Idle, Bradford; father a maltster.
1901	Hebden Bridge: fustian clothing finisher, aged 30.
1907 Feb	joint secretary, Hebden Bridge WSPU branch.

Cohen, Leonora

1873 Jun	born Hunslet, Leeds, daughter of Jane and Canova Throp, sculptor.
	death of father; Jane works as seamstress, Leonora assists.
1887	leaves school; millinery apprentice, Leeds.
1900 Mar	at Bridlington, marries Henry Cohen, watchmaker and jeweller; son of President of Jewish Synagogue, Leeds.
	daughter Rosetta dies; son Reginald born.
c. 1909–10	Leeds WSPU branch, selling papers and fund-raising.
1911 Nov	WSPU deputation, on Caxton Hall platform; throws stone at Local Government Board window; sentenced to 7 days.
1912 Mar	WSPU window-smashing, but evades arrest.
from 1912	selling *Suffragette* outside Leeds Town Hall, helped by Reg.
1913 Jan	on deputation of working women to Lloyd George at Treasury.
1913 Feb	smashes glass display case at Tower of London; jury acquits her.
1913 May	WSPU procession, Woodhouse Moor, Leeds; detectives note her speeches, arrested under 1861 Malicious Damages Act; agrees to be bound over.
1913 Nov	smashes Labour Exchange windows on Asquith's visit to Leeds; Armley gaol, hunger and thirst strike.
1913 Dec	released under Cat and Mouse Act; Henry protests to Home Secretary.
	Cohens remove to Harrogate; opens a 'Reform Food' boarding house.
1914 May	shelters Lilian Lenton; assists her escape, lending Reg's clothes.
1914–18	munitions work.
1920s	becomes magistrate; receives OBE.
1970s	*Shoulder to Shoulder* publicity; interviews and reminiscences.
1978 Sep	death, aged 105, north Wales.
Suff Ann, EC.	

Connelly, Dinah

1879 Apr	born, Keighley, xx.
1907	signs ILP *Manifesto* to WSPU.
1907 Mar	Women's Parliament, age given as 24, sentenced to 14 days.

Fielden, Mary

1908 Aug	NUWSS organiser; caravan tour, Yorkshire.
1909	NUWSS organiser for Yorkshire; caravan tour with Isabella Ford. leaves tour for Cleveland by-election campaign.

Ford, Bessie

1848	born (*see* Isabella Ford, *below*), family lives at Adel Grange, Leeds. treasurer, Leeds Suffrage Society.
1919	death.

Ford, Emily

1850	born (*see* Isabella Ford, *below*), lives at Adel Grange, Leeds.
1908	'Factory Acts' design published by Artists' Suffrage League.
1911	for Coronation Procession, designs banners (local town councils).
1930	death.
EC.	

Ford, Isabella

1855 May	born, Leeds, youngest child of Hannah and Robert Lawson Ford, solicitor and landowner.
	Aged 10, family moved out of Leeds to Adel Grange.
1889	portrait, *Yorkshire Factory Times*, in recognition of work for women workers.
1890	helps form Leeds Women's Suffrage Society.
1893	joins ILP; helps organise Special Appeal, signed by women only.
1890–1901	three novels published, to mixed reviews; her scrapbook closes.
1900s	long-serving member of NUWSS executive, representing it at IWSA congresses.
1909	joins caravan tour of Yorkshire dales.
1913	through NUWSS, campaigns for EFF e.g. Keighley by-election.
1924	death, aged 70.

Suff Ann, EC, *DNB*. *D Lab Biog*.

Foster, Mary

	Roundhay, Leeds, graduate teacher, ILP member.
	Secretary, Leeds Suffrage Society briefly, then resigns.

Gardner, Emilie

	Cambridge history graduate; becomes NUWSS organiser.
1908 Sept	NUWSS caravan tour, speaking at Bridlington.

Gawthorpe, Mary (Nellie)

1881 Jan	born Nellie, Leeds, daughter of Annie and John Gawthorpe, leather worker.
1894	thirteenth birthday, becomes pupil teacher.
1899	passes Queen's Scholarship with distinction.
1902	Government Certificate as Acting Teacher, double first; moves to Beeston Hill.
1904	hears Christabel Pankhurst at Labour Church, Leeds.
1905	writes to Christabel; questions Herbert Gladstone MP.
1906	addresses suffrage meetings with Isabella Ford; writes to *Yorkshire Weekly Post*; tea at Adel Grange; organises Pethick-Lawrence meetings; Cockermouth by-election; becomes WSPU organiser.
1906 Oct	demonstration for opening of Parliament, sentenced to 2 months.
1906 Nov	Huddersfield by-election campaign.
1907 Jan	addresses Halifax WSPU meeting.
1907 Feb	at Women's Parliament: badly knocked about and could not appear in court.
1907 Nov	Hull West by-election campaign: rehearses children's choir.
1908 Feb	South Leeds by-election; WSPU Self-Denial Week, Leeds.
1910	ill-health, retires as WSPU organiser; by 1911, resigns from WSPU.
1912 Feb	breaks Home Office window as protest against William Ball's forcible feeding; in prison, hunger strike, quickly released.
1912	involved with *Freewoman*, writes for Orage's *New Age* journal.
1916 Jan	sails to America with mother.
1921	marries John Sanders; lives Whitestone Landing, Queens, New York.
1931	correspondence with Sylvia Pankhurst; contributes to Suffragette Fellowship.
1973	death.

Suff Ann, EC, *DNB*.

Gray, Almyra

1862	born, daughter of chairman Vickers Ltd.
1882	marries Edwin Gray, Under Sheriff of Yorkshire.
1898	York Board of Poor Law Guardians.
1900s	helps form York NUWSS branch; President 1908, 1909.
by 1913	President, NUWSS North and East Riding Federation.

Suff Ann.

Higgins, Annie

1866	born Derbyshire; marries 1895, 2 daughters.
1906	becomes interested in suffrage on Mary Gawthorpe's visit to Sheffield. helps form WSPU branch, Sheffield; becomes its treasurer.
1907 Mar	Caxton Hall, sentenced to 14 days. leaves WSPU and joins WFL.

Suff Ann.

Illingworth, Margaret

1842	born Cullingworth, Bradford, daughter of Sir Issac Holden.
1866	marries Alfred Illingworth, industrialist, leading Bradford Liberal.
by 1913	President, Bradford NUWSS branch; vice-president, NUWSS; vice-president, London Society; houses in Bradford and London.

Suff Ann.

Kenney, Annie

1879 Sep	born, Springhead, Saddleworth, West Riding; xx.
1905 spring	drawn into WSPU by Christabel Pankhurst.
1905 Oct	with Christabel at Free Trade Hall meeting, Manchester and imprisoned.
1906	addresses Halifax meetings during tram workers' strike.
1907	appointed WSPU organiser, based in Bristol.

Suff Ann, EC, *DNB*.

Key, Edith

1872 Jan	born Eccleshill, Bradford; mother Grace Proctor, father Joseph Fawcett, mill owner.
1872 Mar	'Agreement as to Child', Grace Proctor & Joseph Fawcett.
1881	Eccleshill, Bradford; Edith, 8 years, scholar, living with 3 aunts; Grace, 24 years, general domestic servant, Britannia Inn, Bradford.
1885	Huddersfield School Board, Edith's thirteenth birthday, leaves school. Almondbury, Huddersfield, knotter.
1891 Mar	marries Frederick Key, blind musician.
	Birth of two sons, Lancelot and Archie.
	Family music shop on 43 West Parade, Huddersfield.
1907	secretary, Huddersfield WSPU branch.
1908	New Year, writes annual report, Huddersfield WSPU branch.
1913–14	hides suffragette 'mice' in her West Parade attics.
1937	death, Huddersfield, aged 65.

Key-Jones, Violet

c. 1883	born Ireland; father, army Surgeon Major; mother from Water Fulford Hall, York.
1909	imprisoned and goes on hunger strike at least twice.
by 1911	WSPU organiser, York office.
by 1913	by early summer, moves to Doncaster, renting suburban house, 15 Osborne Road, accommodating local suffragettes; meetings subject to rowdyism; *see also* Lilian Lenton.
1914	WSPU Doncaster office, runs self-denial week; York, organises *café chantant*; also has a WSPU base Darlington.

Lenton, Lilian

1891 Jan	born Leicester, daughter of carpenter-joiner; eldest of at least 5 children.
	trains as a dancer.

1912 Jan	twenty-first birthday; volunteers to break a window.
1912 Mar	as 'Miss Ida Inkley', in WSPU window-smashing raid; sentenced to 2 months.
1913 Feb	volunteers to burn empty buildings; arrested for burning Kew Gardens pavilion; forcible feeding, accidentally into lung, collapses, hurriedly released; case becomes *cause célèbre*.
1913 Jun	as 'May Dennis', takes part with Harry Johnson in attempt to fire 'empty' building, Balby. Doncaster court appearance; transported to Armley, hunger-strikes, probably covertly photographed; released under Cat and Mouse Act; escapes in disguise from Rutters' house, Leeds via Harrogate to Scarborough.
1914 May	tracked down to Liverpool, transported to Leeds, hunger and thirst strike; Leeds Assizes, addresses jury, sentenced to 12 months. Released under Cat and Mouse Act; escapes disguised from Cohens' house in Harrogate, via coal chute.
1914–18	works in Serbia, Scottish Women's Hospitals Unit.
1920s	speaker for Save the Children Fund and for WFL. Remains active in Suffragette Fellowship.
1972	death.
EC.	

Lockwood, Florence

1861	born Plymouth, daughter of navy doctor; Plymouth High School.
1887	enrols at Slade, University College, London. rents own attic studio in Bloomsbury.
1901	visits sister in Huddersfield, meets Josiah Lockwood, Colne Valley manufacturer.
1902	marries Josiah, St Giles', London; after honeymoon, to Black Rock, Linthwaite.
1907 Jun	Colne Valley by-election: encounters Emmeline and Adela Pankhurst. joins local Women's Liberal Association and Huddersfield NUWSS branch.
c. 1910	designs Huddersfield NUWSS branch banner (dating unclear). President, Colne Valley Women Liberals; Poor Law Guardian, Linthwaite.
1912	writes *The Enfranchisement of Women* pamphlet.
1913	attends IWSA congress, Budapest.
1914 Jun	local 'Friends' recruitment campaigning; joins NUWSS pilgrimage in Wharfedale.
1914 Aug	Active Service League campaigning.
1924	widowed; leaves Linthwaite for London. gives paintings to Huddersfield.
1937	death, London.

Lowenthal, Bertha
> Daughter of successful German-born Huddersfield wool merchant; lives at the Grange, Huddersfield.
> Member of NUWSS branch; later member of Huddersfield WSPU branch.

McKay, Jessie
1908 Feb   arrested Old Palace Yard, Westminster; aged 30, model, Leeds.

Mahony, Amy and Lottie
1901   Lottie aged 14 and Amy aged 8, daughters of engine-stoker, Middlesbrough.
               active members of WFL branch, Middlesbrough.
1912   in WFL branch, Lottie challenges militancy, Amy supports it.

Martindale, Louisa
1872   born; educated by English and German governesses.
1890s   studies at London School of Medicine for Women.
c. 1900   joins Mary Murdoch (*see below*) as partner in her Hull practice.
1904   co-founding Hull NUWSS branch.
1906   leaves Hull for Brighton.
Suff Ann, DNB.

Meyer, Georgiana
1870   born West Huntingdon Hall, York.
by 1913   Organising Secretary, North and East Riding Federation, NUWSS.

Morris, Molly
1890 Jun   born Ethel, Leyland near Chorley, Lancashire.
               family moves to Salford, father deserts.
               Ethel works in bakery-confectioner's shop.
c. 1906   aged c.16, taken by mother to WSPU meeting, Manchester; arrested for chalking pavements, soon released.
c. 1908–10   works with Mary Gawthorpe (*see above*) in Manchester; changes name to 'Molly'.
1912–13   reading *Suffragette*; becomes WSPU organiser, Sheffield; works with Elsa Schuster (*see below*); runs WSPU shop, firing pillar-boxes.
               resigns from WSPU post; works for a medical supply agency.
1914–18   qualifies and works as nurse.
1921   marries Jack Murphy; sets off for Moscow; one son; joins Communist Party.

Murdoch, Mary
1864   born Elgin, Scotland, daughter of a Liberal solicitor.
1888   studies at London School of Medicine for Women.
               appointed house surgeon, children's hospital, Hull. Later becomes GP.

1900	meets Dr Louisa Martindale – who joins Mary's Hull practice.
1905	founding-president, Hull NUWSS branch.
1907 Nov	Hull West by-election campaign, drives carriage carrying colours.
1909	sympathetic to suffragette militancy and resigns from NUWSS.
1916	death, aged 51.

EC, *D Lab B, DNB*.

Noble, Alice

1890 Mar	born Beeston, Leeds, daughter of brick-maker, originally coal miner, x.
1907 Feb	at Women's Parliament aged 16, domestic servant, Leeds; imprisoned.

Older, Ann

1901 Apr	aged 23, Ann Alice Sykes, Slaithwaite, marries Charles Older, stoker, Golcar, near Huddersfield.
1908 Feb	Women's Parliament, London, aged 30, Honley; sentenced to 6 weeks.

Pankhurst, Adela

1885 Jun	born Manchester, third daughter of Emmeline and Richard Pankhurst, barrister.
	family moves to Russell Square, London.
1893	family moves back north; attends Manchester Girls' High School.
1898	death of father; family moves to 62 Nelson Street, Manchester; attends Board School, Ducie Avenue.
1903	becomes pupil teacher, Urmston, near Salford.
1903 Oct:	WSPU founded in her home.
1905	speaking for WSPU.
1906 Apr	*Labour Leader* short story published.
1906 Jun	arrested at Liberal meeting, Belle Vue, sentenced to 7 days; Boggart Hole Clough meeting.
1906 Oct	demonstration at opening of Parliament, sentenced to 2 months.
1907	Hebden Bridge fustian weavers' strike; Colne Valley by-election campaign.
1907 Nov	harasses Haldane in Sheffield; Hull West by-election campaign.
1908 Feb	South Leeds by-election; speaks Hunslet Moor rally.
1908 Jul	Woodhouse Moor, Leeds, 1¼-hour speech; becomes WSPU organiser for Yorkshire; campaigns Bradford and Leeds.
1908 Oct	disguised as kitchen-maid, tries to enter McKenna meeting, Sheffield.
1909	Sheffield Attercliffe by-election campaign.
	Scotland, and friendship with Helen Fraser; health deteriorates.
1910 Jan	General Election campaign, Scarborough; works with Helen Archdale.
	lives Sheffield; helps form WSPU branches in neighbouring towns.
1911	loses voice, gives up; to Scottish health resort with Helen Archdale, then London.
by 1912	involvement with WSPU ends; attends Studley horticultural college.

1914 Feb   sails to Australia, fare paid by mother.
1917   marries widower Tom Walsh, union organiser
                 3 step-children and 5 children.
c. 1927   writes 'The story of my life' (no date).
Oct 1928–1929 writes 'Looking Backwards', *Stead's Review*.
1933   writes 'My Mother'.
1934   writes 'The Philosophy of the Suffragette Movement'.
1961   death, as widow, Australia.
EC, *DNB*.

Pechey-Phipson, Edith
1845   born, Essex, daughter of a Baptist minister.
1869   aged 24, studies medicine at Edinburgh University.
                 practises medicine in Leeds; then travels to India.
1905   returns to England from India with her husband.
1906   represents Leeds Society at IWSA Congress, Copenhagen.
1907   takes part in NUWSS 'Mud March', London.
1908   death; suffrage banner commemorates her achievement.
DNB.

Phillips, Mary
1880   born Hampshire, daughter of a Glasgow doctor.
1907   becomes WSPU organiser, including 1909 Bradford and Leeds.
c. 1912   vigorous correspondence with editor of *Yorkshire Post*, defending
                 WSPU window-smashing.
1956   death, Sussex.
Suff Ann, EC., *DNB*.

Pinnance, Elizabeth
c. 1879–80   born Paddock, near Huddersfield.
c. 1889–90   half-timer, rug weaver.
1899   marries Bob Pinnance, cloth-presser and trade unionist.
1901   Elizabeth (21), rug-weaver; Robert (23) cloth-presser; William (1).
1907   member, WSPU Huddersfield branch.
1907 Mar   to Westminster, aged 27, sentenced to 14 days.
1908 Feb   South Leeds by-election, speaks Hunslet Moor rally.
                 presented with illuminated testimonial, signed by Emmeline Pankhurst.
1959 Aug   death, Marsh, Huddersfield.

Quinn, Bertha
1908 Oct   arrested Leeds, outside WSPU's Liberal leaders' meeting.
                 organiser for clothing workers' union, Leeds.

Renton, Helena
by 1913   organiser, NUWSS West Riding Federation; EFF work including
                 lobbying miners' lodges.

1913 Jul   NUWSS pilgrimage through Yorkshire (e.g. Rotherham).

Robertson, Margaret
                  literature graduate; resigns teaching post to become a NUWSS
                  regional organiser.
1908 Aug   NUWSS caravan tour, speaks Whitby harbour; Sept at Bridlington.

Rowlette, Miss
1904–5   NUWSS speaker, Yorkshire.

Rutter, Frank
1876   born London.
1912   Director, Leeds Art Gallery.
                  See Lilian Lenton for his role in her escape.
DNB.

Saltonstall, Lavena
1881 Sep   born Hebden Bridge, daughter of Mary and John Saltonstall, fustian
                  dyer.
                  family removes frequently around Hebden Bridge area.
1891 Sep   tenth birthday, probably begins as a half-timer tailoress in clothing
                  factory.
1890s   leaves school for full-time work; death of a brother and a sister.
1901   aged 19, 28 Unity St, Hebden Bridge, machinist fustian clothing
                  tailoress.
early 1900s;   five shadowy years, with little known.
1906   Women's Labour League meetings, Halifax tram workers' strike.
                  Moves to Haugh Shaw Rd, Halifax.
1907 Feb–Mar   *Hebden Bridge Times* controversy with Pankson Baines.
1907 Mar   Westminster, Halifax weaver, imprisonment 14 days.
1908 Feb   WSPU Women's Parliament; no occupation given; sentenced to 6 weeks.
1908 Apr   North West Manchester by-election; seems to distance herself from
                  WSPU.
1908 May   'Suffragettes on Tramp', with Laura Wilson, *Halifax Labour News*.
1911   'The Letters of a Tailoress', *The Highway* (WEA).
1914   dispute with Ethel Carnie over workers' educational entitlement.
1917 Jun   marries George Baker, private soldier, Unitarian Chapel, Halifax;
                  moves to Bradford.
1957 Sept   death, widow, St Luke's hospital, Bradford.

Scawthorne, Mary
1907 Mar   Westminster, aged 40, from Huddersfield, sentenced to 14 days.

Schofield-Coates, Alice
1881 May   born Prestwich; becomes trained teacher, teaching in Manchester.
                  hears Emmeline Pankhurst speak in Manchester, joins WSPU.

by 1906	organiser for WSPU; speaking for Middlesbrough ILP on suffrage.
1907	leaves WSPU to join WFL.
1908	becomes WFL organiser in north-east, Teesside.
1909	arrested in Downing Street, imprisoned in Holloway for one month.
1910 Feb	marries Charles Coates, brother of Marion Coates (*see above*).
1912	remains leading member of WFL branch, despite Marion's resignation.
1920s	with husband, opens vegetarian restaurant below WFL Middlesbrough office; becomes Labour councillor and magistrate.
1975	death, Middlesbrough.

Suff Ann, D Lab B.

Schuster, Elsa M.

	born, Leipzig, Germany (possibly daughter of wealthy German-born merchant banker, west London).
1910 Nov	takes part in 'Black Friday'; arrested for stone-throwing, sentenced to 14 days.
c. 1912–13	secretary-cum-treasurer, Sheffield WSPU branch.
	works with Molly Morris (*see above*) in Sheffield WSPU campaigns.

Suff Ann.

Stevenson, Blanche

| | born York. |
| 1907 Feb | at Women's Parliament, housekeeper, Garforth near Leeds, aged 40; sentenced to 14 days. |

Stevenson, Elsie May

| 1888 Aug | born south-east Leeds, father elementary school teacher. |
| 1907 Feb | aged 18, typist, Leeds; at Women's Parliament, gives age as 21, sentenced to 14 days. |

Studdard, Helen

1856	born Cambridgeshire.
1879	marries Joseph Studdard
	forms first Huddersfield women's suffrage society; Hon. Secretary, Huddersfield Women's Liberal Association.
	Secretary, Huddersfield NUWSS branch.
	attends IWSA congresses in Amsterdam, London and Stockholm.

Suff Ann.

Sunley, Agnes

c. 1849	born, Leeds; marries packer in asbestos factory
1882	employed as suffrage canvasser of Leeds women householders.
1890	present at meeting of Leeds Suffrage Society.
1905 Nov	postcard to Mary Gawthorpe.

1924   death, due to 'exhaustion'.
EC.

Sykes, Annie
1880 Oct   probably born Lockwood, Huddersfield, father a sizer and beamer.
1907   Huddersfield WSPU member; niece of Ellen Beever.
1907 Feb   at opening of Parliament: aged about 27, housekeeper, gives age as 37;
                sentenced to 7 days.

Taylor, Mary
1885 Mar   aged 21, marries Arthur Taylor, blacksmith, Halifax.
                Arthur, engineers' union, experiences victimisation.
                elected Poor Law Guardian; active in Halifax ILP branch.
1906–7   supports Halifax tram workers' strike.
1907 Feb   at 'Women's Parliament' demonstration; aged 40, sentenced 14 days.

Thewlis, Dora
1890 May   born Honley, daughter of Eliza (*see below*) and James Thewlis,
                woollen weaver.
by 1907   working as weaver, joins Huddersfield WSPU branch.
1907 Mar   arrested; on *Daily Mirror* front page; age given as 17 (aged 16),
                remanded in custody 6 days; accompanied home by wardress;
                Shamrock postcard produced.
before 1914   with elder sisters and other Huddersfield girls, emigrates to
                Australia; works in blanket-weaving in Melbourne area.
1918   marries Jack Dow, Australian; 2 children.
1976   death.

Thewlis, Eliza
1860 Oct   born Woodbridge, Suffolk, mother xx; father coal porter.
1880   aged 19, millhand, Meltham Mills, marries James Thewlis, 20 yrs,
                weaver.
1890s   at least 7 daughters, 1 son; family removes to Slaithwaite, Colne Valley.
1900s   family removes to Hawthorne Terrace, Huddersfield.
                founder-member of Huddersfield WSPU branch committee.
1907   WSPU branch invites her to resign.

Titterington, Amy
1885 Jun   born Armley, Leeds; mother Mary (*see below*), father shopkeeper and
                bootmaker.
1908 Feb   at WSPU Women's Parliament: shop assistant aged 23, sentenced to 6
                weeks.

Titterington, Mary
1907 Feb   at 'Women's Parliament' demonstration, 50-year-old draper, Leeds,
                sentenced to 14 days.

1908 Feb   at WSPU Women's Parliament: arrested and sentenced.
1913 Jan   on deputation of working women to Lloyd George, Treasury (*see* Leonora Cohen).

Varley, Julia
1871 Mar   born Bradford, daughter of worsted mill engine feeder.
                  aged 12, becomes half-timer, working in textile mill, Bradford; becomes active in weavers' union.
1904–07   Poor Law Guardian, Bradford.
1907 Feb   at Women's Parliament, aged 34, Bradford, no occupation given, sentenced to 14 days.
1909   leaves Bradford for Birmingham as trade union organiser.
D Lab B, DNB.

Whitworth, Edith
1870   born 1871, Aston Netherthorpe, Yorkshire.
1893   marries postal telegraphist; 2 children.
1906   foundation member of WSPU branch, Sheffield; branch secretary.
1907 Feb   at Women's Parliament, aged 34, sentenced to 14 days.
1908   leaves WSPU, for Sheffield branch of WFL.
Suff Ann.

Wilson, Agnes
                  leaves NUWSS over condemning militancy, joins WSPU.
1912 Mar   Whitehall, breaks Agricultural Offices window; sentenced to 2 months hard labour; hunger strike.
by 1913   literature secretary, Harrogate WSPU branch.
Suff Ann.

Wilson, Helen
1864   born Mansfield; father, Liberal MP for Holmfirth.
                  trains at London School of Medicine for Women.
                  President, Sheffield NUWSS branch.
Suff Ann, DNB.

Wilson, Laura
1877 Aug   born Halifax; father dyer's labourer, mother xx.
1899   worsted coating weaver; marries George Wilson, iron turner; Halifax.
1906   chairs Christabel Pankhurst meeting; to Huddersfield by-election.
1907   'violent and inflammatory' speech charge during Hebden Bridge fustian weavers' strike; sentenced to 14 days, Armley.
1907 Mar   to Westminster, aged 29, arrested and sentenced to 14 days.
1907 Oct   attends meeting of WSPU rebels, who form WFL.
1908 May   'Suffragettes on Tramp' with Lavena Saltonstall.

APPENDIX 3

Bibliography and sources

Place of publication is London unless noted otherwise.

PRIMARY SOURCES

Collections of Personal Papers

Cohen: Leonora Cohen papers, Abbey House Museum, Kirkstall, Leeds.
Fawcett: Millicent Garrett Fawcett papers, Archives Department, Central Reference Library, Manchester.
Gawthorpe: Mary E. Gawthorpe papers, Tamiment Library, New York University.
Key: Edith Key papers, Kirklees District Archives, WYAS, Huddersfield Library.
Pankhurst: Adela Pankhurst Walsh papers, National Library of Australia, Canberra.
Sennett: Maud Arncliffe Sennett papers, British Library, London.

Records of Organisations

Home Office papers, National Archives, Kew, London.
ILP Manchester Central branch, minutes, Manchester.
NUWSS postcard collection, Women's Library, London.
Leeds Women's Suffrage Society, Fourth *Annual Report*, 1896, Leeds Library.
Westminster Police Court, Register of the Court, London Metropolitan Archives.
Suffragette Fellowship collection, Museum of London, London.
Middlesbrough Women's Freedom League branch, minutes-books, Women's Library.
Women's Freedom League, *Report* to the Second Annual Conference of WSPU now the WFL, 12 Oct 1907, Women's Library.
WSPU, *Annual Reports*, Women's Library.
WSPU, Huddersfield WSPU branch, minutes-book, Edith Key mss, Kirklees, West Yorkshire Archive Service (WYAS).
Women's Suffrage Collection, Archives Department, Central Reference Library, Manchester.

Journals, Newspapers

Colne Valley Guardian
Common Cause
Daily Mail
Daily Mirror

Doncaster Chronicle
Doncaster Gazette
Halifax Evening Courier
Halifax Guardian
Halifax Labour News
Hebden Bridge Times
Highway
Huddersfield Examiner
Huddersfield Weekly Examiner
Huddersfield Weekly Express
Hull Daily Mail
Labour Leader
Labour Record and Review
Leeds Mercury
Manchester Guardian
Radio Times
Scarborough Mercury
Sheffield Daily Telegraph
Sheffield Independent
Suffragette
The Times
Todmorden News
Votes for Women
Worker: the organ of the Huddersfield Socialist Party
Yorkshire Evening News
Yorkshire Evening Post
Yorkshire Observer
Yorkshire Post
Yorkshire Weekly Post

Autobiographies

Gawthorpe, Mary, *Up Hill to Holloway*, Traversity Press, Penobscot, Maine, 1962.
Kenney, Annie, *Memories of a Militant*, Arnold, 1924.
Lockwood, Florence, *Private Diary*, 13 parts (variously titled), privately printed.
Lockwood, Florence, *An Ordinary Life 1861–1924*, Echo Press, Loughborough, 1932.
Martindale, Louisa, *A Woman Surgeon*, Gollancz, 1951.
Mitchell, Hannah, *The Hard Way Up*, Faber, 1968 and Virago, 1977.
Montefiore, Dora, *From a Victorian to a Modern*, Edward Archer, 1927.
Moyes, Helen, *A Woman in a Man's World*, Alpha Books, Australia, 1971.
Murphy, Molly, *Molly Murphy: Suffragette and Socialist*, Institute of Social Research, Salford, 1998.
Pankhurst, Emmeline, *My Own Story*, Hearst's International Library, USA, 1914 and Virago, 1979.
Turner, Ben, *About Myself 1863–1930*, Humphrey Toulmin, 1930.

Novels and other writings

Grahame, Kenneth, *The Wind in the Willows*, 1908.

Hodgson-Burnett, Frances, *The Secret Garden*, 1911.

Marcus, Jane (ed.), *The Young Rebecca: writings of Rebecca West 1911–1917*, Virago, 1983.

Nietzsche, Friedrich, *Thus Spoke Zarathustra*, 1883–5 and Penguin, 1961 and 2003.

Wells, H. G., *Ann Veronica*, 1909.

West, Rebecca, *The Sentinel*, written *c.* 1909–11, ed., Laing, Kathryn, European Humanities Research Centre, Oxford, 2002.

West, Rebecca, 'Adela', in Antonia Till (ed.), *Rebecca West: The Only Poet and Short Stories*, Virago, 1992.

Histories Written by Participants

A.J. R. (ed.), *The Suffrage Annual and Women's Who's Who*, Stanley Paul, 1913.

Pankhurst, Sylvia, *The Suffragette: the history of the women's militant suffrage movement 1905–1910*, Gay and Hancock, 1911 and Source Book Press, New York, [1970]

Pankhurst, Sylvia, *The Suffragette Movement: an intimate account of persons and ideals*, Longman, 1931 and Virago, 1977.

Strachey, Ray, *The Cause: a short history of the women's movement in Great Britain*, 1928 and Virago, 1978.

SECONDARY SOURCES

Biographies

Clark, David, *Labour's Lost Leader: Victor Grayson*, Quartet, 1985.

Coleman, Verna, *Adela Pankhurst: the wayward suffragette 1885–1961*, Melbourne University Press, Melbourne, 1996.

Dictionary of National Biography, Oxford University Press, Oxford, 2004.

Groves, Reg, *The Strange Case of Victor Grayson*, 1946 and Pluto, 1975.

Hannam, June, *Isabella Ford*, Blackwell, Oxford, 1989.

McPhee, Carol, and Fitzgerald Ann (eds), *The Non-Violent Militant: selected writings of Teresa Billington-Greig*, Routledge, 1987.

Malleson, Hope, *A Woman Doctor: Mary Murdoch of Hull*, Sidgwick and Jackson, 1919.

Pankhurst, Richard, *Sylvia Pankhurst: artist and crusader*, Paddington Press, 1979.

Pugh, Martin, *The Pankhursts*, Allen Lane, Penguin Press, 2001.

Purvis, June, *Emmeline Pankhurst: a biography*, Routledge, 2002.

Rubinstein, David, *A Different World for Women: the life of Millicent Garrett Fawcett*, Harvester Wheatsheaf, 1991.

Vellacott, Jo, *From Liberal to Labour: the story of Catherine Marshall*, McGill-Queen's University Press, Kingston and Montreal, Canada, 1993.

Suffrage Histories

Abrams, Fran, *Freedom's Cause: lives of the suffragettes*, Profile, 2003.

Cowman, Krista, *'Mrs Brown is a man and a brother!' women in Merseyside's political organisations 1890–1920*, Liverpool University Press, Liverpool, 2004.

Crawford, Elizabeth, *The Women's Suffrage Movement: a reference guide 1866–1928*, UCL, 1999 and Routledge, 2001.

Crawford, Elizabeth, *The Women's Suffrage Movement in Britain and Ireland: a regional survey*, Routledge, 2005.

Holton, Sandra, *Suffrage Days: stories from the Women's Suffrage Movement*, Routledge, 1996.

Hume, Leslie, *The National Union of Women's Suffrage Societies 1897–1914*, Garland, New York, 1982.

Liddington, Jill, and Jill Norris, *One Hand Tied Behind Us: the rise of the women's suffrage movement*, Virago, 1978 & Rivers Oram, 2000.

Liddington, Jill, *Respectable Rebel: the life and times of Selina Cooper 1846–1964*, Virago, 1984.

Liddington, Jill, *The Long Road to Greenham: feminism and anti-militarism in Britain since 1820*, Virago, 1989.

Marlow, Joyce (ed.), *Votes for Women: Virago Book of Suffragettes*, Virago, 2000.

Neville, David, *To Make their Mark: the women's suffrage movement in the North East of England 1900–1914*, University of Northumbria, Newcastle, 1997.

Raeburn, Antonia, *The Militant Suffragettes*, Michael Joseph, 1973 and NEL, 1974.

Rosen, Andrew, *Rise Up, Women! the militant campaign of the Women's Social and Political Union 1903–1914*, Routledge, 1974.

Tickner, Lisa, *The Spectacle of Women: imagery of the suffrage campaign 1907–14*, Chatto and Windus, 1987.

Other Histories

Binney, Marcus, and others, *Satanic Mills: Industrial Architecture in the Pennines*, Save Britain's Heritage, n.d. *c.* 1978.

Burke, Peter (ed.), *New Perspectives on Historical Writing*, Polity Press, Cambridge, 1991 and 2001.

Clark, David, *Colne Valley: radicalism to socialism*, Longman, 1981.

Croft, Linda, *'This is the District, we are the people': a history of the WEA in Yorkshire*, Workers' Educational Association, Leeds, 2003.

Haigh, Hilary (ed.), *Huddersfield: a most handsome town*, Kirklees Cultural Services, Huddersfield, 1992.

Hey, David, *Yorkshire from AD 1000*, Longman, 1986.

Jowitt, J. A., and A. J. McIvor (eds), *Employers and Labour in the English Textile Industries, 1850–1939*, Routledge, 1988.

Laybourne, Keith, and David, James, (eds), *'The Rising Sun of Socialism': the Independent Labour Party in the Textile District of the West Riding of Yorkshire 1890–1914*, West Yorkshire Archive Service, 1991.

Mumby, Zoe (ed.), *Raising our Voices: 100 Years of Women in the WEA*, WEA, Sheffield, [2003].

Pelling, Henry, *Social Geography of British Elections 1885–1910*, Macmillan, 1967.

Rose, Jonathan, *The Intellectual Life of the British Working Classes*, 2001 and Yale University Press, New Haven and London, 2002.

Spencer, Colin, *The History of Hebden Bridge*, Hebden Bridge Literary and Scientific Society, Otley, 1991.

Steele, Tom, *Alfred Orage and the Leeds Arts Club 1893–1923*, Scolar, Aldershot, 1990.
Thompson, Paul, *The Edwardians: the remaking of British society*, Weidenfeld and Nicolson, 1975 and Routledge, 1992.

Journal Articles

Bowley, A. L., 'Wages in the Worsted and Woollen Manufactures of the West Riding of Yorkshire', *Journal of the Royal Statistical Society*, Mar 1902.
Cowman, Krista, '"Crossing the Great Divide"; inter-organizational suffrage relationships on Merseyside, 1895–1914', in Eustance, Ryan and Ugolini (eds), *A Suffrage Reader*, Leicester University Press, 2000.
Cowman, Krista, '"Minutes of the last meeting passed"': the Huddersfield Women's Social and Political Union minutes book January 1907–1909, a new source for suffrage history', *Twentieth Century British History*, 13:3, 2002.
Cowman, Krista, 'A Footnote in History? Mary Gawthorpe, Sylvia Pankhurst, *The Suffragette Movement* and the writing of Suffragette history', *Women's History Review*, 14:3 and 4, 2005.
Crawford, Elizabeth, 'Police, Prisons and Prisoners: the view from the Home Office', *Women's History Review*, 14:3 and 4, 2005.
Davin, Anna, 'Imperialism and Motherhood', *History Workshop Journal*, 5, 1978.
Eddyn, Sarah, 'Alice Schofield Coates: suffragette and Middlesbrough councillor', *Bulletin*, Cleveland and Teesside Local History Society, 1987.
Hannam, June, '"I had not been to London"': women's suffrage – a view from the regions', in June Purvis and Sandra Holton (eds), *Votes for Women*, Routledge, 2000.
Holton, Sandra, 'The Suffragist and the "Average Woman"', *Women's History Review*,: 1992.
Hunt, Karen, 'Rethinking the Early Years of the WSPU', *Bulletin of the Marx Memorial Library*, 139, 2004.
Liddington, Jill, 'Era of commemoration: celebrating the suffrage centenary', *History Workshop Journal*, 59, 2005.
Kean, Hilda, 'Searching for the Past in Present Defeat: construction of historical and political identity in British feminism in the 1920s and 1930s', *Women's History Review*, 3:1, 1994.
Mayhall, Laura, 'Creating the "Suffragette Spirit": British feminism and the historical imagination', *Women's History Review*, 4:3, 1995.
Shannon, Issy (ed.), *Milltown Memories*, 2002–5, Hebden Bridge.

Theses and Dissertations

Copley, John, *The Women's Suffrage Movement in South Yorkshire*, Sheffield City College of Education, 1968.
Greenwood, Tom, 'The Origins and Development of the Clothing Industry in Hebden Bridge', Ruskin College Labour Studies Diploma, 1982.
Halliday, Peter, 'The WSPU and the rise of female militancy in the Halifax area 1906–1910', long essay, Leeds University SCE, 2000.
Pemberton Joss, Vine, 'Suffrage in Leeds, 1908', long essay, Leeds University SCE, 2003.

Oral History

Brian Harrison, Oral evidence on the suffragette and suffragist movement, interviews
recorded *c.* 1974–1981, Women's Library.
Interviews recorded by the author.

Ancestor	*descendant*	*relationship*	*date of interview*	*place of interview*
Florence Lockwood	Mary Lockwood	niece	May 1984	Huddersfield
Dinah Connelly	Laura Mitchell	daughter	1988	Halifax (class discussion)
Elizabeth Pinnance	Joyce Bradley	grand-daughter	Aug 2003	Huddersfield
Elizabeth Pinnance	Margaret Pinnance	grand-daughter	Aug 2003	Huddersfield
Edith Key	Julia Mitchell	great-grand daughter	Oct 2003	Huddersfield
Mary Gawthorpe	Betty Meissner	great-niece	Dec 2003	Boston, US
Mary Gawthorpe	Betsy Meissner	great-gt-niece	Dec 2003	Boston, US
Dora Thewlis	Mabel Carey	daughter	Dec 2003	Melbourne, Australia
Adela Pankhurst	Susan Pankhurst Hogan	grand-daughter	Dec 2003	NSW, Australia
Leonora Cohen	Duncan Honeyborn	Henry's great-nephew	Jun 2005	phone convers-ation (Dorset)

APPENDIX 4

List of illustrations

Illustrations are reproduced by the very kind permission of:

Women's Library: 23, 24, 26, 27, 28, 29, 30, 31, 32, 33, 34 and 40.
Mary E. Gawthorpe Papers, Tamiment Library, New York University: 5, 6, 7, 22, 25 and 47.
Leonora Cohen collection, Abbey House Museum, Leeds: 37, 38, 39, and 41.
Mirrorpix, *Daily Mirror*: 9, 13, 14, 18, 19 and 42.
Museum of London: 4 and 8.
Sheffield Local Studies Library, Sheffield Picture Collection: 35 and 44.
The National Archives image library: 43 and 45.

  1 The Colne Valley, Slaithwaite, 1922, watercolour painted by Florence   9
     Lockwood. Huddersfield Art Gallery, Kirklees.
  2 Isabella Ford, *Yorkshire Factory Times* supplement, 1.11.1889.   11
  3 Adela Pankhurst, about her fifth birthday, Clacton-on Sea, *c.* 1890.   18
     Mary Evans Picture Library, London.
  4 WSPU Membership Card, designed by Sylvia Pankhurst *c.* 1906.   28
  5 Nellie Gawthorpe, aged 18, 1899.   36
  6 Thomas Birtwhistle Garrs.   39
  7 Mary Gawthorpe, Leeds, Feb 1908.   65
  8 Adela Pankhurst, portrait, 1908.   66
  9 Mary Gawthorpe cheered by a huge crowd of boys and girls, Huddersfield   77
     by-election, *Daily Mirror*, 30.11.1906.
 10 Women sewing in machine room, Hebden Bridge.   85
     Alice Longstaff collection, Hebden Bridge.
 11 Hebden Bridge, showing Unity Street.   86
     Photographer: Fay Godwin, *Remains of Elmet: A Pennine Sequence*, 1979.
 12 *Manifesto to the Women's Social and Political Union*, ILP, New Year 1907.   95
 13 *Daily Mirror*, front page, Thursday 21 March 1907.   125
 14 Dora Thewlis, *Daily Mirror*, 28 March 1907.   129
 15 'A Lancashire Lass in Clogs and Shawl being "Escorted" through Palace   134
     Yard', Dora Thewlis. Shamrock postcard.
 16 The approach to Black Rock House, Linthwaite, from a sketch by Florence   141
     Lockwood, 1903. Illustration in *An Ordinary Life*.
 17 Florence and Josiah Lockwood, 1902. Illustration in *An Ordinary Life*.   143
 18 'Polling in the Colne Valley Division Yesterday', *Daily Mirror*, 19 July 1907.   154
 19 'Colne Valley Mill Girls Wait for the Election Result', *Daily Mirror*, Saturday   156
     20 July, front page.

20 Huddersfield NUWSS banner, embroidered by Florence Lockwood, Tolson   160
    Museum, Huddersfield. Courtesy of Kirklees Community History Service.
21 'Dr Murdoch in her writing room', Hull. Illustration in *A Woman Doctor*.   169
    Courtesy of Kingston-upon-Hull City Libraries.
22 Mary Gawthorpe, Hull West by-election campaign, Nov 1907.   173
23 Alice Schofield, Women's Freedom League.   178
24 Women's Freedom League banner, 'Dare to be Free'.   178
25 Self Denial Week 15–22 February 1908, Leeds. Mary Gawthorpe.   197
26 'Factory Acts', 1908, designed by Emily Ford, Artists' Suffrage League.   198
27 'The Bugler Girl', designed by Caroline Watts, Artists' Suffrage League,   200
    advertising the procession, 13 June 1908 and other NUWSS events.
28 Banners carried on the NUWSS procession, 13 June 1908.   202
    A: 'Leeds for Liberty', watercolour, design by Mary Lowndes.
    B: 'Charlotte Brontë, Emily Brontë', banner, unidentified designer.
    C: 'Edith Pechey-Phipson MD', banner designed by Mary Lowndes.
29 NUWSS caravan at Whitby, 21 Aug 1908, suffragists speaking. Postcard   206
    collection, TWL.2002.318.
30 NUWSS caravan at Goathland, n.d. probably 1908. Postcard collection,   207
    TWL.2002.295.
31 NUWSS caravan at Bridlington, Margaret Robertson speaking, Sept 1908.   208
    Postcard coll, TWL.2002.295.
32 Probably Emilie Gardner and Margaret Robertson, probably 1908.   209
    Postcard collection TWL.2002.293.
33 NUWSS caravan rural scene, probably late Aug 1908. Postcard collection, 210
    TWL.2002.303.
34 NUWSS caravan at Pickering, with Isabella Ford, June 1909. Postcard   212
    collection, TWL.2002.309.
35 Adela Pankhurst addressing factory workers at Attercliffe by-election,   222
    Sheffield Daily Independent, 23 April 1909.
36 'Miss Pankhurst at Grassington', Upper Wharfedale Museum, probably   226
    spring 1910. I am grateful to Adrian Bailey and Grassington Museum.
37 Leonora Cohen: 'Leaders of the Suffragist Rioting before the furious   237
    onslaught last night', *Daily Sketch*, 22 Nov 1911.
38 Leonora Cohen: 'After my release from Holloway Prison wearing the   241
    prison badge.' Rosemont Studio, Bond Street, Leeds.
39 Leonora Cohen: WSPU deputation of working women to Lloyd George,   254
    Treasury, *Daily Sketch*, 24 Jan 1913.
40 NUWSS acorn.   262
41 Leonora Cohen: WSPU Procession to Woodhouse Moor, Leeds, 4 May 1913.   271
42 Harry Johnson and Lilian Lenton, alias 'May Dennis': Doncaster court,   279
    Daily Mirror, 11 Jun 1913.
43 Lilian Lenton alias 'May Dennis', photographed covertly in prison,   280
    probably Armley gaol, Leeds, June 1913. Home Office papers, AK1/528.
44 Suffrage pilgrims leaving Sheffield along Pinstone Street, *Sheffield Daily*   284
    Independent, 8 Jul 1913.
45 Lilian Lenton and other suffragettes photographed unawares in prison,   291
    1913. Home Office papers AK1/528.

46 Adela Pankhurst Walsh, *Pioneers*, 1929.   302
    I am grateful to Verna Coleman and Melbourne University Press.
47 Mary Gawthorpe, passport photograph, 1915.   302
48 Dora and Jack Dow, 1920, Australia.   303
    I am very grateful to Mabel Carey, Melbourne.
49 'Shoulder to Shoulder', *Radio Times* Special, front cover, 1974.   311
50 'Freedom Fighters', Leonora Cohen aged 100, *Radio Times*, front cover, 1974. 330

APPENDIX 5

Acknowledgements

The research and writing of *Rebel Girls* has been completed fairly swiftly. However, because it draws upon a longer gestation period, I have built up over the years debts of gratitude to suffrage historians and others, and these I would like to acknowledge.

In particular, thanks to: Sandra Holton, for doing more than any other historian in the last decade to reinvigorate suffrage scholarship. Elizabeth Crawford, for always so generously sharing with me her wisdom and encyclopaedic knowledge. In Leeds, Vine Pemberton Joss, with whom I paced out a suffrage walk across the city, and whose enthusiasm I always value; and Veronica Lovell for sharing her knowledge of Leonora Cohen.

On other local suffrage research, I would like to thank Linda Croft and Peter Halliday for generously helping piece together the Lavena Saltonstall story, and for walking round Hebden Bridge with me, tracing the suffragettes' footsteps.

For the Huddersfield chapters, I am most grateful to Thelma Singleton who was exceedingly generous in sharing her knowledge of local suffragettes; to Cyril Pearce, Colne Valley historian; and to Julia Mitchell, who grew up in the very same house as her great-grandmother Edith Key, and could thus explain to me about its so-convenient attics. Also, for allowing me to interview them about their suffragette ancestors, I am grateful to Margaret Pinnance and Joyce Bradley, granddaughters of Elizabeth Pinnance. In Sheffield, to Marina Lewycka for her hospitality and to Anne Summers in London for hers.

The talented suffrage diaspora seventy years ago took my suffrage trail to America; I am most grateful to Betty Meissner and her daughter Betsy, both in Boston, for their kindly help with following the Mary Gawthorpe story. And in Australia, Susan Pankhurst Hogan was also generous with her time; in Sydney, Guy Harber and Bev Cooper were enormously hospitable; and in Melbourne, Judy Anderson kindly guided me round the city. I would also like to thank the Institute for Historical Research for a Scouloudi Historical Award research grant, which helped toward travel costs of this global suffrage detective trail.

Librarians, curators and archivists have been unfailingly professional and helpful, both during the research period and later in making available their illustrations. I am particularly grateful to Samantha Flavin at Abbey House Museum, Leeds, for generous access to the Leonora Cohen papers; Gail Cameron and her colleagues at the Women's Library, for responding to my many requests and queries; to Beverley Cook at the Museum of London for all her help; in New York, Gail Malmgreen and colleagues gave me invaluable access to the Gawthorpe papers; in Canberra, I am grateful for access to the Pankhurst Walsh papers.

Local history librarians merit far more recognition than they often receive; and I would particularly like to express my gratitude to them – notably in Halifax and Huddersfield, Sheffield and Doncaster, York and Scarborough, Middlesbrough and Manchester – all of whom helped me to piece together this hitherto neglected suffrage picture.

Historians who have kindly read and commented upon large sections of the book include Timothy Ashplant, David Doughan, Tom Steele and June Hannam.

In writing *Rebel Girls* I wanted to reach a wider readership than is often, sadly, reached by many works of orginal scholarship. So I am particularly grateful to two friends – journalist Kerry McQuade and writer Angie Cairns – whose comments after reading earlier drafts helped ensure my writing style was accessible and clear.

I'm grateful to my agent, Jane Conway Gordon, who believed in this book from the beginning and was there with a cheering word when needed. And especially to Lennie Goodings, my editor at Virago who, from the initial book proposal, always offered encouragement and invaluable suggestions for strengthening the book and making its meaning much clearer. Also at Virago, thank you to Elise Dillsworth and Vanessa Neuling for their help in processing the complex manuscript, and to Robyn Karney for scrupulous copy-editing.

And finally thanks to my partner, Julian Harber, whose computer search skills he generously shared, time after time. His enthusiasm infected me, and I began to see how electronic web-searches could open up the suffrage past. And, one more time, he's given house-room to – on this occasion – some Yorkshire rebel girls.

Over the last few years, I have used sections of this book in teaching, in articles and talks, and in conference papers; the discussion after each has always been stimulating and helped me shape my mass of original research and see broader patterns and comparisons. I am greatly indebted to friends, students and other historians for helping me to present a picture of Edwardian suffrage that, I hope, succeeds in capturing the vivid sense of place and heady Edwardian excitement of all the rebel girls.

ABBREVIATIONS

APW	Adela Pankhurst Walsh papers, National Library of Australia.
DNB	*Dictionary of National Biography*, Oxford University Press, Oxford, 2004.
EC, *Reference*	Elizabeth Crawford *The Women's Suffrage Movement: a reference guide 1866–1928*, UCL, 1999 and Routledge, 2001.
EP	Emmeline Pankhurst.
ESP, 1931	Sylvia Pankhurst, *The Suffragette Movement: an intimate account of persons and ideals*, Longman, 1931 and Virago, 1977.
HB Times	*Hebden Bridge Times.*
HFM	Helen Fraser Moyes correspondence, Museum of London.
Hx G	*Halifax Guardian.*
Hfld D Ex	*Huddersfield Daily Examiner.*
H'fld br mins	Huddersfield WSPU branch minutes book.
LC coll	Leonora Cohen collection, Abbey House Museum, Leeds.
LL	Lilian Lenton
MG, *Up Hill*	Mary Gawthorpe, *Up Hill to Holloway*, Traversity Press, Maine, 1962.
MG mss	Mary Gawthorpe papers, Tamiment Library, New York University.
M'bro br mins	Middlesbrough WFL branch minutes, Women's Library.
One Hand	Jill Liddington and Jill Norris, *One Hand Tied Behind Us: the rise of the women's suffrage movement*, Virago, 1978 and Rivers Oram, 2000.
Pugh, *Pankhursts*	Martin Pugh, *The Pankhursts*, Allen Lane, Penguin Press, 2001.
Purvis, *Emmeline*	June Purvis, *Emmeline Pankhurst: a biography*, Routledge, 2002.
SF	Suffragette Fellowship collection, Museum of London.
WHR	*Women's History Review.*
WYAS	West Yorkshire Archive Service.
Ykshr Ev News	*Yorkshire Evening News.*

NOTES

Note: where there is a double surname, often symbolising two names joined in equal partnership through marriage, these are always hyphenated here.

Preface

1 These historiographical and comparative themes are discussed in more detail in chapter 16 and in Appendix 1; all titles referred to are given in full in the Bibliography.

2 For instance, Joyce Marlow (ed.), *Votes for Women: Virago Book of Suffragettes*, 2000, back cover.

Introduction: Edwardian Ancestors

1 *Oxford Dictionary of National Biography*, 2004; words by Arthur C. Benson.

2 Reissued by Virago, 1983. Roy Hattersley, *The Edwardians*, 2004, cover: Winifred, Duchess of Portland, by John Singer Sargent.

3 Liddington, *Long Road to Greenham*, chap 3.

4 ESP, 1931, p. 156; for Edith Key mss, see chap 8.

5 Anna Davin, 'Imperialism and Motherhood', 1978, p. 15.

6 Also available on line at www.esds.ac.uk/qualidata/online/data/edwardians including 444 interview summaries.

7 See Liddington, 'Era of commemoration: celebrating the suffrage centenary', 2005.

8 See Appendix, 'Suffrage Detective' for full references.

9 Fords: 1851 and 1861 household census; two daughters died young; thanks to Ursula Ford for her family tree. Pankhursts: 1891 census.

10 Henry Pelling, *Social Geography of British Elections 1885–1910*, 1967 (e.g. pp. 22–3 and 30) lists all constituencies with over twenty-five per cent female domestic servants per 1,000 households; of course, the pattern was more complex than just a north-south distinction (e.g. residential Harrogate: thirty-five per cent).

11 David Hey, *How our ancestors lived*, 2003, pp. 14–15.

12 F. Hodgson-Burnett, *The Secret Garden*, 1911, chap 3 'Across the Moor'.

13 Census, 1901, Occupations of Males and Females, County of York.

14 Jonathan Rose, *Intellectual Life*, 2001, though he bangs an anti-feminist drum.

15 The novels were: *Miss Blake of Monkshalton* (1890), Whitman was told by Yorkshire socialist Edward Carpenter; *On the Threshold* (1895); and *Mr Elliott* (1901). Alfred Orage (see chap 2) reviewed the second as absent of plot and weak of style, though readable.

16 Kathryn Laing (ed.), *The Sentinel*, p. lxiv.

17 In a few rural constituencies like Colne Valley, it may have been as high as seventy-five per cent. Clark, *Colne Valley*, pp. 4–5. Gawthorpe, *Up Hill*, pp. 31–2 and 110.

18 June Hannam, *Isabella Ford*, 1989, pp. 36–41. For Isabella's scrapbook, see chap 2 note 36. Helen Cordelia Ford had married Isabella's lawyer brother; her Commonplace book for 1902 is in WYAS, Leeds.

19 Leeds Women's Suffrage Society, Fourth *Report*, 1896, president: Mrs Edward Walker; I worked at Springfield Mount, now on the edge of Leeds University campus.

20 *One Hand*, pp. 71–7.

21 Hannam, *Isabella*, pp. 36–41.

22 *One Hand*, pp. 142–7.

23 Kenneth Grahame, *The Wind in the Willows*, 1908, chap vii.

24 Rebecca West, 'Adela', in Antonia Till (ed.), *Rebecca West: The Only Poet and Short Stories*, 1992, pp. 44–5. See Chap 10 for West's contact with Adela Pankhurst. H. G. Wells, *Ann Veronica*, 1909, also captures the new woman spirit.

Chapter 1: Adela Pankhurst

1 Dora Montefiore, *From a Victorian to a Modern*, 1927, p. 210.

2 ESP, 1931, pp. 90–1; anarchists included Malatesta, and incendiarists Louise Michel, the *pétroleuse*.

3 An older son, Frank, had died in 1888, aged 4.

4 The photograph is reproduced in Pugh, Purvis, David Mitchell and Richard Pankhurst, usually giving 1890 as the date. Verna Coleman, *Adela Pankhurst: the wayward suffragette 1885–1961*, 1996, p. 12, suggests Adela was 6, but this seems less likely.

5 Adela Pankhurst Walsh papers [APW], 'Looking Backwards', for *Stead's Review*, Oct 1928, pp. 1–5. I have occasionally altered AP's punctuation, to assist clarity.

6 APW, 'Looking Backwards', Nov 1928, p. 1.

7 APW, 'My Mother: an explanation and vindication', 1933, p. 17.

8 APW, 'Looking Backwards', Nov 1928, p. 10.

9 APW, 'Looking Backwards', Feb 1929, p. 2.

10 The building has the carved initials 'M.S.B.', Manchester School Board, still prominent over the entrance.

11 EP to Nodal, 27.11.1902 ff, quoted in Purvis, *Emmeline*, pp. 60–63.

12 APW to Helen Fraser Moyes [HFM], 11.2.1961, Museum of London. APW was extremely vague about her age then.

13 APW, 'Looking Backwards', Feb 1929, pp. 1, 3 and 7. Again, AP is misleading about time: '2 years' was only 6 months – but then time does go four times more slowly when waiting for a reluctant parent to agree.

14 APW, 'My Mother', p. 32. HFM to David Mitchell, 24.3.1965, Museum of London.

15 APW, The Story of my Life', p. 4; APW, 'My Mother', p. 32.

16 *One Hand*, pp. 162–4. Its full name was the Lancashire & Cheshire Women Textile & other Workers' Representation Committee, democratically inclusive, yet decidedly unwieldy.

17 *One Hand*, pp. 168–75. Under 1902 Education Act, School Boards were replaced by local Education Committees.

18 See Karen Hunt, 'Rethinking the Early Years of the WSPU', *2004, pp. 7–23*.

19 For her suffrage years, Adela has three biographers: Coleman, *Adela*, 1996, p. 33; Fran Abrams, *Freedom's Cause: lives of the suffragettes*, 2003, p. 88, echoing this; and Pugh, *Pankhursts*, 2001, p. 107. See also Purvis, *Emmeline*, p. 67; and APW to HFM, 11.2.1961, Museum of London.

20 E.g. *Labour Leader*, 31.10.1903, quoted in *One Hand*, p. 176. Also C McPhee and A. Fitzgerald (eds) *The Non-Violent Militant: selected writings of Teresa Billington-Greig*, 1987, pp. 92–3 and 102.

21 APW, 'My Mother', p. 33.

22 McPhee and Fitzgerald, *Non-Violent Militant*, pp. 94–5.

23 Annie Kenney, *Memories of a Militant*, 1924, pp. 30–2.

24 Montefiore, *Victorian to Modern*, p. 117; letter dated 19.2.1905. Billington-Greig, p. 104, spring 1905.

25 APW, 'The Story of my Life', p. 4. Again APW is blurry about age; it felt like she was 18, but more likely 19–20? (However, some of her biographers have rather taken Adela at her word: Coleman, *Adela*, p. 35, no source, and Abrams, *Freedom's Cause*, p. 88, talk of her spending summer/autumn 1905 'as one of her mother's

"suffrage missionaries"' across the North: this is enticing – but unlikely, as yet.) AP often subtracts a year or two from her age later, probably because she felt younger than she was.

26 APW, 'Looking Backwards', May 1929, p. 6.

27 APW, 'Looking Backwards', July 1929, p. 1. *Labour Leader*, 20.10.1905.

28 Hannah Mitchell, *The Hard Way Up*, 1968, p. 132.

29 APW, 'Looking Backwards', July 1929, pp. 2–3. *Labour Leader*, 5.1.1906.

30 Adela Pankhurst, 'The Turning', *Labour Leader*, 13.4.1906. For Piper at the Gates of Dawn, see Introduction note 23.

31 *Labour Leader*, 2.3.1906, Thornhill Lees and West Salford, and 6.4.1906, Glossop and Hadfield.

32 APW, 'Looking Backwards', July 1929, p. 3 (though AP was unlikely to have reached Bradford yet, i.e. this is probably later).
For dating the membership card, the consensus seems to be late 1906 or possibly early 1907.

Chapter 2: Mary Gawthorpe

1 See Tom Steele, *Alfred Orage and the Leeds Arts Club 1893–1923*, 1990, from which this chapter draws. Sandra Holton, *Suffrage Days*, offers an able account on MG; this chapter is similar, though with – inevitably – slightly different emphases.

2 Mary Gawthorpe, *Up Hill to Holloway*, 1962, pp. 16–18. Occasionally MG's punctuation has been slightly altered, to aid clarity.

3 1906 OS map: in the space of one mile – *leather*: 3 tanneries, 3 leather works, 1 glue mill, 1 leather and glue works, and 1 boot works; *textiles*: 1 dyeing mill, 1 woollen mill, and 1 or 2 other mills.

4 MG, *Up Hill*, pp. 28–30.

5 Photograph in MG mss of St Michael's, Buslingthorpe, 1933. Jackson (1840–1917) was MP for North Leeds till 1902; a 'leather lord', he then became Leeds' first business peer, Baron Allerton. MG, *Up Hill*, pp. 31–2 and 110.

6 MG, *Up Hill*, pp. 26–7, the chronology of which is not always clear.

7 MG, *Up Hill*, pp. 50.

8 MG, *Up Hill*, pp. 88–9 and 95

9 MG, *Up Hill*, pp. 97, 98. MG mss e.g. Leeds School Board Pupil Teachers' Centre, 1898; her mother, understandably so very proud of her talented daughter, kept many of Nellie's laboriously diligent classroom notes, only slightly doodled on. Unlike Adela's mss (where queries remain) this new archival evidence generally confirms *Up Hill*'s accuracy, just correcting its sometimes baffling chronology.

10 MG, *Up Hill*, pp. 101–2. 'His brandied breath I never could stand', p. 120.

11 MG, *Up Hill*, p. 172 suggests this photograph might be 1900s, but this seems unlikely; it was perhaps taken at her scholarship time.

12 MG, *Up Hill*, pp. 105–6.

13 MG, *Up Hill*, p. 148.

14 MG, *Up Hill*, pp. 120–1. Nellie's brother Jim went to the Central Higher Grade School for two years, their mother managing to save the money to enable him to stay on at school.
The Gawthorpe household is captured by the 1901 census: John (50) is a leather currier; Annie (49), no occupation recorded; Mary E. Gawthorpe (20) is listed as

'school mistress'; and James (17) as a surveyor's clerk (*Up Hill* says he worked in a piano shop; the exact age he left school is confused). The heads of neighbouring households were: general labourer, leather dresser, grocer, and cloth tenter (i.e. respectable working-class).

15   MG, *Up Hill*, pp. 64–5. Probably late 1900.

16   MG, *Up Hill*, pp. 145 and 148 (then, after eighteen months' probationary teaching, she would receive the coveted Government Certificate.)

17   MG, *Up Hill*, pp. 146–7. However the picture of 'Catlin's Pierrots, 1904' among the MG mss is later (and does not appear to include her).

18   MG, *Up Hill*, pp. 150 and 151–2.

19   MG, *Up Hill*, pp. 154 and 157.

20   Thanks to Tom Steele & Sandra Holton. MG, *Up Hill*, pp. 155, 160, 165 and 168.

21   MG, *Up Hill*, pp. 170, 172, 206. MG mss includes Nellie Gawthorpe, Cert[ificated] Assistant, 1903–4 *Scheme of a Year's Work*; by 1904–5 her handwriting has grown more experimentally curly, but she was still working within a fairly old-fashioned rigid pedagogic framework; also University *Extension Lectures* prospectus, 1906–7.

22   MG, *Up Hill*, pp. 173–5.

23   MG, *Up Hill*, pp. 173–4.

24   MG, *Up Hill*, p. 176.

25   MG, *Up Hill*, pp. 97, 176–7, 180, 186.

26   MG, *Up Hill*, pp. 188–9, 206; MG mss, Zion Rambling Club, Bramley, Syllabus and Member's Card, 1906–7.

27   Quoted in Steele, *Alfred Orage*, 1990, p. 26.

28   Steele, *Orage*, pp. 32 and 45–50; Friedrich Nietzsche, *Thus Spoke Zarathustra*, 1883–5 and Penguin 1961 and 2003, p. 41.

29   Nietzsche, *Zarathustra*, 2003, pp. 18 and 91–2. Later Orage took study leave from the School Board and, with Bernard Shaw's support, embarked on his first books, *Nietzsche: the Dionysian Spirit of the Age* and *Nietzsche in Outline and Aphorism*, both published 1906.

30   A. R. Orage, *Nietzsche in Outline and Aphorism*, Foulis, Edinburgh, 1911 (third edition), p. 49. Orage presented a more subtle Nietzsche, but within the Club, another member, Albert Waddington, took *Zarathustra* to its chilling extremes.

31   Kelly, *Directory of Leeds*, 1904; also Theosophists and Fabians. Steele, *Orage*, pp. 49, 68.

32   MG, *Up Hill*, pp. 196–7.

33   MG mss, *The Leeds Arts Club, Syllabus*, Feb–May 1908, by which time the Club had moved to 8 Blenheim Terrace, Woodhouse Lane; MG, *Up Hill*, pp. 191, 193.

34   MG, *Up Hill*, pp. 199 and 200–1. Contrast Millie Price, *This World's Festival: an autobiographical effort*, typescript [date?], pp. 62, 111–16, 151.

35   MG, *Up Hill*, pp. 203,

36   Isabella Ford mss, scrapbook, West Yorkshire Archive Service [WYAS], Leeds. This subsequent personal reticence has proved very tricky for historians and biographers.

37   *One Hand*, pp. 148 and 153, quoting the Central Society for Women's Suffrage pamphlet, *Working Women on Women's Suffrage*, 1902; radical suffragist Sarah Reddish (Bolton) also played key role.

38   Elizabeth Wolstenholme Elmy to Harriet McIlquham, quoted in EC, *Reference*, p. 226. Also, NUWSS Central Society for Women's Suffrage, *Annual Report*, Nov

1902, pp. 4–6. Twenty-two per cent of Yorkshire women textile workers signed, undoubtedly encouraged by trade union leaders Allen Gee and Ben Turner.

39 Isabella Ford, 'Women and the Franchise', *Labour Leader*, 1.3.1902; Mrs Ann Ellis, Batley; Mrs K. May, Slaithwaite; Miss Mitchell, Keighley; Miss Wormald, Heckmondwike; Mrs Whitwham, Great Horton, Bradford; Mrs Grew, Mrs Hollings and Mrs Heaton, Bradford; Mrs Guest, Morley; Miss France, Huddersfield; Mrs Watson, Yorkshire Textile Union; Miss Agnes Close, Leeds. Also, *Yorkshire Factory Times*, 28.2.1902; *One Hand*, pp. 151–2.

40 Leslie Hume, *The National Union of Women's Suffrage Societies 1897–1914*, 1982, pp. 22–4. Gray Heald of Leeds (who helped form the Huddersfield branch with Roper and Alan Gee – see next chapter) exemplified this: she was both a leading suffragist *and* President of the Leeds Women's Liberal Association (*Labour Leader*, 19.1.1906). Agnes Close had emigrated to Canada in autumn 1902, a real loss to the Leeds petition momentum.

41 *Labour Leader*, 18.11.1904; Hannam, *Isabella*, pp. 92 and 108–9. At the debate, ESP described Isabella, who now seemingly experienced some ageist unkindness, as a 'plain, middle-aged woman, with red face and turban hat crushed down upon her straight hair'.

42 MG, *Up Hill*, p. 181; oddly there are no references to IOF in the Club, in an otherwise honest autobiography. Steele, *Orage*, p. 95.

43 *Yorkshire Post*, 14 and 20.10.1905.

44 Hannam, *Isabella*, p. 113.

45 MG, *Up Hill*, p. 207.

46 *Labour Leader*, 26.1.1906; the meeting was in Stanningley near Bramley. Price, 'Festival', p 180. Agnes Sunley, Armley, to Mary Gawthorpe, Bramley, 8.11.1905, MG mss. On the reverse of the postcard was a picture of Manchester's Peterloo massacre in 1819, under which was hand-written: 'History repeats itself. Remember Meeting at Free Trade Hall Manchester Oct 13 1905!!!'

47 *Labour Leader*, 15.12.1905.

48 Pugh, *Pankhursts*, pp. 133 and 109.

49 *Leeds Mercury*, 11.1.1906, quoted in MG, *Up Hill*, p. 208.

50 Isabella Ford to Millicent Fawcett, 14.1.1906, Fawcett mss, Manchester Archives Department. (Was IOF ever tempted to join the WSPU, or at least take dual membership? Was she taken financial advantage of?)

51 MG, *Up Hill*, p. 209.

52 MG, *Up Hill*, p. 209. Also leaflet, Leeds Women's Suffrage Society, Annual meeting, 7.3.1906, MG mss. (It was still apparently dominated by Liberals such as Gray Heald.)

53 MG, *Up Hill*, pp. 209–10. (IOF had worked for Snowden in Blackburn, and attended wedding, JH p. 111.)

54 *Yorkshire Weekly Post*, 3 and 10.1.1906. MG's interesting Nietzschean premise seems overlaid with a big dose of J. S. Mill's *Subjugation*, perhaps more Isabella Ford than Orage. MG was paid £2.

Chapter 3: Suffragettes released: Adela and Mary

1 Paul Thompson, *The Edwardians*, 1975 and 1992, p. 223.

2 Ada Nield Chew is a good example of a genuine adultist then; later she converted, working for NUWSS.

3   Margaret Ashton of Manchester was one leading Liberal suffragist, now alienated by WSPU; Gray Heald of Leeds is an example of a leading Liberal suffragist in Yorkshire NUWSS. *Halifax Guardian*, 17.3. and 26.5.1906, as an example of education as the priority, not women's suffrage.

4   Leeds WSS, 'Annual Meeting' leaflet, 7.3.[1906], MG mss; emphasis added.

5   Pugh, *Pankhursts*, p. 137; Purvis, *Emmeline*, p. 82; Hannam, *Isabella*, p. 116–17; *Hx G* 28.4.1906.

6   *One Hand*, pp 206–8; significantly, after the 33,000 Yorkshire textile workers' petition signatures just four years previously, none apparently spoke, suggesting the fragility of regional organisation.

7   MG to ESP, 11.5.1931, MG mss.

8   MG, *Up Hill*, pp. 209 and 214–16. MG also suggests, less persuasively, it might be their writers' pique. MG was also very involved in the new Women's Labour League [WLL].

9   MG, *Up Hill*, p. 221.

10 MG, *Up Hill*, p. 217–18. *Labour Record and Review* started in March 1905, showing only passing interest in women's suffrage to March 1906, after the P . . .-L . . . s returned from Africa. Frederick Pethick-Lawrence, *Fate has been Kind*, p. 70. August 1906 for Yorkshire meetings.

11 MG, *Up Hill*, p. 218–19. Holton, *Suffrage Days*, p. 123 suggests that possibly this was a paid position.

12 APW, 'The Story of my Life', p. 5, APW mss.

13 'Looking Backwards', July 1929, p. 3, APW mss, which offers the date of 17 June, confusingly. This is one of most dramatic incidents in AP's life, yet little is known about it because Sylvia was not there (e.g. ESP, 1931). Contrast ESP, *The Suffragette*, 1911, p. 88 which says a little more.

14 Mitchell, *The Hard Way Up*, pp. 142–6.

15 WSPU *Annual Report* 1906–7, suggests confusingly 21 June as the date of both Belle Vue and London (Asquith's doorbell) arrests; but the *Manchester Guardian*, 25.6.1906 gives 23 June for Belle Vue.

16 Mitchell, *Hard Way*, pp 142–6; also *Manchester Guardian*, 5 .7.1906, which states AP was fined 5s or 7 days. Mrs Morrissey's husband, a Liverpool councillor, was persuaded to pay his fine and go home on account of his job. The court case of Annie Kenney and two others was held the same day.

17 Mitchell, *Hard Way*, pp. 147–9; APW, 'Looking Backwards', July 1929, pp. 6–7, and Aug 1929, p. 6.

18 Mitchell, *Hard Way*, p. 150.

19 *Labour Record*, Aug 1906. APW, 'Looking Backwards', Aug 1929, p. 7; punctuation slightly altered. *Manchester Guardian*, 16.7.1906 gives a similar account.

20 Mitchell, *Hard Way*, p. 151.

21 APW, 'Looking Backwards', Oct 1929. Generally, HM and AP accounts confirm each other closely. Oddly, even Coleman, *Adela*, dismisses this event in a single sentence.

22 For press coverage see *Manchester Guardian*, 16.7.1906; 'The Storm', *Labour Record,* Jul 1906, six women in prison (3 in London, 3 in Manchester).

23 APW, 'Looking Backwards', Oct 1929, pp. 1–5. It is problematic that AP ('Story of My Life' p. 4) conflates June 1906 arrest into Oct 1906 arrest etc. AP's reminis-

cences' chronology is again unclear (e.g. had already had 1 week in prison, and how this fitted into school summer term).

24 MG, *Up Hill*, p. 223.
25 MG, *Up Hill*, p. 225. *Labour Leader*, 24 and 31.8.1906.
26 *One Hand*, p. 212; considerable correspondence in *Labour Leader* on Cockermouth (e.g. Marion Coates-Hanson).
27 MG, *Up Hill*, p. 227.
28 MG, *Up Hill*, pp 227–9. Orage left Leeds for London 1906–7, *DNB*.
29 EC, *Reference*, Organisers.
30 *Manchester Guardian*, 27.8.1906.
31 MG mss, Box 11 Artifacts, child's tiny brown leather gloves, with note 'worn by Sydney when helping Auntie['s] Suffragette Work 1906', Leeds being surely the most likely location for this.
32 MG, *Up Hill*, pp. 231 and 236.
33 I have been unable to find surviving photographs of MG between aged 19 & this one of Feb 1908, other than blurry news pictures (e.g. Huddersfield).
34 Kenney, *Memories*, p. 101.
35 APW, 'The Story of My Life', p. 5; also Coleman, *Adela*, pp. 38–9.
36 AP, 'The Strike at Daubhill, Bolton', *Labour Record*, Sept 1906.
37 The comparison is more with Esther Roper and Eva Gore-Booth, but is given a new twist with WSPU's stress on industrial *conflict*.
38 For instance, Hilda Kean, 'Searching for the Past in Present Defeat: construction of historical and political identity in British feminism in the 1920s and 1930s', *Women's History Review*, 1994, for historiography and narratives of moments of Pauline conversion.
39 Teresa Billington, 'Suffragette Chat', in Carol McPhee and Ann Fitzgerald (eds), *The Non-violent Militant: selected writings of Teresa Billington-Greig*, 1987, pp. 100–1; date of writing probably (much) later.
40 APW, 'Looking Backwards', Oct 1929, pp. 4–5. APW confusingly says one day's leave of absence, but she must have known she was jeopardising her teaching post. Sadly, this account ends abruptly with 'to be continued' – but doesn't appear to be. Why does she stop here? *Hx G*, 2.2.1907, has AP a school-teacher till a couple of months earlier (i.e. to Nov/Dec 1906).
41 MG, *Up Hill*, p. 239.
42 *Daily Mirror*, 24.10.1906
43 Mitchell, *Hard Way*, p. 160.
44 Quoted in MG, *Up Hill*, p. 239.
45 MG, *Up Hill*, p. 239.
46 *Daily Mirror*, 24.10.1906.
47 Dora Montefiore, *From Victorian to Modern*, pp. 93–4. Coleman, *Adela*, p. 40.
48 MG, *Up Hill*, p. 243. Seems a bit early for a suffragette picture postcard?
49 *Labour Record*, quoted in MG, *Up Hill*, pp. 241 and 243; emphasis added.
50 *Labour Record*, quoted in MG, *Up Hill*, pp. 242–3.
51 MG, *Up Hill*, p. 247; Montefiore, *Victorian to Modern*, p. 97.
52 McLaren to Fawcett, 25.10.1906, M50/2/1/231; and reprint from *The Times*, 27.10.1906, M50/2/1/234, Fawcett mss, Manchester CRL.
53 *The Times*, 29.10.1906, reprinted in Montefiore, *Victorian to Modern*, pp. 100–4.

54 MG, *Up Hill*, p. 245–6.
55 *Labour Record*, Nov 1906, 'Women Suffragists in Prison', also Dec 1906; ESP, 1931, pp. 228–40 provides an extremely graphic account of Sylvia's own time in prison.
56 M50/2/1/230–43, Fawcett mss, Manchester CRL; for Gore-Booth and Esther Roper see *One Hand*, p. 210. Montefiore, *Victorian to Modern*, p. 108.
57 *Huddersfield Daily Examiner*, 21, 22 and 23.11.1906. Also Mitchell, *Hard Way*, pp. 162–3. The L&CWToWRC had put up a candidate at the General Election, but decided not to contest Huddersfield.
58 *Daily Mirror*, 24 and 26.11.1906; *HDE*, 26.11.1906. Home Office files HO144/837/145641, 24.11.06 for eleven-pages of legal opinion and legal precedents, confirming how very nervous was the Liberal government.
59 *HDE*, 26.11.1906. *Daily Mirror*, 27.11.1906. Mitchell, *Hard Way*, p. 164.
60 *Daily Mirror*, 28.11.1906. *HDE*, 28.11.1907. MG, *Up Hill*, p. 249.
61 *Daily Mirror*, 29.11.1907.

Chapter 4: Lavena Saltonstall

1 For the search for such elusive suffragettes as Lavena, see Appendix 1, 'Suffrage detective'.
2 Birth certificate, 3.9.1881; census, Apr 1881. See biographies, Appendix 2, for full details.
3 Hebden Bridge UD, 1901 occupations census: men aged over 10 – 340 in cotton, 370 in fustian, 433 in clothing; total 1,143 out of 4,572 occupied.
4 John Sottenstall (his surname was still variously spelt then); see 1881 census, Old Town, Wadsworth.
5 Marriage certificate, 8.9.1880, Halifax Parish Church, Mary Black aged 26, spinster, and John Sottenstall, 26, dyer. Mary's birthplace: 1891 Dundee. As 'Emily Saltonstall' (1881 census) her birthplace is given as Scotland; 1891 as Sunderland; as 'Emily Black' (1901 census) birthplace is given as Durham.
6 Colin Pooley, 'On the Move: continuity and change in internal migration', *Ancestors*, 24, 2004; work was the single most important motivation for migration, along with family needs.
7 1891 census, Wood Top; Emily 15, Lavena 9, William 5, Richard 4, Amelia 2.
8 Death certificates, 9.3.1894 and 21.3.1896, cause of death was tabes mesenterica.
9 Hebden Royd UDC, Analytical reports on water supplies, e.g. 3.9.1885, 31.8.1894, 15.2.1906. For schools e.g. Hebden Bridge UD School Board, Nov 1902 and Jan 1903.
10 Hebden Bridge UD School Board figures, Nov 1902 and Jan 1903; the figures for the early 1890s were likely to be higher.
11 1901 occupational census; a further 68 worked as dressmakers & milliners; 1894 White's *Directory*.
12 See note 20.
13 Robinson, *Halifax and district directory*, 1905–6.
14 1905–6 Street directory; the 'tin tab' was Methodist.
15 1901 census, 28 Unity Street. Emily had changed her name from Saltonstall back to her birth-name, Black, suggesting she had asserted her own identity over her step-father?
16 1901 census: only a handful of married women locally worked outside the home.

Todmorden News, 12.4.1907, for slender hints of Primrose Dames (and noting friendship with Rev. George Crookenden).

17 Hebden Bridge UD, Science, Art, Technical, Commercial, and Domestic Classes, 1902–3.

18 LS, 'The Letters of a Tailoress', part I, *The Highway*, Jan 1911.

19 5¼ missing years: April 1901 (census) in Unity St to Aug 1906 (Halifax)!

20 Fustian machinists in the clothing factories were unlikely to have joined a trade union. However, the Amalgamated Union of Clothiers Operatives (AUCO) formed 1894, took root in Leeds, and in 1897 a branch was formed in Hebden Bridge. It was not till 1900 that nine women/girls joined, each paying 3d a week, compared to men 6d, including Lilian Cobbe. AUCO Contribution Book includes an Emma Saltonstall among its members, but not apparently Lavena. However, all female members had lapsed by 1903. Then in late May 1906, the Hebden Bridge Trades and Labour Council plus AUCO invited to speak Ada Nield Chew of Rochdale, organiser for the Women's Trade Union League. 'At the conclusion of the meeting a few members were enrolled'. Suddenly, in June 1906 eleven new women members – including Lilian Cobbe – at 3½d each, joined the AUCO branch, and by August this had risen to seventeen; by early 1907 the branch had over sixty members (rising to seventy-eight), thirty-seven of whom (nearly half) were women and girls. Tom Greenwood, 'The origin and development of the Clothing Industry in Hebden Bridge', 1982.

21 *Hebden Bridge Times*, 23.3.1906. Ironically, Ada Nield Chew, an adult suffragist, had recently battled with Christabel Pankhurst over women's suffrage in the *Clarion*; see *One Hand*, chap. 10.

22 LS, 'The Letters of a Tailoress', part II: 'Some Aspects of Modern Life', *The Highway*, Feb 1911.

23 LS, 'The Letters of a Tailoress', Part I, *The Highway*, Jan 1911.

24 Laybourne and David (eds), *Rising Sun of Socialism*, pp. 54, 57–9, 65.

25 *Hx G*, 31.3.1906; *Labour Leader*, 22 and 29.9.1905; also 2.2.1906. Mary Taylor at the ILP Conference seconded the resolution for the immediate enfranchisement of women, *Labour Leader*, 20.4.1906.

26 *Hx G*, 11.8.1906.

27 *Hx G*, 1.9.1906.

28 Kenney, *Memories*, pp. 114–15, an ingenuous account.

29 *Halifax Evening Courier*, 3.9.1906.

30 *Halifax Evening Courier*, 21.9.1906 and *Hx G*, 22.9.1906.

31 *Hx G*, 29.9.1906

32 *Halifax Courier*, 3.10.1906. The 'parson' was probably Crookenden, whom Lavena knew.

33 *Halifax Evening Courier*, 17.10.1906.

34 *Hebden Bridge Times*, 3, 17 and 24.8.1906.

35 *HB Times*, 2.11 and 14.12.1906,

36 *Huddersfield Examiner*, 4.5.1907.

37 *Labour Leader*, 14.12.1906, also 7.12.1906.

38 *Labour Leader*, 4 and 11.1.1907; Ethel Snowden retaliated: 'we never asked the men of the ILP to interfere', and it was increasingly difficult for women socialists to remain members of the ILP compared to the 'splendid work' of WSPU. The

editor, insulted, replied tetchily about the WSPU's *negative policy at elections*. Also 18.1.1907 for angry letters.

39 *Manifesto to the Women's Social and Political Union*, Dec 1906 – Jan 1907, p. 1. Other signs of rush include the fact that no other Calder valley ILP branches respond. Lavena herself did not sign, suggesting, although sympathetic to ILP, she may not formally have been a member.

40 *Halifax Guardian*, 5.1.1907. The Wilsons had moved to Illingworth, north Halifax.

41 Conceivably the link was made by Lavena corresponding with Adela.

42 *HB Times*, 1.2.1907; also *Todmorden Advertiser*, 1.2.1907.

43 *HB Times*, 1.2.1907. *Halifax Guardian*, 2.2.1907.

44 *HB Times*, 8.2.1907.

45 Why were Adela Pankhurst (and Mary Gawthorpe) *not* arrested then for inciting public disorder? Had the local constabulary been instructed to use a light touch?

46 *Hx G*, 2.2.1907.

47 *HB Times*, 8.2.1907. Adela Pankhurst, 'The Weavers' Strike at Hebden Bridge', *Labour Record*, Feb 1907.

48 *HB Times*, 8.2.1907.

49 Mitchell, *Hard Way*, p. 149.

50 'The Needs of the Hour', WSPU *Annual Report*, Feb 1907. See next chapter.

51 *Hebden Bridge Times*, 15.2.1907.

52 Unusually, her late father was an elementary school teacher; he perhaps left the family impoverished after his death. I am grateful to Linda Croft for disentangling the Cobbe sisters.

53 Lavena Saltonstall, *The Highway*, Feb 1911.

54 *HB Times*, 22.2.1907.

55 *Hx G*, 23.1.1907.

56 *HB Times*, 22.2.1907.

57 *HB Times*, 1 and 8.3.1907.

58 *Daily Mirror*, 23.3.1907; sadly no such prison diary appears to have survived.

59 *HB Times*, 15, 22 and 29.3.1907.

Chapter 5: Dora Thewlis

1 WSPU, First *Annual Report*, 28 February 1907.

2 For useful comparisons with two other WSPU minutes books, see Krista Cowman, '"Minutes of the last meeting passed": the Huddersfield Women's Social and Political Union minutes book January 1907–1909, a new source for suffrage history', 2002, p. 301.

3 See Holton, 'The Suffragist and the "Average Woman"', 1992.

4 Photographs include Marcus Binney *et al.*, *Satanic Mills: Industrial Architecture in the Pennines*, Save Britain's Heritage, n.d. (*c.* 1978), p. 13. See also Fay Godwin photograph, illustration 11. Mills calculation based on 1907 OS map, 25 inches to the mile. Town-centre mills were predominantly woollen mills, some worsted and some cotton; Colne Valley mills and dye works were mainly woollen, a few cotton. See also David Jenkins, 'Textiles and other industries 1851–1914', in Haigh (ed.), *Huddersfield; a most handsome town*, 1992, pp. 241–52.

5 Miss Grace Proctor v Mr Jos[ep]h Fawcett, 'Agreement as to Child', 23 Mar 1872; thanks to Julia Mitchell for help with her family history.

6   Archie Key, *Once Over Lightly*, chap 1, 'Blind leading the Blind', typescript, Edith Key mss, KC1060/5 and Introduction to KC1060, WYAS.

7   Birth certificate, Lancelot Key, Nov 1891, Paddock; 1901 census, 43 West Parade, Huddersfield.

8   Archibald Key, KC1060/5(b); Lancelot Key, KC1060/4.

9   *The Worker: the organ of the Huddersfield Socialist Party*, 21.7.1905.

10   In Huddersfield, a male wool weaver would earn 26/- [£1.30] or female 13/- to 17/- [65p – 85p]. The Lancashire cotton figures were 25/- [£1.25] and 21/- [£1.05] respectively. In other words, wages of male weavers were comparable, but for female weavers wages were thirty per cent higher in Lancashire cotton than West Riding wool. See A. L. Bowley, 'Wages in the Worsted and Woollen Manufactures of the West Riding of Yorkshire', *Journal of the Royal Statistical Society*, Mar 1902, pp. 118–19; for Lancashire, *One Hand*, p. 79.

11   *Huddersfield Weekly Examiner*, 30.3.1907.

12   Taped interview with Joyce Bradley, Aug 2003.

13   Birth certificate, Lockwood, Huddersfield, Oct 1880. Ellen Brooke, West End, Wooldale, is less easy to pin down.

14   Tony Jowitt, 'The Retardation of Trade Unionism in the Yorkshire Worsted Textile Industry', in Jowitt and McIvor (eds), *Employers and Labour*, p. 85.

15   Ben Turner, *About Myself*, pp. 130–1. Originally the Huddersfield and District Power Loom Weavers and Woollen Operatives' Association, Jowitt and McIvor, p. 89.

16   Turner, *About Myself*, p. 93.

17   Subtitled *The organ of the Huddersfield Socialist Party*, changed to *and Labour News* from 1906.

18   Rob Perks, 'Late Victorian and Edwardian Politics in Huddersfield', in Hilary Haigh (ed.), *Huddersfield*, pp. 503, 507–9 and 519.

19   G. M. Wood, *Milnsbridge Memories*, pp. 7–11 [n.d., *c.* 2000?].

20   *Huddersfield Examiner*, 21.1.1904; the branch was re-formed in 1904, supported by Esther Roper, Emily Siddon, Gray Heald and Bertha Lowenthal. Ironically, suffrage in West Yorkshire could rely upon the support of textile trade unionists, in contrast to the cotton union leaders; *One Hand* pp. 205–6.

21   *Huddersfield Weekly Examiner*, 30.3.1907.

22   *Hfld Ex*, 19.12.1906. Unclear exactly how many enrolled at this founding meeting.

23   It looks as if Eliza Thewlis's name had been added to an existing six-strong committee. The exception is Bertha Miss Lowenthal, the Grange, Edgerton.

24   This is difficult to disentangle, as an Ann Sykes married a Charles Older, becoming Ann Older.

25   *Worker*, 19 and 26.1.1907. Since the *Huddersfield Examiner* decided on a news-blackout policy, we rely on the *Worker* for more sympathetic coverage.

26   Also a Mrs Hellowell from Lockwood and a Mrs Mosley from Deighton.

27   For Leeds arrests, see chap. 9.

28   Maud Arncliffe Sennett mss, National Convention notice and letter from WSPU, 5.1.1907.

29   *Daily Mirror*, 14.2.1907.

30   *Hfld Ex*, 23.2.1907. 56 women and 2 men arrested.

31   *Daily Mirror*, 14.2.1907; Metropolitan Police District, Register of the Court, 14 Feb 1907.

32 *Daily Mirror*, 15.2.1907. Ben Turner, Batley, 14.2.1907, HO 144/847/149245.

33 *Hfld Ex*, 23.2.1907.

34 *Hfld Ex*, 23.2.1907.

35 Holton,'The Suffragist and the "Average Woman"'.

36 WSPU, First *Annual Report*, to 28.2.1907 (exact date unclear, as it includes 20.3.1907 arrest figures).

37 Kenney, *Memories*, pp. 113–15.

38 *Worker*, 9.3.1907.

39 The others were Mrs Calpin, Mary Scawthorne, Annie Hopson, Sarah Pogson, Lillie Hellowell and two Mrs Tinkers. It is difficult to be precise about Ellen Brooke, and whether age given at arrest is correct.

40 *Worker*, 23.3.1907. Reference to hiring the 2 wagonettes omitted, as it seems really to have been Lancashire women only, led by Annie Kenney.

41 *Daily Mail*, 21.3.1907, quoted by Rosen, *Rise up, women!* p. 82.

42 *Daily Mirror*, 21.3.1907.

43 *Worker*, 23.3.1907.

44 Alfred Orage was later discharged.

45 *Daily Mirror*, 21.3.1907. Metropolitan Police District, Register of the Court, 21 Mar 1907.

46 For a few like Julia Varley of Bradford, the sentence was increased to a month.

47 *Daily Mirror*, 22.3.1907 and *Holmfirth Express*, 23.3.1907; both papers must have had access to shorthand writers in court, as the dialogue is intriguingly similar. Historians often find trials and interrogations invaluable as sources to illuminate otherwise hidden worlds of the socially invisible like Dora; see Peter Burke, *New Perspectives on Historical Writing*, 1991.

48 In fact, the NUWSS just had; for the 'Mud March' see next chapter.

49 *Hfld Weekly Express*, 30.3.1907.

50 *Hfld Weekly Ex*, 30.3.1907

51 *Hfld Weekly Ex*, 30.3.1907. Dora's pre-dating her involvement in the WSPU branch (which was of, at most, four months' duration) to 1903, suggests her youthful confusion and hyperbole – and perhaps some revealing confusion between WSPU and, say, local ILP activity.

52 *Daily Mirror*, Thurs 28.3.1907; also *Hfld Weekly Ex* 30.3.1907.

53 *HWE*, 30.3.1907.

54 *Hfld Ex*, 30.3.1907, *Daily Mirror*, 29.3.1907. Dora was still vague about her age.

55 For Pinnance, see interview with Joyce Bradley, Aug 2003; and golden wedding press cuttings, 1959 e.g. 'She was gaoled as a suffragette'. *Hx [G]*, 6.4.1907; Laura Wilson went via the ILP conference; Lavena stayed in London briefly, to visit Crookenden.

56 *Hfld Exp*, 28.3.1907 and 4.5.1907. Other women on platform were Scawthorne, Pogson, Hellawell, Fielding, Hopson.

57 WSPU Huddersfield branch minutes, KC1060/1, WYAS, Kirklees; see also note 2 above. There was the full painstaking ritual of a proposer and seconder for every resolution, however trifling, very much in political movement tradition.

58 2 Jul 1907, KC1060/1.

59 Given the context of the Colne Valley by-election, it is difficult to identify precisely the cause of the tension; Cowman, 'Minutes', pp. 312–13, gives greater detail. Certainly Eliza Thewlis 'rather exceeded her duties' in answering questions asked of Laura Wilson, *H'fld Worker* 22.6.1907.

Chapter 6: Florence Lockwood

1   Huddersfield WSPU branch minutes book, Annual Report, Jan–Dec 1907.

2   NUWSS, *Annual Report*, 1907. This chapter and those following provide detailed microcosms (e.g. Halifax, Huddersfield and Colne Valley) to test suffrage historians' notions about fluidity and friendships across organisations.

3   Tickner, *Spectacle of Women*, pp. 56 and 74. There had been earlier meetings, e.g. Trafalgar Square, May 1906.

4   Padma Anagol, *DNB*; *Huddersfield Express*, 5 and 13.2.1907.

5   Tickner, *Spectacle*, pp. 16 and 74–78.

6   Florence Lockwood, *An Ordinary Life 1861–1924*, 1932, pp. 15–16. Its wording is almost identical to the diaries, printed earlier; see chap. 13.

7   Lockwood, *Ordinary Life*, pp. 24–6.

8   Lockwood, *Ordinary Life*, p. 37.

9   For a while Isabella Ford had lived there as a lodger with a German wig-maker and his family: 1881 census, IOF aged 25, Torrington Square.

10 Lockwood, *Diaries*, Part II, *A Record*, p. 8.

11 Lockwood, *Ordinary Life*, pp. 72 and 78.

12 1901 census, 8 North Crescent, Chenies St; plus a general servant.

13 Lockwood, *Ordinary Life*, pp. 87–8.

14 Lockwood, *Ordinary Life*, p. 90.

15 Lockwood, *Ordinary Life*, p. 97. 1871 census, Lower Clough, Linthwaite (which was undoubtedly the entrance to Black Rock); 1878, marriage certificate, Slaithwaite parish church; 1888, death certificate, Southport, Lancashire.

16 1891 census, Causeway Side, Linthwaite.

17 Lockwood, *Ordinary Life*, pp. 94 and 95–6.

18 Lockwood, *Ordinary Life*, pp. 96–7.

19 Kelly's *Directory of the West Riding*, 1908.

20 David Howell, *Independent Labour Party*, p. 176; David Clark, *Colne Valley: radicalism to socialism*, p. 80.

21 Lockwood, *Ordinary Life*, pp. 122–3. In fact, FL did open local bazaars on at least one occasion: to raise money for Linthwaite prize-winning brass band, *Hfld Ex*, 4.4.1907.

22 David Clark, *Labour's Lost Leader: Victor Grayson*, 1985, pp. 156–7.

23 Reg Groves, *The Strange Case of Victor Grayson*, 1946, pp. 7–15 and 18. This early biography is more romanticised, less thoroughly researched, than later ones; I have drawn from it because what is important here is not so much what Grayson did, but what Edwardians and others thought he did.

24 ILP Manchester Central branch, minutes, 15.11.1904; from notes taken by Jill Norris, 1976.

25 Neither of Emmeline Pankhurst's recent biographers, Martin Pugh and June Purvis, note this – nor the symbolism of Grayson's election.

26 131, Pollard St Dwellings.

27 ILP Manchester Central branch, minutes, 4.9.1906, 19.3 and 23.4.1907. See also *One Hand*, pp. 212–2.

28 David Howell, 'Victor Grayson', *DNB*.

29 the *Worker* regularly advertised Grayson meetings from late 1905, including a 1906 May Day rally.

30   Mitchell, *Hard Way*, p. 129; perhaps *c.* 1905?
31   *Worker*, 19 and 26.1.1907.
32   Groves, *Grayson*, p. 72.
33   Clark, *Radicalism to Socialism*, pp. 199–200.
34   Clark, *Grayson*, p. 28. [is this true??] *Worker*, 26.6.1907.
35   *Colne Valley Guardian*, 5.7.1907.
36   Florence says tantalisingly little after Ward and before the Colne Valley by-election; she is unlikely to have attended any WSPU meetings.
37   Lockwood, *Ordinary Life*, pp. 123–4. (With Adela was perhaps Miss Glyde, Keighley, or more likely Nellie Martel.)
38   How could Black Rock House not have heard stories of Dora's arrest? Did they have no impact, or had they been somehow forgotten as of no moment?
39   Groves, *Grayson*, p. 36; this account is probably somewhat romanticised – see note 23 above.
40   *Daily Mirror*, 19.7.1907.
41   Groves, *Grayson*, p. 37, and the *Colne Valley Guardian* report, upon which this is based. Or one boy could be Elizabeth Pinnance's son; her grandson had a photograph of her on the celebration waggon when Grayson was elected.
42   *Colne Valley Guardian*, 26.7.1907; Groves, *Grayson*, pp. 37–8. Clark, *Radicalism*, p. 157.
43   *Daily Mirror*, 20.7.1907.
44   Oddly, the branch meeting 23.7.1907 makes no reference to the Grayson result (possibly because the political bitterness brewing over Eliza Thewlis over-shadowed it).
45   *Women's Franchise*, 25.7.1907, quoted in Mitchell, *Queen Christabel*, p. 103. But we should not read this at face value, but rather as good propaganda for keeping ardour of foot-soldiers aflame?
46   *Colne Valley Guardian*, 26.7.1907. Hannah Mitchell suffered a nervous breakdown about this time.
47   Lockwood, *Ordinary Life*, p. 124.
48   Lockwood, *Ordinary Life*, p. 125.
49   NUWSS, *Annual Report*, Oct 1907; *H'fld Examiner*, 5.2.1907.
50   1901 census; Helen Studdard attended the IWSA congress in Copenhagen.
51   The one exception is Bertha Lowenthal of The Grange, Edgerton; she had originally been elected NUWSS branch secretary – and had rather tentatively agreed, perhaps feeling she'd been dumped on? But soon she joined the WSPU branch. *H'fld Examiner*, 21.5.1904. See next chapter.
     The NUWSS agreed, on Isabella Ford's oddly optimistic suggestion, to send workers to help Grayson; but if this happened, it was scarcely visible or effectual. It remained the Victor and Adela show!
52   Lockwood, *Ordinary Life*, p 125.
53   *Worker*, 28.9.1907.
54   *Colne Valley Guardian*, 6.12.1907.
55   Lockwood, *Ordinary Life*, pp 140–1. FL dates this later to 1910.
56   Lockwood, *Ordinary Life*, p 125.
57   Textile conservationists have discovered earlier lettering: it was not originally 'Votes for Women' but 'Votes for Homes'; this intriguing alteration was perhaps to distance Grayson's demand to 'nationalise marriage', and nearer to something

the Linthwaite Lockwood clan would feel more comfortable with?

58 The Colne Valley by-election has been mainly recorded by local *labour* historians; Sylvia Pankhurst, the key suffragette chronicler, was not present; and her 1911 and 1931 histories say very little (e.g. ESP 1931, p. 367, dismisses Grayson as 'unstable' and 'ephemeral'). Even the biography of Adela (who *was* there) offers only one line (p. 42). Yet it was a key contest for the early WSPU.

59 Dating the banner is tricky. Was it carried in the June 1908 procession? The first direct evidence I have found is from 1911, suggesting its first national outing was more likely the 1911 Coronation Procession; see *Common Cause*, 16.2.1911, which reproduces it, giving a detailed account, and noting that Florence's banner 'raises the cry of VOTES FOR HOMES', which significantly was its *original* wording.

Chapter 7: Mary Murdoch and the Coates clan

1 See Biographies, Appendix 2.
2 Pugh, *Pankhursts*, pp. 163–4, is insightful about the two WSPUs, yet critical. Purvis, *Emmeline*, p. 109 offers a more loyalist take on WSPU branches' autonomy.
3 Huddersfield WSPU minutes, 30.7.1907; this was meeting which agreed to write to Eliza Thewlis; picnic 7.8.1907.
4 Huddersfield WSPU minutes, 13.8.1907 and 18.9.1907.
5 Huddersfield WSPU minutes, 1 and 22.10.1907.
6 Report to the Second Annual Conference of the WSPU now the Women's Freedom League, 12.10.1907. Because of the frenzied decision-making in Halifax, Laura's delegate credentials were queried when she arrived.
7 Pugh, *Pankhursts*, p. 167: 'the evidence suggests a more even split'.
8 1901 census.
9 WSPU Annual Report, Feb 1907; given as 'Miss D Coates, Roman Road, Linthorpe', round corner from Coates-Hansons' house; as Marion had no known sisters with initial 'D', this may be a misprint.
10 Report to the Second Annual Conference of the WSPU now the WFL, 12.10.1907.
11 Middlesbrough WFL minutes book does not start till November 1910.
12 Hope Malleson, *A Woman Doctor: Mary Murdoch of Hull*, 1919, chap. II; a hagiographical, uncritical biography. See also *DNB*.
13 Malleson, *Woman Doctor*, p. 56–7; letter written shortly after Mary's death.
14 Malleson, *Woman Doctor*, pp. 59–61; she was also an appalling driver.
15 www.brightonourstory.co.uk. Mabel subsequently adopted a child with a woman friend.
16 Louisa's mother had long been involved in the suffrage movement in Sussex and, like Marie Corbett, worked to get more women elected as parish councillors, and was now on the NUWSS executive.
17 www.womenofbrighton.co.uk/louisamartindale. Louisa Martindale, *A Woman Surgeon*, 1951, pp. 43 and 101.
18 NUWSS Annual Report, 20.10.1905, Hull.
19 Martindale, *Woman Surgeon*, pp 142, 102, and 228.
20 Malleson, *Woman Doctor*, pp 87–8.
21 NUWSS Annual Report, 25.10.1907.
22 Malleson, *Woman Doctor*, pp. 90–3.
23 Malleson, *Woman Doctor*, p. 93; more probably Tuesday.

24   Holton, *Suffrage Days*, p. 132.
25   *Hull Daily Mail*, 25.11.1907. Also present at the by-election was Selina Cooper, for the Lancashire Women Textile Workers' Representation Committee, appealing to industrial workers to support Holmes; see *Daily Mirror*, 28.11.1907.
26   *Hull Daily Mail*, 26.11.1907. EC, *Reference*, p. 235 notes 'Suffragette' card game, invented by Kensington WSPU branch, probably late summer 1907, described in *Votes for Women*, Nov 1907.
27   *Hull Daily Mail*, 27.11.1907.
28   *Hull Daily Mail*, 27.11.1907. Later, the Labour candidate was warmly received — though most of the suffragettes seem to have left by then.
29   Malleson, *Woman Doctor*, pp. 93–4. This biography gives a rather different gloss on the election campaign, skimming over her handling of such WSPU hecklers; and confidently positioning the NUWSS campaign centre-stage. She reported how someone told one WSPU speaker, 'that no one would even have heard of the suffrage [question] if I had not come to Hull and taught them all about it'.
30   Malleson, *Woman Doctor*, pp. 64 and 95–6. Martindale, *Woman Surgeon*, pp. 102–4.
31   Malleson, *Woman Doctor*, pp. 95–6; she may have again been persuaded by Louisa Martindale and her mother, who were inspired by suffragettes braving prison.
32   Sarah Eddyn, 'Alice Schofield Coates', 1987, pp. 20–1; also *Dictionary of Labour Biography*.
33   Middlesbrough WFL minutes book, e.g. 15.12.1910.
34   M'bro WFL mins, e.g. 17.2 and 29.5.1911.

Chapter 8: Edith Key and Lavena Saltonstall

1   Sylvia Pankhurst, *The Suffragette*, 1911, p. 178.
2   H'fld br mins, 1 and 15.10.1907. Key was blind, but their two sons came to do bodyguarding.
3   H'fld br mins 19 and 26.11.1907.
4   *H'fld Ex*, 7.12.1907.
5   H'fld br mins, undated; annual meeting, 7.1.1907, Clarion Club Room.
6   Adela Pankhurst presided at AGM; also Yorkshire report by Adela, printed in *Votes for Women*, 9.1.1908, 'Haunted House' issue.
7   *Halifax Evening Courier*, 18.1.1908.
8   *Daily Mirror*, 12.2.1908. Nearby, women had hidden inside two furniture vans, and sprung out, though Lavena doesn't mention this. Also arrested were Ann Older and Ellen Brooke, Westminster Police Court, Register, 12 Feb 1908.
9   *Halifax Evening Courier*, 12.2.1908. *Daily Mirror*, 12.2.1908, photograph 'Suffragettes Try to Rescue one of their Comrades' arrest outside the House of Commons. Lavena was at the centre of such an incident, and so this blurry image may possibly be the only photograph of her.
10 *Halifax Evening Courier*, 15.2.1908.
11 H'fld minutes book, 11.2.1908 and letter 16.2.1908.
12 Purvis, *Emmeline*, pp. 105–6.
13 *Hebden Bridge Times*, 27.3.1908.
14 H'fld br mins, 17.3.1908, 5.5.1908 etc.
15 Pugh, *Pankhursts*, pp. 174–5. Herbert Asquith, *DNB*.
16 *Halifax Guardian*, 25.4.1908.

17 Turner, *About Myself*, p. 278; date not given, but must have been the by-election. Also, *Halifax Labour News*, 22.4.1909. The Liberal was returned (though with a reduced majority) and Turner came bottom. *Daily Mirror*, 24.4.1908 has photo of suffrage campaigners at polling station. Contrast Lancashire trade unionists' lack of real suffrage sympathy.

18 H'fld br mins, 31.3.1908, 5 and 19.5.1908.

19 H'fld br mins, 12, 19 and 26.5.1908; see Cowman, 'Minutes', p. 307, citing *Worker*, 30.5.1908.

20 *Votes for Women*, 1.10.1908. H'fld br mins, 28.7.1908, 19.1 and 14.2.1909.

21 KC 1060/5(b), typescript.

22 KC 1060/4, typescript.

23 See chap. 13 for skulduggery.

24 She also moved out of lodgings and round the corner to Park Place, Halifax.

25 Lavena Saltonstall, 'Suffragettes on Tramp', *Halifax Labour News*, 24.4.1909. Chronology unclear, seems to be about 1908. Why Lavena waited 11 months to report this escapade is unclear. Thanks to Linda Croft for her research here.

26 *Halifax Labour News* Apr/Dec 1909 on suffragettes; *Halifax Evening Courier*, 19.7.1910 suffrage letter; 15.4.1911.

27 Linda Croft, *Raising our Voices: 100 Years of Women in the WEA*, p. 22.

28 *Hx G*, 18.11.1911.

29 Saltonstall, 'The Letters of a Tailoress', *The Highway*, Feb and Jan 1911. I am grateful to Linda for Lavena photocopies.

30 An exception is the East End of London.

32 *Cotton Factory Times*, 20.3.1914 ff; quoted in Rose, *The Intellectual Life of the British Working Classes*, p. 267; this chapter on the WEA is particularly good, even if this much-praised book uneven.

Chapter 9: Isabella Ford and her sisters

1 1911 population figures for county boroughs: Leeds 446,000, Sheffield 455,000, Bradford 288,000, Hull 278,000, Huddersfield 108,000 and Middlesbrough 105,000.

2 Leeds Arts Club, *Syllabus*, Feb–May 1908, MG mss papers; whether she was still in close contact with Thomas Garrs is less clear.

3 NUWSS *Annual Report*, 1904–5: Secretary, Mrs Nixon, Shaw Lane, Headingley; 1907 and 1908, Secretary, Miss Foster, Oakwood Nook, Roundhay.

4 WSPU, *Annual Report*, 1906–7: Miss Rhys Davids, Cliff Road, Hyde Park.

5 Westminster Police Court, Register, 14 Feb 1907.

6 H. C. G. Matthew, *DNB*, a valuable, sympathetic biography, if not immediately recognisable to suffragette historians.

7 Sylvia Pankhurst, *The Suffragette*, 1911, p. 178; probably Nov 1907.

8 *The Times*, 13.2.1908; there is some confusion about the length of the sentences.

9 *Yorkshire Post*, 12.2.1908. Thanks to Peter Halliday.

10 Emmeline Pankhurst, *My Own Story*, p. 96, a rather romanticised source. *Yorkshire Post*, 13.2.1908.

11 *Yorkshire Evening Post*, 15 and 19.2.1908.

12 Also in MG mss, Box 11.

13 Quoted in Tickner, *Spectacle*, p. 245.

14 NUWSS Annual Reports, 1904, 1907.

15 One of the few active converts was Mary Foster; a graduate teacher and an ILP member, she was branch secretary, though only for a while before she resigned; Hannam, *Isabella*, p. 126 and e.g. p. 136.

16 Dec 1907, reiterated Jan 1908; quoted in Rosen, *Rise up, Women!* p. 98.

17 Feb 1908, on Stranger's bill, quoted in Purvis, *Emmeline*, p. 104.

18 Tickner, *Spectacle*, p. 81.

19 Whether her banner was finished by then remains unclear; see end of chap 6.

20 *Labour Leader*, 24.4.1908, quoted in Hannam, *Isabella*, p. 129.

21 NUWSS *Annual Report*, 1909.

22 *Daily Mirror*, 13.6.1908.

23 *Daily Mirror*, 15.6.1908. Tickner, *Spectacle*, p. 88. Sadly, the *Yorkshire Post*, 15.6.1908 ran only a general report, and the *Yorkshire Evening Post* seemed to ignore it.

24 Bessie Ford to Kate Salt, 15.6.1908, Carpenter mss, quoted in Hannam, *Isabella*, pp. 129 and 130.

25 *Halifax Guardian*, 20.6.1908, though with no reference to a WSPU branch there.

26 WSPU handbill, MG mss; in the collection, there is also an internal pledge card pre-26.10.1908, including WSPU Bradford office (61, Manningham Lane) and publicity for 26.10.1908.

27 *Daily Mirror*, 22.6.1908. Tickner, *Spectacle*, pp. 91–7.

28 Tickner, *Spectacle*, pp. 97–8.

29 Handbill, MG mss. *Yorkshire Post*, 22.7.1908. Thanks to Vine Pemberton-Joss for alerting me to this. If this figure was correct, it would make it a momentous Yorkshire demonstration.

30 Liddington, *Respectable Rebel*, pp. 193–4. They were joined by the daughter of a high sheriff, peripatetic Alice Abadam; she left the WSPU for the WFL and now took her speaking talents to the NUWSS.

31 Exact date not clear; did Mary Fielden join the tour in 1908, or is it 1909 and a return visit to Goathland?

32 Postcard, CT/005, to Miss E. W. Gardner, postmarked Hull. A Miss H. Gardner, perhaps another relative, was secretary of the Newnham suffrage society.

33 Postcard, CT/011, Sat Sept 12 [1908], Driffield, TWL.2002.300. The exact route is difficult to plot with certainty. Postcard dates are Beverley (9.9), Driffield (12.9), then Malton (14.9), then Pickering (16.9); Bridlington (possibly early Sept). If so, this would (with a quick gallop from Goathland to Bridlington late Aug or early Sept) have given the vanners a concise anti-clockwise perambulation round Yorkshire Wolds.

34 It was edited by Helena Swanwick of Manchester.

35 Crawford, *A Regional Survey*, 2005, p. 52. *Common Cause*, 17.6.1909. The postcard was sent on to Mary at Ripon post office, possibly to be collected by her en route.

36 *Common Cause*, 17.6.1909.

37 EC, *Reference*, p. 279; *Common Cause*, 24.6.1909.

38 'Yorkshire Caravan', *Common Cause*, 1 and 5.8.1909. Another photograph (probably 1909) shows Haverfield leading the pony, Fielden seated, and either Costelloe or Ford standing.

39 *Common Cause*, 5 and 12.8.1909.

40 Alice Clark, quoted in Holton, *Suffrage Stories*, p. 161.

Chapter 10: Adela and Mary

1. West, *Adela*, in Till (ed.), *Rebecca West*, pp. 18 and 20; it was left uncompleted; it is interesting to compare to H. G. Wells's *Ann Veronica*, 1909, though the heroine is slightly older and living in London suburbs.

2. West, *Adela*, in Till (ed.), *Rebecca West*, pp. 26–33. West, *The Sentinel* written *c*. 1909–11 (ed, Laing, 2002), pp. xvi–xxi.

3. The *Clarion*, 24.1.1913, in Marcus (ed.), *The Young Rebecca*, pp 4 and 149.

4. Elsa Gye, Suffragette Fellowship, to Adela Pankhurst, 1.11.1934, APW mss: 'she never got over that frightful kick in the stomach' from a policeman 'in the early days'.

5. *Votes for Women*, e.g. Oct 1907, Jan and Feb 1908, 18.2.1910.

6. West may already have encountered Adela in Scotland in 1907–8 (e.g. Aberdeen, with Helen Fraser).

7. West, *Adela*, in Till (ed.), *Rebecca West*, pp. 17–18.

8. Dr Helen Wilson 1864–1951, scrapbook, Women's Library; sadly, this is largely just news-cuttings of public speeches.

9. Copley, *South Yorkshire*, pp. 45–6; branch formed Jan 1907; Feb–Mar 1907 arrests were Mrs Whitworth, Mrs Higgins and Miss Lockwood.

10. *Sheffield Daily Telegraph*, 9.11.1907 ff.

11. *Sheffield Daily Telegraph*, 21.11.1907; Adela Pankhurst, 'Yorkshire Report', *Votes for Women*, Dec 1907, Copley, *South Yorkshire*, pp. 47–8. In Leeds, Herbert Gladstone meeting following eve (21 Nov).

12. Adela Pankhurst, 'Yorkshire Report', *Votes for Women*, Dec 1907.

13. Quoted in Abrams, *Freedom's Cause*, p. 92.

14. Demonstration in St George's Hall, 26 Oct 1908, see MG mss.

15. *Votes for Women*, 15 and 22.10.1908. Others from Leeds arrested were Bertha Quinn, Theresa Garnett etc, given 5 days in Armley. Baines was sentenced to 6 weeks, 22.10 released from Armley. I am grateful to Vine Pemberton Joss for this information.

16. Rosen, *Rise Up, Women!*, p. 111.

17. *Sheff Indep*, 30.10.1908. The Sheffield police, unlike Leeds and London, had seemingly decided on low-key arrest policy for suffragettes.

18. *Sheff D Tel*, 24.10.1908. Copley, *S Yorkshire*, p. 52. Mrs Styring was particularly anti-militant. Helen Wilson also tried to start a local branch of the Men's League for Women's Suffrage, concerned that voters needed to be visible in persuading other voters. Sadly, records and minutes books of WFL Sheffield branch, held in Women's Library, have not survived pre-1916.

19. *Sheff D Indep*, 22.4, 3 and 6.5.1909 (H. Wilson letter). Copley, *S. Yorkshire*, pp. 53–4. In May 1909, Asquith visited Sheffield, talking up Lloyd George's reforms; outside the hall, skirmishing on the crowded street grew wild, the local paper describing it as 'little short of being a protest riot', with one suffragette's 'clothes rucked up almost to her waist'; *Sheff D Indep*, 21 and 22.5.1909.

20. See Crawford, 'Police, Prisons and Prisoners', 2005.

21. Helen Moyes, *A Woman in a Man's World*, 1971, p. 30. EC dates this to early 1907.

22. Scottish Office Prison Commission files, quoted by Abrams, *Freedom's Cause*, p. 94. Marcus (ed.), *Young Rebecca*, p. 367.

23   Moyes, *A Woman*, p. 32.

24   Copley, p. 51. 7,560 signatures in Barnsley; the photograph is reprinted on the cover of Crawford, *A Regional Survey*, 2005.

25   *Scarborough Mercury*, 7 and 21.1.1910; *Votes for Women*, 7 and 21.1.1910.

26   AP to Mrs Addy, on WSPU notepaper, 15.7.1911, Addy Coll, Sheffield Archives.

27   ESP, 1931, p. 367. In Jan 1911, Emmeline Pankhurst writes Preface to ESP's suffragette history, May 1911 published, June 1911 reprinted.

28   APW, 'My Mother', pp. 35–7.

29   Abrams, *Freedom's Cause*, p. 95.

30   ESP, 1931, p. 406; APW, 'My Mother', pp. 41 and 45. Helen (Fraser) Moyes, 22.10.1964 and AP to HFM, 11.2.1961, Suff Fell coll. EP to HA, 14.7.1912, quoted Purvis, *Emmeline*, pp. 191–2.

31   MG to ESP, 11.5.1931, MG mss.

32   *The New Age*, 12.9.1912.

Chapter 11 Leonora Cohen:Such smashing girls 1911–1912

1   Winston Churchill, *DNB*.

2   Tickner, *Spectacle*, pp. 123–4 and 130. M'bro WFL br mins, 29.5.1911; it had approached local council about the Conciliation Bill, 9 and 17.3.1911.

3   Holton, *Suffrage Days*, p. 175, which clarifies the complex politics here. Sadly, M'bro WFL br mins pages are left blank for these weeks.

4   Brian Harrison interview, LC, Oct 1974; listened to recording, Women's Library, May 2001; attended Veronica Lovell's talk on LC at Thoresby Society, Mar 2004; and conversation with VL, May 2005.

5   1891 census, Leonora aged 17, probably recorded as milliner.

6   1891 census, Henry aged 24, jeweller's assistant; 1901 census.

7   *Yorkshire Post*, 15.6.1973.

8   *Yorkshire Evening Post*, 13.3.1973.

9   *Yorkshire Evening Post*, 13.3.1973, 'A Suffragette message to women's lib'.

10   *Votes for Women*, e.g. 18.2.1910.

11   It is difficult to pin her down: was she any relation to Mrs Dodgson, pres of Leeds NUWSS *c.* 7 years earlier?

12   Quoted in Rosen, *Rise Up, Women!*, p. 155.

13   Brian Harrison interview, tape 6.

14   'Suffragette Violence Renewed. Frenzy and Hysteria. Fierce Attempts to Enter St Stephens', *Yorkshire Post*, 22.11.1911.

15   *Ykshr Ev News*, 13.11.1963; *The Times*, 28.11.1911; *Suffrage Annual & Women's Who's Who*, 1913. It is difficult to disentangle the details of this incident, whether the claim that the stone was thrown only as last resort was slightly disingenuous, and whether this note *is* from her first arrest.

16   *Yorkshire Post*, 22.11.1911. Also a Nancy Norton, Bradford.

17   *Ykshire Ev News*, 13.11.1963.

18   *The Times*, 23.11.1911. Metropolitan Police charge sheets: 21.11.1911, Cannon Row, (malicious damage, bail £2); 22.11.1911, Bow Street (malicious damage, bail £10); 24.11, Bow Street ('police', £10), LC coll. Or possibly Leonora had thrown a second stone i.e. was charged with a second more serious offence?

19   'The Suffragette Police Cases. Defendants from the North', *Yorkshire Post*, 28.11.1911;

and *The Times*, 28.11.1911. (See note 15 above, about this speech perhaps being rather disingenuous.)

20 *Votes for Women*, 1.12.1911.
21 Harrison interview, and V Lovell information.
22 Rosen, *Rise Up Women!*, p. 154; Pugh, *Pankhursts*, p. 232. Purvis, *Emmeline*, p. 174.
23 See for instance, Holton, *Suffrage Days*, p. 178.
24 Holton, *Suffrage Days*, pp. 177–8, and EC, *Reference*.
25 *Votes for Women*, 12.1.1912; close links with Women's Lab League and Socialist Institute.
26 *Votes for Women*, 1.3.1912, *The Times*, 2.3.1912; there may have been some conflation here.
27 *Votes for Women*, 8.3.1912. *Suffrage Annual*, 1913; because she was not arrested nor in court, there is little evidence in Leonora's papers.
28 *The Times*, 2 and 5.3. 1912; *Yorkshire Post* correspondence columns.
29 HO144/1195/220196 e.g. 20.3.1912, 13.4.1912.
30 For instance, Rubenstein, *Fawcett*, p. 176–7,
31 M'bro WFL br mins, from 29.11.1910, e.g. 9.3.1911 and 15.9.1911; 19.2.1912, 1.4.1912; 19.6.1912, 15.7.1912, 2.12.1912. Members also belonged to other societies: Marion to the ILP, others to labour groups, two to the WSPU (which may still have had a tiny presence in the town).
32 M'bro WFL br mins, e.g. 9 and 22.4.1912, 6 and 21.5.1912. Possibly after defeat of Conciliation bill, despondency and personal difficulties come to surface e.g. Despard accused of being autocratic, though supported by rank-and-file, and it is she who remains, as president, and 7 resign.
33 M'bro WFL br mins, 17.12.1912, 20.1.1913. This WFL branch candidly record the tensions and strains; yet these were in all probability mirrored by other suffrage branches then.
34 *Yorkshire Evening Post*, 13.3.1973; Brian Harrison interview, tape 6, and Veronica Lovell.

Chapter 12: Molly Morris and Leonora: 1912–1913

1 WSPU *Annual Report*, 1914 (to 28 Feb 1914).
2 1864 birth certificate, Whitechapel; 1881 census, Hulme, Manchester.
3 1871 census, Hulme; 1881 and 1891 census, Salford. Clara's grandfather had been a scavenger.
4 1886 marriage certificate; 1890 birth certificate; 1891 census, Leyland; 1901 census, Salford.
5 Molly Murphy, *Molly Murphy: Suffragette and Socialist*, 1998, pp. 1–6.
6 Murphy, *Molly*, pp. 9–10; possibly 1906?
7 Murphy, *Molly*, pp. 11–12.
8 Murphy, *Molly*, pp. 13–15 and 16.
9 Murphy, *Molly*, pp. 19 and 21; punctuation altered slightly for clarity. I have not so far been able to identify this exact advertisement. However, there is one possible advertisement slightly later (7 Feb 1913): 'WANTED by Suffrage Society, SECRE-TARY. Typewriting, shorthand, clerical experience', replying to Box 138 c/o *Suffragette*, Lincoln's Inn House, London. However, that would mean that Molly's suffrage sojourn in Sheffield was slighter than the later autobiography suggests.

10 Murphy, *Molly*, p. 19.

11 *Votes for Women*, e.g. 12.1.1912, 6.9.1912, *Suffragette*, 7.3.1913.

12 She may have been the eldest daughter of a very wealthy German-born mer-chant banker living near the Brompton Road in west London, though it is difficult to track her on the census; she was possibly a member of the WSPU's strong Kensington branch.

13 Murphy, *Molly*, pp. 22–3; *Suffragette*, 4.7.1913 (one of the very few references to Molly), implies Molly was in shop Mon–Thurs, and out selling the *Suffragette* Fri-Sats, for which days Schuster asks for replacement.

14 Murphy, *Molly*, pp. 23–4. Copley, *S Yorkshire*, p. 67.

15 Murphy, *Molly*, p. 24; punctuation slightly altered; sadly this autobiography is not always reliable. Copley, *S Yorkshire*, p. 67 gives Dec 1912 as start of local postbox fir-ings; it seems likely the firings started or increased when Molly arrived (i.e. to date her arrival to late 1912).

16 Copley, *South Yorkshire*, p. 72, Apr 1913.

17 Murphy, *Molly*, pp. 26–7; no replacement for Molly was found.

18 Purvis, *Emmeline*, p. 207, 10 Jan 1913, Craigie coll.

19 [*Yorkshire*] *Evening News*, hand-written note added: 20 Jan 1913, but probably 23 Jan, LC coll.

20 *Votes for Women*, 31.1.1913; also *Suffragette*, 31.1.1913.

21 Interview, Brian Harrison; *Daily Mirror*, and *Daily Sketch*, 24.1.1913, LC coll.

22 Metropolitan police account of WSPU meeting, quoted by Purvis, *Emmeline*, p. 209.

23 Purvis, *Emmeline*, p. 209, Pugh, *Pankhursts*, p. 258.

24 Raeburn, *Militant Suffragettes*, p. 204; *Yorkshire Evening News*, 13.11.1963.

25 *Yorkshire Post*, 15.6.1973.

26 Green card label and purple velvet ribbons, very faded writing, overleaf 'Jewel House Tower of London', LC coll. 'Evidence', 1 Feb 1913, LC coll; *Yorkshire Evening News*, 13.11.1963 and *Yorkshire Post* 15.6.1973; also Raeburn, *Militant*, pp. 204–5, inter-view recorded about 1970. Good consistency between the contemporary documents in LC mss and 1960s-70s press interview; discrepancies only in minor details.

27 Charge sheet, witness statements ('Evidence'), 1 Feb 1913, LC coll. Rosina Mary Pott stood bail.

28 Possibly *Lloyd's News*, *c.* 3.2.1913, LC coll. LC had the endearing yet confusing habit of dating her cuttings to the event rather than to the press date.

29 *The Times*, Mon 3.2.1913.

30 However, this does not quite fit with words still just about legible on label in LC coll.

31 Hand-written note added to typed 'Procedure at the Sessions', LC coll.

32 Hand-written note, Joseph Rmumens, LC coll. Raeburn, *Militant*, p. 205 says Henry secured this estimate.

33 [8?].2.1913, *Times* and *Yorkshire Post*, brief paragraph, 8.2.1913; no *local* report. And (oddly brief) in *Suffragette* and *Votes for Women*, perhaps because there were so many imprisonments, or because LC was a lone maverick?

34 HO mss re 21 and 26 April.

Chap 13: Florence Lockwood and Lilian Lenton: pilgrims and fugitives: summer 1913

1   Jo Vellacott, *From Liberal to Labour with Women's Suffrage*, 1993, particularly records the role of Catherine Marshall of the Lake District, with the influence of the London Society and old guard now more balanced by northern societies. NUWSS figures from Hume, *National Union*, appendices.

2   George Lansbury, committed socialist MP for Bromley and Bow, had recently lost his seat, vociferously championed free speech.

3   Bertha Quinn, full-time organiser for the Leeds branch of AUCO, moved a resolution at Leeds Trades Council protesting against the Cat and Mouse Act; Hannam, *Isabella*, p. 154. Also Julia Varley, Bradford, but she had left for Birmingham by this time. The support of trade unionists like Ben Turner and Alan Gee must have helped. However, the situation was now made more complicated by WSPU attacks on labour leaders e.g. Philip Snowden was heckled; joint ILP/Women's Labour League and WSPU membership grew difficult.

4   She was daughter of the Chairman of Vickers Ltd; also Georgiana Meyer, Organising Secretary of the North and East Riding Federation, also of York; see A.J.R. (ed.), *Suffrage Annual*, 1913.

5   Influential Eleanor Rathbone of Liverpool was among the strongest of opponents of EFF. For regional differences see chap 16, Analysis.

6   Rubinstein, *Fawcett*, pp. 177–8; Hannam, *Isabella*, pp. 148–9. Holton, *Suffrage Days*, p. 183 ff argues for continued flexibility at a local membership level, but it is hard to uncover evidence of this in Yorkshire.

7   Liddington, *Rebel*, pp. 231–2 and 235–6.

8   Liddington, *Rebel*, pp. 238–9, quoting Catherine Marshall mss, Cumbria Record Office.

9   Helen Wilson's scrapbook, never personally revealing at the best of times, ended in 1910.

10 Lockwood, *Ordinary Life*, pp. 141–2.

11 Lockwood, *Ordinary Life*, p. 165.

12 Lockwood, *The Enfranchisement of Women*, pp. 5–8, n.d., but after Sept 1912. It mentions sweated labour and living wage but still not the labour-suffrage pact, let alone EFF.

13 Lockwood, *Ordinary Life*, p. 175.

14 Liddington, *The Long Road to Greenham*, pp. 73–4.

15 1891 and 1901 census.

16 Recorded London, Mar 1960, interview by Lady Street; typescript pp. 2, 16 and 28–9, Museum of London. Thanks to Beverley Cook. It is difficult to be precise about dates.

17 *Votes for Women*, 8.3.1912.

18 Interview, Mar 1960, p. 3; Olive Wharry 1886–1947 a.k.a. 'Joyce Lock' (who flung papers and a book at the chair of magistrates).

19 Interview, Mar 1960, pp. 3–4.

20 Italian anarchists like Malesta were in London. Stone-throwing etc started by impetuous rank-and-file suffragettes, but Mrs Pankhurst visited them, and such tactics became imbedded in WSPU practice.

21 *Suffragette*, 7.3.1913, 'Victim of the Government', Lilian Lenton in bed recovering; also *Votes for Women*, 28.2.1913. ESP, p. 452 notes she had 'come up from the provinces to join the working women's deputation', but this seems to confuse her with Cohen etc. Interview, Mar 1960, Lilian Lenton understandably refuses to talk about this incident – when she nearly died.

22 *The Times*, 18.3.1913; *Suffragette*, 7.3.1913 and *Votes for Women* 21.3.1913.

23 *H'fld Examiner*, 12.4.13, Longley.

24 Liddington, 'Celebrating', p. 205, also PRI.COM 7/252.

25 This reported speech and those that follow are quoted from press reports of the court case, press-cuttings book, LC coll.

26 *Yorkshire Post*, 4.5.1913, LC coll. In the photograph, it is unclear which one is Leonora Cohen and who are others e.g. Bertha Quinn; also how much this was co-ordinated by the WSPU organiser, and how much a Leeds branch initiative?

27 *Yorkshire Post*, 12.5.1913.

28 City of Leeds (copies), 9.5.1913, LC coll.

29 Cross-questioning of witness notes, LC coll.

30 *Yorkshire Post* and other press, 15 .5.1913, LC coll (names altered slightly for clarity).

31 Words amalgated from press reports; LC's keeping the peace was pending a decision on the Lansbury case; Corr file, 1913, box 32, LC coll.

32 HO files. See Crawford 'The View from the Home Office'.

33 Lancelot Key is cryptic re to Sir Charles Sykes having spot of bother at his house at Fixby. This is confused with hatching a supposed plot to burn a house at Howarth: 'I was deputed to deliver a hot-water-bottle filled with kerosene to two feminist arsonists', a distance of 20 miles cross-country!

34 Archibald Key, KC 1060/5 (b and d), typescript, Key coll; this may be confused with a firing by Edith Rigby, a Preston suffragette.

35 Interview recorded with Julia Mitchell, Mirfield near Huddersfield, Oct 2003.

36 Laurence Housman, quoted by Holton, *Suffrage Days*, p. 196.

37 It is unclear whether Leonora attended the funeral.

38 LC coll papers not titled.

39 Marriage certificate, York, 1875, Harriet Key gives her father's occupation as clerk in holy orders; 1881 and 1901 census; 1891 family probably in Ireland. William Key, Fulford Hall, Water Fulford, York, censuses 1871–1901.

40 Hunger Strike medal, 4 Sept and 8 Dec 1909, Suffragette Fellowship collection; thanks to Beverley Cook.

41 *Votes for Women*, 10.11.1911, 8 New St; *Suffragette*, 7.3.1913, Colly Chambers, Coppergate. *York Herald*, 25.2.1911 for theatricals, directed by Mr W. H. Key-Jones of Bishopthorpe.

42 *Doncaster Gazette*, 19.6.1908 and 23.5.1913.

43 *Doncaster Chronicle*, 30.5.1913; *Sheff Indep*, 3.6.1913.

44 A suffragette lived at Albany Rd, Balby. *Sheff Indep*, Tues 3 Jun 1913. PRI.COM 7252: photographing 'without the knowledge of the prisoner' Augusta Winship Johnston + Harry J, HO to Govenor Leeds Prison, 6 Jun 1913.

45 1960 interview: Lilian wanted to help the wrongly accused woman.

46 *Sheffield Independent*, 10.6.1913; *Doncaster Chronicle*, 13.6.1913.

47 *Daily Mirror*, 10.6.1913, which includes a small portrait of LL.

48 *Sheffield Independent*, 11.6.1913.

49 Copley, *South Yorkshire*, p. 74. They only caught up with him in November, in London.
50 PRI.COM 7/252, 13.6.1913; for photography, see Augusta Winship instructions, 6.6.1913, Home Office to Prison Governor, Leeds.
51 *Sheffield Independent*, 17 and 18.6.1913 etc. Elizabeth Crawford, 'Police, Prisons and Prisoners: the view from the Home Office', 2005, is a very helpful overview.
52 EC, *Reference*, definite on this, but Leonora's memories may be a little more confused, blurring this incident with Lilian's 1914 escape via the Cohen's house at Harrogate (see next chapter).
53 Sympathetic report, possibly *Yorkshire Observer*, press-cuttings book, LC coll.
54 *Suffragette*, e.g. 23.5 & 4.7.1913; 1913 WSPU sec was Nora Vickerman, 33 St Nicholas Cliff, Scarborough.
55 *Sheffield Independent*, 20.6.1913. EC, *Reference*, notes the Leeds police file breathless report to Home Office on 20 June detailing how they were out-manoeuvered. July: Lilian escapeed to France in private yacht; Criminal Record Office issued 'wanted' photo, very pretty, with loose hair. For general press interest see for instance *Daily Express*, 20 and 24.6.1913.
56 *Sheffield Independent*, 14.7.1913.
57 PRI.COM 7/252, 22.5.1913 and HO 45/12915, 7.8.1913; see Liddington, 'Celebrating', p. 205.
58 Liddington, *Rebel*, pp. 243–4; Hume, *National Union*, pp. 197–8.
59 Copley, *S Yorkshire*, pp. 69–70.
60 *Sheff Indep* 5 Jul 1913..
61 Copley, *S Yorkshire*, pp 74–6, citing *Sheff Indep* 7 Jul 1913.
62 Hume, *National Union*, p 199; Hannam, *Isabella*, p. 156.
63 Holton, *Suffrage Days*, p. 194–61, Hannam, *Isabella*, p 158. *Common Cause* notes Mrs Illingworth's chauffeur was there, so possibly a bargain was struck.
64 Barnsley WSS min bk, 4.12.1913, 18.3 and 9.4.1914; EC, *Reference*, gives a more sympathetic reading, and Barnsley banners in Women's Library coll suggest energy.
65 See next chapter for references.

Chapter 14: Leonora, Lilian and Florence again: Unsafe city: 1914

1 M'bro br mins, e.g. 20.10.1913, 26.1 and 2.2.1914.
2 *Suffragette*, e.g. 5.12.1913.
3 *Suffragette*, 5.12.1913.
4 Press-cuttings book, LC coll; precise dating is difficult.
5 Prisoners (Temporary Discharge for Ill-health) Act, Leonora Cohen, 1 Dec 1913, to attend at court 3 Dec 1913, signed by Governor, Leeds Prison, LC coll.
6 Press-cuttings book, LC coll, *The Times*, 29.11.1913; *Suffragette*, 5.12.1913; exact dating remains difficult.
7 Undated draft letter, Prisoners Temporary Discharge 'Cat & Mouse Act', file, LC coll. (However, dating is still difficult, perhaps because Henry had also sent another angry letter, probably to the local judiciary, about Leonora, free speech, and his having acted as co-surety.)
8 Home Office to HC, 9 and 10.12.1913, LC coll.
9 Undated draft letter, LC coll. Minor punctuation added to assist meaning.
10 Thanks to Veronica Lovell for help here.

11 E.g. *Suffragette*, 26.6.1914.
12 Confidential memorandum, Prison Commission to all Prisons, 10.3.1914, PRI.COM 7/252.
13 See Crawford, 'The View from the Home Office'. The Museum of London holds a similar but different set of photographs taken of suffragettes in prison; the relationship between two sets of images not yet clear.
14 Leonora may also have acted as a bodyguard for Mrs Pankhurst. *Suffragette*, e.g. 7 and 15.5.1914.
15 *Suffragette*, 15.5.1914. Also, lengthy cuttings in LC's scrapbook.
16 WSPU handbill, LC coll.
17 Interview, Mar 1960, p. 9.
18 *Harrogate Advertiser*, 24.6.1914, hand-written note in scrapbook, LC coll.
19 Brian Harrison interview. LL interview, Mar 1960, pp. 10–13; there are unsurprisingly some inconsistencies about the disguise as Reg and the escape via coal chute.
20 Purvis, 'Representations of Emmeline and Christabel Pankhurst', *WHR*, 5:2, 1996, p. 261, suggests about 1,000 nationally from 1912. The exact number across Yorkshire is hard to gauge.
21 *Suffragette*, 12.6 to 31.7.1914.
22 See Crawford, 'The View from the Home Office', p. 503.
23 Lockwood, *Ordinary Life*, pp. 185–90; this is the same as her printed diaries, except for last section, which draws upon her leaflet, 'World Mending on the First Day of the War'. There was also a garden party at Miss Siddon's house.

Chapter 15: Living with the memory

 1 Rubinstein, *Fawcett*, p. 242; Purvis, *Emmeline*, p. 307. Certain franchise restrictions still applied to women over 30.
 2 Purvis, *Emmeline*, pp. 233 and 248, EP to HA, 2.9.1913 and 27.1. 1914, Jill Craigie coll. APW, 'My Mother' (1933), p. 43.
 3 Purvis, *Emmeline*, p. 257, EP to HA, Good Friday [1914], Jill Craigie private coll.
 4 APW, 'My Mother', p. 43, and she blamed Sylvia.
 5 Coleman, *Adela*, p. 55.
 6 Ursula Young to David Mitchell, 12.4.1966, Mitchell mss, Museum of London. Coleman, *Adela*, p. 114; her youngest child died shortly after birth. Also, Elsa Gye corr., APW mss, 1934, pp. 15–16; and Susan Hogan interview, Dec 2003.
 7 *Huddersfield Chronicle*, 28 May 1993, for Mabel Carey and Thelma Singleton.
 8 Croft, *Raising our voices*; marriage certificate, 1917.
 9 Despite sending a letter of appeal for information Aug 2005 to *Yorkshire Post*. York Library has information about Violet Key-Jones's pre-1914 suffrage activities.
10 Murphy, *Molly*, pp i–iii.
11 EC, *Reference*.
12 Eddy, 'Alice Schofield Coates', pp. 22–3. In the war, Alice consulted Mary Murdoch about establishing a Child Welfare Centre.
13 Lockwood, *Ordinary Life*, p. 256. Interview recorded with Mary Lockwood, May 1984.
14 Sylvia Pankhurst, *The Suffragette: the history of the Women's Militant Suffrage Movement 1905–1910*, 1911, pp. 70, 5, 87–8 and 97; Adela eventually makes a brief appearance in June 1906, when she is given a walk-on part at the Belle Vue meeting in Manchester.

15 Emmeline Pankhurst, *My Own Story*, 1914, p. 12.
16 Annie Kenney, *Memories of a Militant*, 1924, beautifully bound in purple, green and white. Copies are now so rare and expensive, I have had to book-share.
17 Ray Strachey, *The Cause*, 1928; no reference to Mary Gawthorpe, Adela Pankhurst, Colne Valley by-election etc. etc.
18 Pugh, *Pankhursts*, 419.and 410.
19 Pugh, *Pankhursts*, pp. 424 suggests 1931 or after; however internal evidence (ages of her children) suggests *c*. 1927.
20 APW, 'The Story of my Life', n.d., pp. 5–6 (however Adela post-dates her birth by three years).
21 APW, 'Looking Backwards', serialised in *Stead's Review*, a conservative monthly magazine, Oct 1928, p. 5; Feb 1929, p. 3; Aug 1929, p. 7; Oct 1929, p. 5. See chapters 1 and 3.
22 Coleman, *Adela*, pp. 114–16.
23 ESP, 1931, pp. 594–5. I can remember the first time I read it being knocked out by the account of hunger and thirst strikes.
24 APW, 'My Mother', pp. 1 and 40.
25 APW, 'The Philosophy', 6 Oct 1934, pp. 1–2 and 27. My reading of this is of two forces (a) politics – APW has moved from ESP's socialism to EP's conservatism, 7 (b) family – rivalry between the daughters.
26 ESP to MG, 1.1.1931; MG to ESP, 11.5.1931, MG mss.
27 MG to ESP, 8.2.1932 and subsequent correspondence; ESP to MG and to solicitors, Lamartine Yates & M, both 11.12.1935; MG to Silvio Corio, 9.8.1936, MG mss. MG was particularly concerned about this in relation to US immigration formalities.
28 For this lengthy correspondence and its Suffragette Fellowship context, see Krista Cowman, 'A Footnote in History? Mary Gawthorpe, Sylvia Pankhurst, *The Suffragette Movement* and the writing of Suffragette history', *WHR*, 2005.
29 See Suffragette Fellowship collection, Museum of London. An excellent analysis is found in Laura Mayhall, 'Creating the "Suffragette Spirit": British feminism and the historical imagination', *WHR*, 1995, e.g. p. 330.
30 The S.F. typescript is Christmas 1931; I am grateful to Beverley Cook for this dating. These two accounts of MG's early years are similar; 'The Man' of S.F. becomes 'F.L.' in autobiography; and S.F. account perhaps shows more sympathy with her father's talents and ambitions, while the book is more sympathetic to her mother. The S.F. account takes the story further forward (to William Ball etc.), suggesting another volume of autobiography was possibly planned; however, it did not materialise.
31 Elsa Gye, S.F., Record Room, Minerva Club to APW, 30-page letter, 1.11.1934, p. 14, APW mss.
32 I cannot give the full WFL story here: it is less important in Yorkshire (outside Middlesbrough) than NUWSS, WSPU and ASL etc. See Hilda Kean, 'Searching for the Past in Present Defeat: the construction of historical and political identity in British feminism in the 1920s and 1930s', *WHR*, 1994.
33 For full details of all titles, please see Bibliography.
34 *Yorkshire Post*, 31 Mar 1937. She had been vice-president of Huddersfield Art Society.
35 Also APW correspondence with Helen Fraser Moyes.
36 1961 invitation plus Jul 1970 cuttings, LC coll. Lilian Lenton was also editor of the WFL *Bulletin*, to which LC subscribed.

37   EC, *Reference*, e.g. film, *Fame is Spur*, 1947. In 1950–1 the collection was taken over by the Museum of London, now in the Barbican.

38   D. Mitchell's assiduous research (e.g. tracking APW in Australia) and his notes are deposited with Museum of London. A. Raeburn provides no references to her sources.

39   Dame R. West, 'Shoulder to Shoulder', *TV Guide*, Oct 1975, cutting in LC coll, Leeds. ESP (1931) republished by Virago Press, 1977; this paperback edition added to its popularity. The final section, episode 6, focused on Sylvia Pankhurst in the East End.

40   Recent examples include Purvis, *Emmeline*, Introduction; her main criticism of ESP's 1931 book is its 'socialist feminism' rather than its metropolitan leanings. For a critique of the 'London-centred' narratives see Hannam, in Purvis and Holton (eds), *Votes for Women*.

Chapter 16: Rebel Girls: writing narrative history

1   Occasionally I trace in more detail the story beyond these geographical boundaries, particularly Adela's early days, hence the Belle Vue and Boggart Hole Clough meetings. I also include others who were born elsewhere, but who campaigned across Yorkshire: Molly Morris, Lilian Lenton, Alice Schofield and Violet Key-Jones. Helpful here are Giovanni Levi, 'On Microhistory', about microhistory and the problem of narrative; also Burke, 'History of Events and the Revival of Narrative' on micro-narrative; both in Peter Burke (ed.), *New Perspectives on Historical Writing*, 1991.

2   Except Molly Morris, who seemingly managed to scurry away from 'firing' her Sheffield pillar-boxes, so evading arrest.

3   Laura and Leonora each had just one son and supportive husbands; I have included Leonora Cohen here because, although older, many of her experiences were similar.

4   Others with German links include Molly Morris's family and (by marriage) Marion Coates-Hanson.

5   I am very grateful to Timothy Ashplant for discussion of these shared biographical themes.

6   Also the Fawcett Society plus Women's Freedom League; and Adela's friendship with Helen Fraser, now Helen Moyes.

7   The issues of a 'collective biography' is complex, not least because the rebel girls' circles described here do not form a single self-identified grouping like, for instance, the Lunar Society, Bloomsbury Group or 'Red Clydeside'.

8   It is possible Adela had met nearly all of them (e.g. although she left Sheffield before Molly Morris arrived, the two may have already met in Manchester).

9   Mary Murdoch's switch of allegiances makes her trajectory slightly different. Though sharing identical suffrage aims and both leading NUWSS members, Florence Lockwood may well not have 'known' Isabella Ford (even though they had attended the same IWSA congress in Budapest) according to FL's autobiography.

10   For the Lancashire cotton towns (as opposed to Manchester): Annie Kenney is from the West Riding; Jennie Baines from Stockport, Cheshire; Hannah Mitchell from Derbyshire.

Within the cotton towns, for the three mass actions (Feb and March 1907, Feb 1908) only Preston, where charismatic doctor's wife Edith Rigby ran the WSPU branch, accounted for a number of arrests, including at least one weaver; and Rochdale, where arrests included at least two weavers.

11 Of active trade unionists e.g. Julia Varley (Bradford) and Bertha Quinn (Leeds), see chapter 13 note 3.

12 See Crawford, *A Regional Survey*, 2005. Jo Vellacott suggests that there are almost two NUWSS by then, though this was much marked in Yorkshire. I have found it difficult to identify any Yorkshire NUWSS branches which are exceptions.

13 June Hannam, '"I had not been to London": women's suffrage – a view from the regions' in Purvis and Holton (eds.), *Votes for Women*, 2000, p. 231.
Another issue which has exercised suffrage historians recently is the relationship between NUWSS plus WSPU and WFL. The Lancashire evidence suggests some distrust. The Yorkshire evidence suggests some flexibility, with some supporters switching allegiances. In 1907, of course, WSPU rebels formed WFL e.g. Alice Schofield and her sister-in-law Marion. Traffic between WSPU and NUWSS was two-way; for Mary Murdoch, Bertha Lowenthal etc., see Biographies.

14 Huddersfield WSPU min book ends Feb 1909, with the steam seemingly gone out of the branch.

15 Krista Cowman, '"Crossing the Great Divide"', in Eustance, Ryan and Ugolini (eds), *A Suffrage Reader*, 2000, p. 41. Cowman, *'Mrs Brown is a man'*, 2004, p. 80–1.

16 Though, of course, unlike the cotton towns, its coal industry produced miners, rather than organised women workers. David Neville, *To Make their Mark*, 1997 (e.g. Ethel Bentham, Elizabeth Simm).

17 Cowman, *'Mrs Brown is a man'*, pp. 74–5.

18 Though still largely led by elite Liberal women; it would be interesting to know exactly who were the new 'Friends' recruited across Yorkshire.

19 'Shoulder to Shoulder', *Radio Times* Special, p. 13.

20 See also Cowman, *'Mrs Brown is a man'*, pp. 90–4 for the Merseyside contrast between pre-1912 (socialists and bohemians) and post-1912 (bombs placed in public buildings), for the width of support (e.g. small donations), shop, and new recruits helped by a WSPU organiser.

Appendix 1: Suffrage detective.

1 J. Liddington, 'Who was Annie Kenney?', *Spare Rib*, 1975.

2 This long frustrated suffrage historians: the biography, *Isabella Ford* by June Hannam, was not published until 1989.

3 Journals, notably *Gender and History* from 1989; *Women's History Review*, from 1992, which includes some excellent suffrage historiographical discussion.

4 Sandra Holton, 'The Suffragist and the "Average Woman"', pp. 11 and 20.

5 Sandra Holton, *Suffrage Days*, pp. 3–4.

6 Krista Cowman, '"Crossing the Great Divide"', p. 38. Also, Neville, *To Make their Mark*, 1997.

7 *THES*, 25.1.2002.

8 I am grateful to Veronica Lovell for copies of Leonora's obituaries.

9 Also enterprising research and exhibition by Thelma Singleton, Huddersfield.

10   Interview with Julia Mitchell, Oct 2003; she was 5–6 years old when great-uncle Lance died.

11   Also helping to build the picture of Huddersfield's community suffragettes, Dora Thewlis' niece from Australia made contact.

12   False leads and web-trails took me to the wrong Careys, including three Careys living in Warrnambol, and the novelist Peter Carey. I eventually tracked down the current address in Victoria State Library. The family family snapshots, now dog-eared, were all taken after emigration to Australia.

13   MG's mother's loyal hoarding; this collection even includes MG's 1890s pupil-teacher exercise books.

14   Interview recorded with Betty Meissner, Boston, Dec 2003, pp. 3 and 6.

15   Interview recorded with Betsy Meissner, Boston, Dec 2003, pp. 3–4.

16   Robert F. Wagner Labor Archives, The Tamiment Library, New York University also includes the papers of Elizabeth Gurley Flynn and Emma Goldman. Betty and her sisters also produced family research on their great-aunt (2001).

17   Coleman, *Adela*, Melbourne UP, 1996; however, note David Mitchell, *The Fighting Pankhursts*, 1967, which again concentrates on Adela's post-emigration years.

18   There are suggestions on some political weeding of the papers.
Compare Pugh, *Pankhursts* (2001), p 243 says 'though little contemporary evidence survives of Adela's activities for this period, she had continued her work in the provinces'. Researchers do need to read the 'provincial' press. Also Copley, *South Yorkshire* thesis is under-used by suffrage historians, in contrast to certain accessible over-quoted sources.

19   Again, the detective trail was tricky, involving some false clues.

20   Interview with Susan Pankhurst Hogan, Dec 2003, NSW, pp. 1 and 9. She felt understandably critical of how previous biographies had imposed their own personal agendas upon APW.

21   *Yorkshire Post*, 1.1.1966, with Grace Rowe, LC coll. The scrapbook, endearingly but infuriatingly, has added in hand-written dates – which refer to the action date not to the press date, making reconstructing a chronology frustrating.

22   However, there are interpretive and corroborative problems; it can be misleading (e.g. re 'bombs') and overlaid by subsequent CP-ish overshadowing by her husband (e.g. in records of Labour History Museum, Manchester); Molly appears of a generation of women who later felt a worthlessness and suffered from depression.

23   Undated; probably some years after her 1907 imprisonment.

24   Even Leonora Cohen remained invisible to the survey, now housed in the Museum of London; I am most grateful to Beverley Cook for this information, Sept 2003.

25   Copy in Leonora Cohen coll, Abbey House Museum, undated.

26   Alan Travis, 'Big Brother and the Sisters', *Guardian*, 10.10.2003; also BBC News website, 'Spy pictures of suffragettes revealed', 3.10.2003. See J. Liddington, 'Celebrating the Suffrage Centenary', 2005.

27   *Halifax Courier*, 2004. Only Dinah Connelly, who played a rather minor role compared to the other Halifax suffragettes, really survived in local popular memory, largely because her daughter became mayor, and, as chair of the Health Committee, was immortalised with a clinic in her name.

Another letter appealing for information about Lavena, in the *Bradford T & A*, also produced no further leads.

28 BBC *Radio Times*, 9–15 Oct 2004 cover story on 'Who Do You Think You Are?' (BBC2), with Jeremy Clarkson displaying two family portraits. In the second series, Jeremy Paxman was among the participants.

29 I am most grateful to Dan Weinbren, Open University, for his thoughts on this. Oral history of course continues to play a significant role in suffrage historiography, e.g. see the mesmerising interview recorded with Lilian Lenton (1960) and interview with Leonora Cohen by Brian Harrison (1974).

30 I have adhered to the Edwardian boundaries of Yorkshire's three Ridings, slightly different from post-1974 alterations. Thus Sheffield and Doncaster are part of old West Riding, and Middlesbrough falls within the North Riding. This gave me firm criteria for inclusion or omission of both individuals and events. Those that fell within these boundaries were included; those that fell outside were omitted.

31 A number of research frustrations remain. It would be helpful to be able to read behind the pages of the *Suffragette* for what life in the WSPU was really like locally then. Sometimes identifying corroborative evidence is still difficult; and we are still left with Lavena Saltonstall's missing 5½ years, plus little further information about slippery Violet Key-Jones.

32 Bradford is the only major Yorkshire community which has been largely omitted as little evidence survives after Julia Varley's departure. Isabella Ford, post-scrapbook and with so little personal information, remained tricky – but she is featured in chapter 9. The Coates clan also proved difficult, with oddly little personal information; they share chapter 7 with Mary Murdoch. There is less on Middlesbrough and WFL than I had originally envisaged, and so discussion of local campaigners there has been kept brief.

INDEX

Actresses' Franchise League, 163, 177.
Adela, 8, 13, 215–7.
adult suffragists, 54, 115, 117.
America: & suffrage, 12, 267,; & emigration 301–2, 310.
anarchists, 17, 231, 251.
Annakin, Ethel (Snowden), 35, 41, 56; & ILP *Manifesto*, 85–6, 115–6; & suffrage, 203, 213.
anti-suffragists, 163, 213.
Archdale, Helen, 225–8, 300–1.
archives, 108, 102, 194; & suffrage detective, 327, 328, 329, 330; & film, 3, 333.
arrests: *see* courts, prisons.
Artists' Suffrage League (ASL), 136, 159, 199–201.
Asquith, Henry MP, 2; becomes PM, 186, 199; obduracy, 203–4, 219; provocative, 232, 255; Leeds visit, 232, 255; *see also* Reform Bill.
Astor, Nancy, 299.
Australia: & suffrage, 12, 62, 98; & emigration, 300–1, 303, 306.
autobiography, 2, 137, 246, 305–7, 308, 309–10, 311; & suffrage detective, 325, 331.

'Baby Suffragette', *see* Dora Thewlis.
Baines, Jennie, 97–104; in Leeds, 195–6, 219–221.
Ball, William, 242.
banners, 8, 137, 159–60, 178, 182, 295; in

1908 procession, 200–2; *see also* Florence Lockwood, Mary Lowndes, Emily Ford.
Barnsley, 136, 225, 283, 285.
Barran MP, Rowland, 37, 50.
Becker, Lydia, 10.
Beever, Ellen, 117–121, 131.
Benson, Arthur, 2.
Berkley, Lizzie, 103–4, 123–4, 131.
Billington-Greig, Teresa: & WSPU, 25–6, 28, 64–5, 67; breaks to form WFL, 164–6.
biographies, 309, 329; group, 313, 317; *DNB*, 321.
Bloomsbury, 136–40.
Board Schools, 20–3,
Boer War, 1–2, 4.
Bondfield, Margaret, 47, 299.
Boyd-Dodgson, May, 236–7, 240.
Bradford, 5, 11, 31, 109–10, 136, 203,
Brontes, 91, 202.
Brooke, Ellen, 184, 195.
Brown, Kathleen, 277.
Butler, Josephine, 10.
by-elections: North Leeds 1902, 37; Cockermouth, 1906, 62–3; Huddersfield, 1906, 74–77, 115; Colne Valley, 1907, 132, 149–57; Hull, 1907, 168–176; N W Manchester, 1908, 186–7; S Leeds, 1908, 195; Sheffield Attercliffe, 1909, 222–3; Holmfirth, 1912, 264; Keighley, 1913, 285.

Campbell-Bannerman, Henry, 1; Prime
    Minister, 53–4, 69, 123, 135; deputation
    to, 55.
Carpenter, Edward, 40, 42, 43, 64.
'Cat and Mouse Act', 260–1, 267, 269, 272;
    suffragettes let out on licence under,
    279, 287; 'mice' sheltered, 274–5, 281–2,
    292–3.
Cause, The, 211, 305.
census, 3–4, 21, 140, 333–4.
Chew, Ada Nield, 319.
Churchill, Winston, MP: interrupted, 26,
    27; heckled, 49, 58; & N W Manchester
    by-election, 186–7; & strikers, 231.
Clarion, 8; & cycling, 19–20.
Close, Agnes, 46.
clothing workers' union, 88.
Coates-Hanson, Marion, 166–7, 177–8, 304.
Cobbe, Lilian, 88, 98, 100, 123–4, 131.
Cobbe, Louie, 88.
Cobden-Sanderson, Mrs & Mr, 69–75, 116.
Cohen, Henry, 234 ff, 245, 258, 272–4;
    writes to Home Secretary, 288–9.
Cohen, Leonora, xiv, 3, 5, 6; childhood,
    233; milliner, 234; marries Henry
    Cohen, 234–5; & suffrage, 235–6; to
    Westminster, & throws stone 236–9; to
    Holloway, 240–1; window smashing,
    243; in Leeds WSPU, 245; deputation to
    Lloyd George, 253–4; smashes glass
    case at Tower of London, 255–7; trial by
    jury, 258–60; in Leeds detectives note
    her speeches, 270–1; in court for
    incitement, 272–4; stone-throwing
    during Asquith's visit, 286–7; in
    Armley & ness, 287–8; to Harrogate &
    shelters 'mouse'; 289–93; JP & OBE,
    304–5; & Suffragette Fellowship, 310;
    elderly woman, 325; death, 327; papers,
    330; on Radio Times cover, 330.
Cohen, Reg, 235, 241, 245, 292.
Coleman, Verna, 25, 301, 329.
Colne Valley, 109, 131, 137, 140–57, 265; see
    also Florence Lockwood, Victor
    Grayson.
Common Cause, 211–2,
Conciliation Bill, 231.
Connelly, Dinah, 95, 104, 123–4, 131, 326.

Cooper, Selina, 12, 24, 263–4, 285, 313.
co-operative shops, movement & Guild,
    86, 142, 202.
courts, magistrates': 59, 71; Todmorden,
    102–3; Westminster, 119, 124–5, 183–4;
    Bow Street, 240; Thames, 257; Leeds,
    272–4, 287; Doncaster, 277–9; jury
    trials, 258–60, 291–2; lone suffragette
    voices heard in, 325.
Crawford, Elizabeth, 326.
Cromer, Lord, 163, 213.

Daily Mail, 55, 278.
Daily Mirror, 55, 69–70, 72, 75–77; & Dora
    Thewlis, 123, 125, 128–9; & Grayson
    campaign, 154–6; & Doncaster case,
    278–9, 335.
Davison, Emily Wilding, xi, 275, 280.
Despard, Charlotte, 67, 69–70, 117, 129–30;
    leads WFL, 164–6.
Dewsbury, 187, 190.
Dickenson Bill, 121–2.
doctors, women: see Edith Pechey-
    Phipson, Mary Murdoch & Helen
    Wilson.
Doncaster, 225, 276–80, 293.
Drummond, Flora, 181, 306.

education, 7, 87; see also Board Schools,
    universities.
Edward VII, 1.
Edwardians, 1–7, 314.
Election Fighting Fund (EFF), 261, 285, 294;
    problems in Yorkshire, 263, 283, 320.
elections: see by-elections, general
    elections.
electoral pact, secret, 54.
electronic internet searches, & suffrage
    detection, 3, 333–4.
Elgar, Edward, 1, 13.
emigration: see Adela Pankhurst, Mary
    Gawthrope, Dora Thewlis.
Europe & suffrage, 12, 267; see also German
    connections.

family history: see census & electronic
    internet searches.
fathers, 4, 34–37, 315.

Fawcett, Millicent (Mrs), xii, 2, 10–11; & NUWSS, 12, 45, 50; supports suffragettes, 72, 74, 135–6; leads NUWSS, 136, 201; grows critical of militancy, 263, 267; celebrates victory in 1918, 299.

Fawcett Society & Fawcett Library, 309, 329.

Fenwick-Miller, Florence, 73–3.

Fielden, Mary, 207, 211–3, 222.

Ford, Bessie, 10, 11, 45, 197, 202–3, 213, 283.

Ford, Emily: artist, 8, 45, 213; & ASL, 136, 197–8, 231–2.

Ford, Isabella, 2, 4; novelist, 7–8; & suffrage, 10–11; & ILP, 11, 47; & NUWSS, 12, 45–48; & Mary Gawthorpe, 50, 56, 63; conciliatory approach, 195–8, 201, 214; & IWSA, 203; & vanning, 211–3; & EFF, 263, 283, 285; death, 304, 309; comparisons 319.

forcible feeding, 223, 255, 269; see also prisons.

Fraser, Helen, 223–4, 227.

Free Trade Hall, Manchester: 1904, 26; 1905, 27–8, 47–8.

Freewoman, The, 8, 228.

fustian workers, 82, 94, 97–103.

Gardner, Emilie, 205–210.

Garrs, Thomas, 38–41, 43–4, 48, 57; afterwards, 64, 73.

Gawthorpe, Annie (mother), 32 ff, 64.

Gawthorpe John (father), 8–9, 32 ff, 76.

Gawthorpe, Mary (Nellie), xiii, 2, 3, 5, 9; Leeds childhood, 32–4; as pupil teacher, 34–6; as teacher, 36, 55; & Leeds Arts Club, 44–5, 47; & Christabel Pankhurst, 47–8; questions Liberal politicians in Leeds; 49–50; journalism, 51–2; takes tea at Adel Grange, 56; & Pethick-Lawrences, 56–7; & Women's Labour League, 62–3; joins WSPU, 63; becomes organizer, 64–7; arrested at Parliament demonstration, 68–70; in prison, 71–5; released and to Huddersfield byelection, 75–77, 117; in Halifax, 96–7; in Hebden Bridge, 100–1; arrested at Women's Parliament, 119;

to Hull byelection, 172–5; organizing in Leeds and Bradford, 195–7, 203–4; illness & retires from WSPU, 228; journalism, 228, 242; & William Ball, 242; with Molly Morris in Manchester, 248–9; emigrates to America, 301; marries John Sander, 302, 309; marginalized in Sylvia's history, 307–8; writes autobiography, 308, 327, 328; death, 310; descendants, 311, 328; papers deposited, 328.

Gawthorpes, other, 196–7.

Gee, Alan, JP, 113–15, 157.

General elections: 1900, 2, 41; Jan 1906, 52, 53; Jan 1910, 224–5; Dec 1910, 231; 1918, 299.

German connections, 132, 164, 247, 250, 267, 315; & war, 219, 294.

Gladstone, Herbert MP, 41, 48–9, 54; as Home Secretary, 194, 199, 213.

Goldstein, Vida, 300.

Gore-Booth, Eva, 11–2, 24, 26, 28; critical of militancy, 74–5.

Grassington, 225–6, 294.

Gray, Almyra, 263.

Grayson, Victor, 132,146; with Pankhursts in Manchester ILP, 147–8; stands in Colne Valley by-election, 149–50; suffragettes support 151–55; election victory, 156–7; fizzles out, 160.

Grey, Sir Edward, MP, 27, 28.

Gye, Elsa, 309, 316–7.

half-timers, 84, 110.

Haldane, Lord, 217–8.

Halifax, 89–90; tram workers' strike, 90–3; Mary Gawthorpe arrives, 96; WSPU branch, 96–7, 166; NOW course, 325; see also Laura Wilson, Lavena Saltonstall.

Hamilton, Cicely, 177.

Harberton, Lady, 122–6.

Hardie, Keir, MP, 18, 53; supports suffrage, 27, 46, 54, 55, 60; barracked by WSPU, 293.

Harrogate, 213, 281–2, 289–90, 292–3.

Haverfield, Hon Mrs Evelina, 212–3.

health, 2, 4, 32–3, 83–4.

Hebden Bridge: 'fustianopolis', 82–3; &

Lavena Saltonstall grows up in, 84–8; fustian weavers' strike in, 94–5, 97–103; Emmeline Pankhurst speaks in, 98–9; WSPU branch, 103.

Holton, Sandra, 232, 326–7.

Home Office surveillance tactics, 223, 233, 280, 290–1; files, 260, 269; papers uncovered, 332; *see also* Reginald McKenna.

How-Martyn, Edith, 120, 129–30, 165.

historiography, suffrage: 310, 311–2, 319–20, 321–2.

Huddersfield, 5, 107–9; by-election 1906, 74–5; released suffragettes arrive in, 76–77; NUWSS branch, 75, 115, 157; WSPU branch, 107–8, 115–6, 121–2, 131–3, 135; & Grayson campaign, 150–7; WSPU branch under strain, 165–6, 179–81, 187–8; *see also*, Edith Key, Dora Thewlis.

Hull, 5, 136, 168–9, 171; 1907 by-election, 168, 172–6, 201.

hunger strikes, 223, 275; *see also* forcible feeding.

Hunt, Henry, MP, 9.

Ibsen, Henrik, 32, 43, 244.

illegitimacy, 7, 83, 109–10.

Independent Labour Party (ILP), 2, 18; & suffrage, 24–6; in Leeds, 41, 45, 51; supports Adela & other suffragettes, 59–61; *Manifesto*, 95–6, 107, 115–6; & Grayson campaign, 147–60; lobbying Labour leaders on suffrage, 232, 264.

Intellectual Life of the British Working Classes, The, 7, 332.

International Woman Suffrage Alliance (IWSA), 136, 201, 203; in Budapest, 266–7, 283.

Irish politics, 231, 287, 291.

Jackson, Holbrook, 42.

Jackson, W.L., MP, 33, 37.

Jewish communities, 42, 234, 247.

Johnson, Harry, 277–9.

Kenney Annie, 7; & WSPU, 26–9, 47–8; as WSPU organizer, 57, 64–5, 67, 121; in Halifax, 91, 93; in Huddersfield, 116, 131; in Sheffield, 217–8; autobiography, 305; comes from Springhead, West Riding, 325, 334.

Key, Edith, 2; childhood, 109–11; as secretary of WSPU branch, 115–7, 122, 132–3; & Grayson campaign, 150–4; & WSPU branch tensions, 165–6, 184–5, 187–9; shelters 'mice', 274; descendants & papers, 327–8.

Key family, 110–11, 154, 188–9, 274.

Key-Jones, Violet, xiii; family, 275; in Doncaster, 276–9; WSPU organizer & 'railway suffragette', 282, 286, 293; remains elusive, 303.

Kitson, Sir James, MP, 145, 149.

Labour Church, 40.

Labour Leader, 27–8; Adela writes for, 29–30; & suffrage, 47, 48–9; suffrage correspondence in, 63, 115

Labour Party, 53, 262; electoral pact with NUWSS, 232, 255, 261, 264; *see also* EFF.

Labour Record, 57, 65, 69–71, 74, 101.

Labour Representation Committee, 12

Lancashire Women Textile Workers' Representation Committee, 24, 76.

landscape, xiv, 86, 193–4, 316, 334–5; Pennine, 82–3, 107.

Lansbury, George, MP, 167, 262.

Leeds, 5, 33, 42, 193–4; suffrage society, 10, 45, 54; Arts Club, 32, 43–9; NUWSS branch, 136, 193, 201; WSPU branch, 193–5, 204, 236 ff, 242; meetings and procession, 270–2, 286; unsafe city, 286–7; *see also*, Isabella Ford, Mary Gawthorpe, Leonora Cohen.

Lenton, Lilian, xiii, xiv; dancer, 267; dreams of being twenty-one, 268; arsonist, 268–9; & forcible feeding danger, 269; as 'May Dennis' to fire building in Doncaster, 277; drama in court, 278–9; in Armley, 280; covertly photographed in prison, 280–1, 290–1; escapes from Leeds in disguise, 281–2; addresses jury during trial in Leeds, 291–2; escapes from Cohens', Harrogate in disguise, 292–3; remains a fugitive, 293;

Lenton, Lilian – *continued*
    too young to vote in 1918, 299; & WFL,
    304; & Suffragette Fellowship, 310;
    death, 310.
lesbian relationships, 170–1.
Liberal Party, 47; reform agenda of, 53–4,
    224; *see also* Lloyd George.
Liberalism, 10, 18, 45. 114–5, 120, 145.
Liddiard, Victoria, 3,
Lloyd George MP, David, 2, 58; as
    Chancellor of Exchequer, 53, 222, 231;
    deputation to, 253–4.
Linthwaite, 141–6; *see also* Florence
    Lockwood, Colne Valley.
Liverpool & Merseyside, 5, 320.
Lockwood, Florence, xiv, 2, 8, 137;
    childhood, 138; painter in Bloomsbury,
    139–40; meets Josiah, 140–2; moves to
    Linthwaite, 143–6; listens to Mrs
    Pankhurst, 152; encounters Adela in
    hay-field, 153; & Colne Valley by-
    election result, 156–7; joins NUWSS,
    157–9; elected Guardian, 159; makes
    suffrage banner 160; & Liberalism,
    263–4; writes *Enfranchisement* pamphlet,
    265–6; to Budapest, 266–7;
    campaigning & pilgrimage, 285, 294;
    outbreak of war, 294–5; widowhood,
    304; autobiography, 309, 325; death,
    310.
Lockwood, Josiah, 141 ff, 152–3, 156, 265.
Lost World of Mitchell and Kenyon, The, 3, 333.
Lowenthal, Bertha, 132, 163–4, 179, 188.
Lowndes, Mary, 159, 200–2, 231.

MacDonald, Ramsay, MP, 53, 54,
MacDonald, Mrs, 57,62.
McKenna, Reginald, MP, 219–20; as Home
    Secretary, 252, 269, 282; *see also* Home
    Office.
McLaren, Walter, MP, 72.
Mahony, Amy & Lottie, 244.
Manchester, 5, 7; & suffrage, 10–12, 17,
    24–9; NUWSS Federation, 264; *see also*
    Pankhursts, Molly Morris.
manhood suffrage, 8, 232; *see also* Reform
    Bill.
Markiewicz, Constance, 186, 202, 299.

Martel, Nellie, 131–2, 154, 173–5.
Martindale, Louisa, Dr, 170–1, 176.
Men's suffrage leagues, 163, 232, 281.
Middlesbrough, 166–7; WFL branch, 167,
    177–8, 232, 243–4, 275, 286.
migrations, economic, 6, 83, 109, 112.
militancy: *see* WSPU.
Mill, John Stuart, MP, 10, 120, 265.
milliners: *see* Leonora Cohen.
Mitchell, Hannah: joins WSPU, 28, 103–4;
    with Adela in Manchester, 58–61; in
    Huddersfield, 75–6, 116, 121–2, 131–2;
    in Colne Valley, 148–9; critical of
    WSPU, 164.
Montefiore, Dora, 62, 70–4.
Morris, Molly, xiii, xiv, 246; family, 247–8;
    & WSPU in Manchester, 248–9;
    organizing for WSPU in Sheffield,
    249–51; firing pillar-boxes, 251–53;
    becomes a nurse, 303–4; marries Jack
    Murphy, 252, 304; autobiography, 331.
Morrissey, Mr & Mrs, 58–60.
mothers, 5, 7, 104, 235, 315; *see also* Mary
    Gawthorpe, Leonora Cohen.
'Mud March', 136–7, 158, 200.
Murdoch, Mary, Dr, xiv; Hull doctor,
    168–9; runs NUWSS branch, 170; &
    Hull by-election, 172–4; chairing
    election meeting, 174–7; supports
    militancy, 176–7; death, 304; biography,
    309.

narrative history, xiv, 313, 322, 335–6.
National Union of Women's Suffrage
    Societies (NUWSS), xii, 12, 45, 46–7; &
    Liberal government, 54; branches,
    growth & regional federations, 136,
    168, 211; 1908 procession, 199–203;
    caravan tours across Yorkshire, 1908,
    205–210, & 1909, 211–3; increasingly
    critical of militancy, 210, 214, 243; other
    campaigns, 222–3; feels betrayed by
    Asquith, 255; electoral pact with
    Labour, 232, 255, 261; expansion, 261–2;
    traditional Liberalism of, 263, 285, 320;
    pilgrimage, 283–4; Friends & Active
    Service League, 284–5, 294–5; &
    NUSEC, 309; *see also* Mrs Fawcett, EFF.

'new woman', 32, 41; *see also* rebel girls.

Nietzsche, Friedrich, 32, 42–3, 228.

Noble, Alice, 193.

North East region, 320.

North of England Society for Women's Suffrage, 24.

North & East Riding Federation (NUWSS), 263.

occupations, 7, 22, 34, 123; *see also*, tailoresses, textiles, pupil teachers.

O'Grady, James, MP, 51, 53.

Older, Ann, 184.

Oldham, Springhead, & Annie Kenney, 325.

One Hand Tied Behind Us, xi–xii, xiv, 312, 313–4, 325.

Orage, Alfred, 32, 42–45, 47, 123, 228.

oral history, 325, 327–9, 334.

Pankhurst, Adela, xiii, 2, 4; early childhood, 17–19; death of father, 20–21; as pupil teacher, 22–25; & WSPU formed in her home, 25–6; speaking for WSPU, 26–29, 30–1; writes story in *Labour Leader*, 29–30; & Mary Gawthorpe 55–6; & Annie Kenney, 57–8; arrested at Belle Vue, 58–9; & rowdies at Boggart Hole Clough, 60–1; teaching & speaking, 62, 65–7; at opening of parliament, 68–70; in prison, 71–5; in Hebden Bridge, 100–3; in Huddersfield, 116–7; & Grayson campaign, 147, 151–2, 154; encounters Lockwoods in hay-field, 153; as WSPU organizer, 195, 216, 218; campaigning in Sheffield, 217–223; in disguise as kitchen-maid, 220–1; on hunger strike, Scotland, 223–4; to Scarborough for General Election, 224–5; returns to Sheffield, 225–6; illness, 224, 226; leaves WSPU, 227–8; 'banished' to Australia, 300; marries Tom Walsh, 301; erased from Sylvia's histories, 305, 307, 309; own autobiographical writings, 306–7; death, 310; descendants, 311, 329; papers deposited, 329.

Pankhurst, Christabel, xii, 17–21; & early WSPU, 41, 47–8, 51; leads WSPU strategy, 62, 65–6; speaker, 88, 90, 180; at Westminster, 119–20, 123; arrested, 219; suspicious of Adela, 226–7; & further militancy, 241; in exile, 245, 286, 293; stands for parliament, 299; *see also Suffragette*, WSPU.

Pankhurst, Emmeline, xi–xii, 2, 4, 9, 10; marriage, 19; widowhood, 20; founds WSPU, 24–27; inspirational, 64, 66; at Huddersfield, 75, 116; speaking during Hebden Bridge fustian weavers' strike, 97–8; at Women's Parliament, 117; & Grayson campaign, 147, 151–5; star speaker, 172–3, 195; arrested, 219; to Sheffield, 222; & further militancy, 255; re-arrested, 280, 290, 291; stands for parliament, 299; autobiography, 305; death & statue, 305–6; *see also* WSPU, Suffragette Fellowship.

Pankhurst, Harry: childhood, 17–21; & Adela, 68; death, 224.

Pankhurst, Richard, 4, 10, 17; death, 20.

Pankhurst, Sylvia: childhood, 17–21; artist, 28; imprisoned, 71; & East London, 286; expelled from WSPU, 291; WSPU historian, xii, 305; controversy over *The Suffragette Movement*, 306–9, 310–1; death, 310; *see also Shoulder to Shoulder*.

'Pankson Baines', 8, 104–6.

Parker, James, MP, 90.

photography, xiii, 129; covertly in prison, 260, 269–70, 274, 282; instructions on, 280, 290–1; 'spy pictures' discovery in news, 332; see also *Daily Mirror*.

Pechey-Phipson, Edith, Dr, 136–7, 157, 202.

Peterloo, 9.

Pethick-Lawrence, Emmeline & Frederick: & Mary Gawthorpe, 56–7; in Manchester, 60–1, 63, 67; at Westminster, 68–71, 107, 119–20, 123; to Huddersfield, 180; ousted from WSPU, 249; stands for parliament, 299.

Phillips, Mary, 236, 240, 243.

Pinnance, Elizabeth, 113, 122–4, 131, 195; descendants, 311, 327, 331; illuminated testimonial of, 331.

Poor Law Guardians, 9, 71, 159.

postcards, picture, 133–4, 205–12, 329–30; see also photography.

prisons: Strangeways, Manchester, 28, 48, 59–60; Holloway, London, 71–5, 119–20, 184–5, 240; Armley, Leeds, 103; forcible feeding in Holloway, 269, 278; forcible feeding & Armley, 280, 286, 287–8; shared memories of, 316–7.

procession, coronation, 231–2; see also Mud March, NUWSS, WSPU.

pupil teachers, 22; see also Adela Pankhurst, Mary Gawthorpe.

Pugh, Martin, 305, 327.

Purvis, June, 327.

Quakers, 295; see also Isabella Ford.

Quinn, Bertha, 263.

Rathbone, Eleanor, 320.

rebel girls, xii–xiv, 13, 313; as a group, 314–5; shared experiences & dreams, 315–7; suffrage aims of, 316; as friendship network, 317–8.

Reform Acts, 8; Reform Bill, 232, 255, 267–8.

regional suffrage histories, xii, xiv, 311–2, 314; comparisons, 318–20; & regional boundaries, 334, 335–6.

Renton, Helena, 264, 283.

Representation of the People Bill: women over 30 (1918) & over 21 (1928), 299, 305.

research techniques, see suffrage detective.

Robertson, Margaret, 205–10.

Roper, Esther, 11–12, 24–26, 28; critical of militancy, 74–5, 313, 319.

Rowlette, Miss, 50–1.

Rutter, Frank, 281,

Sackville-West, Vita, 1.

Salford, 5, 23,

Salisbury, Lord, 1,

Saltonstall, Lavena, xiii, xiv, 6, 81; family in Hebden Bridge, 82–3; as tailoress, 84–7; writings, 8, 87–90, 103–4; Women's Labour League & Halifax tram strike, 91–3; & Hebden Bridge fustian strike, 97–103; & 'Pankson Baines'

correspondence, 104–6; arrested at Westminster, 123; sentences to fourteen days, 124, 131; WSPU Women's Parliament, 182; arrest & prison again, 183–5; N W Manchester by-election, 186–7; on tramp with Laura Wilson, 189–90; in WEA, 190–1, 303; marriage, 303; remains one of the 'disappeared', 332–3.

Scarborough, 224–5, 281–2.

Scawthorne, Mary, 131.

Schofield-Coates, Alice, xiii, 177–8, 244, 304.

School Boards, 7, 9, 71, 110; see also Board Schools …

Schuster, Elsa, 250–2, 286.

Secret Garden, The, 5.

servants, female domestic, 3–4, 5; see Pankhurst, Ford & Lockwood households.

Shackleton, David, MP, 102.

Shaw, George Bernard, 42, 43,

Sheffield, 5, 216–7; Adela Pankhurst & WSPU branch, 217–8; Adela & McKenna meeting, 219–221; Adela returns to, 225–6; Molly Morris in, 249–53, 286, 293; NUWSS branch, 217, 283–4; WFL branch, 168, 217, 221–2.

Shoulder to Shoulder, 310–11, 320, 321, 328–9, 330.

Siddon, Emily, 157.

Slade, the, 136, 139–40, 159.

Smith, Mary, 9.

Snowden, Philip, MP, 53, 111, 262, 264; see also Ethel Annakin.

socialism, 19, 11, 113; see also, ILP, Labour Leader.

Special Appeal, 10–11.

Stevenson, Elsie May, 193.

Stevenson, Blanche, 194.

Studdard, Helen, 115, 158–9.

Strachey, Ray (Costello), 211–2, 305.

suffrage detective, xiii, xiv, 3, 81, 325–7; startling new discoveries, 327–30; visit Pinnance descendants, 331; & Home Office papers, 332; & census, 333–4; & Yorkshire, 334; pacing streets, 335; & local press, 335.

Suffragette Fellowship, 308–9, 310, 316–7, 332.

suffragettes, xi, 55, 104–6; community, 120, 160, 164, 191–2, 316–7; maverick, 228, 232–3, 316–7; see also WSPU.

Suffragette Movement, The, (1931), xii, 306–8, 310–1.

Suffragette, The, newspaper: 245, 249, 286, 289, 290, 293; see also Christabel Pankhurst.

suffragists: radical suffragists, xi–xii, 313–4, 318; democratic, 228, 232; pioneer, 315, 317, 318; see also NUWSS.

Sunley, Agnes, 10, 48–9.

Sykes, Annie, 113, 117–20, 131.

tailoring, 7, 84–5; see also Lavena Saltonstall.

tailoresses' union, Leeds, 11, 46, 253–4.

Taylor, Mary, 90–3, 95–6, 97–9; & Women's Parliament, 103, 117.

temperance, 55, 115, 136.

textiles, 7, 107–8, 112–4, 142–4, 263; in Lancashire & West Riding, 318–9.

Thewlis, Dora, xiii, xiv; childhood, 112; & suffrage, 116; to Westminster, 122–3; remanded, 124–6; on *Daily Mirror* front-page, 123–5, 129, 133–4; released, 129–30; emigrates to Australia & marries, 303; descendants traced, 328.

Thewlis, Eliza, 7; childhood, 112; & suffrage, 115–6, 122; & Dora, 126, 133.

Thewlis family, 6, 112.

Thompson, E.P., 334.

Thompson, Paul, 3.

Thus Spake Zarathustra, 42–3.

Tickner, Lisa, 199–200, 326.

Times, The, 72–3, 243, 258, 335.

Titterington, Amy, 195.

Titterington, Mary, 194–5, 253.

trams, electric, 87, 140, 317.

Turner, Ben, 113–5, 119, 187.

university, women at, 11–12, 20, 24, 40, 51.

Up Hill to Holloway, 2, 308, 327, 328; see also Mary Gawthorpe.

vanning, see NUWSS caravan tours.

Victoria, Queen, death of, 1.

Virago Press, 335.

Votes for Women, 185, 210, 240, 248, 305.

Walsh, Tom, 301, 306; see also Adela Pankhurst.

Ward, John, MP, 146, 157.

weavers, see textiles, fustian workers.

West, Rebecca, 8, 13, 215–7, 228, 310.

West Riding, xiv, 5, 6, 318–9; & suffrage, 107, 120; see also Yorkshire.

West Riding Federation (NUWSS), 263–4, 283.

Whitby, 136, 205–6.

Whitman, Walt, 7, 20.

Whitworth, Edith, 217, 220–22.

Wilson, Helen, Dr, 217, 221–2, 263, 264.

Wilson, Laura: living in Halifax, 89; & Women's Labour League, 90; & Halifax tram strike, 90–3; & suffrage, 94; signs *Manifesto* to WSPU, 95; becomes secretary of WSPU branch, 96; & fustian strike, 97, 99; summonsed,101; in court, 102–3; in prison, Armley, 104; to Westminster & arrested again, 123–4, 131–2; & local tensions, 166, 180, 182; on tramp with Lavena Saltonstall, 187, 189–90.

Winship, Augusta, 277–8.

Women's Freedom League (WFL): formed, 166–8; campaigning, 177–8, 202, 205, 221–2, 243–5; see also Middlesbrough branch.

Women's Labour League, 62–3, 90–2.

women's Liberal organizations, 136, 158–9.

Women's Social & Political Union (WSPU), xii, 17; formed by Mrs Pankhurst, 24–5; early recruits, 25–6; at Free Trade Hall, 27–29; & Isabella Ford, 47–8; heckling Liberal politicians, 49–50; moves to London, 55; employs organizers, 64–7, 216; at opening of Parliament 1906, 67–9; arrests, 69–74; branches, 94–6, 103, 121, 216; Women's Parliament, 1907, 103, 117–20; internal tensions about democracy, 164–6; Hyde Park demonstration 1908, 187–8, 203; & stone-throwing, 204, 210, 214; & hunger strikes, 223; & forcible feeding, 223, 255, 269;

Women's Social & Political Union
   (WSPU) – *continued*
   shops, 225, 236, 250; & window-
   smashing, 232, 239–43, 255; & war on
   'coalition government', 245, 293; &
   rhetoric of personal sacrifice, 246; &
   arson attacks, 258, 260, 266–9;
   precariousness on eve of War, 293, 322;
   on militancy, 314.
women voters: over 30 (1918) & over 21
   (1928), 299, 305.
Women Writers' Suffrage League, 177,
   201–2.

Wollstonecraft, Mary, 73.

York, 275; NUWSS branch, 136, 263; WFL
   branch, 168; WSPU branch, 276.
Yorkshire, xii, xiv, 5, 7, 316; *see also* West
   Riding, landscape, textiles, NUWSS
   caravan tours.
Yorkshire Factory Times, 11.
Yorkshire Post, 38–9, 73, 238–9, 241, 243.
Yorkshire Evening Post, 47, 257.
Yorkshire Weekly Post, 51, 56.
Yorkshire women textile workers'
   petition, 46–7, 319.